THE
AMAZING WORLD
OF
SUPERSTITION, PROPHECY, LUCK, MAGIC & WITCHCRAFT

THE
AMAZING WORLD
OF
SUPERSTITION,
PROPHECY,
LUCK, MAGIC &
WITCHCRAFT

Two Volumes in One

Leonard R.N. Ashley

BELL PUBLISHING COMPANY
New York

Originally published in separate volumes under the titles:
The Wonderful World of Superstition, Prophecy, and Luck,
copyright © 1984 by Leonard R.N. Ashley
The Wonderful World of Magic and Witchcraft,
copyright © 1986 by Leonard R.N. Ashley

This 1988 edition is published by Bell Publishing Company
distributed by Crown Publishers, Inc., 225 Park Avenue South,
New York, New York 10003, by arrangement with Dembner
Books, a division of Red Dembner Enterprises Corp.

Printed and Bound in the United States of America

Library of Congress Cataloging-in-Publication Data

Ashley, Leonard R. N.
The amazing world of superstition, prophecy, luck,
magic, and witchcraft / Leonard R.N. Ashley.
    p.   cm.
    Reprint (1st work). Originally published: The wonderful
world of superstition, prophecy, and luck. New York :
Dembner Books, c1984.
    Reprint (2nd work). Originally published: The wonderful
world of magic and witchcraft. New York : Dembner Books,
c1986.
    Includes indexes.
    ISBN 0-517-66566-2
    1. Occultism.   I. Title
BF1411.A84   1988   88-19317
133—dc19   CIP

h g f e d c b a

SUPERSTITION, PROPHECY & LUCK

Volume 1

For Raymond William Ayre
si placeo, tuum est

Contents

Foreword

A great American humorist once said that it ain't what we don't know that hurts us, it's all the things we do know that *ain't true*.

For example, most people are absolutely convinced that hot water will freeze faster than cold water. Under certain special circumstances—outdoors in Alaska in a styrofoam cup—this is true. In your freezer it is not, so if you put hot water into your ice trays, don't expect it to make ice faster than cold water does.

This makes an interesting point about belief in the supernatural—in any and all of its many colorful forms. The striking aspect of *hot* water *freezing* and freezing *faster than cold* makes it stick in the mind, and we greatly enjoy the unusualness of the idea. This accounts for ignorant and irrational belief in many of the phenomena in this book—the stubborn insistence of people in believing in the fantastical even when it has been proved that it *ain't true*. Faith welcomes miracles.

Superstition is a sort of faith. In *De divinatione*, Cicero said that superstition is a parody of religion, that it poisons and destroys all peace of mind. Edmund Burke called it "the religion of feeble minds." Wrote Francis Bacon:

> Such is the way of all superstition, whether in astrology, dreams, omens, divine judgments, or the like; wherein men, having a delight in such vanities, mark the events where they are fulfilled, but where they fail, though they happen much oftener, neglect and pass them by.

Nonetheless, occult matters are colorful and men do have "a delight in such vanities," and that is what this book is about. The first half is devoted largely to folk beliefs: the people's magic, charms and incantations and cures and omens and wonder working carried out by ordinary people according to their own rules. The second half takes up "educated" forms of the occult: pseudo sciences developed and practiced and studied by learned men down through the ages. Both kinds of superstition have their adherents; both have their skeptics. Both are interesting for what they reveal of human nature.

But this is, above all, a book to be enjoyed. So scoff at our ignorant and wildly imaginative ancestors. Or pause before some item of folk wisdom here and wonder if perhaps there may not, after all, be something in it. . . . Whatever suits you best.

And if you happen to hit upon something equally intriguing that I have omitted, why not write to me and tell me about it? I cannot undertake to answer all your letters, but I shall read them with interest. Now, good reading. And good luck.

L. R. N. A.

PART ONE

Superstition

"Crush the Infamous Thing!"

THAT is the great Voltaire's remark regarding superstition, for Voltaire lived in—was the embodiment of—the Age of Enlightenment, and thinkers of his day attempted to apply rationality not only to political and social life but to religion and morality as well. Superstition links causes and effects in ways that defy logic and fail all impartial tests, and thus superstition was at odds with the new scientific way of thinking dominant in Voltaire's time.

Nonetheless, superstition is ineradicable, Frederick the Great assured the philosopher. Superstition has always existed and has formed both the alpha and the omega of religions: the primitive beliefs from which they emerge and the baroque delusions into which they finally fall.

In reality, superstition is the enemy of true religion, as many religious leaders have said. In 1080, for instance, in the very beginning of those Middle Ages so often pointed to as the heyday of superstition, Pope Gregory VII wrote to King Harold the Simpleminded of Denmark to warn him unequivocally that blaming tempests, illness, and other afflictions on witches was heresy. These, he said, were Acts of God, and to punish witches for them was only to injure the innocent and further provoke the wrath of the deity.

There are many people alive today who are far less "modern" and enlightened than Pope Gregory was a thousand years ago. We are often as much in a "dark age" now as our ancestors were in the Middle Ages.

Mankind clings to its superstitions in the face of all intellectual advance, all evidence to the contrary. Mankind has a will to ignore evidence that contradicts its treasured beliefs. Mankind does not want to find out it has been wrong. It searches for ways of holding onto the comfortable, even if incorrect, explanations of the past. One coincidence can make a convert; all instances to the contrary just don't count.

We all have some superstitions, of course, because we are all carrying some of the baggage of the past. No one can be rational and informed all the time. Nobody can be entirely free of ancient fears, or of foolish fancies. Many of the beliefs that follow will seem outrageously silly. Others, however improbable they sound, may draw more on practical experience than we are aware of. Still others may appeal to some romantic streak lurking unrealized in our prosaic modern souls. It is hoped that all readers will recognize at least *some* of what comes next. Knock on wood!

1

People

SHADOWS

The ancients believed that a man's shadow and his reflection in some measure represented his soul. Hence, in legends, vampires and other soulless entities cast no shadow and cannot be seen in mirrors. Hence, too, the ancient tale of the man who sold his shadow to the Devil and the Richard Strauss opera about a supernatural wife, *Die Frau ohne Schatten* (*The Woman Without a Shadow*).

Many people believe that to see one's shadow cast by the moon is bad luck. On the other hand shadows can be used to ward off evil, as is shown by the superstitious natives of Transylvania who in the eighteenth century tried to build a shadow into a wall.

Some Jews believe that if a man cannot see his shadow at nightfall on the seventh day of the feast of Sukkoth, Hoshana Rabbah, he will die within a year. Likewise, in ancient Greece, it was believed that any unauthorized person who entered the sanctuary of Zeus on Mount Lycaeus would lose his shadow and die within a year.

Many different peoples hold the folk belief that injury done to a shadow will inflict the living body to a similar degree. The aborigines of Australia sometimes stab an enemy's shadow as a way of attacking the man; and when they are working magic against an enemy they are careful not to allow their own shadows to fall on the spell object, for fear the curse will turn back upon themselves.

Some Arabs believe that if a hyena steps on a man's shadow, it will deprive the man of speech. A dog could do the same thing to a hyena by

3

stepping on *its* shadow. On the other hand, if a dog were standing on a roof so that its shadow fell on the ground and a passing hyena stepped on it, the dog would be jerked to the ground as if by a rope.

One of the best-known shadow beliefs is that a shadow helps the groundhog (the badger in England) predict the weather. The animal is thought to emerge from hibernation on February 2, and if he sees his shadow—that is, if the day is sunny— he returns to his den, and there will be six more weeks of winter. Headquarters for this prediction is the town of Punxsutawney, Pennsylvania, about seventy miles northeast of Pittsburgh, where the Groundhog Club is located. The superstition is based, however, on an ancient tradition associated with the feast of Candlemas, celebrated on February 2. "If Candlemas Day is bright and clear," men said, "there'll be two winters in the year."

LADDERS

It is dangerous to walk under a ladder, but it is also dangerous to walk on a ladder lying on the ground. If you step over the ladder while making a wish, your wish will come true. In fact, you can walk under a ladder and still be lucky if you cross yourself or cross your fingers and make a wish first.

If a woman walks under a ladder, it's the same as if she sits on a table: She will not get married for at least a year.

CIDER

Makers of homemade cider have many superstitions about the brew. It must be made while the moon is waning or the apples will shrivel up and the cider be sour. There are all sorts of theories about how to make scrumpy or some other drink "work," how much sugar or honey or whatever to add, how adding a few parsnips or beets gives it something to "feed on," and so on. Some country people add half a horseshoe to the cider barrel to "put iron in it." They maintain that when the cider is "done," the metal will be found to have disappeared. (Similarly, some people drop a dime into a churn to make the butter "come.")

DOUBLES

Multiple births have awakened feelings of awe and wonder among many different peoples. Even the statistics are curious. In the United States (and based on statistics collected before the advent of fertility pills), according to the *Encyclopaedia Britannica* there are eighty-six single births for every set of twins, eighty-six sets of twins for every set of triplets, and eighty-six sets of triplets for every set of quadruplets. It is hardly surprising, therefore, that superstitions about twins abound. They go back to the Gemini, and beyond.

The commonest superstition in this connection is some variation on the theme of the Corsican brothers—the idea that twins can somehow feel what happens to each other, even at a distance, that they are really one soul in two bodies. Often, too, it seems that one twin is doubly disturbed and even feels guilty when the other dies.

Many Europeans believe in the *Döppelganger* (double) who looks just like the original but seems to lead an independent existence. Reports are heard from time to time of one man being recognized by friends at the same time in two widely separated places. The record for such multiple appearances is probably held by one Johannes Teutonicus, who one day in 1221 was seen celebrating Mass at Mainz, Halberstadt, and Cologne, all at the same hour. Fortunately these *Döppelgangen* did not meet, for Germans believe that if a man meets his double face to face, he will die.

Similarly the Yoruba of West Africa and the Baganda of Uganda believe that every man has a spirit double, a twin brother or sister, in effect, whose destiny is intricately bound up with his own. Perhaps it has something to do with the high incidence of twins among the Yoruba, much higher than the above-mentioned American rate. It is sad to note that the commonest of all the beautiful Yoruba cult carvings are those to commemorate twins who die in infancy.

HAIR TODAY . . .

Hair has long been a symbol of sexuality, and this has given rise to a number of religious practices concerning it. In times past, nuns, when they took their vows, and Orthodox Jewish women, when they married, shaved their heads and adopted wimples and wigs instead. Sikh men to this day are forbidden to cut their hair and instead bind it up elaborately and hide it under turbans. This practice recently caused some consternation among British motor-safety experts when it was discovered that the crash helmets prescribed for motorcyclists would not fit over the turbans, and the Sikhs refused to abandon the turbans. Eventually Sikh motorcyclists were exempted from the law.

Samson in the Bible seems to have belonged to a religious sect that forbade the cutting of hair. When Delilah cut it for him, it cost him his strength—probably symbolizing the loss of the faith that had formerly upheld him. Today the beards and side curls still worn by some Orthodox Jews are a survival of this religious practice.

In ancient Egypt, pharaohs shaved their chins and then wore fake beards for ceremonial occasions. The Egyptians made no bones about the fact that it was fake; the strap attaching it is plainly shown in portrait statues of these kings. Such a fake beard was even worn by a queen of Egypt, the famous Hatshepsut.

Sidi Mohammed ben Aissa (1456–1533) was a Moroccan holy man who, believing he could study best by night, stayed up all night to read the Koran. To keep himself awake, he tied a lock of his hair to the wall. If he nodded, the pain brought him sharply to attention. Today, his followers, of the Aissawa (or Isawa) sect, wear a long lock in his memory.

Other Muslims wear a single long lock of hair in the belief, it is said, that they will be drawn up to heaven by the hair at the hour of their death. The long tassle on the fez represents this lock of hair.

Hair figures to some extent in customs. Lovers used to keep a lock of the loved one's hair in a locket or the back of a watch, and locks of hair from famous heads are much-valued treasures. (Napoleon in particular was always being asked for souvenir locks, and many of these are still extant.) About the time of the Civil War, "hair pictures" were in vogue—hair wound around bits of wire and bent into the shape of some image, usually a flower. The Confederate Museum in Richmond, Virginia, has a framed bouquet of hair flowers, every "petal" of which is composed of hair from a different Confederate hero.

Naturally hair has given rise to a number of superstitions.

Curly hair is lucky. You can make it curly by eating bread crusts (and carrots and spinach and prunes and virtually anything else that Mother wants her recalcitrant child to finish up).

To "put hair on your chest," eat substantial food, such as meat and potatoes.

Masturbation was once thought to make your palms hairy (a bestial act leading to a bestial appearance was the rationale, obviously).

To make your hair grow longer, brush it a hundred times a day. Rain is also supposed to make your hair grow. So is frequent cutting.

Sailors used to wear tarred pigtails, as protection against back-of-the-neck blows—from cutlasses in battle and from falling spars in peacetime. The apronlike collar of a "sailor suit" was supposed to protect the jacket from the tar on the pigtail. But when sailors did have their hair cut, they preferred to have it done during a storm at sea, which was widely believed to be lucky.

If a hairpin falls out of your hair, a friend is thinking of you. If you lose it, you will make an enemy. If you find a hairpin—as when you find a needle or pin—you must pick it up or you will have bad luck. For best results, hang it on a hook.

If a man has his hair cut when the moon is waning, his hair will dwindle too.

If you eat a raven's egg, it will turn your hair black, and if you suffer a severe fright, it will turn your hair white overnight.

Many people believe hair fibers are extremely fragile—hence, "to hang by a hair," meaning "to be on the verge of falling." Actually, hair is stronger than it looks, having a good half the tensile strength of steel.

Many sports figures, finding themselves in a winning/losing streak will vow not to shave until the streak comes to an end. Winners don't want to take chances with good luck, and losers hope to push themselves on to do better.

LIGHTNING

Lightning no longer impresses most people as evidence of God's wrath, but that does not mean they have abandoned superstitions concerning it.

The commonest belief is that lightning never strikes twice in the same place. This is not true, of course; skyscrapers are repeatedly struck by lightning, and *Life* magazine once published a photographic story showing the Empire State Building being struck six or seven times in one year alone. But many people still believe the old superstition.

To protect yourself from lightning, wrap yourself in a feather bed, sleep with a steel thimble under your pillow, or equip your house with a piece of hawthorn wood cut on Holy Thursday. In Britain they hold that if you can find a piece of coal under a mugwort plant at noon or midnight on

Midsummer Day (June 24), it will prevent you from being struck. In
Germany brands from the Easter bonfire serve the same purpose.

On the other hand, in the American West it is believed that where
lightning strikes, you'll find oil.

THE SUPERSTITIONS OF KIDS

If you see a red truck: "Red truck, good luck." For good luck, put a
penny in your shoe. When you see a ladybug, pick it up gently, put it on
your hand, and for good luck encourage it to fly away, saying, "Ladybug,
Ladybug, fly away home. Your house is on fire and your children alone."

If you see a white horse, *stamp* it: lick your right thumb, touch it to the
palm of your left hand, "paste it down" with a good blow from the right fist.

If you see an eyelash on someone's cheek, have them make a wish and
guess whether it's on the right or the left. If they guess right, the wish will
come true.

When it rains say: "Rain, rain, go away. Come again another day."

If you make a face at the clock as it strikes twelve, your face may stay
that way.

If you see a ghost or a bogeyman, say: "Crisscross, double-cross. Tell the
monster to get lost."

To find out if your sweetheart likes you, the way you like her, pull the
petals off a daisy one by one, reciting, "She loves me, she loves me not."
Whichever it ends up on is the right answer. (Daisies usually have an odd
number of petals.) Or you count apple seeds as you recite:

> One I love, two I love, three I love, I say.
> Four I love with all my heart, five I'll cast away.
> Six he loves, seven she loves, eight they both love.
> Nine he comes, ten he tarries,
> Eleven he courts and twelve he marries.

If you tell a lie, cross your fingers behind your back. If you tell the truth,
wet your index finger in your mouth, take it out and say:

> Is my finger wet?
> Is my finger dry?
> Cross my heart and hope to die.

Blowing out the candles on a birthday cake in one breath will make your wish come true. Hitting a baseball with the label on the bat will split the bat. Stepping on a crack in the sidewalk will cause something awful to happen to your mother.

FIRE

Man has known how to light and use fire since Neanderthal times. The magic powers of a fire were vital to early religion, and belief in them survives today in the form of much superstition.

If the fire draws badly, the Devil must be at hand; to counteract him, place the poker upright against the bars—iron crosspieces enclosing the grate—thus forming a cross. If, after poking, the fire burns brightly, it means an absent loved one is in good spirits.

Oblong hollow cinders are called coffins in England, and if one flies out of the fire, it is thought that a death in the family is imminent. A coming birth is indicated by a cradle—an oval cinder—doing the same thing. In America, a hot cinder popping out of the fire means a guest is coming.

In New England, they believe that if a house burns down, another should not be built on the same spot. A fire in your dreams means that you will soon have a quarrel with someone. But hang an adder's skin in the rafters and your house will never catch fire. Or stand branches of dried seaweed on your mantel to obtain the same result.

On my mantelpiece I have Staffordshire china dogs, which are supposed to guard the fire. In ancient times, the same chore was assigned to the old-fashioned iron fire dogs that supported the logs in a fireplace. Human-figure andirons had no magical purpose; they were just there to fool burglars, who might glance in and be deterred by seeing "people" in the room.

In Torres Strait, New Guinea, however, the figure by the fire has a magical task. Made of stone and resembling an old woman, the figure is superstitiously believed to keep an eye on the fire and prevent it from going out.

WARDING OFF EVIL

The Chinese believe that spirits can travel only in straight lines, so they build zigzag bridges to thwart them. A similar Western belief is that witches cannot cross running water, a fact that saved the life of Robert Burns's fictional hero Tam O'Shanter, who reached the River Doon just in time to escape from pursuing witch Cutty Sark.

Another Western way to stop a ghost is the direct approach. Ask it boldly, "What do you want?" It is then supposed to disappear forever.

In ancient Babylonia, men got rid of demons by making small figures of them, placing these figures in tiny boats, and pushing them out into open water, meanwhile pronouncing a magic formula in hopes the boat would capsize.

Many modern habits are the result of still surviving superstitions and the attempt to change ill chance to good.

If you and another person happen to say the same thing at the same time, link little fingers. If someone gives you a knife, give him a coin in return or the knife will "cut" the friendship. The same thing goes for a pair of scissors—or the donor can drop the scissors and step on them as you drop a penny and step on it.

If you stumble, snap your fingers. If the stumble takes place while crossing someone else's threshold (which used to be taken as a sign that you practiced witchcraft), you must immediately turn around three times and say, "I turn myself three times about, And thus I put bad luck to rout."

In the RAF during World War II, a pilot would pick up a pebble from the airfield before takeoff and put it in the pocket of his flying suit; when he returned from his mission, he put it back. Failure to follow this custom was regarded as a sign that you did not expect to get home. (In one squadron it was the custom, when a pilot did fail to return, for his best friend to take two pebbles along on the next mission, to "make up" for the missing man.) It was also an RAF custom to leave some task unfinished or a letter half-written and to give one's wallet to a friend to hold.

SERVANTS' SUPERSTITIONS

The servants in British houses had a great number of folk beliefs and superstitions. They thought, for instance, that it was bad luck to

enter a house for a job before midday.

cross knives at the table.

let water that had been boiled stand cold in a bedroom.

sweep out a bedroom within an hour of a guest's departure.

return a softboiled egg's shell to the kitchen if the bottom had not been bashed in with a spoon.

start a new job on a Friday.

UP AND AT 'EM

Getting out of bed on the wrong side can ruin your day. What's the right side? The right side is the right side—because the left side is *sinister* (Latin for "left"). In many hotel rooms, if a wall is handy, the bed's left side is placed against it so that the sleeper cannot make a mistake.

Some authorities say you must get out the same side you got in, "otherwise the interrupted 'circle' also suggests symbolically a bad or unpleasant day." Never attempt to avoid difficulties by climbing over the footboard to get into bed. That's extremely bad luck.

ACTORS AND THE STAGE

No aspect of human life has more superstitious people than the performing arts. Luciano Pavorotti always looks for a bent nail on stage before he feels secure singing in opera. John Ford liked to direct films in his "lucky" hat. The Schuberts always tried to avoid opening on an "unlucky" Monday. Walter Hampden, the American Shakespearean, would never speak to other actors backstage while playing Shakespeare.

Many modern actors hold onto ancient folk traditions of the Profession. Here are some of them:

Never whistle in a dressing room.

Never put a hat on a bed or shoes on a table.

Never quote from *Macbeth* or *Hamlet* in conversation or repeat the last line of play dialogue at rehearsal.

Never use real flowers on stage or accept real flowers over the footlights.

Never have lilies or peacock feathers around—perhaps a stage version of antipathy to the Evil Eye.

Never have yellow in a set or green in a costume if it is at all avoidable.

A cane is lucky, but crutches are unlucky onstage.

Knitting on stage is unlucky.

Never remove a wedding ring to go onstage. If a ring is not right for the part you are playing, keep it on, tape over it, and use makeup to disguise the tape.

Never mention the precise number of lines you have in a show, or you'll forget some.

Never open an umbrella on stage.

Never read congratulatory telegrams until after the final curtain on opening night.

Never write on the mirror in your dressing room until after the first performance.

Never send out your laundry until after opening night.

Wigs are unlucky, squeaky shoes lucky.

If the play is a hit, continue to wear the same costume with which you opened. Repair worn places if necessary, but do not change, or the play will lose its appeal.

Call it "Shakespeare's Scottish play," and never say *Macbeth*.

Trip on your first entrance and you'll be lucky.

Don't peek out through the curtain to check the house before a performance.

Bill the straight man over the comedian in a comedy duo.

Spit into your dancing shoes before putting them on.

Never say "Good luck" to a performer. Say "Break a leg!"

TOOTH AND NAIL

Superstitions concerning these parts of the body—the teeth and the toe- and finger-nails—are rife throughout the world.

Wide apart teeth are a good-luck sign. You will travel widely (especially if it's the front teeth that are gapped), prosper, and be happy.

The first baby tooth that falls out should be either burned in the fire or thrown to the squirrels, with an order for them to provide the child with stronger (permanent) teeth.

If the baby's teeth come early, they claim in the North of England, there will soon be fresh toes—meaning a new baby is on the way.

In Britain, if the child's first tooth appears in the upper jaw, it is believed that he will die in infancy. Among the Azande of Africa such a child is called *irakörinde*, "he who has bad teeth," and he is believed to bring bad luck to the crops. They ask him not to eat the first fruits of the harvest, especially peanuts and corn, lest the rest of it be ruined. In Central Asia, in times past, such a child would be taken out and "exposed"—that is, allowed to die or become the victim of a wild animal.

We also have superstitions about fingernails. Almost universal is the fear of allowing nail clippings to fall into someone else's hands, for this will enable an enemy to work magic against you.

If fingernails are broad, it indicates generosity; if long, lack of thrift; if short, that you are a liar. (Specks on them indicate the number of lies).

A whole mystique has developed about when and how to cut nails. If a child's nails are cut before it is a year old, it will grow up to be a thief. (Many mothers, to avoid this fate, bite off their children's nails.) If a sick person's nails are cut, he will never get well. It's bad luck to cut anybody's nails on a Friday or a Sunday. Many cautious people go by the following jingle.

> Cut them on Monday, cut them for wealth;
> Cut them on Tuesday, cut them for health;
> Cut them on Wednesday, cut them for news;
> Cut them on Thursday, a new pair of shoes;
> Cut them on Friday, cut them for woe;
> Cut them on Saturday, a journey to go;
> Cut them on Sunday, cut them for evil,
> And be all the week as cross as the Devil.

WEATHER OR NOT . . .

Mark Twain was wrong—people *do* do something about the weather. Or try to. Here are some popular folk suggestions.

To bring rain: stick a spade in the ground or kill a spider or burn ferns or heather or carry a statue of your favorite saint to a nearby stream and dunk it.

To hold off rain: carry an umbrella or wash your car or water a parched lawn—preparing for rain scares it off.

But most folk beliefs concerning weather involve predicting it.

Signs of rain: Frogs croaking during the day. A halo around the moon. Smoke sticking close to the ground. A greenish sky at the horizon. Spiders deserting their webs. Swallows flying low. Chickweed closing up. Moles casting up their hills. Horses gathering in the corners of fields. Gulls flying inland. Asses braying and shaking their ears. (Almost any kind of excitement or unusual activity among animals is held to be a prediction of a coming storm.) In New England they also say:

Rain before seven,
Clear before 'leven;
Sun at seven,
Rain at 'leven.

Signs of a severe winter: Heavy coats on foxes. Large nut harvest. Skunks coming in early from the woods to make winter homes in barns. Corn husks difficult to pull apart. Oysters bedding deep. Heavy migration of wild geese. Bees laying up large stores of honey. Another New England proverb:

Onion's skin very thin
Mild winter coming in.
Onion's skin thick and tough
Coming winter cold and rough.

Signs of fair weather: Swallows flying high and rooks nesting high in trees. Ants piling up hills early in the morning. Cattle chasing one another about the pasture. Cobwebs on the grass in the morning. Dandelions opening their petals early. Another proverbial jingle:

Red in the morning,
Sailors take warning;
Red at night,
Sailors delight.

SOME AMERICAN SUPERSTITIONS

Never start any enterprise on a Tuesday. Monday is unlucky. Wednesday is the day for weddings.

If three persons are photographed together, the one in the middle will die first.

Don't sleep with your head pointing north or death will follow.

To keep witches from moving, throw salt under their chairs.

Catch a falling leaf, and you will have twelve months of happiness.

It is bad luck to make a new opening in an old house, to wash a garment before it is worn, to comb your hair after dark, to count stars or graves, to drop a book and not step on it, to see a pin and not pick it up, to bring eggs into the house after sunset or sweep the floor before sunrise, to rock an empty chair or to spin a chair on one leg, to sneeze on a Friday or at the dinner table, to get married on a cloudy day or to stumble as you enter your new home as a bride (hence, the husband carrying his bride across the threshold).

SOME BRITISH SUPERSTITIONS

Not to be outdone by their transatlantic cousins—indeed, many American superstitions came to this continent on the *Mayflower* and its successors—the British also have much time-tested folk wisdom. It varies from region to region. Thus:

Anyone appearing in new clothes must be pinched for good luck (North Country).

When an unmarried young person dies, a Maiden's Crown (for bachelors as well as spinsters) should be hung up in the church (Hampshire).

Skipping rope to make the crops grow used to be common but now is seen only on Good Friday at the Rose Cottage, an inn in Alciston (Sussex).

Thursday has one unlucky hour, the hour before the sun rises (Devonshire).

It is good luck to encounter a deformed or retarded person while going fishing (Shetlands).

When you move into a new house, you must carry a loaf of bread and a plate of salt into every room (North Yorkshire).

To give your lover a handkerchief as a gift means that you will soon part. That's just one example of a folk belief widely held throughout Britain.

PINS

Pins, used to attach one thing to another, seem to have intrigued many people, for there are many superstitions concerning them. Both the English and Americans know the old verse:

> See a pin, pick it up;
> All the day, you'll have good luck.
> See a pin, let it lay;
> Bad luck you'll have all that day.

Others say, "Pick up a pin, pick up sorrow," or "Pass up a pin, pass up a friend."

If the point is toward you, don't pick it up at all. If the head is toward you, however, pick it up by the head. In New England this means you will soon be offered a ride.

Never lend a pin. In the North of England, they say, "You can have it— it's a gift. But I'm not lending it."

Brides should never wear pins as part of their wedding outfit, and if there are some on it, they must be thrown away. If a pin is given to a bridesmaid, it means she will not be married before Whitsuntide (the season of Pentecost, usually late May to early June).

Pins were often employed in black magic, usually to stick into a wax image of some person—either to cause him to sicken and pine (the pain would appear in that part of his body that corresponds to the position of the pin) or to draw one's lover to one's side. Devon sailors carried pincushions for good luck. Some practicing witches wore on their persons bags or pads (usually heart-shaped) into which they stuck pins as a way of doing harm to others. "I'll stick in a pin for you" was a potent threat.

If a pin falls and sticks upright, it means a stranger is coming. For good luck, stick a pin in the lapel of someone's coat. To ward off evil, stick an onion or a sheep's heart full of pins. If you want to keep witches from coming down the chimney, hang the pin-stuck object in the flue.

COINS

A lot of superstition is involved with how to get or hold onto money, but for the moment let's speak of the coins themselves.

Some people consider it lucky to carry a coin bearing the date of their birth or some other significant event in their lives. A purse should never be allowed to be entirely emptied of coins; keep at least one in it for good luck. Likewise, never give a purse or wallet as a gift without including a coin of some denomination.

Turning up a coin with the plow is unlucky; spit on both sides of it.

The luckiest coins of all are those that are bent or have a hole in them, especially if they come to you naturally as part of your change. If you have such a coin, carry or wear it on the left side or hang it around your neck. The Chinese used to mint coins with square holes already in them, representing (in the Chinese view of the cosmos) the round sea and the square earth.

Throwing a coin to a wayside beggar brings good luck. So does tossing a coin into a fountain—a belief so widely held that virtually every well, pond, fountain, and reflecting pool available to the public quickly becomes carpeted with tossed coins. At the U. S. Naval Academy, Annapolis, Maryland, middies toss coins at the statue of Tecumseh, for good luck in exams and at sports.

In Greek mythology, the River Styx had to be crossed to get to the Underworld, and the fare, paid to the ferryman Charon, was one obol (a coin of quite a small amount, although not the very smallest). Before a corpse was buried, relatives placed an obol in its mouth.

In England and throughout Europe, coins were placed on the closed eyes of a corpse and buried with it. In the Balkans, there is a superstition that these coins can render a husband "blind" to his wife's extramarital carryings-on; just take them from the corpse, wash them in wine, and induce the cuckolded husband to drink the wine.

GEM STONES

Rubies make excellent amulets, but are said to work best for those born under the sign of Cancer. They bring peace of mind and prevent all evil and impure thoughts. Since they were believed to be strong protectors of chastity, they were often worn by priests in the Middle Ages. On the other hand, being the color of blood, they also attract werewolves.

Jasper will cure madness. If worn as an amulet with certain cabalistic inscriptions, it is supposed to strengthen the intellect.

Agate is supposed to be beneficial to the eyes and acts as an antidote to the poison of spiders and scorpions.

Bloodstone, a variety of chalcedony, is also called heliotrope. In the Middle Ages it was believed that if the stone heliotrope were combined with the flower heliotrope, it would render a man invisible.

Sapphires were thought to make their owner devout, disposed toward peace, and "cool from inward heat." It also helped him sleep.

Emeralds were believed to be found in the nests of griffins (fabulous beasts, half lion, half eagle). Emeralds bestowed on their owner a good understanding, an excellent memory, and riches. If held under the tongue, an emerald enabled a man to prophesy.

Coral, which the ancient naturalist Pliny thought was a plant, was supposed to be able to stanch blood. Like the emerald and the jasper, coral made a man wise. Babies were given it for teething. It was also supposed to be a good preventive against tempests and floods.

Each month of the calendar has its particular birthstone, supposed to be lucky for the person born in that month. Both Englishmen and Americans seem to be agreed on the following list:

January, garnet.

February, amethyst (good for preventing drunkenness).

March, bloodstone or aquamarine.

April, diamond (if held to the left side, it will ward off enemies, madness, wild and venomous beasts, and chiding and brawling).

May, emerald.

June, agate, pearl, or moonstone (pearls are considered unlucky, especially for engagement rings; they bring tears to the marriage).

July, ruby.

August, sardonyx.

September, sapphire.

October, opal (lucky for all those of October birth, but disastrous for others; an opal ring is reputed to have caused the deaths of Alphonso XII of Spain [1857–88], his wife, his sister, and his sister-in-law).

November, topaz (good to ward off grief and "lunatic passion").

December, turquoise.

BABY SUPERSTITIONS

A baby born with teeth may be a vampire.

A baby born with a caul (the inner fetal membrane or amnion) will be lucky.

A baby with large ears will be generous; one with small ears will be stingy. A baby with a big mouth will be a singer or orator; one with a small mouth will be mean.

It is a good sign if the baby cries at baptism, but it is unlucky to change the baby's name after it has been baptised.

If a baby will not take a coin when it is offered, it will grow up reckless with money. Offer a baby a choice of several objects belonging to different family members, living and dead, and its choice will show you whom it will "take after."

To prevent colic, give the baby hot water that has been poured into a shoe.

To keep the baby well, put it out in the first April shower, put a rabbit's foot in its crib, a bag of sulfur around its neck, or sulfur in its shoes.

To bring luck to a newborn, spit on it or rub it all over with lard.

If a baby is born feet first, rub bay leaves on its legs within its first few hours of life. Otherwise it will grow up lame or be lamed in an accident.

Never let an infant see itself in a mirror before it is several months old, or it will die within the year.

Never rock an empty cradle, or the baby to which it belongs will have an early death.

A GRAIN OF SALT

Salt has been recognized, since ancient times, as highly significant in the life of man. Ancient peoples employed it in acts of religious worship. The Greeks burned salt and flesh on their altars. Catholics add salt to water before it is blessed and rendered into holy water (a sacramental and a means of grace).

Superstitions about salt abound also. It is bad luck to spill it. If this should happen, throw a pinch over your left shoulder (where the Devil lurks) as a propitiation.

Salt is the first item to be placed on the dinner table when it is being set, the last thing removed. Concerning salt at the table, there's an old American saying, "Pass me salt, pass me sorrow," and its English version: "Help to salt, help to sorrow."

A pinch of salt was dropped into a churn, so that the butter would "come."

Because salt preserved food, it was thought to purify. In Scotland and Ireland they put salt on the chest of a corpse—up to three handfuls. In the North of England, a young baby, leaving the house for the first time, is given salt—plus an egg, some money, and a piece of bread—so that he will never want for the necessities of life. Similarly, in many parts of the world an arriving stranger is greeted at the threshold of the house with bread and salt.

"ALWAYS A BRIDESMAID . . ."

A comic song of the British music halls used to describe the plight of the bridesmaid who discovered that "wedding bells" were always ringing "for someone else." Being a bridesmaid carries various superstitions of its own, many of them concerned with that very problem—finding a groom of one's own.

To stumble while walking down the aisle is very bad luck, probably leading to old-maidhood. To be a bridesmaid three times used to guarantee that one will never be a bride. Then someone decided that being a bridesmaid *seven* times would break the jinx.

The best way to be sure that you will be the next bride is to catch the bride's bouquet when it is thrown. (In France, a garter is thrown rather than the bouquet.) The bride often takes careful aim, however, so if you are not her choice for the one to follow her down the aisle, you may be out of luck.

If a bridesmaid puts a piece of wedding cake under her pillow, she will dream of her future husband. If a bridesmaid's chances seem really slim in the marrying line, a bride can give her the shoes she wore at the wedding, and these should have been old shoes, anyway. A bride's shoes are a potent charm.

DON'TS

If you want to avoid bad luck, DON'T
   count the stars.
   comb your hair after dark.
   burn apple branches for firewood.
   bring a wild bird into the house.
   dream of cabbages.
   wash new clothes before wearing them.
   make a new opening in an old house.
   watch a person going until they disappear entirely.
   see a crow.
   have your fruit trees bloom twice in a year.
   have your sweet potatoes bloom at all.
   plant a weeping willow.
   have a bat land on your head or touch it.
   take your cat with you when you move.
   get the ASPCA after me for telling you that last one.

2
Animals and Plants

A ROSE IS A ROSE

The national badge of England is the Tudor rose, a popular heraldic device in many coats of arms. The rose is associated with Aphrodite and considered by Christians to be the Virgin's own flower. Yet the rose is often regarded as an unlucky flower.

If roses bloom in the fall, there will be an epidemic of disease the following year. If the Scotch rose blooms out of season, there will be a shipwreck. It is bad luck to scatter the petals of roses, particularly red roses (associated with blood), on the ground.

On the other hand, it was the custom to plant rose bushes on graves—white for a young virgin, red for a person known for charity. And wild roses placed over the gate to a cow pasture will prevent witches from riding on the backs of cows.

In the language of flowers, roses speak of many things but mostly of love: bridal rose, happy love; burgundy rose, unconscious beauty; cabbage rose, ambassador of love; damask rose, brilliant complexion; deep red rose, bashful shame; dog rose, pleasure and pain; rosa mundi, variety; thornless rose, early attachment.

TOADS

In America it's considered bad luck to kill a toad—a belief perhaps derived from the Indians, because throughout tropical America the natives regard the toad as a benevolent water spirit that watches over and ensures the purity of the water (and hence the harvest).

In England and some other parts of the world, however, toads are often feared and loathed as emissaries of the Devil. It was thought that they carried venom like vipers and that touching them could at least cause warts. A farmer who suspected that someone had "overlooked"—bewitched with the Evil Eye—his cattle, burned a toad alive at midnight. This would force the witch to appear. In West Africa, an epidemic is halted by dragging a toad through the village, then casting it—now having absorbed the plague—into the forest.

Despite general mistrust of the toad, the English clung for many centuries to the notion of a "toad stone." This was thought to be a gem stone located in the head of an aged toad, which could indicate the presence of poison by changing color. In *As You Like It* Shakespeare has the banished Duke say: "The toad, ugly and venomous, Wears yet a precious jewel in his head."

Sir Walter Scott's family possessed something reputed to be a toad stone. (The Wizard of the North was supposed to have been descended from a genuine spell-casting and -removing wizard.) Sir Walter once described the family treasure in a letter to a friend: "a toadstone, a celebrated amulet . . . was sovereign for protecting new-born children and their mothers from the power of fairies, and has been repeatedly borrowed from my mother, on account of this virtue."

TREES

Many popular superstitions attach themselves to certain trees. Poplar leaves tremble, according to folk belief, because it was supposedly on a cross of poplar wood that Christ was crucified. Elder is unlucky, too, says another tale, because it is the tree on which Judas Iscariot hanged himself. Cypress trees, frequently planted in graveyards, especially in those of Eastern Mediterranean countries, are said to offer shelter to the dead during bad weather. Western European churchyards often featured yew trees, and it was considered extremely bad luck to injure a churchyard yew, though branches might be stolen for magic wands.

Apple orchards had to be serenaded, and cider-soaked toast left in the branches of the trees "for the robins" (actually, for the god of the orchard). If a dead animal is not buried under the roots of a newly planted tree, it will not bear fruit. An orchard will do better the next year, they say in the West of England, if children are permitted to steal the apples left on the trees after apple picking ("the piskies' harvest"). One must never take *all* the apples off a tree when picking.

All pruning and grafting of fruit trees must be done at the increase of the moon. Thomas Tusser, a sixteenth-century English writer on agriculture—he wrote his *Husbandrie* entirely in verse—gave this advice to farmers:

> From moon being changed
> Till past be the prime,
> For graffing and cropping
> Is very good time.

Around the world, many trees are said to be the habitations of good and evil spirits and to grant blessings or magical dreams to those who touch them. Greeks believed in Dryads, oak nymphs who inhabited woods and ravines and romped with satyrs. Some people will not touch an unlucky tree and, even when cutting down a tree, will first ask forgiveness of the spirit who lives in it.

In Darjeeling, India, there is a sacred tree of Poona. Some years ago an old woman named Shelibai ran around it a million times to ensure the birth of a grandson. When the boy was born, the news took three months to reach the grandmother, so she made 200,000 laps too many.

The Mogul emperor Hamayun (1508–56) wanted a magic carpet but settled instead on a tree house. He had a platform built up in a tree, and there he sat to conduct all his business.

Tree advice from Rev. Daniel Stock, minister at Carlisle, Pennsylvania, in 1850–1867: To make a fruit tree bear, "Bore a hole with a half-inch auger into the heart toward sunrise; then put sulphur in and knock a pin on it." For greatest durability of the wood, cut oak and chestnut in the month of August, in the forenoon, and after full moon. Hickory, pine, maple, or other white wood should be cut in the month of August, in the forenoon, and between new moon and the full of the moon.

PEACOCK FEATHERS

Many people like the elegant look of peacock feathers but somehow fear that the "eye" may have something to do with the Evil Eye. In ancient times the peacock was considered sacred to the goddess Juno, and the "eyes" were thought to represent the eyes of Argus, her hundred-eyed watchman. When her husband Jupiter fell in love with Io and changed her into a heifer to preserve her from his wife's machinations, Juno set Argus to watching the animal, to prevent her from escaping to be with Jupiter. Hermes, sent by Jupiter, lulled Argus to sleep, killed him, and freed Io. In memory of her faithful servant, Juno set his hundred eyes in the tail of her sacred peacock.

Many people use peacock feathers as decorative devices or stand them upright in vases. One late Victorian householder had a ceiling entirely covered with their splendor.

Other people will not have the feathers in the house, perhaps believing, as the ancients did, that where peacock feathers are, no child will be born. Theater people are notoriously uneasy about them, too, and will not have them on the stage. The great Shakespearean Sir Henry Irving didn't even like them in the audience. One night, during the first act of *Othello*, he noticed a woman in the stalls carrying a feathered accessory. He sent her a note: "For heaven's sake, take your peacock-feather fan out of the theatre to save disaster."

CRAZY LIKE A FOX

The cunning of the fox is proverbial and has been for centuries. Though hunted for sport and as a farmland pest, it has managed to survive by artful maneuvering rather than speed—by keeping many "earths" into which to dive, by crossing watercourses to throw foxhounds off the scent, by backtracking its own trail, by running along fence rails or walls, by taking to thin ice, by running through a flock of sheep, occasionally by taking refuge in nearby houses.

Naturally the fox is the subject of many superstitions. Some people believe that thick fur on foxes in the fall presages a bad winter. Others tell stories of how foxes sling stolen goose carcasses over their shoulders to carry them off. Foxes are occasionally believed to rid themselves of fleas by backing into the water, a leaf held in their mouths, until they are entirely submerged, so that the fleas must retreat to the leaf or be drowned. For relief from respiratory ailments, eat a fox's lungs. To see one fox is lucky, but to see many is unlucky. (Foxes are normally solitary, but mates do stay together throughout the breeding and kit-rearing season.) The bark of a fox presages death. To wear a fox's tongue as an amulet cures shyness.

ACORNS

Great superstitions from little acorns grow. The Norsemen associated the oak with Thor, god of storms, who made thunder by flinging his great hammer around the heavens. So they put acorns on their windowsills to protect the house from Thor's anger.

In modern times people put little acorns on the pullstrings of window shades, sometimes encasing real acorns in carefully crocheted jackets, sometimes substituting wooden imitations. Unwittingly they are trying to ward off thunder and lightning.

As for the oak itself, it remains dangerous.

> Beware of the oak.
> It draws the stroke.
> Beware of the ash.
> It courts the flash.
> Creep under the thorn.
> 'Twill protect you from harm.

They say lightning will never strike the elm, or the walnut tree.

FOR THE BIRDS

The bluebird signifies happiness and good luck. The raven croaks of evil. The sparrow kept in a cage in the house will bring bad luck; William Blake said that "puts all Heaven in a rage." A robin flying into your house brings good luck. To kill a dove brings terrible luck, and to rob any bird's nest is to invite disaster. If a bird strikes one of your windowpanes, or if an owl hoots ominously, death may be near for someone in the house. Old superstition has it that a pigeon frequenting your house is good news, but many people very much dislike them nonetheless. When the rooks leave the rookery, expect the worst—worse than rats leaving a sinking ship, in fact.

"WHEN THE WHIPPOORWILL CALLS . . ."

The whippoorwill, because of its dark color and its nocturnal habits, has long been associated with the occult. Moreover, it is often heard just before

dawn, when evil spirits are considered particularly powerful. The spirits are presumably getting in their last licks before they must disappear with the crowing of the cock.

If you hear a whippoorwill near your house, it may be carrying a message of impending death. Even if you cannot see the bird, point your finger in the direction of the sound and "shoot" it. That will counter the evil.

In spring, a young woman who hears the first call of the whippoorwill should listen carefully. One call means the man of her dreams will turn up. Two calls means she will have to wait another year.

Some Amerindians used to say that if you hear two whippoorwills singing together ("hoin, hoin"), you should shout, "No!" If the birds cease at once, the hearer can expect to die shortly, but if they continue to call, the hearer can look forward to a long life. Two whippoorwills are always a bad sign, but fortunately these birds are nearly always solitary.

Never disturb the nests of any birds (bad luck will follow), but be especially careful not to destroy whippoorwill eggs. For each one you destroy, it is said, a member of your family will suffer misfortune.

DOVE OF HAPPINESS

White doves nesting in the beams of one's house are considered good luck by many Islamic peoples. Ali, son-in-law and cousin of Mohammed, used to wish his friends the blessing of white doves. He is reputedly buried in a mosque in Afghanistan, where, it is said, flocks of white pigeons have guarded his tomb for centuries. It is certainly true that if a pigeon with black feathers in its plumage tries to roost there, the white ones drive it violently away.

NESSIE REARS HER UGLY HEAD

Is the famed Loch Ness "monster" fact or fiction, science or superstition? The long, cold, immensely deep Highland lake has been thought for many centuries to be the home of a supernatural "water horse." In recent times, hundreds of people claim to have sighted "Nessie" surfacing, diving, or swimming. Dozens of photographs have been taken, purporting to show a long reptilian neck and a muscular series of "humps" along the creature's back. Divers, exploring the murky depths, occasionally report encountering large moving objects which they cannot identify. Persons of expertise and scientific stature have been sufficiently interested to mount five separate expeditions to explore the loch, equipped with the most modern cameras, recording instruments, and research facilities.

Theories to explain the recorded phenomena range from some sort of giant fish (such as an eel) to a surviving prehistoric marine saurian to masses of decayed vegetation, propelled to the surface and then across it by escaping marsh gas. Nothing has yet been proved, but more and more people are becoming convinced that there'e "something" in Loch Ness.

"ASH GROVE, FAIR ASH GROVE . . ."

My own name, *Ashley*, derives from "ash trees" in a "lea" (field). The ash was revered by the ancient Druids, who worshipped in a sacred grove of ash trees. Think of the charming Welsh folksong "The Ash Grove." Yggdrasil, the great tree of the world in Norse mythology, whose branches extended through the heavens and the earth and the underworld, was an ash tree, and the ash was sacred to many Teutonic peoples. Thus in time there emerged a number of superstitions concerned with the ash.

In ancient rites, people crept through a cleft ash tree, as they did under the dolmen or through the "hole of stone" in the West Country of Britain, to stimulate a kind of new birth and to leave behind disorders and diseases. The ash tree was, as Edmund Spenser wrote, "for nothing ill," so ash was used for the magician's wand (if hazel was not available) and for other magical purposes.

In *Witchcraft and Black Magic*, Montague Summers tells of Cornish children suffering from rupture being "passed through a slit in an ash before sunrise fasting," after which the slit portion was bound together, and this sympathetic magic supposedly caused the rupture to heal. Summers also wrote of country people carrying "a splinter of ash to protect themselves against ill-wish, or as a grand specific for rheumatism." He added:

> The reason for giving ash sap to new-born children in the High-
> lands of Scotland is, first, because it acts as a powerful astringent,
> and, secondly, because the ash, in common with the rowan, is
> supposed to possess the property of resisting the attacks of
> witches, fairies, and other imps of darkness.

The ash had sinister attributes in the opinion of other peoples. In *The Black Arts*, Richard Cavendish says that "the ash, yew and cypress are associated with death and graveyards," though he also notes that a magic circle is consecrated with "a bunch of vervain, periwinkle, sage, mint, valerian, ash, basil, and rosemary." Ash branches are among the things burned in ritual magic, for even the ashes of ashes are powerful!

Legend has it that the Virgin Mary used ash twigs to make a fire to warm the Christ Child at the Nativity, so ash is often used for cradles, and Anglo-Saxon mothers used to hang the cradles of their children from the branches of the ash trees. If you want your child to grow up to be a good singer, bury its first fingernail parings under an ash tree. Many people in England still believe in that.

WOLVES AND MAN-WOLVES

According to ancient legend, Romulus and Remus, founders of Rome, were suckled by a she-wolf. For many centuries, Romans thought of themselves as Sons of the Wolf, and in other countries legends persist of human children reared by wolves. Such a "wolf-boy" was picked up in Lucknow, India, in 1954, and there have been others. Evidence to prove this, however, is often vague, unreliable, and based on assumption without proof.

The ancients believed it was bad luck just to catch sight of a wolf and that, if he saw you before you saw him, you would lose your voice. If you spoke of a wolf, one would appear—probably with hostile intent. He would not attack a flock of sheep, however, if the shepherd kept a careful count of them. As moderns speak of having a tiger by the tail, Romans said, *Lupum auribus tenere*, "To hold a wolf by the ears."

Belief in werewolves is as old as the Roman Republic and very widespread. Virgil wrote in the Eighth Eclogue, *His ego saepe lapum fieri . . . vidi*, "By means of these [poison plants] I often saw him turned into a wolf. . . ." In France today they speak of the *loup-garou*, in Spain of *lobombre*, in Italy of *lupo mannaro*. In parts of Sicily it is believed that if you can somehow get a wolf's skin to wear, it will give extraordinary courage. In men's minds, the wolf seems to symbolize power.

In Norwegian legend we have the saga of Sigmund the Volsung and his son, Sinfjötli. Adventuring in the forest, they come upon a house in which two men, with great gold rings, are sleeping, and on the wall hang two wolf skins. Sigmund and his son put on the wolf skins as garments and are transformed by their magic into wolves, howling at each other but understanding each other as if they spoke words. They run off into the forest and slay many men. On the tenth day, weary with slaughter, they are back at the house, where they shed the skins and the spell that they had taken over from the two sleeping men, who turn out to be the king's sons, under enchantment. This story obviously has something to do with the wild Vikings who, dressed in furs, went berserk and ravaged the countryside, despoiling, raping, destroying.

OTHER MAN-ANIMALS

In other cultures, men were believed to turn into other animals who represented wildness and strength. In Greece they had a wereboar, in Walachia (Rumania) a weredog, in China a werefox, in other parts of the Orient a weretiger, in Java and Malaya a wereleopard, in Central America a were-eagle and a wereserpent, in Chile a werevulture, and among American Plains Indians a werebuffalo.

DOGS

Dogs, which have lived so close to man for so many eons, have given rise to even more superstitions than wolves. Ghostly dogs protect long-dead people, demon dogs accompany witches, headless dogs run rampant in legend, and even real dogs are involved in superstitions.

In Tibet, people in bad health or out of luck make little human figures out of dough and throw them to the dogs as "ransom"—a cheap and effective way to escape one's troubles. (Tibetans might consider purchasing American "people crackers," canine tidbits in the shape of mailmen and other people frequently attacked by dogs.)

Fernand Mery in *The Life, History and Magic of the Dog* recounts a number of superstitious beliefs about the dog. He says dogs were venerated in ancient Egypt and since then often believed to have a kind of ESP:

> A dog was fast asleep on the terrace of a villa at Antibes when [an eyewitness] saw it suddenly leap up and run howling to the railings. It was called back and quietened, but then it began to behave even more strangely. It crouched under the bed of its master and wailed incessantly. It so happened that at the same moment when the dog was wrenched from sleep on the terrace, its owner was killed in a car accident several miles from Nice.

The loyalty of dogs to their masters is proverbial, of course, the most famous being that of Greyfriars Bobby, a small Scots dog who slept for fourteen years, 1858–1872, summer and winter, on the grave of his master. Not one of the many eminent Scots buried in this Edinburgh churchyard is as famous throughout the world as Bobby.

Superstition caused dogs to be used to pull up mandrake roots. These roots—shaped like a man, our ancestors thought—were believed to have magical powers, but when they were torn from the earth they made a sound so like a human cry that it was thought it would drive a man insane. Therefore, the plant was tied to a dog's tail, and *he* pulled it up, for dogs were believed to be immune.

Dogs were often regarded as the familiar spirits of witches and wizards. They were considered to be emissaries of the Devil in animal form, bestowed upon their earthly masters to do their bidding. In Goethe's *Faust*, Mephistopheles first approaches Doctor Faustus in the form of a dog. Cornelius Agrippa, a sixteenth-century German student of the occult, had a large black dog that followed him everywhere—worked with him, slept with him. People were convinced that the animal was really a demon in disguise.

BANANAS

In recent years American teenagers went through the Mellow Yellow period, when hippies were convinced that smoking banana peel would get you "high." Methods were handed around among subculture groups for preparing the peels for "tripping," and many young people did indeed claim to have taken off on banana skins—either from too little oxygen or too much imagination.

In New Britain, Bismarck Archipelago, banana skins are taken even more seriously. If you thoughtlessly discard a banana skin, a witch can retrieve it, burn it, and thereby cause you to die a painful death.

RUN, RABBIT, RUN

Alexander Severus, Roman emperor from 222 to 235, attributed his lifelong good looks to the fact that at every single meal he ate rabbit. Down the centuries there have been many superstitions connected with this attractive little animal. If a rabbit crosses the road behind you, it is good luck (trouble is behind you), but if one crosses in front of you, it could mean problems. To avoid the problems, cross yourself, or make an X in the road, spit on it, and walk backward over it before continuing on your way.

In countless tales and folk legends, the rabbit symbolizes the common man—forever persecuted, forever cunningly outwitting his betters. Joel Chandler Harris's *Uncle Remus* stories are literary retellings of West African folktales. Beatrix Potter in *Peter Rabbit* and Richard Adam in *Watership Down* have continued the tradition. It's no wonder that one of modern man's most persistent superstitions concerns the importance of carrying a rabbit's foot.

FLOWER TIME

In Europe chrysanthemums are regarded as flowers of death. Never give them as a present. (A variety of chrysanthemum, pyrethrum, contains an ingredient important in insecticides.) In China, however, they are considered the symbol of autumn, and in Japan their resemblance to the sun makes them virtually sacred.

Some people think the first time you visit people, especially for a dinner party, you should bring along white flowers (no other color). Others say one should never bring white flowers into the house.

Don't let florists put fern along with a bouquet, for fern should never be brought into a house. Other people say fern is a protection against witches.

Never pick the earliest flowers in spring, or ivy or Canterbury bells or a single violet or a hyacinth or a white lilac or one lily of the valley or a leaf off a barberry bush or a pansy with the dew still on it.

Lavender, marigolds, snowdrops, and carnations are all lucky, all associated with the Blessed Virgin. Asters are associated with Venus, the cornflower with the goddess Flora, the daisy with Saint Margaret of Antioch, the lily with Eve, and the shamrock, of course, with Saint Patrick; they are all bringers of good fortune, as are primroses (associated with British Prime Minister Benjamin Disraeli) provided you have a pretty big bunch of them and not just a few.

Many flowers have interesting tales connected with them. The hyacinth is supposedly the metamorphosis of a friend of the god Apollo, who was accidentally slain—the red spot is his blood. The thistle saved the Scots from a Viking invasion, it is reported, when a Norseman in the dark stepped on one and let out an involuntary yelp, which roused the Scots to defend themselves. It is now, of course, the national badge of Scotland as the rose is of England.

Crowns of flowering hazel (which will make your wishes come true) and flowering hawthorn (though legend says hawthorn was used for the Crown of Thorns) are especially lucky.

THE GENTLEMAN WHO PAYS THE RENT

The "gentleman" of the above title is the Irishman's pig, for that was the way the Irish tenant farmer used to refer to this useful beast. Cheaply fed and easily reared, he was often a poor farmer's only cash source, so that the money from his sale might well be the family's only means of scraping up the rent money.

Pigs are often treated with great respect in Ireland, and when the Irish began to emigrate to America they took their pigs along. ("As Irish as Paddy's pig," Americans used to say.) Some superstitions about pigs probably went with them:

It is bad to kill a pig when the moon is waning. The flesh may not take salt (and consequently won't cure), and the bacon will shrink in the pan. Pigs are considered good weather predictors. If you see a pig running with a straw in its mouth, rain is coming; if a pig squeals loudly a storm is on the way—pigs "see wind." If a pig runs off, sickness is coming to the family. If you dream of pigs, you will be asked for money. If you have a run of bad luck and wish to break it, pull a pig's tail. And if you own a pig figurine, break it. Even piggy banks are unlucky. Chip yours a little or, better yet, knock one ear off.

Several religions regard the pig as unclean, but this is a canard. The animal is actually much cleaner than a horse or cow, but it does roll in mud to cool itself off, because it does not have sweat glands.

In some languages it is unlucky to refer to the pig directly. The Chinese call him "the long-nosed general." Among the fisherman of northeast Scotland, one does not mention pigs at sea. Just as touching wood can prevent evil on land, so at sea if a pig is mentioned (especially when baiting the lines, which could ruin the catch), one touches iron. "Even in church," it has been reported, "whenever the story of the Gadarene swine was read, the stalwart fisherman would reach for their bootnails and mutter, 'cauld airn' [cold iron]."

Pigs, being more intelligent than dogs, make good familiars for witches and are supposed sometimes to accompany those who have sold their souls to the Devil. If the appropriate charms are used, they will dig up truffles for you. The natives of Sumatra save the jawbones of the pigs they have eaten and suspend them from the ceiling. This is thought to guarantee the salvation of each little porker's soul.

CATS

The Egyptians had a cat god, Bast. She was the goddess of pleasure and protected men against contagious disease and other evils. In Bast's honor, they mummified cats.

The ancient Hebrews believed the ashes of a black kitten would enable one to see demons. Today people are afraid when a black cat crosses their path. In Britain it's unlucky to say the word *cat* while you're down in a mine. In Texas they say you're lucky if a black cat comes into your house, provided it stays. In Lancashire, it's unlucky if a cat dies in your house. It's bad luck for a family to move a cat. Among the Azande of Africa, some women are supposed to give birth to cats; nobody can deny this, for to see one of them is to die. The Chinese emperors slept on cat-shaped pillows for luck.

Buddhists will tell you where cats come from. A rat ate part of one of Buddha's scriptures, so the Enlightened One rubbed a little skin off the inside of his arm and from that made the first cat. The proof? Rats are still afraid of cats.

RATS

Rats are another animal, like foxes, about whom many queer stories are told. They are thought to free one another from traps by gnawing away caught tail tips or by springing the mechanism. Witnesses have reported seeing rats transport a stolen egg to their nest through a cooperative technique: one lies on its back, clinging to the egg, the other pulls its friend across the floor by its tail.

There are many traditional methods of ridding a building of an infestation of rats. In New England, you write the unwanted creatures a letter, telling them that they must leave your premises and suggesting a nearby house where they might be more comfortable. You then grease the paper to make it more palatable to them and push it into the rathole. It is soon digested. So, superstition says, is the message on it.

Rats are perhaps most famous as foretellers of maritime disaster. Rats leaving a sinking ship are a classic symbol of escape from falling fortune. In July 1889, three hands aboard the *Paris C. Brown*, a riverboat plying between Cincinnati, Ohio, and Plaquemine, Louisiana, saw some rats leaving the ship, and in a panic they walked off too. They turned out to be the sole survivors of the *Brown*, for after sailing it was never heard from again. Literally. Not even wreckage of the *Brown* was ever found. The vessel disappeared—completely, permanently, mysteriously.

FISH

St. Malo, the French seaport, still sees fishermen throw back the first fish of the season, for luck. But first they pour a lot of wine down its throat.

The idea is that it will tempt all the other fish to hurry up and get caught so they, too, can get drunk.

Most dreams of fish are said to forecast good luck. The fish is a symbol of life, fishing is a sign of peaceful life, and to see a fish in the water is to receive unexpected favors. A dead fish means loss, and cleaning and dressing a mackerel stands for "deceit and evil tidings."

DRAGON BONES

The belief that many ills can be cured with "dragon bones" in powdered form has cost China a precious, irreplaceable part of its ancient history.

For decades, farmers digging in their fields in Anyang have unearthed certain old bones inscribed with designs that the modern scholar Liu Ngo finally identified as the ancient writing of the Shang people. But before the nature and value of these records could be established by archaeologists, much of this treasure was sold to apothecaries, who pulverized the bones and sold them as "dragon bones."

About 1928, the importance of these finds (and ceremonial vessels of bronze and other artifacts) was established. Well-organized scientific expeditions disinterred treasures from one hundred tombs, ten of them sites of elaborate royal burials. Thus some of the Shang heritage was preserved, but much of China's distant past was lost with the inscriptions on the old "dragon bones."

STORKS

Centuries ago there was already a superstition that a stork flies over a house where a birth is about to take place. It's a small step from that to the legend of the stork as the bringer of babies and of good luck.

So valued are storks as symbols of domestic bliss—for which their habit of mating for life provides a good example—that when these birds began to disappear recently from parts of northeastern Europe, whole regions cooperated in campaigns to induce the birds to return. Pollution controls were instituted, telephone lines raised or lowered so that they would no longer interfere with the birds' flight patterns, and new buildings provided with stork-attracting chimneys. The stork population has begun to rise again, and so have the hopes of their delighted hosts.

EGGS

In Siberia it was believed that shamans (witch doctors) were born from iron eggs laid in larch trees by a large mythical bird.

It's unlucky to use the word *egg* aboard ship.

Eggs are symbolic of life and fertility. Our Easter eggs represent the Resurrection and the renewal of life that comes with spring. In Washington, D.C., they roll them on the White House lawn. In the Ukraine they still decorate them with symbols that recall the ancient days of sun worship.

China's best-known eggs are the so-called hundred-year-old ones, a delicacy. (Actually they have been preserved for considerably less time than that, probably ten years.) Chinese also decorate a baby's layette with designs featuring eggs for good luck. These eggs have eyes to "see" that the child is protected.

A GALLIMAUFRY

The reason a horse blows on water before drinking at night is that water sometimes sleeps, and if an animal were to drink sleeping water, it would die. Blowing wakes the water up.

If you try to kill a snake after dark, it will not die.

Never kill flies toward the end of the year, for you will suffer a $100 loss for each fly killed.

German farmers dread turning up a turnip in the shape of a shriveled hand.

A black lamb means good luck for the flock.

It is bad luck to meet a white horse.

If a rooster crows while facing the door, expect the visit of a stranger.

Leap year, say the Scots, was never a good year for sheep.

Certain mushrooms grow in a circle, called a fairy ring. The Irish believe these rings are caused by the Good People circling in round dances.

3

Medicine and Health

CHARMS AND PREVENTIVES

The common man of yore, who had no access to doctors, knew that his best hope of living for a long time lay in not falling ill. Therefore, innumerable charms were thought up for warding off disease.

Rheumatism. Carry an animal's foot bone (preferably a hare's right forefoot) or an amber charm. Or wear an eelskin around the waist. Or carry in your pocket a potato that has been begged or stolen from someone else. Or carry buckshot in your pocket, or a horse chestnut. Or carry a piece of mountain ash. Or wear a ring made from a silver coffin handle. Or tie a brass wire around your wrist. Or avoid "unclean" habits in youth (advice from the Delaware Indians).

Fits. Carry ash twigs in silk bags. Or go to the parish church at midnight on June 23 (that is, as Midsummer Day is about to break), walk three times up and down each aisle and crawl three times under the Communion table from north to south—this last as the clock is striking twelve. Or grate a small portion of human skull and sprinkle it on the potential sufferer's food. Or collect nine silver coins and nine sets of three halfpennies from nine bachelors (if the sufferer is a woman, from maidens if the sufferer is a man). The silver coins should be made into a ring for the epileptic to wear, and the halfpennies are given to the jeweler or whoever makes the ring.

Colds. Catch an oak leaf before it touches the ground. Or rub yourself with bear grease.

Ague. Tie a red ribbon to someone else's gate. The affliction will then attack him instead of you. Or cut off a lock of hair, wrap it around a pin, and

37

stick it in the bark of an aspen tree; then say, "Aspen tree, aspen tree, I pray thee shake instead of me."

Tuberculosis. Smear yourself with dog's fat. Or swallow baby frogs before breakfast.

Toothache. Carry a double nut in your pocket. Or wear around your neck in a little bag a tooth taken from a corpse. Or do the same with the forelegs and one hind leg from a mole. Or put on stockings or trousers right leg first.

For all-around good health, wear around your neck a pebble exposed for three nights to the beams of the moon. Or wear a stone with a natural hole in it—a powerful charm, especially against witchcraft and fairies.

WARTS

There are almost too many cures for warts to count. Many of them work, too, for warts often disappear spontaneously, no matter what you do. Here are some things superstition recommends for warts.

Steal a dishrag and hide it in a stump. Or rub the warts with "stones, peas, beans, or seeds" and then throw the latter away. Or tie as many knots in a string as you have warts and bury the string; as the string rots, the warts will disappear. Or put vinegar on your wart and on a penny at the same time; as the copper corrodes, your wart will vanish.

Rub a wart with corn, then bore a hole in a tree, insert the corn, and plug up the hole. Or fill your mouth with corn, dig a hole, spit the corn into the hole, and cover it up. Or rub the wart with a sassafras leaf or soda bread or a piece of onion (then throw it away). Or rub the wart with a penny.

Capture a large black snail, rub it over your warts, then hang it up on a thorn; do this nine nights in succession. Or rub your wart with raw meat (preferably stolen), wrap the meat in paper, and throw it away in a spot where a dog will find it.

Cut a notch in a stick for each wart and burn the twig. Or say your prayers backward over the wart. Or take a nail you have touched to the wart and make a cross with it on a pecan tree. Or wash your warts in water in which eggs have been boiled. Or put a drop of blood from the wart into a hollowed-out kernel of corn and throw the kernel to the chickens.

Or kill a cat and bury it in a black stocking. Or steal a piece of steak and bury it where three roads meet. Or bury a rooster's comb. Or rub the wart with a peeled apple and then give the apple to a pig.

When a funeral is passing, rub your warts and say, "May these warts and this corpse pass away and nevermore return."

SALIVA

From very ancient times human saliva was thought to have the power to cure wounds, to ward off evil, to attract good luck. Dancers spit into their ballet shoes, workmen spit on their hands before launching into a job, actors spit on either side of you to bring you luck. Fighters spit on their hands for luck.

Christ used His saliva to heal the sick, to bring back sight to the blind.

Businessmen spit on the *Handsel*, the first money taken for the day. (To be lucky, the *Handsel* must be "well wet.") A successful bettor spits on his winnings.

Spittle is an ingredient in many charms. It was mixed with dirt and oil and smeared on foreheads. It was spat into water in which two persons had (presumably inadvertently) washed. It was used to moisten dry ingredients in poultices and doses, somehow conveying to them the power of life.

Spitting to change bad luck to good is almost a worldwide practice. Some Australian aborigines spit whenever a dead man's name is mentioned. Ancient Greeks spat three times at the sight of an epileptic or madman. Old women in Greece and Rome would spit three times to ward off the Evil Eye, especially if it was thought to be threatening a child. English rustics spat three times if they saw a piebald horse, a dead dog, or a person lame in the right leg.

METALS AS MEDICINE

Certain metallic elements were thought to contain important magic properties and to ward off or cure illness.

Iron was hated by fairies and witches, who would not approach it. (It was suspected that these supernatural creatures were, in fact, survivors of Bronze Age people, inimical to newcomers who possessed iron tools and weapons.) To preserve the family from spells and prevent fairies from carrying off newborn children, a piece of iron was laid on the threshold or a horseshoe tacked up over the door. When something evil or dangerous was mentioned, men touched iron (as moderns knock on wood). To prevent disease, men wore iron rings or amulets.

But it was considered bad luck to bring old iron into the house. No plant with magical virtues should be cut with iron. In some parts of Europe it was considered bad luck to plow with iron-tipped plowshares, and many buildings, especially sacred ones, were erected without the use of iron nails.

Gold and silver were associated with the sun and the moon respectively, often male and female as well. Gold ruled the heart and was prescribed by early physicians—for wealthy patients, it need hardly be said—as a tonic and a cordial, a strengthener of the heart. Silver ruled the head and was prescribed for melancholia, failure of memory, and epilepsy.

Antimony, mercury, lead, sulfur, tin, bismuth, zinc—all these had passing phases as medicines. Today the chief mineral prescribed for health and human diet is iron. No wonder fairies are seen no more.

SNEEZING

Gesundheit means "health," and it's what Germans (and many others) say when people sneeze. Why? Because of an old superstition that when a person sneezes his soul for an instant flies out of his body. A quick blessing will prevent the entry of a demon at this awkward time.

Some people like to sneeze. Truman Capote claims that seven sneezes in a row are as good as an orgasm. (Not everyone agrees with him.)

Sneezes were often signs of good things. If a sailor sneezed on the starboard side of a vessel as it embarked, it would have a lucky voyage. If he sneezed on the port side, it would encounter foul weather. If you sneeze in the morning before breakfast, you will receive a present before the week is out. If you sneeze before you get up on Sunday, it means that a wedding is approaching. If a sick person sneezes, he will recover. Sneezing three times in a row is a sign of good luck.

But it's bad luck for a bride or groom to sneeze during the wedding ceremony.

The Scots believed that a newborn baby was under a fairy's spell until it gave its first sneeze; then the spell was broken. Scots midwives often carried snuff with them to induce sneezing.

A once familiar rhyme summarizes the meaning of sneezes:

Sneeze on Monday, sneeze for danger;
Sneeze on Tuesday, kiss a stranger;
Sneeze on Wednesday, get a letter;
Sneeze on Thursday, something better;
Sneeze on a Friday, sneeze for sorrow;
Sneeze on Saturday, see your sweetheart tomorrow.
Sneeze on Sunday, your safety seek,
Or the Devil will have you all the week.

The Zulus believe that a sneeze summons *makosi* (spirits). The natives of Calabar say, "Far from you!" and make a gesture of shooing away evil. Some Christians cross themselves. Some say, "Bless me!" The Samoans say, "Life to you."

Sir Thomas Browne, writing of superstitions, mentioned the belief that when the king of Monomotapa sneezed, blessings were broadcast all over the sky.

Garcilaso de la Vega, Peruvian historian, records that when the native chief Guachoya sneezed, all his courtiers cried, "Save you!" prompting the great explorer Hernando de Soto to remark, "Do you not see all the world is one?"

In fact, all the world does seem to be "one" on some of these remarkably universal superstitions.

BURNS

A wide variety of folk remedies are advocated for treatment of burns. American Indians used honey, an infusion of pine bark, or wilted Jimson-weed leaves (applied externally, of course, for Jimson weed is a deadly poison if ingested).

A poultice of mashed potatoes is an American remedy (and possibly a useful one, for the puree must seal off the injury from infection and keep it moist while healing).

Goose dung mixed with the bark of the elder tree was an English cure for burns, as was touching the burn with some item of church linen such as an altar cloth or chalice napkin. But in Great Britain people relied mainly on charms for healing burns.

Lay your hand over the burned spot, blow on it three times, each time saying, "Old clod beneath the clay, burn away, burn away. In the name of God, be thou healed." That's an Irish charm.

In the Shetland Islands, one says:

> Here come I to cure a burnt sore;
> If the dead knew what the living endure,
> The burnt sore would burn no more.

And in the West of England:

> Three Angels came, from North, East and West,
> One brought fire, another brought frost,
> And the third brought the Holy Ghost.
> So out fire and in frost,
> In the Name of the Father, Son, and Holy Ghost.

ITCHING

The presistent torment of itching has driven many people to attempt either to cure it or explain it. Hence the following folk beliefs:

An itchy right palm means money is coming, and an itchy left that money is slipping away. You can break the spell of the latter, however, by rubbing the offending left hand on wood. An itchy right hand can also mean a friend is coming, that you will soon be shaking hands with a stranger, or that you will be having company. If the thumb pricks, however, it portends evil. "By the pricking of my thumbs," says the second witch in *Macbeth*, "something wicked this way comes."

If your nose itches, you will shortly meet a fool and be injured by him. If your right ear itches, someone has said something nice about you; if it's your left, someone has said something not so nice about you. If your right eye itches, you are shortly going to laugh; if it's your left, you are shortly going to cry. If your upper lip itches, you will be kissed by someone tall; if it's your lower, by someone short.

If your knee itches, you will soon be kneeling in a strange church. If your foot itches, you will soon be treading strange ground. If your elbow itches, you will soon be sleeping with a strange bedfellow.

CURES

If, even after all the precautions you have taken, you still manage to fall ill, there are still some measures to be taken. Here are a few folk remedies:

Cramp. Wear an eelskin around the leg to relieve leg cramps. Or wear a moleskin around your left leg. Or tie a cotton string around your ankle. Or lay your shoes across the aching member. Or use cork; wear cork garters or lay pieces of cork between the sheet and the mattress of your bed. Or stand on the leg that has cramp and recite the following:

> Foot, foot, foot is fast asleep;
> Thumb, thumb, thumb, in spittle we steep;
> Crosses three we make to ease us;
> Two for the thieves and one for Jesus.

Best of all for cramp was a cramp ring, usually made from the nails, hinges, or handles of a coffin or—in the American West—from a bent horseshoe nail. Edward the Confessor had a cramp ring, supposedly an aid to stomach cramps; it was handed down for several generations of kings before being lost. Tudor kings revived the fashion, consecrating pieces of silver and gold each Good Friday, which metal was then made into rings. The custom was abandoned by Edward VI.

Rheumatism. Have the patient treated by a woman who has given birth to a child by "footling presentation" (that is, feet first). Or rub pepper into the finger- and toenails (a Javanese cure). Or crawl under bramble bushes, thus "scraping off" the ailment. Or bury the patient up to the neck in a churchyard (old version) or give him a hot mud bath (modern version). Or chew a thistle. Or carry a haddock bone (the haddock has long been considered a "sacred" fish because of the two dark marks just behind its head, said to be the fingermarks of Saint Peter). Or induce bees to sting the affected area—a remedy recently rediscovered under respectable auspices, for bee venom is now thought to counteract the pain of this condition.

Fever. Drink gin, flavored with powdered mole, for nine consecutive mornings. Or chew a turnip. Or place an agate stone on the forehead. Or eat watermelon. Or imbed the fingernail parings of the patient in a ball of wax and stick the wax on a neighbor's door, thus "transferring" the fever to him. Or make three knots in a thread, rub the sufferer with the knots, then throw part of the thread with two of the knots into the fire, saying, "I put the sickness on top of the fire," and tie the rest of the thread with the third knot around the patient's neck.

Toothache. Apply the boiled root pulp of the sumac tree. Or drive a nail into an oak tree (especially one struck by lightning). Or bite off at ground level the first fern that appears in the spring. Or catch a frog, spit into its mouth, and then throw it away. Or apply gunpowder and brimstone. Or apply a splinter from a gallows on which a murderer has been hanged. Or drink water from a human skull. Or touch your mouth with the finger of a dead child. Or take clay from the grave of a priest and say a Paternoster ("Our Father") and an Ave ("Hail, Mary").

Stomach disorders. Tie a cormorant skin to the stomach. Drink an infusion of pine bark.

Headache. Bind the head of a buzzard or the cast-off skin of a snake around the forehead. Or clutch some scraped radish pulp. Or find some moss grown on a human skull, dry it to powder, and use it like snuff. Or nail a lock of the sufferer's hair to a tree, preferably aspen or ash. Or wear a rope noose with which a man has been hanged.

Bleeding. Apply cobweb. Or (for nosebleed) push a cold key down the back or hold a table knife to the upper lip. Or wear a dead toad in a bag around the neck or a lace from the shoe of a member of the opposite sex. In fairness to folk beliefs, however, it ought to be pointed out that ordinary people at least tried to stanch bleeding; their "betters," the learned doctors who attended the rich and important, often deliberately caused bleeding in the belief that it relieved fever and released the demons of disease, the humours.

Epilepsy. Every two hours, take a concoction of pulverized horse hook. Or wear a ring made from a half-crown donated to a church collection. Or take the victim's nail parings and a lock of his hair and bury them together with a live cock at the spot where the victim fell down in his last seizure. Or drink an infusion of mistletoe. Or wear a necklace made from nine pieces of elder wood. Or eat the heart of a black jackass on toast. Or drive a nail into the ground at the spot where the epileptic fell. Or for nine days in a row eat the heart of a crow beaten up with its blood.

Boils. Place a poultice over the boils for three days and nights; then place the poultices with their cloths in the coffin of somebody about to be buried. Or hang three nutmegs or a camphor bag around the neck. Or induce a friend to go to a cemetery for you and walk six times around the grave of a recently interred corpse. Or steep the petals of the madonna lily in brandy, then apply to the boil, rough side down.

Injuries or sores. Keep the instrument or weapon bright until the wound heals. Cut a slit in the stomach of a freshly killed animal and thrust the sore member into it; as the stomach cools down, the sores will heal. Or sleep on a bearskin.

Colds. Boil sumac leaves in beer and drink the brew. Or stuff a thin slice of orange rind up each nostril. Or eat dried rats' tails.

Erysipelas. This streptococcal infection, highly contagious, is characterized by high fever and outbreaks of rough, reddened areas on the skin. It used to be much more common than it is today, and hence there were a number of spells for curing it. Apply sheep's dung as a poultice to the eruptions. Or strike sparks from stone and steel in such a way that they will touch the face. Or cut off one ear of a cat—or its tail—and allow the blood to drip on the affected part. Or wear a piece of elder wood around the neck; it must be a piece cut between two knots on which the sun has never shone. Or pass a red-hot poker near the face three times, chanting:

> Three holy men went out walking;
> They did bless the heat and the burning;
> They blessed it that it might not increase;
> They blessed it that it might quickly cease;
> And guard against inflammation and mortification,
> In the Name of the Father, the Son, and the Holy Ghost.

Miscellaneous cures. For earache: blow tobacco smoke in the ear or prick a snail and apply a drop of the moisture that comes out. For gout: take hairs from the affected leg, plus the sufferer's nail parings, put them into a hole made in an oak, and seal it with cow dung. For jaundice: eat nine lice on a piece of bread and butter. For wens: touch a dead man's hand. For baldness: drink sage tea or anoint the bald spot with goose dung. For drunkenness: put a live eel or the eggs of an owl in the drunken man's drink. (To prevent herself from marrying a drunkard, a girl should make sure she never gets wet when doing the laundry.) For colic: stand on your head for fifteen minutes or jump through a midsummer bonfire, or drink wolf dung mixed with white wine. For sore eyes: apply tea or rainwater that fell on Holy Thursday or an ointment made of salt, human milk, and crushed bed bugs. For scarlet fever: cut some hair from the patient's head and stuff it down the throat of a donkey. For frostbite: apply a poultice of cow manure and milk. For goiter: take a common snake by head and tail and draw it nine times across the swelling; then put the snake, alive, in a bottle.

General sickness. Wash the patient and throw the water over the cat. Or make a chalk mark on an iron kettle and put it on the fire; as the mark burns off, the disease will be driven out. In Tibet, if a doctor happens to be out of the precise remedy you require, he writes your prescription on a piece of paper; then you take the prescription—literally. You swallow the piece of paper, for it's considered the same as taking the medicine itself.

HANDS

The hand, along with upright posture, imagination, reasoning ability, and fear of the future, is one of the marks that distinguish man from animals. It is not surprising that the hand is involved in many superstitious beliefs.

A moist hand is supposed to be the sign of an amorous nature. Cold hands are a sign of a warm heart. If two people wash hands in the same basin at the same time, they will soon quarrel and part. It is lucky to have a left-handed pitcher in baseball. If a baby's hands are washed before it's a year old, he will never have money. Shake hands with the right, and you'll have good luck; with the left, bad luck. If four people shake hands with the pairs crossed, a wedding is in the offing. But if the hands of two people cross while reaching for something, look for a quarrel between them. A hand must cover the mouth when you are yawning, or the Devil may enter through it.

The Romans had names for the four fingers, indicating their uses: index finger, *salutaris* (healthy, useful); middle finger, *medius* (middle), but also *impudicus* and *infamis* (shameless, disgraceful) because indecent gestures were performed with it, ring finger, *anularis* (ring); and little finger, *parvus* (little). Images of hands were frequently used as amulets, usually to signify power. To ward off the Evil Eye, of course, one made signs with one's hands.

The laying on of hands was regarded as a most potent gesture of healing, particularly if the person who did the laying on was powerful or holy. The touch of kings was considered especially efficacious. The royal touch for curing diseases probably got its start with Louis IX (1215–70), crusader and lawgiver, canonized as Saint Louis by Boniface VIII in 1297. This pious king of France was credited with miracles even while he was alive, and he cured many of scrofula, tuberculosis of the lymph glands, by the touch of his hand.

French and English royal families frequently intermarried, so the blood of Saint Louis ran in the veins of the English kings as well. Therefore English kings also used to "touch for the scrofula," or "king's evil." After they more or less gave it up, the eighteenth-century earl of Chesterfield took it up for a while, until the embarrassment of his friends called a halt.

Today many still believe in the efficacy of touching in faith healing. You can see it in many churches and at revival meetings and "crusades" and even on televised religious shows. Many cures are claimed.

The laying on of hands survives in the father's blessing, in the ritual by which a bishop ordains a priest, even in a sense in the friendly touch that demonstrates caring, affection, sympathy.

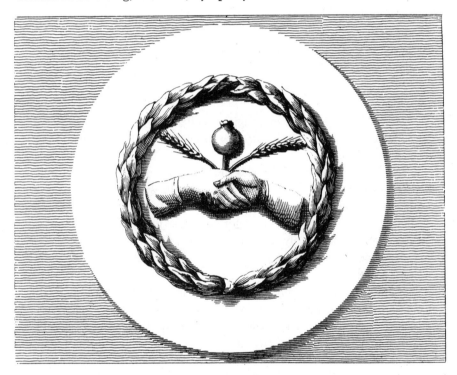

4

Places

WELLS

Many superstitions and religious beliefs are associated with wells, perhaps because water carries strong connotations of life-giving and rebirth to so many people.

Drinking well water will make you grow tall, many Americans believe. In Cornwall, they say that a child baptised with water from the well of St. Ludgvan will never be hanged. If you go to Gulval Well in the same county on the eve of the feast of Saints Peter and Paul (June 28) and ask the water, "Water, water, tell me truly, Is the man I love duly, On the earth or under the sod, Sick or well—in the name of God?" the water will bubble and boil if the news is good.

If a cross of palm fronds is tossed into the well at Little Conan (also in Cornwall) and it floats, the one who throws it will live out the year. The Silver Well at Llanblethian in Glamorganshire was the place for sweethearts to test one another out. A blackthorn twig was thrown into the water; if it floated, the lover was faithful, and if it sank, he was not. If it whirled around, your lover was cheerful; if it stayed put, he would be sullen.

At Altarnum (Cornwall), lunatics were dunked in the waters of St. Nun's Well and tossed until the frenzy left them. St. Tecla's Well water cured epilepsy. So did that of St. Fegla's Well, Caernarvonshire. Eglys Well in Lleyn, Wales, granted wishes; but first you had to descend the steps to the well, fill your mouth with water, walk up again, and walk around the church without spilling a drop. St. Servan's Well was good for the eyes and the toothache, but after washing in the water, the patient had to sleep all night in the chapel. At St. Madron's Well, near Penzance, shingles, wild fire, and other skin complaints were cured by a dunking; afterward, the patient (usually a child) was carried nine times around the spring and then a piece of his garment was left behind.

At the Llanbedrog Well in Lleyn, you could learn the name of a thief. You threw a piece of bread into the water and then named the persons you suspected. When you came to the right name, the bread would sink.

Britain has a number of "granny" wells dedicated to Saint Anne, grandmother of Jesus, as well as wells dedicated to such local saints as those mentioned above. Pious people still deck these wells with garlands on certain festive days.

In Derbyshire, wells are often decorated with streamers, farm produce, flower petals pressed into wet clay, and such. About June 25 each year, parishioners at Brislington process to the ruins of St. Anne's Well. Around Ascension Day, wells are dressed at Tissington; in June at Wicksworth, Ashford-in-the-Water, Youlgrave, Tideswell, and Hope; in July at Buxton and Marsh Lane; in August at Bonsall, Stoney Middletown, Bradwell, Barlow, Eyam, and Wormhill.

OUTCROPS AND WONDER ROCKS

There's magic and myth in stones—especially large, oddly shaped, or out-of-place boulders (such as those carried by glaciers many miles from where they were picked up). Here are the tales told of some of these formations.

Perhaps the best-known geologic formation in the world is the Giant's Causeway, near Bushmills in Antrim, Northern Ireland. It is a mass of hexagonal basaltic columns standing bolt upright, ground level to forty feet in height. Some parts of it extend seven hundred feet out to sea, hence the name "Causeway." The Irish say that once, long ago, the giants built a bridge from Ireland to Scotland, and that this is what remains of it.

At Shebbear in Devonshire, every November 5 (Guy Fawkes' Day), people make a public ceremony of turning over a large stone that lies under an ancient oak. This is said to prevent bad luck during the following year, for the stone is supposed to have been dropped into the village square by the Devil himself.

Starved Rock on the Illinois River, near Ottawa, Illinois, is a high, isolated, free-standing mesa. According to legend, it was here in the 1680s that a remnant of the Illinois Indians took refuge from the marauding Iroquois and held them off until food supplies ran out.

East of Edinburgh and within sight of Holyrood Palace is an eight-hundred-foot hill known as Arthur's Seat. Tradition says that it was from this elevated spot that King Arthur surveyed the surrounding region and watched his knights defeat the Saxons in a great battle.

In the sandy southern regions of Australia's Northern Territory, an astonishing outcrop of rust-colored rock juts up 1,143 feet above the plain. Ayers Rock is regarded by the aborigines of the continent as the home of their original ancestors, and the lair of hare-wallaby men, poison-snake people, and other denizens from their tribal legends.

In southwestern Arizona are located the aptly named Superstition Mountains, the site, if so immense an area can be called a site, of the famed Lost Dutchman mine. This fabled gold strike, reputedly the richest in the world, has been found and lost, found and lost so many times that prospectors believe it to be cursed. No one, having once located it and left it to get help in working the claim (the belief goes) has ever been able to find it again.

GARDENS

Garden lore, like that for farming, depends heavily on folk beliefs. Here are a few common ones.

Planting. Above-ground crops should be sown as the moon is on the wane; root crops, such as turnips, potatoes, carrots, etc., should be planted when the moon is waxing. Algonquian Indians planted corn when the leaves of the tree were the size of the mouse's ear. English farmers tested the temperature before sowing grain by pulling down their pants and sitting on the ground; if the soil was not too cold for them, it was not too cold for the barley. Some recommend that turnips and rampion be planted by a naked man. But, in any event, never sow the last three days of March—unlucky— and beans must be planted before May. And sow thickly:

> One for the rook, one for the crow;
> One to die, and one to grow.

Good friends and bad friends. Foxglove and camomile are said to be helpful and sustaining to other plants that grow nearby, whereas ash trees are bad for some neighboring plants, and walnuts must not be allowed to sprout near tomatoes or they will spoil the flavor.

Here are some things you can expect from your vegetable patch.

Beans. Accidents and the onset of lunacy are more common when the broad bean is in flower. However some people believe that the flowers of this plant smell so sweet that they must contain the souls of dead men. When eaten, they give you bad dreams.

Parsley. This is an unlucky plant. The ancient Greeks regarded it as a symbol of mourning, and it was most unfortunate to encounter a growing patch of it while you were marching to war. In England, there were taboos against cutting it, transplanting it, giving it away, and even growing it at all.

Asparagus. The wild variety was used in ancient Greece for wedding garlands, so it is regarded as a lucky plant. Always leave one stem uncut and allow it to blossom.

Cabbage. If it grows double—two shoots from one root—it is very lucky, as are cabbages that grow with widely opened leaves. A leaf tied around the throat is a cure for sore throat, and the juice (mixed with honey) eases hoarseness and laryngitis. In parts of France and Belgium it is believed that newborn infants are grown in the cabbage patch—boys in white cabbages, girls in red. (At least that's what children are told. One little French girl the author has heard of, learning that a new baby was on the way, went out and cut down all the red cabbages. She wanted a baby brother.)

Lettuce. Some people regard lettuce as a kind of contraceptive—an excess of it in one's garden, and the woman of the house will not conceive. On the other hand, Juno is thought to have conceived Hebe after eating lettuce, so it seems to work both ways.

Peas. A peapod containing only one pea is lucky. One with nine peas must be thrown over the shoulder while you make a wish, which will then come true.

Carrot. This can be an ingredient in love potions.

Endive. Even if you don't like this vegetable in salad, plant it as a kind of clock. Its leaves open at eight in the morning, it is said, and close at four—an eight-hour day.

Cress. Eating this will make you witty.

Onion. This vegetable is regarded as an aid to deafness and good in a sickroom. To dream of eating onions means that you will have much domestic strife.

Potato. Plant these roots with the eyes up, so that they can see to grow.

When you dig the first potatoes of the season, all the family must partake of them, or the rest of the potatoes will not keep.

Cucumber. In addition to its reputation for coolness, still with us today, cucumber was considered an aid to love affairs and a cure for rabies.

Strawberry. This is one of many plants of which the Virgin is said to be particularly fond. Fairies and elves like the fruit also, and in Bavaria farmers used to tie the leaves to the horns of their cattle to protect them from spells.

Here are some things to expect from your herb garden.

Rosemary. This herb is a great comforter to the heart and, if worn about the person, an aid to memory.

Sage. This plant was considered to be good for virtually everything: the liver, the blood, the brain, the muscles, the stomach, the heart, and the nerves. "Why should a man die whilst sage grows in his garden?" ran a medieval saying. But if, in spite of everything, a sage-eating man died, it was considered sage to plant sage on his grave.

Centaury. Anxiety will not bother the person who eats centaury, and if a girl washes her face in a decoction of the plant, it will take away freckles.

Vervain. This herb will cure grief, can be used in a love potion, and (if the latter is successful) makes an excellent bridal wreath.

Bay. The leaves purge a man of choler and phlegm. If thrown on the fire and found to crackle, that's a good sign; if they burn silently, you will have bad luck. Placed under pillows, they give sweet dreams. Or wrap a bay leaf around a wolf's tooth and put it under the pillow, and your dreams will tell you where your stolen money has been hidden.

Rue. Make a disinfectant from this herb. Plant it next to sage to help that useful herb to thrive. Some Turks consider rue a good luck symbol. (Edie Gormé, who is part Turkish, is said to carry a growing rue plant with her on tour.)

Borage. Mixed with hellebore, this plant will "purge the veins of melancholy, and cheer the heart of those black fumes which make it smart." It is also supposed to heal abscesses. Incidentally, it produces a tall handsome plant with exquisite blue flowers.

Bugloss. This herb is good for "harmful wicked moistness of the lung," for coughs, and for swollen feet. When mixed with hot water it "maketh a man to have a good mind."

Pennyroyal. This variety of mint is supposed to cure nausea, "cold humor in the head," boils, and cramp.

Briony. Considered a "martial" plant, briony was often an ingredient in witches' spells (the berries contain a dangerous poison), but the tender young sprouts could be pickled safely and the roots made a useful cathartic.

MINES

People who descend into the bowels of the earth every day and earn a hard living in semidarkness can hardly help but develop folk beliefs of many sorts. The oldest perhaps is their belief in small supernatural creatures who work near them underground but can seldom be seen.

The Cornish tin miners believe in the Knockers, diminutive creatures in miners' leather clothes who can be heard working away with their picks in nearby galleries. By following the sounds of these knocks, men can locate the richest veins of ore. Sometimes the Knockers also warn miners of impending cave-ins or other disasters. However, one must never mark a cross underground, for the Knockers are enemies of Christianity and will resent it.

In Germany dwarfs are believed to live underground, mining and storing up treasures of gold, silver, and (especially) gems of all kinds. (The seven little men in "Snow White" were miners of this sort.) Do a kindness for one of these creatures, and he will reward you with what looks like a heap of coals, but when you get the heap home it will turn out to be a collection of jewels.

More prosaic beliefs of those who work in the mines are concerned with good luck and bad luck, like those of their neighbors above ground. To meet a woman on the way to the pit or a cross-eyed person or a rabbit (especially if you are on the night shift) is very bad luck. The same goes for seeing a snail, although one can drop a bit of tallow from one's candle and thus ward off that evil. It is bad luck to return to one's house after setting out for work. Superstitious miners, having forgotten their packed lunches, often work without food all day rather than go back to fetch them. A dove or robin flying around the pithead foretells disaster; many miners will not go to work if they see that. A dream of broken shoes is also bad luck. Washing his back will bring a miner trouble, possibly cause a cave-in.

IRELAND

Many places in Ireland are "magical" sites, often of pre-Christian origin. At Arboe, County Tyrone, there are both a Christian cross and a pagan wishing tree, the latter studded with nails driven in by believers. At Armagh, site of the primate since Patrick's time and earlier a center of pagan witchcraft, a museum contains items of folkloric interest, some documenting early superstitions which have not entirely died out in Ireland even to this day.

Lough Larne in Northern Ireland is said to be the site of a ferry inaugurated by Saint Patrick himself. In fifteen hundred years, no drowning has ever been recorded there.

On Slemish Mountain, Antrim, Patrick was a swineherd slave and worked his boyhood miracles. On Mount Cuilcagh, Fermanagh, is a rock throne used from time immemorial for investing the chiefs of the Maguires. At the Giant's Causeway, where early settlers believed the prehistoric giants had been at work, there is a famous wishing seat.

Near Downpatrick, there is a "tomb" of Saint Patrick, though he is not actually buried there. Downpatrick also contains some pre-Christian holy wells.

Derry ("grove of oaks") was probably the site of Druidic practices. The Seven Mountains of Mourne were left by Patrick, they say, as perpetual guardians of Ireland.

On Rathlin Island, seven miles off the coast of Antrim, Robert the Bruce is said to have watched a spider in a cave try over and over again to construct a web. The arachnid's persistence impressed and inspired Bruce, and he found the courage to return to Scotland and renew his war for his country's independence.

The Cloughmore, or large stone, near Rostrevor is said to have been put there by Finn MacCool, the legendary giant. The hole in it became filled with water, and thus Carlingford Lough was created.

And, of course, most famous of all is the Blarney Stone, which is found in the ruins of Blarney Castle (built 1446) in County Cork. Anyone who wants to acquire sophistication, charm, and eloquence can do so by kissing the stone, but he must hang upside down to do it. There's also a fairy glen nearby.

TOMBS AND GRAVES

Concern for the welfare of the dead in the afterworld dates from the very earliest periods that man has occupied the earth. The vast bulk of what we know today about prehistoric peoples has been learned from the artifacts and human remains uncovered from interment sites. Many customs, from very ancient times, have survived in some form to the present day.

To have a stillborn infant buried in the coffin with you is a sure ticket to heaven, many people believe. Place a coin in the coffin so that the deceased can pay his fare across the River Jordan (an obvious survival of the ancient Greek belief in Charon and the River Styx). Bury a woman all in black, and she will return to haunt her family.

The corpse must be taken from the house feet first; if it is able to look back at the family, it may beckon someone else to follow. On the way to the burying ground, the coffin must be carried with the sun behind it, even if this means taking the long way around. The grave itself should be dug on an east-west axis, so that the deceased will face east—toward Gabriel when he blows his horn for the resurrection. The grave should also lie on the south side of the church. Rain falling on the coffin or a clap of thunder at the conclusion of the obsequies means that the deceased has reached heaven.

The first person buried in a newly dedicated cemetery is claimed by the Devil. Never plow up land that was once a burying ground, no matter how long ago. To annoy the dead, urinate on their graves. To raise them, sprinkle the tomb with blood and call them by name.

Troubled by a vampire? Find out where it "lives"—a white horse can lead you there. Dig it up (by daylight) and drive a stake through its heart. Or decapitate it. Or both. Or pour boiling water (to which some vinegar has been added, perhaps a parody of offering wine to the dead) over the grave.

Just as some reliquaries of Christian saints are supplied with openings, so that the faithful can reach in and touch the relics, so in Islam some tombs of holy men are left open at the top so that prayers may reach them. In the Sahara, the dead man's belongings are left at his gravesite: a plate and pitcher, perhaps an ostrich egg. An American Indian's property is so intricately bound up with his person that, unless he specifically wills an item to a relative, all his possessions are burned at his death.

The tomb figurines from Chinese burials represent servants provided for the dead. In some cultures figurines came to be used in place of actual persons sacrificed at the burial of VIPs. In Egyptian tombs, *ushabti* figurines in the form of mummies were provided to be agricultural laborers in the other world.

The strangest death figurines may be the *mulongo* ("double") venerated by African natives. In Britain's Horniman Museum there is a bark-cloth case from the Baganda tribe containing the umbilical cord of a prince, "supposed to retain the ghost of the afterbirth, which was the prince's double."

THE SEA

The lonely sea—the barren sea, as the ancient Greeks called it—kept men from their homes for many months, even years, at a stretch, endangered their lives, often crippled them or caused them to die of scurvy or other diseases, and yet it never lacked for men to sail it. They concentrated their natural anxieties in numerous superstitions.

In ancient times men would not launch a ship, especially a man-of-war, without first blooding its keel. Slaves or prisoners of war were strapped down to the ways, and as the vessel slipped down them to the sea, it crushed the sacrifices. Today, we christen a ship with a bottle of champagne or other wine instead, which both bloods the keel and represents a libation to the gods of the sea.

It is bad luck to sail on a Friday, the first Monday in April, the second Monday in August, and December 31. Friday commemorates the Crucifixion, of course, and the other three are supposed to be anniversaries of the slaying of Abel, the destruction of Sodom and Gomorrah, and the suicide of Judas.

> Sunday sail, never fail.
> Friday sail, ill luck and gale.

If, on your way to the dock, you encounter a barefoot woman or one in a white apron, turn back. The voyage would be unlucky. The same belief holds if you find your earthenware basin turned upside down or if a hawk, owl, or crow alights in the rigging. (But bees and small birds are welcome.)

Once aboard, superstitions thicken. You must not bring an umbrella with you. You must not lend any of the equipment of your ship to another without damaging it slightly. Otherwise all your luck will go out of your ship with it. You must not lose a bucket or mop overboard. You must not mend a flag on the quarterdeck or hand one to another sailor through the rungs of a ladder. During a voyage, you must not wear the clothes of a sailor who has died at sea, or you will follow him overboard. (But once back ashore, they can be worn with impunity.) You must not carry your seaboots over your shoulder, only under the arm. You must not carry flowers aboard ship. If you do they are destined to become a wreath either for a shipmate or for the entire vessel (a superstition particularly strong among submariners). Your friends and family must not watch your ship out of sight, or it will never be seen again. Never stick a knife into a deck.

Beware of Jonahs (ships' jinxes). Among fishermen, a small catch following the signing on of a new hand means that he's a Jonah. Or if a man comes aboard carrying a black valise, that's a jinx. Jonahs bring bad luck to an entire vessel.

So do women and clergymen. The sight of a woman angers the sea—unless she is naked, in which case she can cause gales to subside. (This is supposedly one reason why so many figureheads were images of bare-breasted women.) The clergy were disliked because of their association with death and burials. Even worse was a corpse; a ship cannot make headway with a dead man aboard.

Above all, never change a ship's name. A deadly curse will follow the ill-fated vessel if you do.

To counter all this bad luck, carry the caul of a newborn infant or a feather from a wren killed on New Year's Day (a potent charm against mermaids and sirens). Nail a horseshoe to the mast. Pierce your ears! That is supposed to improve eyesight. Toss a piece of silver at the foot of the mast; better yet, if possible, see that the mast, when stepped, rests on a silver coin.

Sighting a phantom ship such as the *Flying Dutchman* is supposed to mean death or at least blindness for the one who sees it. (However, on July 11, 1881, sixteen-year-old Prince George of England, then a young naval cadet, was reputed to have sighted the *Dutchman*, and it certainly did him no harm for he eventually ascended the throne as King George V.) St. Elmo's fire, a brush discharge of electricity often seen at the masts of ships, was considered to be a benevolent warning of storms. If it was seen to play around the person of a man such as the lookout, however, he would probably die within twenty-four hours.

It is unlucky to whistle aboard a ship, for it will bring a wind, probably blowing foul for the voyage you are on. But if you are becalmed in a sailing vessel, then whistling is useful, and to make sure it blows from the right quarter, stick your jacknife in the mast.

If you encounter a sailor, touch his collar for good luck.

SHRINES AND STATUES

Many religions have established special sites at which the faithful gather to worship, to do reverence to holymen and deities, and to pray for aid or favor.

The church at Broualan, France, was erected in 1483 by a wife whose husband had deserted her. She prayed, and the husband returned. Since then, many abandoned wives have repaired there to pray for the return of their wayward spouses.

A statue of Mateo, the sculptor who designed the portico in the cathedral of Santiago de Compostela, one of the great historic shrines of Christendom, is put to an odd use by Spanish mothers. They bang their children's heads against it, hoping to knock some sense into them.

In Katmandu, Nepal, stands a big red statue to Hanuman, the Monkey God of the epic *Ramayana*, beneath a ceremonial umbrella. Nearby is a stele, centuries old, inscribed in sixteen languages. If you can read them all, superstition says, milk will flow from a tap.

More effective is the statue of Bhairab, God of Fear. Criminals dragged before him to give their testimony believe that, if they lie, they will instantly be struck down. So firm is this belief that many confessions have been exacted there, and some criminals must have lied, for they dropped dead of fright.

But most shrines specialize in cures. A statue in the public fountain at Braga, Portugal, has water flowing from its ears that is believed to improve the hearing of all those drinking it.

At St. Joseph's Oratory in Montreal, many crutches and braces attest to recoveries. This gigantic basilica was erected on its hill in Montreal at the behest of a saintly monk, Brother André, to whose intercession many cures have been attributed. So large is St. Joseph's dome that water condenses on its inner surface and it sometimes "rains" inside.

Asiatics, like Europeans, have many specialized shrines. The tomb of Nasir-ud-Din in Amroha, India, is where you go if you want to recover your ass. (Stray donkeys are supposed to get there eventually.) There are many that offer miraculous cures and spiritual benefits but few that compete with the temple of Arakan, Burma, which guarantees a cure from snakebite if you just touch it. For skin ailments, throw mud at the wall of the temple in Kashgar, Chinese Turkestan.

Perhaps the most famous shrine in the world is that at Lourdes at the foothills of the Pyrenees in southern France. Established in 1858 after a fourteen-year-old peasant girl, Bernadette Soubirous, reported that she had seen the Virgin Mary and been directed to locate a certain spring, the shrine acknowledged fifty "miraculous" cures in its first hundred years. As techniques of diagnosis have become more sophisticated and the authorities more skeptical, the cure rate has slowed down, but now and then a miracle—such as regeneration of dead bone tissue, plainly visible on X rays—is still accepted.

The Roman Catholic Church used to offer indulgences (remission of some punishment for sins that had been confessed and forgiven) for visiting certain shrines. Similarly, in India, anyone who walks around the courtyard of the temple at Tiruvidaimarudur earns merit equal to that of having visited all the other temples of India. Anyone who sees the *chorten* ("shrine") of Tashiding, Sikkim, is immediately cleansed of all sin.

There used to be a gate in Baghdad that the natives believed would give untold wealth to anyone who happened to pass through it at one particular instant in certain twenty-four hour periods. The crowds struggling to take advantage of this opportunity became so unmanageable that the gate had to be bricked up in 1906.

IMAGINARY PLACES

In the days before the globe was as thoroughly explored and mapped as it is today, geographers believed in many dim and distant regions at the rim of Creation. They gave these lands names and locations, and here are some of them.

Atlantis. In two Dialogues, *Timaeus* and *Critias*, Plato mentioned a continent larger than Asia Minor and the known parts of Africa (which would make it about the size of modern Europe). It was reported to lay in the Atlantic Ocean. An idyllic place, perfectly governed, wealthy and peaceful, the island-continent was overwhelmed by jealous aliens and destroyed by earthquakes, but is supposed to lie today somewhere under the sea. Scientists think Plato and his contemporaries may be misremembering the location of an actual island (Mediterranean Thera) that was destroyed by violent volcanic eruptions in 1450 B.C., but other people believe in the literal truth of the story. Some even think the place continues to survive under the sea.

The land of Prester John. Prester (a corruption of the Greek word *presbyter*, "elder") was supposedly a priest-ruler of a mighty Christian empire somewhere in the far reaches of Asia or Africa. There *were* isolated Christian communities in these regions—in Abyssinia (cut off from Christian Europe by the Islamic lands to the north and east), in India (where Christianity was supposedly planted by Saint Thomas the Apostle), and in an area below the Gobi Desert. One of the motivations for early voyages of exploration—motivations at least for the pious monarchs financing them— was to locate the fabled kingdom of Prester John. Long after seamen had brought back facts concerning the Far East and the East Coast of Africa, learned men continued to believe that the land of Prester John lay somewhere out there.

El Dorado. This name actually means "the Gilded Man" and originally referred to a native king of some remote Indian nation who was said to appear on ceremonial occasions with his body covered with gold dust. There actually was a village, located in what is now Colombia, where the chieftain was so decorated at times, but in Indian tales (as they reached Spanish ears) this practice became magnified and rumor persisted of a land so fabuously rich that gold dust was a kind of face powder. For nearly a century this tale lured *conquistadores* high into mountains, deep into jungles, farther and farther from home in search of fabulous wealth. In time "El Dorado" came to mean some mystic land of riches or dreams in quest of which men spent their lives. Even in modern times expeditions have vanished in Latin American jungles, hunting for the Gilded Man and his gold-rich people.

The Northwest Passage. Explorers of the sixteenth and early seventeenth centuries could not bring themselves to believe that what Columbus and his successors had stumbled across was a string of new continents. Rather, South, Central, and North America must be (they thought) a string of islands, like those in the Caribbean. They were convinced in particular that, to the north, there lay a strait—similar to the Strait of Magellan only not situated so far from the temperate climate—that would grant them quick and easy passage to China. The Hudson, the Delaware, and Chesapeake Bay were each in turn thought to be the fabled strait. The French were once convinced that the St. Lawrence would ultimately lead them to the Orient.

Unknown South Land. *Terra Australis Ignota* appeared on many early maps because cartographers felt it *ought* to be there. Surely there had to be something south and west of South America to balance the land masses of the north. Once Australia was discovered, it was named for this supposed land mass, but learned men refused to accept it as a substitute, and *Terra Australis* continued to appear on maps well into the nineteenth century.

5

Events

NEW YEAR'S DAY

Whatever day is celebrated as the first of a new year people regard as a day of fresh beginnings, of expelling old sins and old evils and starting afresh.

In parts of Scotland, it was the custom to usher a dog to the door, give him a piece of bread, and then drive him away, "Get away, you dog!" All the ills that were destined for the following year were supposed to have been laid on the animal's head and thus cast out of the community.

In the Western Himalayas, the Bhotiya people still carry out a similar ceremony. They first feed the dog spirits, bhang (marijuana), and sweets, then lead it around the village, turn it loose, and chase it. When the poor animal is caught and beaten or stoned to death, it is thought that no disease or misfortune will visit the community during the forthcoming year.

Other superstitions in regard to New Year's Day concerned the importance of keeping the fire going. If that was allowed to go out, that was bad luck for the whole year. No neighbor would contribute a coal to start a new one, for that would be giving away her own luck, and to steal fire from someone else was to call even worse luck down on one's head.

Fire was not the only thing that was not to be taken out of the house on New Year's Day. Nothing was to leave—not even refuse.

Another New Year's superstition concerned the British custom of first footing—that is, being the first person to enter the house as the new year dawns. In many parts of Britain it was the custom, as soon as midnight had struck, to make calls on neighbors. If the first footer was a woman, that was bad luck. A fair-haired man was not very popular either, and in parts of the country married men were considered less desirable first footers than bachelors. Ideally, the first footer should be a dark-haired bachelor, and in some communities these lucky individuals made the rounds of all the houses, being warmly welcomed in each. In some regions the first footer was also expected to bring coals, a contribution to keeping the fire going.

In addition it is believed that if your cupboards are bare on New Year's Day, you will have an impoverished year. The same thing holds for being out of money—expect to be broke all year. However, the last drink out of the bottle on New Year's Eve brings good luck to the one who consumes it.

CANDLEMAS, FEBRUARY 2

An ancient Druidic festival was taken over by the Christian Church as the feast of the Purification of the Virgin. It was also the day on which the Church blessed the candles to be used in services throughout the coming year, hence the name "Candlemas." Nevertheless, it—along with its eve, the feast of Saint Brigid—retained many of its old superstitions.

In Scotland, on February 1, women used to dress up a sheaf of oats in women's clothes, lay it in a basket, and say, "Brigid, Brigid, come in—your bed is ready." This Christian saint is thus made to represent the pagan bride of spring, wedded to the soil.

Before Candlemas proper, all Christmas decorations must be removed from the local church. If so much as a leaf or berry is left, the family that occupies the pew where it remains will suffer a death during the next year.

Candlemas was also an important weathercock day. If the sun shone on February 2, it meant a long winter and bad luck. This too:

> When the wind's in the east on Candlemas Day,
> There it will stick till the second of May.

GOOD FRIDAY

Good Friday beliefs seem to be about equally divided between good luck and bad.

To obtain good luck: Make hot-cross buns; eat some and preserve the rest to prevent whooping cough. (If your husband is a fishermen, have him carry one with him as a safeguard.) Bake bread and save some of it to cure other illnesses; bakings of Good Friday will never go moldy. Have a ring blessed and wear it to prevent illness. Sow parsley, and it will come up double. Move bees only on this day.

To avoid bad luck: Do not hammer iron (it recalls the Crucifixion). Do not put iron into the ground (do not plow or spade up the earth) or nothing will grow in that field that year. Do not hang out clothes, or you will find them spotted with blood.

EASTER

The greatest religious festival of the Christian year, celebrating the Resurrection of Christ, is Easter. But because it comes in the spring, many pre-Christian customs—concerned chiefly with fertility and the renewal of life—have become clustered around it. Hence the many folk beliefs concerning Easter.

Wearing new clothes on Easter will insure good luck for the year. It's not only the rich who follow this tradition and show off their finery in Fifth Avenue's Easter Parade. Sociologists report that, among the very poor, the struggle to obtain new Easter garments for every member of the family often borders on the desperate.

The sun is important in Easter beliefs. At dawn on Easter, many people claim, the sun dances. Others say that at sunrise one can see the Agnus Dei (Lamb of God, a lamb holding a cross or a banner) in the center of the sun. (But don't try looking for it except through smoked glass—gazing directly into the sun can do severe damage to the eyes.) If the sun shines on Easter, it will also shine on Whitsun (Pentecost); if it rains on Easter, it will rain the next seven Sundays, and produce little good hay.

The egg, symbol of new life, is still synonymous with Easter. Decorating Easter eggs is considered a fine art in many parts of Europe, particularly in the Ukraine and Hungary and other parts of Eastern Europe. And in the days of Carl Fabergé (1846–1920), jeweler to Czar Nicholas II, it *was* a fine art, for this gifted goldsmith created enameled and jewel-encrusted Easter eggs that were marvels of beauty and ingenuity.

The ancient Teutons believed that, at Easter, rabbits laid eggs. That's the origin of our Easter bunny. To refuse a gift of an Easter egg was to refuse the friendship of the person offering it. An Easter egg with two yolks meant great prosperity for the fortunate recipient. Eggs blessed at Easter warded off illness. Rolling Easter eggs downhill was a favorite Easter game, the idea being to cross the finish line first with an unbroken shell; if all the eggs were broken, then the winner—who would be rewarded with a year of good luck—was the one whose shell held out longest. The most famous egg rolling today is probably that held on the White House lawn. Few of those who participate, it can be assumed, have any knowledge of the pagan customs dimly recalled in this pleasant occupation.

MAYDAY OR BELTANE

The ancient Druids, or priests of the Celtic peoples of Britain, celebrated four great fire festivals every year equivalent to our Candlemas (February 2), Beltane (May 1), Midsummer (June 23–24), and All Hallows Eve (October 31). Beltane and All Hallows were the big days; then fertility rites were carried out. Giant frameworks of willow were built in the shape of a man, sacrifices of animals and sometimes even human beings were penned up inside them, and they were set afire. Later, in parts of Europe, the wicker effigy was carried in procession as a figure of fun or replaced by young boys dressed in summer greenery who went from house to house collecting fuel for a bonfire. It was called the Beltane fire.

These holidays were often the occasion of much rural mumming and cavorting, people dressing up in masks and costumes and parading about the village. A favorite "character" of such celebrations was the hobby-horse—a crude boat-shaped body of canvas and lath, painted, decorated with ribbons, and topped with a horse's head, which became a central figure in much of the romping. From such antics we derive our term "horseplay."

Mayday superstitions seem to be further survivors of ancient Beltane rites. Washing your face in dew gathered at daybreak on that morning was thought to preserve a woman's complexion. Slavic peasants gathered dew to wash their cows as a preventive against witchcraft. In Spain and France, people rolled naked in dewy grass to protect themselves from skin diseases. Others sniffed it as a cure for vertigo.

If your head is rained on, come May 1, you will have no headaches throughout the year. If you eat sage on Mayday, you will live forever. If you wear a garland, you will find love during the coming year.

On the other hand, cattle were in danger unless you took certain precautions on the first of May. You had to place a green branch against the side of the house or set up a maypole near the cowbarn to ensure plenty of milk. You were well advised to singe cattle with lighted straw on Mayday eve, and bleed them on Mayday itself, the blood then to be burned. You decorated the barn with pieces of rowan. You killed all hares found near the cows, because they were thought to be witches intent on harming the beasts.

In many parts of the world, Beltane fires are still lighted, danced around, and jumped over. In England the celebrations more often feature the maypole, although the dancing nowadays is usually by members of folklore societies, not the simple peasants of former years. The last maypole to be formally erected in London was 130 feet high and took more than four hours to raise with block and tackle. It stood in the Strand for more than half a century, then was taken down in 1717 and sold; Sir Isaac Newton bought it as a support for his new telescope.

WEDDINGS

As one might expect, wedding traditions abound in superstitions, most of them conscientiously followed even by people who would laugh at the notion that they really believe in such things. It would hardly be a proper wedding, they feel, if the bride did not wear "Something old, Something new, Something borrowed, Something blue, With a six pence In her shoe."

Don't get married on February 11, any day in May (it brings poverty), any day in Lent, June 2, November 2 (All Souls' Day), December 1, or December 28 (Holy Innocents' Day). Whatever date you settle on, stick to it. Postponement brings bad luck. "Happy is the bride that the sun shines on," but if it rains go through with the ceremony anyway.

The marriage will be ill-fated . . . if the groom sees the bride on the wedding day, before they meet at church . . . if the bride sees herself in the mirror after she is dressed and before the ceremony . . . if a dog passes between the couple on their wedding day . . . if the wedding party meets a funeral cortege en route to the church . . . if the bride tears her gown or bursts a seam (she will be mistreated by her husband) . . . if it rains . . . if a stone rolls across the path of the newly married pair . . . if the bride stumbles on the threshold of her new home (hence the groom carrying her inside). . . .

The marriage will be happy and blessed . . . if a cat sneezes in the bride's home on the wedding eve . . . if the wedding takes place at the time of the new moon . . . if a hen cackles in the couple's new home . . . if the bride weeps bitterly on her wedding day . . . if the bride wears old shoes . . . if the bridesmaids lay out the bride's stockings (on the wedding night) in the shape of a cross. . . .

It is considered a bad omen if there is an open grave in the churchyard during the wedding ceremony. However, in 1826 in Salisbury, Vermont, when Elizabeth Kelsey married Jonathan Titus, not only was there an open grave but the wedding took place right beside it. The brother of the bride had wanted to attend the nuptials but had died the previous night.

Wedding rings are popular objects of superstition. To cure a stye, rub the ailing eye with a wedding ring. To cure warts, prick them with a gooseberry thorn, thrust through the ring. Turn the ring around three times, and your wish will come true. Never remove the ring except for emergencies. If a wife loses her ring, she will lose her husband; if it breaks, she and her husband will die. A borrowed wedding ring enables an unmarried woman to determine if she will ever marry; suspended over a glass of water from a south-running stream by a hair from her own head, it predicts spinsterhood if it hits the rim of the glass, marriage if it turns quickly around, and two marriages if it revolves slowly.

By the way, it is a popular belief that the ring is worn on the third finger because a vein or a nerve runs from there to the heart. Not so, say Mona and Edmund Radford in their *Encyclopedia of Superstitions*. The third finger is a practical choice, because it is difficult to straighten out unless other fingers are also straightened; thus, since it cannot be extended independently (as all other fingers can, even the pinky) it is the safest finger on which to wear a valuable item of jewelry.

At Jewish weddings, the couple stand under a *huppah*, or wedding canopy, which symbolizes the wedding tent of ancient times. After the bride and groom have both drunk from a wedding glass, it is dropped, and the groom treads on and smashes it, a ceremony that dates back to the fifth century A.D. There are various interpretations of what this symbolizes, perhaps the destruction of the Temple, perhaps simply a reminder that life is fragile. Or perhaps it is to prevent any less happy persons from drinking out of the same fortunate vessel. It has been jokingly suggested that this is included in the wedding ceremony in order to give the husband his last chance to put his foot down. After the glass is broken, the guests cry, "*Mazel*

Tov!" ("Good luck!"), after which the bride, her parents, and her sponsors circle the groom seven times, carrying lighted candles, perhaps marking a mystic, cabalistic circle.

In the Greek Orthodox Church, jeweled crowns are held over the heads of the bride and groom, signifying that the couple are the lord and lady of procreation. They may exchange rings. He receives a gold one; hers is silver.

Many folk beliefs concerning weddings are involved with the struggle to determine which partner will wear the pants in the family. In the Middle Ages, the bridegroom stamped on his new wife's toes. In modern Germany, bride and groom compete to see which one can step on the other's feet, the winner to become dominant. In parts of Britain, the one to retain the mastery will be the one who first steps over the threshold of the church, or the new home.

Wedding cake should be saved by an unmarried young woman and placed under her pillow; she will then dream of her future husband. Whatever she dreams, if dreams come three nights in a row, the third dream will come true.

ASCENSION DAY

This Christian feast, celebrated on a Thursday forty days after Easter, commemorates the ascension of Christ into Heaven.

Rain on Ascension Day portends a poor harvest and sick cattle, but collect the rainwater—it's good for eye troubles. Sunshine, on the other hand, foretells a whole summer of good weather; make a wish as the sun rises. If you do not take a holiday from work on Ascension Thursday, you can expect an accident to occur.

In Saxony peasants used to hold a ceremony called Carrying Out Death. In it a straw effigy (similar to the Scots "Saint Brigid") was dressed in women's clothes, carried through the streets by girls, and then torn apart by boys. In Switzerland, girls climb church towers and ring bells on Ascension Day to ensure a good flax harvest.

BAD DAYS

Numerology, astrology, and almost every other form of superstition believes that people have their good days and their bad days. Arthur

Hopton's *A Concordance of Years*, published in 1612, devotes a whole chapter to "the infortunate and fatall dayes of the years." For instance, in January look out for the first, second, fourth, fifth, tenth, fifteenth, seventeenth, and nineteenth. The *really* "fatall" days are January 3, April 30, July 1, August 1 and 31, and October 7. Hopton says, if you fall ill on one of those days, you will "hardly or never escape."

The following about Evil Days is translated from the Latin of the old Sarum (Salisbury) Missal:

January.	Of this first month, the opening day And seventh like a sword will slay.
February.	The fourth day bringeth down to death; The third will stop a strong man's breath.
March.	The first the greedy glutton slays; The fourth cuts short the drunkard's days.
April.	The tenth, and the eleventh too, Are ready death's fell work to do.
May.	The third to slay poor man hath power; The seventh destroyeth in an hour.
June.	The tenth a pallid visage shows; No faith nor truth the fifteenth knows.
July.	The thirteenth is a fatal day; The tenth alike will mortals slay.
August.	The first kills strong ones at a blow; The second lays a cohort low.
September.	The third day of the month September, And tenth, bring evil to each member.
October.	The third and tenth, with poisoned breath, To man are foes as foul as death.
November.	The fifth bears scorpion-sting of deadly pain; The third is tinctured with destruction's train.
December.	The seventh's a fatal day to human life; The tenth is with a serpent's venom rife.

MIDSUMMER AND MIDSUMMER EVE

The summer solstice usually occurs on June 22 but is celebrated over June 23–24. This recalls the great Druidical festival of Midsummer and is commemorated all across Europe with bonfires and cavortings.

The original intention was to assist the fields to produce a good harvest, and though most such bonfires are considered pure fun today, in some areas they are still lighted so that the smoke blows across the growing crop. In parts of Wales, a cartwheel is wrapped with straw, the straw set afire, and the wheel sent rolling downhill; if it reaches the bottom before the fire goes out, that means the harvest will be a bountiful one.

In some areas, lighted brands were carried through the pastures or the cattle were driven through the smoke. Ashes were later scattered on the crop.

Midsummer Eve is the day on which a girl may meet the man she will later marry. She must fast all day, then at midnight set the table with a clean cloth, bread, cheese, and ale, and sit down as though to eat. Her future husband will then enter and bow to her. Or she must pluck a rose and put it away; if it is still fresh on Christmas Day, she must wear it to church, and her future husband will appear and take it from her.

CORONATIONS

The crowning and annointing of a king has, from ancient times, been a sort of magical ceremony in which the political is united with the sacred and a priest-king is elevated and consecrated. Virtually the sole survivor of this once universal rite is the coronation of British monarchs, a ceremony still retaining much of its ancient beauty and ritual. Naturally many superstitious beliefs have become attached to it.

At his coronation in 1199, King John, an irreverent man, contemptuously threw aside the white spear that symbolized sovereignty over the duchy of Normandy and jeered as they placed the crown of England on his head. A few years later, he lost the duchy in a war with the French king, and eventually, crossing that inlet of the North Sea called The Wash, he was overwhelmed by high tides and lost all his baggage, including the crown.

After his death, he was turned out of his grave by superstitious people, who thought he was a werewolf. *John* is a very common English name, but it is unlikely it will ever be born by another British sovereign. Too unlucky.

James II was crowned on April 23, the feast of Saint George, patron of England. That day in 1685 ought to have been lucky for the new monarch, but the crown, too large, slipped down over James's head, and witnesses interpreted that as a sinister omen. Sure enough, within three years, James was forced to flee his kingdom, to be replaced by his Dutch son-in-law, William III, and his daughter Mary. James's son, called James III by devoted followers and the Old Pretender by his enemies, attempted to regain the throne in 1715 but failed miserably. So did the rebellion in 1745 of the Young Pretender, James II's grandson, affectionately called Bonnie Prince Charlie by the Scots. Thereafter, the Stuart line died out in exile.

And now, of course, Saint George himself has been repudiated by the Roman Catholic Church, one of those early saints whose existence (like that of Nicholas and Christopher) is in doubt.

Against all advice, Charles I wore white, England's unlucky color, at his coronation in 1625. Twenty-four years later, he wound up in another white garment (actually two white shirts, for he was afraid he would be cold and his shivering might be misconstrued as fear) on the scaffold. He was the only British monarch to have his head chopped off—and the most mourned. White used to be the mourning color. Black came later.

At Queen Victoria's coronation in 1838, elaborate preparations were made to assure that all would pass off smoothly. The prime minister had even hidden sandwiches and drinks behind the high altar for his refreshment during the ceremony. But the ring with which the young queen was to wed the nation was too small for the correct finger. Believing that to put it on any but the traditional finger would be unfortunate, the archbishop forced it on her ring finger anyway, and for hours after the ceremony, while others celebrated, she had to sit with her hand in ice water. All the other omens were excellent, however, and her reign was the longest in British history.

After the monarch has been anointed with oil, while the choir sings the Handel anthem "Zadok the Priest," he (or she) is presented to the peers. (In olden days, a king was lifted on a shield and carried aloft.) The peers are asked if they will accept "your undoubted lord," and the traditional response is "God Save the King!" (At the coronation of Edward VII, many peers, so accustomed to Victoria, forgot themselves and shouted, "God Save the Queen!")

At the coronation of one of the Hanoverians, the question was not asked loudly enough, and instead of acclaiming George the king, the crowd of peers was silent. The new monarch looked alarmed, whereat a dowager peeress nearby is said to have electrified Westminister Abbey with the loudest whisper on record: "Does the old fool think with so many drawn swords that anyone will say nay?" This was regarded as an inauspicious beginning for the reign.

MICHAELMAS, SEPTEMBER 29

This feast of Saint Michael the Archangel is associated in Britain with the eating of goose for dinner. As an explanation for this, it is said that Queen Elizabeth I was eating goose on this day when news was brought her of the defeat of the Spanish Armada in 1588, but that can hardly be true, since the Armada had been done away with by the end of July. Whatever the reason, if you eat goose on Michaelmas you will never lack money for the next year.

Michaelmas is also associated with blackberries. In Ireland people claim that on this date the Devil puts his foot on the blackberry, so many people will not pick these berries on the archangel's day.

There is also a folk belief that on Michaelmas Eve at midnight the bracken produces a small blue flower. Actually bracken, a variety of fern, does not flower at all.

The age of the moon—that is, the number of days from the appearance of the new moon—governs the number of days of flood that will follow Michaelmas.

HALLOWEEN OR ALL HALLOWS EVE

The name "All Hallows Eve," which has become worn down to our modern "Halloween," means that it is the eve of All Saints' Day (November 1), when the Church venerates the entire host of those she has canonized as holy. But it coincides in date with the great fall festival of the Druids, in the middle ages was considered one of the great witches' Sabbaths, and today is synonymous with tales of goblins and witches and spooks.

The wind, blowing across corpses, predicts the future on Halloween night. It can be heard sighing against the windows of those who will die

within the twelvemonth. If you go to a crossroads and listen to it, you will
learn all the things that will happen to you in the coming year. Refine that by
sitting at the crossroads on a three-legged stool and wait until the local
church clock strikes midnight, and you will hear the names of the parish
doomed spoken aloud.

The Irish are particularly strong believers in the evil of Halloween. The
dead walk that night, they say; therefore, if you hear footsteps following you,
you must not look around for if you meet the glance of the walking dead you
will die too. A gambler who wishes to change bad luck to good should hide
under a blackberry bush and invoke the aid of the Devil on Halloween;
thenceforward he will always win at cards.

In Scotland it's fairies you have to watch out for on Halloween night.
Force all your sheep and lambs through a hoop of rowan and make a circuit
of the cropland carrying lighted torches.

Much more common, however, are Halloween spells or games to
foretell who will be one's mate. A man is advised to crawl under a blackberry
bush, and he will see the shadow of his future wife. A girl should wash her
chemise and hang it over a chair beside her bed; if she stays awake long
enough, the image of her future husband will enter the room and turn the
chemise. Or she should take a willow branch in her right hand or a ball of
wool yarn, slip out of the house unseen, and run three times around it,
saying, "He that is to be my goodman [husband], come and grip." On the
third circuit the proper image should appear and take hold of the other end.

Or a girl can stand before a mirror, combing her hair and eating an
apple, and her future husband's face will appear in the mirror beside her
own. Or she can catch a snail, leave it under a covered dish all night, and
next morning see what initial has been traced out by its slimy trail. Or,
having peeled an apple, she can throw the peel over her left shoulder; the
peel should then form the initial. (It is to be hoped that she has her heart set
on someone named Charles or Christopher or whatnot, for apple peels tend
to form Cs.)

Apples are important in Halloween lore, particularly in America. A girl
can take several apple seeds, give each the name of a potential suitor, place
them over or near the fire, and see which is the first to pop; that's the name
she wants. Or a group of young people can gather on Halloween night, tie
apples to pieces of string, and then whirl them about; the first apple to fall
down indicates which person is to be married first. Or each of the group can
contribute an apple to a tubful of water and then "bob for apples" (the origin

of what is now just a bit of high-spirited horseplay); hands held behind his back, each contestant had to seize an apple in his teeth tightly enough to lift it out (the best way to do this, if one didn't mind ducking, was to pin it against the bottom of the tub), and the person whose apple he managed to catch was his future mate.

HARVEST FESTIVAL

Harvest festivals, in which gratitude is expressed to the life-giving force, whether it is Mother Earth or God the Father, are commonplace throughout the world. Though pagan in origin, they have been taken over by many churches and modern religions. The Jewish feast of Tabernacles, Sukkoth, is still celebrated by many Jews with the setting up of tentlike structures in backyards or in houses or on the balconies of apartment buildings and the setting out of harvest fruits. Every autumn in Britain, parish churches are still decorated with produce of the fields, and a special service is held, at which the congregation sings:

> All good gifts around us
> Are sent from Heaven above,
> So thank the Lord, thank the Lord
> For all His love.

This pagan festival was resurrected in the Church of England in the 1840s by the Reverend R. S. Hawker, who served a remote parish in Cornwall. In their Celtic past, Cornishmen had sacrificed to the Druids' gods of fertility by sprinkling blood in the fields. Mr. Hawker revived this ancient attitude toward the fruits of the earth, giving it the sanction of the Church.

But this does not mean that unabashedly pagan beliefs concerned with the harvest do not still abound. To have a big crop next year, make the last sheaf of harvest a big one. For good luck, make sure one sheaf is bound by a woman. Make a corn baby (a symbolic image out of straw) and set it up in the house.

Many American communities still hold Harvest Home festivals, although this is usually combined with Halloween parties. In the past it was popular to celebrate with a corn-shucking bee. Before the advent of corn hybridization, an occasional red-kerneled ear (nicknamed "Indian corn") would turn up in a crop of normal yellow ears. It was considered highly lucky to find such an ear; it won you a kiss from your sweetheart, and you saved it until the following harvest as a charm. Today people may buy colored ears at the supermarket and affix them to their front doors.

Some people consider the American festival of Thanksgiving as a kind of harvest festival. However, its late date (the original was held in December, 1621, and the modern feast has been established as the fourth Thursday in November) make it unsuitable for a celebration of harvest. Moreover, there seem to be few superstitions in connection with it.

DAYS OF BIRTH

From the days of the ancient cave dwellers to today's earnest followers of astrological horoscopes, the time of a child's birth has been held to be of major importance to its life. Here are some folk beliefs concerning births.

Bad days to be born: March 21, any day between June 23 and July 23, any day in May.

Good days to be born: Sundays, New Year's Day, Christmas Day. The last is particularly desirable, because the child will be psychic. A child born on Sunday cannot be harmed by evil spirits. Many people know this old rhyme:

> Monday's child is fair of face;
> Tuesday's child is full of grace;
> Wednesday's child is full of woe;
> Thursday's child has far to go;
> Friday's child is loving and giving;
> Saturday's child works hard for a living;
> And the child that is born on the Sabbath day
> Is blithe and bonny, good and gay.

Natural phenomena control the good/bad luck of birth. People who live by the seaside believe that a child is not likely to be born until the tide is in (just as old people are not likely to die until the tide is out), and if it is born during the ebb, it will not live long. It is better to be born at night than during the day, especially if the moon if full (if you are born in the dark of the moon, you will not live past puberty). In Sicily it is believed that girls are born under a waning moon and boys under a waxing one. A child born at midnight will be able to see the spirits of the departed. Sunrise is a lucky time to be born, for the child will have a long life; a sunset birth means the child will be lazy.

CHRISTMAS EVE

Christmas is so popular a holiday that whole books have been written about the customs, beliefs, and superstitions connected with it.

Things to do for good luck: Tie wet straw around the fruit trees, so that they will yield well the following year. Bring holly into the house (bad luck if you bring it before this). Hang up mistletoe for a good-luck kiss and after New Year's Day give it to the first cow that calves. (Warning: mistletoe must be burned before Twelfth Night, January 6, or all the couples who kissed under it will be enemies before the end of the year.) At midnight, open the doors and windows to let out evil spirits and welcome in the good.

Things to avoid to escape bad luck: Cutting the Christmas cake before Christmas Eve. Allowing fire or a light to leave the house.

Advice to unmarried girls: Walk backward to the nearest pear tree, walk around it nine times, and see an image of your husband-to-be. Go to the henhouse and tap sharply; if a cock crows first, you will be wed within the year, and if a hen cackles, you won't. Go into the garden at midnight, pick twelve sage leaves, and glimpse the shadowy form of your future husband. Silently make a dough cake, prick your initials in it, and place it on the hearth; at midnight, a vision of your husband-to-be will enter and prick his initials beside yours. Get engaged—very good luck will follow.

Special sights at midnight: All cattle kneeling and lowing. Bees humming the Hundredth Psalm. The rosemary bursting into flower. Familiar faces appearing in the flames of the Yule log. (But if those flames cast headless shadows, beware. The persons whose shadows those are will die before the year is out.)

By the way, never mind what Dickens says in *A Christmas Carol*—ghosts absolutely never appear on Christmas Eve.

CHRISTMAS DAY

Don't go out of the house until a dark man has come to visit (a form of first footing). If a woman appears first, that's very bad luck. Don't turn the mattress. When it's time to go out, wassail the apple trees with cider.

Christmas predictions: A child born on Christmas will never be hanged. If the sun shines through an apple tree on Christmas Day, it will be heavy with fruit next year. Light Christmas, light wheatsheaves; dark Christmas, heavy wheatsheaves (if Christmas is an overcast day, there will be an abundant harvest).

Our symbols of Christmas have come to us from many lands. Mistletoe was venerated by the Druids, especially as it grew on the oak, which was sacred to them. Druids distributed sprigs of mistletoe to people, who hung up these evergreen branches in hope that the nature deities would restore greenery in the spring. A similar reason governed the use of holly and ivy, considered to represent male and female respectively. A fifteenth-century carol depicts a debate between the two over which one held the mastery; it concludes with Holly yielding gracefully.

> Then spake Holly and set him down on his knee,
> "I pray thee, gentle Ivy, say me no villainy,
> In Landes where we goe."

The Yule log comes from Scandinavia, where it was burned as a kind of winter-solstice purification rite. Origin of the word *Yule* is in dispute, but one theory claims that it meant an ancient Teutonic winter season, roughly mid-November to mid-January. Christians took over the practice and made great merriment over dragging it into the hall with singing and dancing. Robert Herrick tells us that for good luck the Yule log had to be lighted from a brand of the previous year's log:

> Kindle the Christmas brand, and then
> Till sunset let it burn,
> Which quenched, then lay it up again,
> Till Christmas next return.

The Yule log crossed the Atlantic and became part of American Christmas traditions, especially in the South. Slaves were allowed to keep holiday as long as the log burned, so it was always thoroughly soaked before being lighted and carefully tended to keep it smoldering for days.

The wassail bowl is an ancient Anglo-Saxon tradition. Carolers carried cups with them, and wherever they stopped to serenade neighbors they held out the cups and cried, "Wassail! Wassail!" At that the family being serenaded was expected to fill the cups with "lambswool," a hot spiced ale with roasted apples floating in it. "You may have it of the costliest wine, or the humblest malt liquor," wrote Leigh Hunt. "But in no case must the roasted apples be forgotten."

And last, but far from least, is the Christmas tree, a relatively recent import from Germany. It did not arrive in Great Britain until Queen Victoria married Prince Albert of Saxe-Coburg (Germany), but it reached American shores a good 150 years earlier than that with the first German settlers. Lighted by small candles (modern Germans still prefer them to electric tree lights), decorated with trinkets and little figures, surrounded by presents, surmounted by a star or an angel figure, it is still the heart of the family's celebration of this most beloved of holidays.

OTHER SPECIAL OCCASIONS

Epiphany or Three Kings' Day, January 6. Take down the Christmas tree. Make a cake containing a ring and a button; whoever gets the ring will marry during the year, and whoever gets the button will not.

Valentine's Day, February 14. Write the names of your boyfriends on bits of paper, stick each one into a ball of clay and drop them into water; the one that rises first will contain your true love's name.

Mardi Gras or Shrove Tuesday (the last day before the start of Lent). Make pancakes for the family and throw one to a rooster. If he eats it all, expect bad luck. If the hens get most of it, good luck will be yours.

Ash Wednesday (first day of Lent). Eat pea soup. Do not sell any cattle.

Lent (forty days of fasting and repentance that precede Easter). "Marry in Lent, live to repent." Until very recently, many Christian churches forbade couples to marry during Lent and Advent.

St. Swithin's Day (July 15). If it rains today, it will rain for the forty days that follow. Swithin was bishop of Winchester, and before he died (in 862) he requested that he be buried outdoors under "the sweet rain of heaven." This request was carried out, but later (when he was canonized) the monks of the nearby abbey tried to move him indoors to a grander tomb (this was on July 15), but it started to rain and did not stop for forty days, so they took that as a sign of the saint's displeasure and returned him to his original grave.

All Souls' Day (November 2). As the previous day commemorated All Saints, so this day commemorated the rest of the dead, and it was believed that all souls still suffering in Purgatory were released for twenty-four hours. If at midnight two people walk around a room in total darkness, in opposite directions, they will never meet and one will be spirited away.

PART TWO

The Future

"The Only Way to Predict the Future Is to Have the Power to Shape the Future"

THE black magician, turning to necromancy, attempts to raise evil spirits in order to learn their deepest secrets, including the nature of the future. With terrifying ceremony, he sacrifices a stolen baby and prays:

> Astoreth, Asmodeus, principles of friendship and love, I invoke
> you to accept as sacrifice this newborn child that I offer you for
> the things I ask; and that you will deny me nothing in return for
> this offering, whether for myself, my relatives, or any of my
> household.

Other men cast horoscopes in hopes of uncovering the great truths of nature and seeing into the future. They read tea leaves, dice, or cards; feel bumps on heads and pore over lines in palms; explore omens and auguries, the Tarot or the *I Ching*. They interpret dreams. They study the peculiarities of chance. They strive to peer beyond the veil of Death itself.

Astrology, the "science" that is studied by more Americans today than any that operate on heavy government funding, goes back to the stargazers of ancient Chaldea. It supplied a good part of early science and the occult lore of masonry, theosophy, and other movements. We may have gone beyond it but we are peculiarly reluctant to leave it behind.

Our traditions of fortune-telling are likewise long-lived, coming to us along with the rest of our culture essentially from our pagan past. Romans, hard-headed though they were in other ways, believed implicitly in fortune-telling and kept state augurs to examine the entrails of animals and the flight of birds and thus predict what was good for the state and what wasn't.

Luck, on the other hand, though believed in almost universally from the beginning of time, has only recently begun to be studied by mathematicians, sociologists, and others interested in the vagaries of chance. Nonetheless, the thing itself has been wooed and fretted over since man lived in caves and learned how to make fire.

Like fortune-telling, interpretation of dreams goes far back into the misty past, inspiring many writers of classical times and earlier to expatiate on what dreams mean. In the Bible, Joseph interprets Pharaoh's dream about cattle. In *The City of God*, Saint Augustine explains the meaning of sexual nightmares.

As for death, when has man not speculated on the meaning of it and what will become of him when his earthly body decays?

In this section, we explore those forms of occult thought that have occupied wonderers from the beginning of time.

6

Predictions and Prophecies

LOOK, WE'VE COME THROUGH!

In just the last few decades, the end of the world has been fairly often predicted. In mid-January 1976, a man named John Nash caused quite a stir in Adelaide, Australia, by predicting that the city, perhaps the world, would soon be destroyed by a giant tidal wave.

Some Aussies fled to the hills, but the prime minister and a host of other optimists gathered on the beach to celebrate what turned out to be the Big Non-Event. Adelaide is still there. So is California, despite dire predictions ("Buy some beach property now in Nevada"), and so is the great Globe itself, despite the men with the signs saying, "The End Is Nigh." We can, in fact, expect many more dire warnings of the Holocaust and Armageddon and nuclear disintegration and so on.

By rights, one of these many predictions of disaster, just by the law of averages, actually ought to coincide with a real event. It is really remarkable that it hasn't. After all, in Tacoma, Washington, a vast bridge was blown down, in Wales a pile of mine dumpings collapsed and smothered a village school, balconies plunged to the lobby of a modern hotel in Kansas City, there have been many calamitous oil spills, and numerous other manmade catastrophes have occurred—not to mention such Acts of God as volcanic eruptions, earthquakes, tidal waves, floods, hurricanes, tornadoes, and the rest. And yet no one warned the public that these specific cataclysms were on the way.

The next Big One to watch out for is the end of the world in the year 2000. Scientists say the world will last to the year 10,000,000,000; the superstitious say no.

A USEFUL VISION

Sometimes clairvoyant episodes stem from the close personal relationships between two persons. *Phantasms of the Living*, a famed collection of such incidents, tells, for example, about a child of ten who, while away from home, had a sudden vision of her mother lying on the floor. The child fetched the doctor, and they ran to the house, where they found the mother exactly as she had been "seen." Their promptness saved her life. "The account does not add," comments novelist Colin Wilson, "that there was a strong bond between mother and daughter, but there undoubtedly was."

A THEORY OF THE SUPERNATURAL

One of the most convincing theories about what makes parapsychological episodes possible occurs not in a learned tome but in a short story—"The Bus Conductor" by E. F. Benson, a literate student of the occult and son of an archbishop of Canterbury.

> Imagine then that you and I and everybody in the world are like those people whose eye is directly opposite a little tiny hole in a sheet of cardboard which is continually shifting and revolving and moving about. Back to back with that sheet of cardboard is another, which also, by laws of its own, is in perpetual but independent motion. In it, too, there is another hole, and when, fortuitously it would seem, these two holes, the one through which we are always looking, and the other in the spiritual plane, come opposite to one another, we see through, and then only do the sights and sounds of the spiritual world become visible and audible to us. With most people these holes never come opposite each other during their life. But at the hour of death they do, and then they remain stationary. That, I fancy, is how we "pass over."

If Benson's theory has some validity, could it be that some people are able to get these "holes" to coincide frequently? If so, it would explain that mysterious power of "second sight" that other people can hardly credit.

MUZA'S FATE

Mlle. Irene Muza of the Comédie Française predicted her own death. And she never knew she had done so.

"My career will be short," she wrote in a trance; no unusual life for an actress, it must be admitted, but she added: "I dare not say what my end will be. It will be terrible."

It was. A few months later Mlle. Muza was accidentally set on fire by her hairdresser; she perished in the flames.

The trance-state prediction had been kept from her by kind friends. But it came true, nevertheless.

FATAL ACCURACY

The German astronomer and astrologer David Fabricius (1546–1617) predicted in 1607 that he would die ten years later; the date he "saw" was May 7, 1617. On that day in 1617 he stayed home with his doors and windows locked, but at midnight he thought he was safe and ventured a walk in his garden. He was set upon by a maniac he had never seen before, who split his skull open with a pitchfork.

PORTENTS

Shakespeare often mentions portents: a lion in the street the night before the death of Julius Caesar, the strange goings-on indicative of the reversal of order presaging the death of King Duncan in *Macbeth*, and so on. Here is a real case, as reported by John Aubrey in his *Miscellanies*:

When King James II first entered Dublin after his arrival from France in 1689, one of the Gentlemen that bore the Mace before him, stumbled without any rub [obstacle apparent] in his way, or other visible occasion. The Mace fell out of his hands, and the little Cross upon the Crown thereof stuck fast between the [cobble] stones in the Street. This is well known all over Ireland, and did much trouble King James himself with many of his chief Attendants.

That the son of James I (who staunchly defended the existence of witchcraft against Reginald Scot's *Discouerie of Witchcraft*, which declared it a delusion) believed in this is perhaps not remarkable. What is notable is that so many other people would take this accident as a portent foretelling the fall of the king. Superstition was rampant among the Jacobites and the Anti-Jacobites alike, so that a thing like that could be bad propaganda indeed.

NIXON AND DIXON

Prognosticator Jean Dixon said in *Parade* on May 13, 1956, that "a blue-eyed Democratic President elected in 1960 will be assassinated." There are many evidences that President Kennedy was told not to drive through Dallas that fateful day, too. But Miss Dixon in 1960 also predicted that Richard Nixon would beat John Kennedy in the election. Neither that nor her prediction of World War III (slated for 1958) came true. The assassination did.

My favorite prediction is the one (not by Miss Dixon) that President Nixon would come to grief over "a piece of tape." Some friends and myself got this one with a Ouija board two years before Watergate (and were wrong by a whole year about the date). When the news of Watergate broke, I thought the White House recorded tapes made the prediction look very important. Later I realized that the "piece of tape" that really brought the President down was the little piece that the Watergate plumbers put over a lock in the offices of the Democrats they were burgling. If *that* had not been noticed by a nightwatchman . . .

SMALL CHANGE

The Maoris still believe that in reciting a spell one little slip of the tongue can be fatal. In Europe it was often said that the smallest error in a spell or magical ceremony would invalidate the whole thing. I have been told by several ritual magicians that the reason certain ceremonies did not work for me was that I sang the magical words to the wrong notes. Had I been better able to carry a tune, I might now be both rich and invisible.

WHAT DO YOU HEAR?

Here's a method for getting news of the future (or the answer to any pressing question). According to Greek geographer Pausanias, it was used at a shrine of Hermes, that of Apollo at Thebes, and that of Zeus at Olympia. The Greeks swore by it.

You went up to the statue of Hermes, lighted the bronze lamps on the hearth-altar (rather like burning a candle in church), put a coin on the altar, and whispered your question into the statue's ear. Then you clapped your hands over your own ears and walked away. The first speech you heard on taking your hands away from your ears was your clue to the answer.

Maybe you'd like to forecast the financial market by using the statue of George Washington on the steps of the U.S. Sub-Treasury building in New York. Run straight over to the Stock Exchange to unblock your ears. This system may work as well as any on Wall Street.

JEWISH DIVINATION

In Biblical times, the Jews believed in official divination to determine the future and the will of God. When officiating at sacred functions, the High Priest wore the ephod, an apronlike vestment, and over it the breastplate of righteousness, or *hoshen*. This breastplate displayed four rows of three stones each, representing and inscribed with the names of the Twelve Tribes of Israel: sardius for Reuben, topaz for Simeon, carbuncle for Judah, emerald for Dan, sapphire or lapis lazuli for Naphtali, diamond or crystal for Gad, jacinth (an orangish stone) for Asher, agate for Issachar, amethyst for Zebulun, beryl for Benjamin, onyx for Manasseh, and jasper for Ephraim. Underneath the *hoshen*, over the priest's heart, was a pouch, sometimes called the pocket of decision, which contained the mysterious Urim and Thummim, sacred lots used for divination or reading the oracles. It is uncertain today exactly what they were or how they worked.

It was when Saul could obtain no information from Urim and Thummim—or from dreams or prophets—that he turned to the witch of Endor to learn why he was out of favor with the Lord (I Samuel 28: 6–19). Magicians who use "the powers" of precious and semiprecious stones today will tell you the ancient Hebrews went about it in the wrong way in arranging these stones; no wonder they didn't work, they say.

YOUR BABY'S FUTURE

Put out a Bible, a silver dollar, and a pack of cards. If the baby touches the Bible, he will be a preacher. If he picks up the silver dollar, he will be a financier. If he touches the pack of cards, he will turn out to be a gambler.

If he picks up all three, perhaps when he grows up he will take a chance on becoming a money-grubbing TV evangelist! Or such is the facetious claim of some people.

OGMA

Ogma was the Celtic god of fertility and healing, of eloquence and prophecy. He is credited with the invention of the Ogham alphabet.

POLYNESIAN PROPHECIES

In Polynesia they set up sticks, each one representing a tribesman, and judged thereby which of their warriors would fall in battle. They also spun coconuts to catch thieves.

DIVINING RODS

Divining rods were once used in France to track criminals or heretics, but a law of 1701 forbade their employment and such evidence was thereafter not admitted in court. Today psychics are occasionally used in trying to track down criminals or find lost persons.

THE END OF THE WORLD

Christianity has been plagued by no end of end-of-the-worldists. In the second century, it was Montanism (a sect of extreme asceticism) that claimed, among other things, that the New Jerusalem (the next world) was soon to appear at the sect's headquarters in Phrygia. The world did not end when predicted, of course, but Montanism continued to gather converts. In the third century, it made its only important one, the ecclesiastical writer Tertullian, but later Church Fathers (such as Origen and Clement of Alexandria) were unimpressed, and eventually the Emperor Justinian proscribed the sect. The Montanists thereupon locked themselves in their churches and set fire to them. That really was the end of the world—for them, at least.

The millenarians forecast the end of the world for the year 1000. They were wrong, too. Neo-millenarians look bleakly toward the year 2000.

POLITICAL PROGNOSTICATION

In 1213 Peter the Wise, a Yorkshire hermit, was hanged because he predicted the death of King John. Treason as well as sorcery, they said—not wise of him at all. In 1580 Elizabeth I passed a law against foretelling the death of the monarch. At that time, rumors such as that could be a lot of help to fomenters of rebellion, such as Mary, Queen of Scots. Mary was well aware of the usefulness of prophecy as propaganda, and she herself called it "the very Foundation of all Rebellion."

The connection of sorcery with politics is a book in itself. I predict someone will attempt it soon.

PREMONITIONS

Everyone has many premonitions; most of them never come true. But every time some spectacular event hits the headlines there are people who claim that they saw it coming all along.

Next time you have a strong premonition, why not get it on record *before* the event? Then you'll find researchers in this field far more interested in it as evidence.

In New York, contact the American Society for Psychical Research, Box 482, Times Square Station, New York, New York 10036. In London, you can write or telegraph the Central Premonitions Register (at the *Evening Standard*) or the Society for Psychical Research, Adam and Eve Mews, London W8.

FATALISM

Che sera, sera ("Whatever will be, will be") is one of the world's most widespread beliefs. Before King Abdullah of Jordan was assassinated in Jerusalem in 1951, he used to quote an Arab proverb: "Until my day comes, nothing can hurt me; when my day comes, nothing can save me." He was right.

Magic, of course, attempts to change events, to force Heaven to its own will. Magic is never satisfied with the idea of things just happening; it wants to *make* things happen. It never pauses to consider that what magicians and seers do is also, perhaps, part of the Great Plan—all dictated from on high, all foreseen and ordained.

COMEUPPANCE

In the year 1370, the road to Canterbury was choked with pilgrims on their way to the shrine of Saint Thomas à Becket. The traffic jam inconvenienced the bishop of London, Simon Sudbury, and he cried out to the throng: "Plenary indulgence for your sins by repairing to Canterbury? Better hope might ye have of Salvation had ye stayed at home. . . ."

Thomas of Aldon, a Kentish squire, was outraged that the bishop should insult England's favorite saint. He shouted back: "My lord bishop . . . I will give up my own salvation if you yourself do not die a most shameful death!"

Eleven years later, Sudbury had attained the highest rank in the English Church, archbishop of Canterbury. But that did not save him. In the Wat Tyler commotions of 1380–81, he was attacked by a mob and ignominiously beheaded on Tower Hill.

The Kentishman did not have to give up his own salvation as offered, for his prophecy, or curse, had come true.

PROPHECIES OF DOOM

English history is full of dire warnings. As a boy King Richard III was warned by a soothsayer that he would die "soon after he gazed upon

Rougemont." One day in 1485 he was startled to learn that a castle he had paused to admire was called Rougemont. A few weeks later, he was slain at Bosworth Field. Many lies were told to and about the enigmatic Richard, but this prophecy seems to have been one important truth.

Thomas Cardinal Wolsey (1475–1530), chancellor of capricious Henry VIII, was warned by a fortune-teller that "Kingston" would mark the end of his life. He deliberately avoided that town name from then on, and on one occasion, when under the king's displeasure, he even gave Henry his glorious palace at Hampton Court in an attempt to placate fate. But one day when the cardinal was ill and worried, a constable arrived, sent by Henry. Wolsey is said to have died of shock on learning that the man's name was Kingston.

CASANOVA'S PROPHECY

Giovanni Casanova (1725–98), who is known chiefly for his sexual conquests, also indulged occasionally in prophecy. One instance involved Sir Thomas Hope, a wealthy merchant, whom Casanova convinced of a vision in which he saw a ship of Hope's. It was heavily laden and safe at sea, although others had given it up for lost. The ship did indeed come in, and Casanova was well rewarded.

Of course, had it been lost, Casanova would have had to make still another of his many midnight departures from foreign cities. As it was, he had all Amsterdam talking about his ability to see into the future, a useful talent in marine insurance.

AN IRISH OCCURRENCE

A story is told of an Irishman who lay down in a field to sleep and who, waking, found himself both deaf and dumb. He could signal messages to his friends, however, and he told them many wonderful things he had never known when he was in possession of all his faculties. He could foretell the future and knew instantly of events at great distances.

In time he recovered his ordinary abilities to hear and speak and in that instant he lost all his paranormal powers. He never could explain what had happened to him.

Think about this story in terms of the folk wisdom enshrined in superstitions, the deep truth of primitive legends, the unsophisticated but subtle insights in the short and simple annals of the poor.

ROYAL PROPHECIES

King Philip II of Macedonia, warned by an oracle to "beware of a chariot," thereafter staunchly refused to ride in one. But at his daughter's wedding (336 B.C.) he was slain by an assassin whose dagger hilt was decorated with a carving of a chariot.

When the mosque of the Sultan Hassan in Cairo was under construction in 1329, a soothsayer warned the monarch that completion of a second minaret would cause his death. He ordered the building to proceed. The second minaret stood, and he congratulated himself on his wisdom. In 1361 that minaret crashed down on an adjacent orphanage, killing three hundred children. They say that when the sultan died thirty-three days later, it was of a broken heart.

When Louis XV attended divine service on March 31, 1774, Bishop Jean de Beauvais (1731–1790) took as the text of his sermon Jonah 3:4: "Yet forty days and Nineveh shall be overthrown." Exactly forty days later Louis XV was dead.

Constantine the Great prophesied that the number 13 would bring down Constantinople. It was eleven hundred years later, when Constantine XIII was Byzantine emperor (he was actually only the eleventh of that name, but some early historians called him XIII) that the Turks destroyed the city. That was in 1453. If you add 1, 4, 5, and 3 the total is 13.

BLAKE THE MYSTIC

Some of the very best English mystical poetry is from the pen of William Blake, the early Romantic poet who not only had visions that he built into such works as *The Book of Thel* and *The Four Zoas* but also claimed he chatted with an archangel in his back garden. He had other psychic experiences. In 1771, as a youth of fourteen, he was apprenticed to William Rylands, then England's foremost engraver, to learn the art of etching. The job lasted only one day, because young Blake could not stand the fact that whenever he looked at his master he saw Rylands dangling dead on a gallows.

It was twelve years before this prophetic vision was explained. Rylands was hanged for forgery on August 29, 1783.

NOSTRADAMUS

It was Merlin, magician at the court of the legendary King Arthur, who is supposed to have said that he would "not speak before our people nor at court save in obscure words, nor will they know what I mean until they see it come to pass." One Michel de Nôtre-Dame (1503–1566) was the past master of this particular form of prognostication. You know him better by his Latin name, Nostradamus.

Though he was named for the Blessed Virgin, Nostradamus came from a long line of Jewish physicians. His grandfather was physician to King René of Anjou. The family converted to Christianity and took the Christian surname "Nôtre-Dame." In spite of the anti-Semitism that raged in Europe in the fifteenth century (and led to the expulsion of the Jews from Spain in 1492), Christian communities experienced a heavy influx of Jewish magic and scientific learning.

Science and magic were then mixed, and Nostradamus, who had a degree in medicine from Montpellier, gained himself a reputation (as did the famous Dr. Faustus) fighting an epidemic of the plague. Like many another physician and banker in the period, he traveled far and wide and picked up extra money spying; Nostradamus was a spy for the kingdom of France and for the duchies of Savoy and Lorraine.

Another sideline was astrology and prediction. In 1555 he published *Centuries*, a book of rhymed prophecies, and attracted the patronage of the powerful queen, Catherine de Médicis, herself no mean plotter and dabbler in the occult.

For her he prophesied:

The young lion shall overcome the old,
On the field of war, in mortal combat.
He will pierce his eyes in a cage of gold.
This is the first of two loppings, then he dies a cruel death.

How's that for obscure? Yet two years later it seemed crystal-clear. In a joust Catherine's husband, Henri II, celebrating the marriage of his daughter, ran against the earl of Montgomery, and the earl's lance pierced the grille of Henri's golden helmet. He died after ten days of excruciating pain caused by a piece of the lance lodged in his eye.

Catherine was interested. She had always wanted to know about the future (and plots, poisons, and other things useful in politics). Anyone who could predict an accident like that could be useful. After forty-five sittings with Nostradamus, Catherine (it is claimed) was visited by an angel who told her everything that would happen to her family, including the fact that the assassination of Henri III would put an end to the dynasty of the Valois—as indeed it did, eventually.

Ordinarily Nostradamus did not produce such extraordinary messen-. gers or such clear-cut messages. He dealt in "obscure words" which were then read, and read into. It was said he predicted World War I, but the prophecy did not seem to mean much until World War I had already begun. In World War II both the British and the Nazis used the ambiguity of Nostradamus's prophecies for propaganda purposes, "reading" them to suit themselves.

If you would like to try interpreting him, there are still many prophecies left dealing with events yet to come, and his 333 quatrains are a lot more readily available today than they ever were in his own time. He is something of a best-selling author in this field.

One quatrain discusses "the Oriental" who is to "pass through the sky" and start what looks like World War III in the very late twentieth century, unless that meant Pearl Harbor in World War II! But if Nostradamus is right, World War III will not be the total annihilation everyone else is talking about, for his prophecies end with A.D. 3797, which means presumably that the world still has some time to run.

THE DEVIL TO PAY

If you want to look into the future, it can be expensive. Remember that Dr. Faustus had to sell his soul to the Devil and then was cheated, too. In the *Rituale Romanum*, liturgical manual for the Roman Catholic Church, the third instruction on exorcism says (in Latin) that a possessing devil reveals himself by the ability of the possessed person to "reveal distant or hidden things." Also, "There are uncountable tricks and frauds that the devil will use to deceive."

Are you sure you wouldn't prefer just to wait and see what happens?

STILL WORKING ON THE CAYCE

To many Americans, Edgar Cayce, the controversial miracle man of Virginia Beach, Virginia, is the prophet par excellence. Nearly forty years after his death (in 1945) the paperback racks of bookstores are crammed with various volumes devoted to his healing arts and prognostications.

The most disturbing prophecy he made concerns the destruction of a great part of the western United States by earthquakes, an event Cayce said would occur in this century and be accompanied by the destruction of much of Europe and Japan.

Undeterred, Americans are flocking west in greater and greater numbers; people from the Frost Belt have been moving to the Sun Belt, the East Coast is losing out to the West Coast. How long this can go on will soon be seen, for Cayce's prophecies speak of the 1990s as the bad times. By the turn of the century New York, too, would be under water, the prophet claimed.

Cayce diagnosed diseases at a distance (over 14,000 cases) merely by going into a trance. Many people credit him with amazing cures. He also undertook to tell people about their "previous lives," for he firmly believed in reincarnation. He gave elaborate, detailed history of the lost city of Atlantis. He predicted that "the temple will rise again" and that "Poseidia will be among the first portions of Atlantis" to be rediscovered. "Expect it in 1968 or 1969," he said (in 1934), and in 1968 ruins that some believed to be the pillars of a massive temple were found off the coast of Bimini in the Caribbean.

ACE OF SPADES

In cartomancy, or fortune-telling by cards, the Ace of Spades relates to love. When it is accompanied by the 10 of Spades, you can expect a lot of trouble. If it appears upside down, the Ace of Spades means pregnancy, and if the Knave of Clubs is also reversed, death. Bad news all around.

PROGNOSTICATION

If you want to find out how the American Federation of Astrologers is going to fare as an organization, you might try making a horoscope for it. Its birth time was May 4, 1938, and the place Washington, D.C.

GROUNDS FOR BELIEF

You have heard of tea-leaf readers. In Macedonia they tell the future from coffee grounds. And in France, using coffee grounds, Mme. Bontemps told the fortunes of Mme. de Pompadour, the duc de Choiseul, and other court figures—with what accuracy I am not sure, but they were satisfied.

THALES

Thales of Miletus, Greek philosopher of the sixth century B.C., requested that at his death he be buried in a certain obscure corner of his native city, for that lonely spot would one day become the forum or center of town. He was, and it did.

HAVE A NICE YEAR

What's going to happen this year, a Chinese astrologer will tell you, has something to do with which of the creatures happens to rule this period. The twelve-animal, twelve-year cycle goes like this:

Rat	Horse
Ox	Goat
Tiger	Monkey
Cat	Rooster
Dragon	Dog
Snake	Pig

1983-5744

The Jewish year beginning in September 1983 is numbered 5744. In traditional Jewish numerology, this spells *DOOM*. "Sheer and utter super-

stitious nonsense," says Dr. Ronald Sobel, rabbi of New York's Temple Emmanuel. If you are Jewish, however, and not Reformed, go worry.

WHAT IS NEEDED

William James, brother of novelist Henry James, was one of the main forces behind the founding in 1885 of the American Society for Psychical Research. As a philosopher, James was interested in new ideas. As a psychologist, he was aware of human gullibility. As a practical scientist, he wanted hard facts. He used to say, "To upset the conclusion that all crows are black, there is no need to seek demonstration that no crow is black; it is sufficient to produce one white crow."

To acknowledge that occult power is at work in some prophets, the world needs at least one list of absolutely specific predictions, all of which come true. That would convince the hardest-nosed statistician and others that the gift for accurate prognostication goes far beyond the so-called laws of probability.

But we are a long way from having it. Every year the *National Enquirer* and other popular papers are chock full of predictions (usually about what entertainment personality is soon to be married or divorced), but the trouble is that most of these prognostications do not come true. When one of them does turn out to be accurate, it is unlikely that anything more than guesswork or chance was behind it.

PRECOGNITION

Can people know things before they happen? Well, everyone has had a hunch from time to time, but some people have experiences of elaborate precognition—rare, hard to explain, and apparently pointless. In 1926 British psychic researcher Dr. S. G. Soal reported just such an incident in *Proceedings of the Society for Psychical Research*. Four years earlier, Dr. Soal was taking part in a séance with the medium Blanche Cooper when he received a "message" purportedly from Gordon Davis, an old school friend of Soal's.

The spirit voice spoke of a row house in "half a street" with *E* somehow important; the house had five or six steps "and a half" leading up to it and a "funny dark tunnel" beside it. Opposite the house was "something" the other houses did not have but "not a veranda."

Inside the house, the voice said, an upstairs room had a very large mirror and pictures of "glorious" mountains and seascapes. Some very large vases and "funny saucers" were mentioned. Downstairs there were "two funny brass candlesticks" and a "black dickie-bird on the piano." A wife and a small son were mentioned.

At the time of the séance, Dr. Soal was under the impression that his old friend Gordon Davis had been killed in action in World War I. So what was this row house? Was it in the next world, or what?

Three years later Dr. Soal discovered that his friend was still in this world—and so was the house. It was located at 54 Eastern Esplanade, Southend-on-Sea, and Gordon Davis was living at that address.

On April 18, 1925, Dr. Soal went to visit his friend in Southend. The house at 54 Eastern Esplanade (the "important" *E*) faced the seafront, with a promenade shelter right across the street (apparently the "something" other houses did not have) and a covered passage or "tunnel" leading to the back between itself and the house next door. There were six steps up to Davis's front door, but the top one was a mere slab, making it more like five and a half steps. Inside the house there were a pair of brass candlesticks and a porcelain kingfisher on the piano, and upstairs there was a room with a large mirror over the fireplace and seven pictures, six of them views of mountains and the sea, as well as five large vases and two plaques that might well have been described as "funny saucers."

Everything was very much as "Gordon Davis" had told Dr. Soal, through the medium Blanche Cooper, back in January 1922. But Gordon Davis was not dead, and he and his wife and small son had not moved into the house described until about a year *after* the séance.

Absolute proof, signed and dated, is available of what was described at the séance in 1922 and of 54 Eastern Esplanade in 1925. The "voice" that spoke to Mrs. Cooper and Dr. Soal in 1922 was describing a place that *did not exist yet*, furnished as described, and yet was to exist in 1925. It was not the voice of Gordon Davis, for he was not *in* the spirit world (in fact, not even in the house) at that time.

HYPNOSIS HELPS

Professor Milan Ryzl taught a course at the University of California at San Diego in 1969 in which 150 students tried telepathy and clairvoyance both before and after being hypnotized. A control group of students who had not undergone hypnosis also tried the telepathic and clairvoyant experiments. Professor Ryzl claimed that hypnosis much increased psychic powers.

In Czechoslovakia, where he came from, he had asked his hypnotized psychics to give him numbers to play in the state lottery. There were forty-nine numbers on the card. His numbers were "good": he did not get the first prize (for that one had to guess six winning numbers) but he did receive a substantial prize for guessing four of the winning numbers. He attributed this to the psychics' help—and he spent his winnings on more laboratory equipment so he could continue to investigate their powers, before and after hypnosis.

Professor Thelma Moss of UCLA reports that some other university faculty are gambling successfully at Las Vegas, as a result of research.

WHAT WILL HAPPEN? SHALL I GET MY WISH?

European witches used orris root (*Iris florentina, Iris germanica, Iris pallida*) to give the answers to questions about the future. The root looks like a little crouching person; a thread was tied around the "neck" and held in the hand, so that the root dangled like a pendulum. Sitting alone at night, the questioner would pose the question and then concentrate. The pendulum would swing clockwise for "yes" and counterclockwise for "no," back and forth for "undecided."

This was a very popular version of coscinomancy (which involved two people balancing a suspended sieve) or cleidomancy (a key on the end of a string used as a pendulum). The pendulum is directed by unconscious or subconscious motions. It can be used over a map to locate treasure, water, and so forth, the pendulum substituting for a dowsing wand.

Experiment with a ring tied to a string and suspended into a glass. Can you *will* it to rotate in this direction or in that? Can you make it stop rotating once it has begun? Some people undoubtedly can move it, apparently at will. *Look Ma, no hands!*

WHERE THERE'S SMOKE, THERE'S LUCK

At Epiphany, celebrations in Tarcento, Italy, climax with a torchlight procession to the top of a nearby hill. This hill is not so famous as the Puy de Dôme in the Auvergne, France, where a temple of Mercury attracted medieval witches in droves, but it is known to have been the site of witchcraft in the past. So the moderns build their bonfire, tossing in their torches, and judge by the volume of smoke that comes from it whether the new year will bring prosperity or not.

REVELATIONS

One basic question people want answered is "When does the world end?" My answer—"when you die"—does not seem to satisfy.

As we have seen, the millenarians were sure the year 1000 was the date, whereas Nostradamus gives us a lot more time. Some people are getting ready for a Big Bang in 2000, and others are gathering on mountaintops to be whisked away at any moment.

In the 1960s, the authors of the musical *Hair* informed us that we were entering the Age of Aquarius, although any good astrologer could have told them differently, and in fact the hippies are not going to be around to enjoy it when it finally does arrive.

If you want a sounder prediction, try this one from a Benedictine monk of the last century, who wrote out a lot of them and sealed them in a lead tube. It was discovered, we are told, by Nicol Rycempel in Berlin when a church was demolished by bombs in 1944. The monk foretold a "trepidation of the spheres" in the eighties, perhaps a shift of the earth's axis "somewhere down the road" or the melting of the polar ice caps or . . . Well, I wouldn't worry about World War III, if I were you. A change of a couple of degrees in the earth's temperature could do a lot more damage to the world as we know it than any manmade catastrophe.

MICH THE WITCH

In an interview in *Playboy*, September 1981, novelist James A. Michener recalled an early period in his life when he was a professional fortune-teller for charity, calling himself Mich the Witch.

When I was in Egypt, I picked up a system of fortune-telling that was really quite extraordinary. I would answer *any* question specifically, in considerable detail. It was fraudulent from start to finish. But I would accidentally hit so close that it really became quite frightening.

There was one dramatic situation where I became sort of famous. This girl came in and the cards were such and such. I said, "How did the operation go?" She said, "What operation?" I said, "Your sex-change operation." Just out of the blue. And it was a guy in drag! It went all over the county. I got in the habit of saying the most outrageous things—and they were true. I got frightened by it. Once, I said, "Don't leave on the trip West Friday." And she left and a few miles from her home, her family was wiped out. When I was in Hawaii, I became very good friends with Henry Kaiser. He would come to have his fortune told. One day I said, "Henry, the banks are going to call your loan for $450,000,000, you'd better get things lined up." He went through the roof. "How did you know about this?!" What do you say to Henry Kaiser? You don't say ten bucks! I have a manuscript completed that will probably be published after I'm dead, about my experience in this. . . . It shows the roots of this mania and how it can be manipulated.

NEWS CONTROL

At Fátima in Portugal in 1917, three shepherd children reported having seen the Virgin Mary on six different occasions. The vision is said to have made certain prophecies concerning the end of the world. The information has been sealed, however, by officials of the Roman Catholic Church. The prophecies are supposed to be so startling that they caused Pope Pius XII to blanch when he read them.

In recent years, someone tried to hold hostages and compel the pope to release this information, but to no avail.

WHAT'S NEXT?

When, in the Babylonian epic of *Gilgamesh*, the hero asks his friend Enkidu how things are with the dead, Enkidu replies:

> I cannot tell it thee; if I were to open the earth before thee, if I were to tell thee that which I have seen, terror would overthrow thee, thou wouldst faint away.

Hamlet's father as a ghost in Shakespeare's play likewise refuses information about the afterlife:

> I could a tale unfold whose lightest word
> Would harrow up thy soul, freeze thy young blood,
> Make thy two eyes, like stars, start from their spheres,
> Thy knotted and combined locks to part,
> And each particular hair to stand on end,
> Like quills upon the fretful porpentine. . . .

Are you so sure, if you could look into the future, you would really want to know about What's Next?

BE OPTIMISTIC

If you suffer a reverse, try to think that in the future you will be glad about what happened. For instance, Napoleon applied for a job in the Russian army, but he didn't get it. He was holding out for the rank of major, and General Tamax thought the rank of captain was about as much as this obscure officer should expect. If Tamax's estimation had been higher, or Napoleon's demand lower . . .

A PRODIGY'S PREDICTION

Like Mozart, Christian Friedrich Heinecken started a brilliant career at the age of four. Few people have heard of "the Infant of Lübeck," however, because he did not live to establish a career, just to start it. He died in 1727 at the age of four, having predicted—in one or more of the several languages he spoke—his own death.

AND, FINALLY . . .

Maybe the best advice is that vouchsafed to historian Arnold Toynbee in a nightmare. He saw a Latin inscription that translates as "Hold on and pray."

7

Astrology

THE ZODIAC

There is no zodiac in the sky. The signs are merely human symbols for some of the celestial bodies we see from the earth. As the planets in their courses pass through the zones alloted to each of the zodiac figures, they are supposed to influence the course of life on earth.

KNOWLEDGE OF THE STARS

Astrology, they say, can give you knowledge of your character and your fate. People have believed that for thousands of years, so we know it *has* to be true, right? But I wonder about it, especially about those astrology columns in the newspapers. All the character delineations are so flattering, all the futures so rosy. Are they really writing and talking about us?

GLORIANA

Henry VIII countenanced strict laws against witchcraft but did not hesitate to consult astrologers about the sex of unborn children. They told him Elizabeth would be a boy. Even with a 50–50 chance, you can't win 'em all.

Elizabeth was luckier in her consultants and her reign (having chosen the date of her coronation with astrological advice). A few scholars allege her faithful John Dee also gave her the date of her death but was a little off. When the time came, she refused to lie down and stood for many hours, surrounded by her courtiers (who could not sit down if she would not), until she died—a little later than scheduled, perhaps, but (*semper eadem*) as determined as ever.

WATCH OUT FOR MARS

Many persons—among them President Theodore Roosevelt—have believed astrologers who warned them of the great dangers Mars can hold when that planet is in certain positions in the heavens.

Astrologers have been contending for many years that the planet to which we have given the name of the warlike god Mars exerts a baleful influence on men who are between the ages of forty-two and fifty-six and produces what has come to be called the midlife crisis.

Recent studies are beginning to clarify for many people the biorhythms, the swings of mood, the stages of mental development, the "passages" of significance in human lives, not just monthly peaks and troughs, not just rough bits in one's horoscope attributed to the actions or influence of Mars or any other planet.

AMERICA'S HOROSCOPE

Evangeline Adams (one of whose clients was Teddy Roosevelt) noted that the United States of America is a Cancer, born on July 4, 1776. She worked out a horoscope for the country. She predicted that the United States would get involved in World War II in 1942, and years later people found out she was twenty-two days off, because it was on December 8, 1941, that America declared war.

HOW OLD IS ASTROLOGY?

The foundation of the art or science of astrology (which, practitioners say, is like medicine, a little of both) may have been the doctrine of *quod superus est sicut quod inferus*, which is to say "as it is above, so it is below." This was the gist of the inscription on the Emerald Tablet said to have been

found in the fist of Hermes Trismegistus, the "thrice-powerful" Egyptian god
of alchemy and magic.

The study of the supposed influence of the stars above on human
mundane affairs below used to be said to be the invention of the Chaldeans
two or three thousand years before Christ (at whose birth some wise men,
generally said to be three but most certainly astrologers, arrived, following
the star to Bethlehem). Now it appears that the lore goes back to the
Sumerians, some four thousand years before Christ.

But Serge Hutin in his learned *History of Astrology* (1970) contends
that what is now popularly called astrology—individual predictions on the
basis of the relative positions of heavenly bodies—was "a slow process, not
appearing in fact before approximately 250 B.C." Those Magi were, in fact,
students of a comparatively new science.

So astrology is both older and younger than its proponents generally
claim. Since 250 B.C. there has been much devolopment of ceremonial
astrology (foretelling the future with the aid of demons) and natal astrology
(horoscopes). Perhaps the greatest astrologers were the Mayans. They said
that time began in 3113 B.C. No sillier than Archbishop Ussher's calculation
on the basis of the Bible that the earth was created in 4004 B.C., or just about
the time that the Sumerians were inventing astrology.

STAR STATISTIC

In 1969, one documentary claimed, Americans spent $800 million on
astrology. Today the figure may be well over $1 billion annually and growing.

DATE OF BIRTH

It is considered lucky to have the greatest distance possible between the
number of your birth day and that of your birth month. Because of an odd
way of calculating these numbers, (you add the second pair, so 27 = 9 and 31
is only 4), the best day of the year on which to be born is January 27. Mozart
was born on that day. But January 18 would also give you a 1–9 relationship.
Al Capone was born on January 18.

"JESUS CHRIST IS BORN TODAY. . . ."

The horoscope of Jesus Christ, wrote Ebenezer Sibley, shows a strong
Libran influence.

I wonder if Mr. Sibley was working with the date December 25, which is just the date of the Saturnalia, taken over by the early Church to replace pagan celebrations with their own festivities. Christ could not have been born in late December if the sheperds were still "abiding in the fields" at the hour of his birth. His part of the country was too cold for that at that season of the year. Also, it turns out that Christ was born *before* the year from which we now calculate our *anno Domini*.

ACADEMIC FASHION

University professors tend to sneer at astrology, once part of the curriculum, but they may be interested to know that their academic gowns go back to the astrologers and students of black arts in twelfth-century Spain. Englishman Robert of Ketene studied at Toledo with Arabs and Jews and went to the University of Pamplona. Then he brought back to England much Arabic lore of astrology. He also brought the long Arab gown which became the familiar academic robe of Western universities.

ALL IN THE FAMILY, PART TWO

Ralph and Carolyn Cummins of Clintwood, Va., have produced five children. Catherine was born on February 20, 1952; Carol on February 20, 1953; Charles on February 20, 1956; Claudia on February 20, 1961; and Cecilia on February 20, 1966.

Something fishy about this? No, but they are all Pisces—just barely. Linda Goodman, author of the popular *Sun Signs*, says that their feet will be "noticeably small and dainty" or "they'll be huge and spread out like a washerwoman's." Their hands will be "tiny, fragile, and exquisitely formed— or else big ham bones that look as if they belong behind a plow." Something fishy about *that* kind of prediction, I think. . . .

RUINED BY A PREDICTION THAT WAS CORRECT

Richard James Morrison (1795–1874) published a number of extremely popular almanacs under the pen-name "Zadkiel." Morrison was ruined by what every astrologer strives for—a prediction that came true.

In 1861 "Zadkiel" announced that the year would see a serious health problem for Queen Victoria's beloved consort, Prince Albert. For a while it looked as if "Zadkiel" had goofed, but in December 1861 Prince Albert attended a function in cold and rain, came home and took to his bed, and died.

Morrison's stock sank to zero. No one likes bad news, even if well predicted.

"Zadkiel" continued until 1931, being taken over by Alfred James Pearce (1840–1923) and others who had better luck, as it were, than Mr. Morrison.

TIMING

People have always had ideas and superstitions about the best times for doing things. One of the earliest documents to be produced from movable type was a calendar, published at Mainz in 1462, which gave the astrological best times for bloodletting (then a very common treatment for unbalanced "humors," which were thought to be the cause of ill health). Of course, one of the most important times in a person's life is when he is born, hence the great emphasis that astrologers place on casting horoscopes for the exact moment a child takes its first breath.

KOHOUTEK

Remember the comet Kohoutek? In Saigon it was blamed for "the steeply rising price of rice, the shelling of Bien Hoa airport, and the imposition of Value Added Tax."

LIKE PARENTS, LIKE CHILD

Probably possessed of the highest I.Q. of anyone alive today, the young Korean genius Kim Ung-Yong (born 1963) may possibly owe some of his ability to the fact that his parents, both university professors, were both born at exactly the same time: 11 A.M. on May 23, 1934. He began talking at the age of five months and reading and writing at the age of seven months, but so far he has not spoken or written about this odd fact.

"THE FAULT, DEAR BRUTUS, LIES NOT IN OUR STARS. . . ."

The professor of agricultural economics at Aberdeen University announced in the 1970s that the 1975 business depression (recession, downward readjustment, panic, crisis—whatever you want to call such things) was due to a combination of heavenly influence and earthly uproar.

A book published some fifty years ago had the theory that sunspot activity, when combined with unusual volcanic activity on earth (filling our atmosphere with particles that blot out certain rays from the sun), adversely affects business cycles. Also, Commander David Williams (U.S.N., Ret.) in *Astro-Economics* (1969) argues that 68 percent of the major aspects of Jupiter, Saturn, and Uranus correlated with the bumpy ride of United States business graphs from 1761 to 1968. His theory of financial astrology was not new, and he admits that a clay tablet found in the ruins of Nineveh translates: "If Jupiter seems to enter the Moon, prices will be low in the country." The British economist W. Stanley Jevons in 1875 found correlations between sunspot activity and commodity price fluctuations. Commander Williams is bullish on America "until February 1992."

If you are interested in financial astrology, go into the market; there your theories will be no wilder than many others widely held. My advice (no charge) is buy cheaply something that inevitably must go up and then avoid mental activity concerned with money for a long while.

PARTRIDGE UP A TREE

Dean Jonathan Swift's satire *Predictions by Isaac Bickerstaff* stated flatly that the most popular astrologer of the day, John Partridge, would die on March 29, 1708. The day came and went, and on March 30, Swift published an account of the death. Mr. Partridge insisted he was still alive, but Swift and his friends blithely ignored that, and Partridge's "death" became a popular joke.

PAPAL ASTROLOGY

"How happy are the astrologers if they tell one truth to a hundred lies," wrote Francesco Guicciardini (1483–1540), a papal diplomat of great importance in the Renaissance, "while other people lose all credit if they tell one lie to a hundred truths."

In a time when most people were utterly convinced, however strong their orthodox faith, that the stars ruled human lives, even the popes relied heavily on astrologers. Julius II, Leo X, Sixtus IV, Adrian VI, and Paul III were just a few of those who would not make a move unless their stars dictated it. When the cardinals wanted Clement V, who had moved the papacy to Avignon, France, to return to Rome, they pointed out to him in astrological language that even the planets did best when in their own houses.

Jacques d'Euse, who reigned as John XXII (1313–1334), had not been able, even with the best astrological advice, to avoid a fatal disaster. He kept hale and hearty to the age of eighty-five despite difficulties all around him, but died when a ceiling fell on him. And the Renaissance popes were not always able to use a knowledge of the stars effectively against dangers that ranged from political intrigue to assassination attempts by witchcraft.

When anyone attacked their astrologers as heretics, as when Pope Honorius IV's physician and diviner Peter of Albano got into trouble in the late thirteenth century, the popes defended them briskly. Even Saint Thomas Aquinas admitted that "astrologers not infrequently forecast the truth by observing the stars" and attempted a pious explanation. Astrology began to be accepted almost universally. It was better than necromancy (which Albertus Grotius performed for Frederick Barbarossa) or the sort of thing that Archbishop Thomas à Becket got involved with to collect prophecies for his master, Henry II (palmistry and watching the flights of birds for auguries).

Then the powerful Council of Trent (1545–1563) ruled out astrological predictions, excepting only agriculture, navigation, and medicine. Sixtus V (pope 1572–85) issued a papal bull against the superstitious astrological charts, horoscopes, and predictions of his contemporaries—and, presumably, his own papal predecessors. The modern disapproval of astrology by the Catholic Church came into existence toward the end of the sixteenth century.

℞

I always thought the ℞ symbol at the head of a prescription was an abbreviation for *recipe*, the Latin for "take." Now I'm told some believe it doesn't mean *recipe* at all but is an "evolution of the astrological sign for Jupiter—an ancient invocation." Any pharmacists Out There ready to comment?

BAD BEGINNING

The horoscope cast for the Empress Maria Theresa's fifteenth child was so discouraging that the celebrations for the birth of the little girl were called off. The baby's name was Marie Antoinette.

KRAFFT ERRING

In World War II, Karl Ernst Krafft (1900–1945) was employed by the Nazis in the Ministry of Propaganda to cast horoscopes for both German and enemy personages. Hitler was a great believer in astrology. When Krafft tactlessly announced that the stars seemed much more favorable to Field Marshal Montgomery than to Field Marshal Rommel, Krafft's own future ceased to be bright. Krafft fell from power and eventually died in transit to the horror camp at Buchenwald; meanwhile the Desert War in North Africa had come out about as he had predicted.

YOUR SIGN

Depending on what time of day you were born on April 20, you're a
Taurus or an Aries.

COLORFUL COMMENT

Avoid these colors: black (sorrow), purple (pride), yellow (lies), and
orange (voluptuousness). Unless, of course, one is your lucky color.
Here is one of many lists that have been made of lucky colors:

Aquarius	(January 20–February 18)	Gray
Pisces	(February 19–March 20)	Blue
Aries	(March 21–April 20)	Red
Taurus	(April 21–May 20)	Dark green
Gemini	(May 21–June 20)	Brown
Cancer	(June 21–July 20)	Silver
Leo	(July 21–August 21)	Gold
Virgo	(August 22–September 22)	Orange
Libra	(September 23–October 22)	Pale green
Scorpio	(October 23–November 22)	Vermilion
Sagittarius	(November 23–December 20)	Sky blue
Capricorn	(December 21–January 19)	Black

In certain circumstances, these are unlucky colors: green (the fairies
prefer it, and resent people using it), white (formerly a color of mourning),
and red in your clothes or your hair (the first because *Leviticus* forbids the
wearing of scarlet and the second because Judas Iscariot was supposed to
have been a redhead).

On the other hand, green means hope, white means purity, and red
means strength. Blue means trustworthiness and loyalty ("true blue"), rose
goes with a gentle disposition, violet with intelligence, and purple with
royalty. You may have to dress right to foretell the future.

Ecclesiastical vestments make use of symbolism in color that may have
originally been connected to some belief in the "powers" of colors, and
magical robes associate earth colors (green, russet), fire colors (scarlet,
orange), water colors (blue) and yellow (for air) with the Four Elements, as
well as assigning colors to the rituals that involve the planets, as follows: Sun

(orange), Moon (violet), Mercury (yellow), Venus (green), Mars (scarlet), Jupiter (blue), Saturn (indigo).

"RAIN, RAIN, GO AWAY . . . ."

A Victorian ecclesiastic in his spare time figured out when Noah's Flood began. In case you're curious, it was November 25, 2348 B.C. It must have been a good thing; the planetary aspects that day were favorable.

PET THEORIES

After astrological cookbooks and such, it was only inevitable there would be a book about astrology and Fido. A few years ago a Los Angeles lady called Dorothy Macdonald obliged with *Astrology for Pets*. Pet-lover Cleveland Amory interviewed her for his syndicated column in 1975. He established with her that Cancer is a good sign for a pet ("very fluid") and that Gemini pets are "good companions, but they're restless." Mr. Amory produced this useful chart, which I reproduce from the May 22, 1975, *New York Post:*

If You Are	Best Pet	Worst Pet
Aries	Leo	Cancer, Scorpio
Taurus	Taurus, Virgo, Capricorn	Gemini, Libra, Aquarius
Gemini	Gemini, Libra, Aquarius	Virgo
Cancer	Cancer, Scorpio, Pisces	Aries, Libra
Leo	Leo, Sagittarius	Aries
Virgo	Taurus	Cancer, Sagittarius
Libra	Libra, Gemini	Aries, Cancer
Scorpio	Scorpio, Capricorn	Cancer
Sagittarius	Sagittarius, Aries, Leo	Pisces, Cancer
Capricorn	Taurus	Aries, Leo, Virgo
Aquarius	Gemini, Aries, Sagittarius	Leo
Pisces	Cancer, Taurus	Virgo

Miss Macdonald said she did not have to see the pet to cast the horoscope: "All I have to know is the approximate date of birth. I do them for horses too. For the next book, I'm going to do a goat."

THEY TOIL NOT, BUT THEY DO SPIN!

Charles IX was told by his astrologer that he could protect his life as many days as he could turn around, spinning on his heel, in an hour. So every morning Charles put in his hour spinning, in full sight of the principal officers of state, who (naturally) had to join in the spinning.

TELEVISION NONSTARS

Did you ever wonder why, with all the interest in astrology, there is nothing about it on television? Gary Marshall, creator of several very successful shows, says it's taboo. "The one absolute ban is anything to do with astrology," says *TV Guide*, and quotes Marshall (August 13, 1983):

> Half the people in this country totally believe in astrology. The other half think its crazy. So either way, if it goes on television, it is sure to offend half the people in this country. No network wants that.

Meanwhile the consumers of pop culture who "totally believe in astrology" will have to make do with the many articles in those checkout-counter magazines they find in the supermarket, though the failure of their predictions, time after time, may be eroding their faith.

RAPHAEL THE ASTROLOGER

"Raphael" published almanacs for nearly a hundred years in England, down to the early 1930s. This is explained by the fact that several men wrote astrological predictions under this archangel's name. They included Robert Cross Smith (1795–1832) and Robert T. Cross (1850–1923).

FLOWER POWER

Each sign of the zodiac is associated with lucky or characteristic flowers. My sign (Sagittarius), for example, has pinks (the romantic side), dandelions (dislike of pretension—and lawnmowing), mosses (from the "rolling stone" aspect contradicted), and holly (prickliness, wariness). It makes a rather strange bouquet. What's yours?

PLACE OF BIRTH

Most people think only the day of the year they are born is astrologically significant but the time of day is important, too, and so is the place.

Robert and Deborah Brown were fans of the Texas Longhorns team and wanted their child to be born on Texas soil. But they lived in Oklahoma, so they got a bag of Texas soil and placed it under the delivery table at Mercy Hospital in Oklahoma City; there Deborah was born on October 4, 1978. How do you calculate *her* horoscope?

PLANET DAYS

In the lore of ancient astrologers, each day of the week had its ruling planet. After all these centuries, we still see evidence of this in these names of the days of the week: Sunday, Monday (Moon Day), and Saturday (Saturn's Day). Mars rules Tuesday (French *mardi*), Mercury rules Wednesday (though we call it after Woden), Jupiter rules Thursday (though our word stresses Thor), and Venus rules Friday (Freya's Day).

MORE ON LIFE CYCLES

Astrologers have long argued that the planets in their courses influence the ups and downs of our lives.

Jerome Cardan was described in *Transcendendal Magic* (first published in 1896) as "one of the boldest students, and beyond contradiction the most skilfull astrologer of his time." That time was the sixteenth century, a great age of astrology building on the work of Tommaso Pisano, Johann Regiomontanus, Johann Stöffler, and others, and featuring such outstanding personalities as Cosimo Ruggiero and Nostradamus. Cardan worked out cycles of 4, 8, 12, 19, and 30 years, based on the date of birth.

To ascertain the fortune of a given year, he sums up the events of those which have preceded it by 4, 8, 12, 19 and 30; the number 4 is that of Venus or natural things; 12 belongs to the cycle of Jupiter and corresponds to successes; 19 has reference to the cycles of the Moon and of Mars; the number 30 is that of Saturn or Fatality. Thus, for example, I desire to ascertain what will befall me in this present year. . . . I pass therefore in review those decisive events in the order of life and progress which occurred four years ago; the natural felicity or misfortune of eight years back; the successes or failures belonging to twelve years since; the vicissitudes and miseries or diseases which overtook me nineteen years [back] from now and my tragic or fatal experiences of thirty years back. . . .

I have left out some details because I do not recommend Cardan's system, but he has one extremely good idea. Before you worry about the future, why not sit down and review the past? Looking back on your life is always worth the effort. If you cannot learn from experience, how can you expect to be able to predict the future?

JANUARY 19 TO JANUARY 26

The "cusp" of Capricorn/Aquarius may be the best time for astrologers to be born, for persons born at this time have a flair for science—and also are "inclined to the fantastic and often support illogical ideas."

YOUR FATE IN THE CZARS

The Baronness von Krüdener, a mystic prominent at the court of Czar Alexander I (1777–1825), predicted both Napoleon's escape from Elba and his final fate. Alexander I was fascinated by such people, and one "Sister Salome" (Mme. Bouche) attended the czar from 1819 to 1821 and persuaded him to distribute solid gold talismans to defeat Napoleon.

On the other side Napoleon himself had some curious ideas; for instance, he dropped a *u* out of his last name so that it would be numerologically more potent.

When Alexander's brother succeeded him as Czar Nicholas I (1796–

1855) the influence of the occult continued. Nicholas depended much on the Polish mystic Hoene Wronski. His son Alexander II (1818–1881) put great faith in Baron Langsdorf's occult abilities. Among other things, the baron told him a bomb would explode at a dinner party in 1880 and persuaded the czar to arrive half an hour late. That saved his life. In 1881 the baron was sent on a mission to Paris; while the baron was away, the czar was killed by a bomb. That time he had no warning. His son Alexander III deeply believed that, had the baron only been present, his father's life would have been saved. Alexander III (1845–1894) had the baron consult the spirits every day via a sort of Ouija board and also was interested in astrological predictions. In 1886 the baron retired from "psychographic communication," due to failing health, and astrologers became more influential.

The last of the Romanovs, Czar Nicholas II, was a little less superstitious than his forebears but was intricately involved with mystics because his wife, the czarina, was completely in the power of the "mad monk" Rasputin. Rasputin knew nothing of astrology and cared nothing for Ouija boards, but his magnetic personality gave him remarkable powers. Among other things, he was the only person who could keep the czarevitch, Nicholas' son, from bleeding to death; hemophilia was a curse of the imperial family. The power of Rasputin ended with his sensational murder by Prince Yussoupov and others who had to poison him, bludgeon him, shoot him, and finally shove him through a hole in the ice-covered river, where at last he drowned. With Rasputin's demise the influence of occultists at court also more or less ended.

No wonder the czar did not see what was coming next.

No reliable evidence exists of any dependence by Lenin, Stalin, or more recent Russian rulers on seers, mediums, and astrologers. But the Soviets still want to know what the future holds. They are conducting scientific research in many branches of parapsychology. They are very interested in astrology, too.

ALL SETTLED

Genethlialogy is the "science" of casting horoscopes at birth, of predicting a person's entire life from the relations of the stars and planets at the exact moment he was born. But in these days when labor can be induced and the moment of birth to some extent controlled, I wonder if anyone undertakes to plan good constellations and a baby's time of arrival.

Perhaps the newspapers ought to give us information to help the unborn rather than the horoscopes they offer now. What is the best moment for conception? What is the best moment today and tomorrow for an infant to emerge? And now that the United States courts are going to have to deal with the problem of when that life actually *begins*, what effect will Congress have on American astrology and its—conceptions?

SCORPIO

If you look carefully, you may find astrological signs where you might not expect them. Charles, Prince of Wales, has a coronet of somewhat mod design that departs from tradition, and incorporated into the design is his sign of the zodiac, Scorpio.

Charles's personal horoscope may be the least favorable since that of William IV, but astrologers would say that a Scorpio is not at all a bad choice for a head of state. They also suggest he will not be able to look forward to taking over soon from Queen Elizabeth II, for no abdication is predicted in the near future, despite the fact that the pearls in her crown are supposed to be unlucky for a Taurus like her.

Theodore Roosevelt and Marie Antoinette were both Scorpios. So were Charles de Gaulle, Douglas MacArthur, and others who do not much seem to fit Linda Goodman's statement that "Scorpios love to travel incognito."

THE RULING PLANETS

In 1981 we entered the first Cycle of the Sun since the eighteenth century. The eighties will be governed as follows: 1981 Sun, 1982 Venus, 1983 Mercury, 1984 Moon, 1985 Saturn, 1986 Jupiter, 1987 Mars, 1988 Sun, 1989 Venus. Note that astrology is based on fewer planets than we now know actually exist, which ought to give us pause. The signs of the zodiac are twelve and run from March 21 through March 20 of the next year. I'm a Sagittarius (with Scorpio rising) with the same birth day as Otto Preminger and Walt Disney. Jupiter governs my sign, which is supposed to give me an exuberant, cheerful disposition. . . .

What about you?

8

Fortune-Telling

IN THE CARDS

Cards are probably the most common method by which fortunes are told these days. People use either Tarot or ordinary playing cards. Among the latter, the Ace of Hearts often signifies good news, the 9 victory. The Ace of Diamonds usually means a message or a document or a letter (favorable or unfavorable contents), the 9 of Diamonds advantage, the 7 good news. The Ace of Clubs is money, the 10 money, the 7 money. Stay away from Spades. The 9 of Spades is the worst card in the pack, but none of the Spades brings much hope.

INFERNO

In the Eighth Circle, near the bottom of Dante's Hell, the greatest Italian poet since Virgil puts usurers, simoniacs and scandalmongers, all sorts of hypocrites and thieves, even Odysseus and a pope (Nicholas III, reigned 1277–1280). Also joining that uncharmed circle are fortune-tellers, who wear their heads backward as a punishment for having tried to look forward too intently.

Dante himself actually engages in some prediction in this part of his poem. He has Pope Nicholas mistake him for Pope Boniface VIII (who did not die until 1303). Dante says that Boniface's arrival in Hell is expected any time, so Nicholas's error was understandable.

RITE ON!

There's hardly an alternative-lifestyle person anywhere these days who is not sitting around throwing the *I Ching* sticks, which the Chinese have given us along with gunpowder, paper, and tea.

Typically, the Chinese improved on something. Earlier people used coins or drew arrows at random from a quiver—like drawing straws. Belomancy (the arrow method) is now practically unknown, although we still draw straws in order to select a "volunteer." The improved Chinese system involved reading the cracks on heated bones or tortoise shells, but for accuracy it demanded real gifts of the reader. The modern *I Ching* comes with an instruction book, though even here some skill is required. Moreover, some latitude is permitted in interpretation, which means that (as with many ways of divining the future) your subconscious mind can come into play.

It could be that fortune-telling is not so much a way of talking to the fates as reaching your own inner self.

For centuries diviners have been trying to do one or both of these things by watching and reading the random way that sticks or cards or stones or tea leaves arrange themselves. The Tarahumares Indians of Mexico use human beings to perform this same kind of divination, called gyromancy. The Tarahumares, topped with wooden headdresses decorated with long streamers (and fueled with something a lot stronger than *yerba maté*), whirl around and around in their traditional dance until they collapse with exhaustion. Thereupon the tribal wisemen predict future events by the patterns formed by the fallen dancers.

Perhaps a combination of the *I Ching*, gyromancy, and rock 'n' roll music could be developed for the counterculture in America. Why not look at the way people "crashed" at a party? What does it tell you? Probably that you, as the only one who is still together, will have to clear up the pad after the love-in.

DICEY FUTURES

Since time immemorial dice have been thrown to tell fortunes. You start with a list of questions. Here is what people usually want to know:

1. Where does my future success lie?
2. Shall I be happy in love?
3. Am I in danger?
4. Will the action I propose succeed?
5. Will I find my lost article?
6. Will I get what I am asking for?
7. What should I now concentrate on?
8. Whom should I believe?
9. Should I change my job?
10. Am I loved by the person I love?
11. Shall I get involved in legal affairs?
12. Am I right to trust a certain person?
13. Shall I receive money owed to me?
14. What does the coming year hold for me?
15. Shall I hear from someone in whom I am interested?
16. Will my secret be discovered?
17. Should I travel?
18. Should I marry?
19. What does the immediate future hold for me?
20. Will he (or she) come back to me?
21. Where can I find happiness?
22. What are the most favorable times for action?
23. How can I get rich?
24. Shall I reach my goal?
25. Is something nice coming to me soon?

Along with this list must go a list of twenty-five responses for each possible combination of the dice. Suppose you throw a 4 and a 3. Consult the 4–3 list of replies. The 3–4 list is usually the same.

In dice games, 2–2 (craps) is not good. Here are the answers for 2–2 on the list provided for the system I am describing:

1. Wherever courage is required.
2. Yes, if your love is true.
3. Danger is always near, but never great.
4. Yes, if you start now.
5. In a hallway or among documents.
6. Eventually.
7. A personal matter such as illness, worry, revenge.
8. Someone whose reliability you trust.
9. Not for at least a few months.

10. Not now, maybe later.
11. Only if it is to your advantage.
12. They are okay except for a few minor details.
13. Don't expect more than part of it.
14. More money and bigger expenditures.
15. Not until your friend returns.
16. Not until it can do you little harm.
17. You will go sooner and more successfully than you have imagined.
18. After some hard times, marriage will turn out all right for you.
19. The answer you have long awaited.
20. When he or she is no longer wanted.
21. Outdoors.
22. Late autumn and early winter.
23. Stop wasting your money and time.
24. Probably, but too much indecision could prevent that.
25. You deserve it but someone is inconsiderate.

Walter and Litzka Gibson, in *Psychic Sciences*, and many others offer shorter or longer lists of questions and answers very like these for 2–2 and full lists of answers for the other dice combinations.

You can see that this requires a book in hand (or a terrific memory—the Gibsons give a list of questions and twenty-one lists of thirty answers in each case) and the replies are less manipulable and satisfactory than one gets simply by memorizing the "meanings" of the fifty-two cards in a pack.

Very few people throw dice any more to find out about their true love, and so forth. Some persist in throwing them to see if they can get rich. . . .

YES AND NO

Does the Ouija board work? Well, yes and no. But it is called Ouija from the French for "yes" and the German for "yes." It is *not* some ancient cabalistic device but a commercial product first patented in 1892 by a Maryland novelty company.

DREAM BOOKS

Many people are devoted to "dream books," which list all the "meanings" of the symbols and situations that crop up in dreams. Psychoanalysts are interested in your dreams, too, but not in oneiromancy (fortune-telling through dreams). *All* your dreams make them rich.

Still the best "dream book" may be that of Artemidorus Daldianus, second-century soothsayer, whose multivolume dictionary of dreams was criticized for offering such latitude that a dream could be interpreted to mean just about anything you wanted it to mean. Or you can check the syndicated column on the interpretation of dreams that runs in hundreds of American newspapers, which is more specific. Or your gypsy handbook. Or even the works of such modern greats as Carl Jung, who concluded that in dreams we use our past and plan our future and get in touch with all that is stored in the attic of our mind.

CRYSTAL BALL

The ancient Jews practiced scrying with bowls of water, but you can use a black mirror, a glass ball, an ink blob, or a real ball of crystal (preferably with a slightly bluish tinge). Any one of them will concentrate the mind. I know one seer who has obtained striking results by staring into the screen of her television set when the set is turned off.

Actually, if you will concentrate on *any* object, you will find that you can summon powers of the mind that you use all too infrequently and may be able to bring to the surface insights and intuitions that will amaze you. Try it.

AUTOMATIC WRITING

Mediums in trance have been able to write, often at incredible speeds, messages "dictated from beyond the grave." One of the most amazing was Mrs. Verrall, who could "transmit" in automatic writing vast quantities of Latin and Greek, languages that she said she did not know. (Of course her husband was a professor of classical languages.)

Others see automatic writing as a way of getting into touch with the subconscious, which may be Another Life just as astounding as that of the Beyond.

Some of William Butler Yeats's poetry was the result of automatic writing. Alfred, Lord Tennyson also used to write in a state of trance. But the results of most automatic writing experiences are less impressive.

GYPSY QUEEN

Everyone was wrong about the origin of gypsies. Their name in English suggests they came from Egypt. Others thought they came from Bohemia, hence *bohemians* for unconventional people. Or even Flanders, hence the Spanish *flamencos*. Today they are believed to have originated in India. In any event, the Romany-speaking people wandered all over Europe, spreading the ancient arts of fortune-telling.

My favorite gypsy fortune-teller in history is Margaret Finch (1631–1740). She lived to be 108, for one thing. For another, she was the gypsy queen of Norwood in Kent, England. Even more striking, for the last forty years of her long life, she crouched on the ground so much that she could not straighten up and had to move from place to place in a sitting waddle. When she finally died, they buried her with her knees still bent, in a square coffin.

ANCIENT ORACLE

Everybody knows about the oracle at Delphi and other marvels of the classical world, but have you heard of the Hypogeum or underground temple of Hal Suflitti (dating from 3000 B.C.) discovered on Malta in 1902? It was found to contain 33,000 human bones and a hole through which the oracle could speak. If those dry bones could speak, what a story they would have to tell!

"ART THERE, OLD MOLE. . . ?"

A mole on the right side of the forehead was thought to indicate talent and promise success. A mole on the left side? You are stubborn, extravagant, dissolute. A mole on the right hand? Money will come to you. A mole on the left hand? Sensitivity and artistic ability.

FATHER BROWN'S OPINION

"If a fortune-teller trades in truth," said G. K. Chesterton's famous detective-priest, Father Brown, "then I think he is trading with the enemy."

HANDS UP!

The ancient art of palmistry would take one or more books just in itself. But look at the nail joint of your thumb. If it is especially bulbous, you are or will be a murderer. A very short little finger indicates mental deficiency, and a long one bodes well for academic success. If your life line shows breaks or splits, move. If your head line terminates under Saturn and your life line shows weakness, expect premature death. If you have the same weak head line, but your life line is stronger, you will just go insane, not die young.

And if you don't know your head line from your life line, why not find an illustrated book on palmistry and give it the once-over as to chirognomy (the general shape and formation of the hand, fingers, and thumb) and chirosophy (the significance of the lines, bumps, etc.)? You may find there some information on whether you have psychic abilities.

Try this. Put your left hand on the table, palm up. The lower right side of your palm has a bump dedicated to the Moon (Luna). Your little finger is dedicated to Mercury. (You see that palmistry and astrology are connected, but we won't get into that, just the names.) You may find a Line of Intuition extending like a crescent from the lowest part of the Mount of Luna to the line that runs up to your little finger, the Area of Mercury. The bend of the crescent should be inward, toward the center of your palm; if it bends the other way, you may have many premonitions and hunches, but they will mostly be wrong. A solid line formation indicates good psychic abilities. If you have similar lines in both hands, you may devote yourself to the occult. If your line of intuition is under your middle (Saturn) finger with a cross, you combine the religious with the occult. If your line of intuition terminates in the upper part of the central palm (Plain of Mars), you have hypnotic powers or at least a charismatic personality. If there is an "island" formed by two lines diverging and then coming together again near the beginning of your line of intuition, you may walk in your sleep. Keep your head line away from your line of intuition if you can. If it crosses it, you'll go at least temporarily insane. If that already obtains and your thumb is small and your hand generally weak, you are probably incurably crazy already.

But this is too difficult to follow, and a hand must be examined in all its aspects. The classic of chiromancy and related arts (or sciences) is *Cheiro's Language of the Hand.* "Cheiro" is the pseudonym for a man who was for many years the leading authority on chiromancy and wrote about palmistry in general while serving also as a reporter, war correspondent, and newspaper editor.

Once Mark Twain went to him to have his hands read. "The one humorous point in the situation is," Mr. Clemens told Cheiro, "that I came here expecting to lose my money by my foolishness, but I have gained a plot for a story which I certainly think should be a 'best-seller.'"

The story became *Pudd'n Head Wilson*. The plot hinges on thumb prints. The famous American author wrote in the London seer's visitor's book; "'Cheiro' has exposed my character to me with humiliating accuracy. I ought not to confess this accuracy, still I am moved to do it."

YOUR CHOICE, YOUR FUTURE

In *Occultism*, expert Julien Tondriau lists more than a hundred ways of fortune-telling and prediction. The nastiest I can think of was tried by Manasseh, king of Judah, 692–638 B.C. He used to tell the future by tearing open young boys and examining the guts. It's called anthropomancy, and worse. The terrible Gilles de Rais in the Middle Ages also practised anthropomancy and murdered hundreds of boys to do it.

SO YOU NEVER WERE ANY GOOD AT MATH?

Mary Russell Mitford (1787–1855), English novelist, at the age of ten dreamed of the number 7 on three successive nights. So she multiplied 7 by 3; and bought a lottery ticket with the number 22. Her arithmetic may have been no good, but her luck was tremendous. She won the equivalent of about $150,000 or $200,000. Of course, had she known her multiplication tables better she would have put her money on 21 and won nothing. There's a moral in this somewhere.

SUITED TO A TEA

For tasseography or teacup reading, use a genuine teacup—that is, a plain cup with slanted sides or one resembling a bowl. (Teacups were first bowls anyway, without handles, as Oriental cups still are.) Drink most of your tea, invert the cup on the saucer, and with your left hand turn the cup around on the saucer three times left to right. There will be some leaves on the bottom of the cup, some on the sides, some near the rim. Those on the bottom indicate the distant future, those near the rim the immediate future. You read with the cup in your left hand, holding the handle, and from the handle to the left and around, getting more and more into the future as you go. The tea stems, if any, represent men and women, respectively long and short.

As to the meaning of the shapes you see, you will need a guidebook or a lot of intuition.

ALL ABOARD!

Jerome Cardan, sixteenth-century astrologer, named the lines on people's foreheads for the various planets known in his time. Hairline to eyebrows in order downward, they were Saturn, Jupiter, Mars, Sun, Venus, Mercury, Moon. Cardan also ascribed attributes to them associated with astrological beliefs. Wavy lines suggested travel by sea, but lines that turned up at the end (travel by air) he had to ignore, since there was no method of flying then available.

The authors of *Psychic Sciences* write: "Today, an airline passenger will do well to note the forehead lines of other persons on the plane. It may be surprising to learn how many turn up at the ends."

I have been watching the corners of the mouths of railway passengers. They tend to turn down, which often indicates that the train is running late.

FIRST STEPS

William Woods's *History of the Devil* (1973) contains these assertions about clairvoyance (clear vision into the future) and precognition (knowing what is going to happen):

The Marquise du Deffand, having been told that St. Denis walked two leagues, carrying his head in his hands, is said to have replied, "*La distance n'y fait rien; il n'y a que le premier pas qui coûte.*" [The distance doesn't matter; it's only the first step that counts.] If [university researcher in parapsychology] Rhine can demonstrate, as he has beyond question, that certain individuals are consistently precognitive, that they can foretell, sometimes against odds of hundreds of thousands to one, the sequence in which certain cards will fall, and that they can do this over and over again, then the case is proved. It does not matter that only one in a thousand can do this. *C'est le premier pas qui coûte.* We may lack the power ourselves, but clairvoyance and precognition exist.

Call it intuitive perception, call it an illogical but consistently accurate leap into the dark, or acuity in the analysis of otherwise imperceptible evidence, or a higher gear in the power of logical reasoning, certain people have always claimed to possess it and most of us have at least superficial evidence that it exists. . . . We simply have to admit that these things happen and that scientific causality has so far been inadequate to explain them. We do not understand. Perhaps we have forgotten even more than we have learned.

A SCIENCE WITH BOTH FEET ON THE GROUND

The Chinese not only read palms, they read feet (podoscopy).

WHICH WITCH?

With a prescription in Exodus not to suffer a witch to live, how could Saul consult the witch of Endor (I Samuel)? Because she was not a witch at all; she was a diviner. Still she was dabbling in forbidden arts, and Saul could only get her to raise the spirit of Samuel for him by promising not to betray her.

THE TAROT

All sorts of people from the barber Alliette to "The Beast" Crowley, from Lord Alfred Douglas to Eden Gray, Bill Butler, "MacGregor" Mathers, Mayananda, "Papus," A. E. Waite, Paul Foster Case, to Arland Ussher and "Eliphas Lévi" have written extensively on the Tarot cards. These fortune-telling cards are sometimes said to have derived from ancient Egyptian mysteries but actually were invented in the late twelfth or early thirteenth century. Playing cards were first banned by Alfonso XI, King of Leon and Castile, in 1332, but the court accounts of Charles VI, King of France, 1392, mention payment for three sets of the Tarot arcana. That French king was insane and superstitious.

The Tarot deck consists of two kinds of cards. First are "minor arcana," resembling our modern playing cards, with four suits, each of ten cards (1–10) and four "face cards" (Page, Knight, Queen, King), as follows:

Pentacles (or Coins) corresponding to our Diamonds.
Wands (or Batons) corresponding to our Clubs.
Cups (or Chalices) corresponding to our Hearts.
Swords (or Epées) corresponding to our Spades.

Then there is a "major arcana" of cards, bearing ancient and much-debated symbols (now twenty-two). So the whole pack consists of seventy-eight cards. Most beginners work only with the major arcana. The minor arcana, ranked Pentacles, Wands, Cups, Swords, the last being highest (as our slang term "in spades" suggests), involve far longer and more complicated procedures for fortune-telling than the major. In recent times, however, people have seemed to seek even larger decks (such as the Morgan deck of eighty-seven cards) and more complexity as well as shorter decks (the Jesus Deck and George Muchery's Astrological Deck each contain only forty-eight cards). The Gypsy Method uses the Fool as "significator" and the twenty-one other major arcana only, while a Planetary Arrangement uses all seventy-eight in *I Ching* trigrams of Fu Hsi. The Churchyard Spread takes out the Fool card, shuffles the remaining seventy-seven, counts out twelve, adds the Fool, and shuffles, and works with thirteen. Mathers's long method in *The Tarot* (1888) uses all the cards and an almost interminable amount of time to run through eleven separate stages of "reading."

I'll spare you a description of that, remarking that fortune-telling by the Tarot is only tangentially related to magic or witchcraft, being neither itself. It is, in fact, only a system for getting into your subconscious. Bill Butler's eminently sensible *The Definitive Tarot* (1975) begins this way:

The cards are not magic. They do not tell the future, they cannot evaluate the past. In the hands of a skilled practitioner they can be used in two different ways for the study of the unconscious mind. The first is for a reader to relate the symbology of the cards as they "fall" in a reading . . . adding as little personal interpretation as possible. The evaluation is performed by the Querent, to whom the question is real and known and the answer is made manifest through the reader . . . [who can be] a relatively unskilled reader.

In the second method the reader, a skilled clairvoyant, uses the Tarot as a vehicle for concentration, a sort of patterned mirror reflecting to an inner eye the features of a landscape in someone else's mind. Both methods rely on the Querent to provide the answer, on the theory that some shadow of events to come is thrown across the unconscious days and perhaps years before the eruption of physical event. As shadows by their nature are not "fixed" it seems likely that shadows of the future are no more fixed. . . .

The Tarot can tell, not compell; it deals in possibilities, not fates. What has not happened need not happen; with knowledge from the Tarot, the questioner may alter the course of the future described. The Tarot simply taps the unconscious. The rule is the same as with computers: "garbage in, garbage out."

To hint at the complexity of dealing with the information stimulated by the symbols on the cards, let us look at one of the most famous, the Hanged Man. Waite suggests this card is full of significance, all veiled, but relates it to willing sacrifice, circumspection, intuition, divination, prophecy.

Magicians will note in the Hanged Man, the twelfth card of the major arcana, a sacrifice to Odin hanging on Yggdrasil (Odin's ash tree), and think of the Hand of Glory, the magical touch of a hanged man's hand, gallows' sweat, and other weird ingredients of ointments, the relation to the Great Work and the turning point in the psychic life, the ambiguity of the lamed but gifted one, etc., bound by Fate but never in pain.

Astrologers will emphasize Neptune (as Case, Crowley, and some others do), Mars acting on Mercury (the Golden Dawn), Scorpio (Mayananda), Libra (Ussher and "Papus"), Pisces (A. E. Thierens), etc. Considerable disagreement here.

Butler gives pages of different interpretations by almost twenty authorities, and he himself in his Introduction says of the "Magician/Fool/Devil/Hierophant/Hermit/Hanged Man," naming some major symbols of the deck, that whatever you call him "he is Hermes, he is Thoth." Grimaud plays down the importance of the Hanged Man; others think him crucial (no pun intended). Many stress that he is always shown in no pain, while Crowley sees "enforced sacrifice, punishment, loss, fatal and not voluntary, suffering." Clearly, one reflects one's own personality in "reading" this or any other card. I see joyous sacrifice, renunciation leading to revelation, transition to triumph, surrender to enlightenment. Even in the Chariot, along with war, vengeance, and trouble, I see victory, equilibrium, solution, and as the seventh card I cannot deem the Chariot very unlucky. Now the thirteenth, Death, is another matter; the best that even an optimist can see there is "sudden change."

What do you see?

Remember, if you will, what eighteenth-century German satirist Georg Lichtenberg said of a mirror: If a monkey looks into it, you cannot expect an angel to look out.

But if you are ready to look into yourself and face what you find, the Tarot is there, not as something magical, but just as a mirror of innermost thoughts, feelings, insights, intuitions.

Here is the shortest explanation I can make of a simple reading. Take the twenty-two cards of the major arcana and place the Fool as "significator" right side up in front of the Questioner (seated opposite the Reader). Place the rest of the cards in numerical order, all right end up (top at the top):

I The Magician/Juggler	XII The Hanged Man
II The High Priestess	XIII Death
III The Empress	XIV Temperance
IV The Emperor	XV The Devil
V The Heirophant/Pope	XVI The House of God/
VI The Lovers	Tower Struck by Lightning
VII The Chariot	XVII The Star
VIII Justice	XVIII The Moon
IX The Hermit	XIX The Sun
X The Wheel of Fortune	XX Judgment
XI Strength	XXI The World

The Questioner, emptying his or her mind of all other thoughts or desires except the question to be silently asked, shuffles the cards face down as much as desired and places the pack face down in front of the Reader. The Reader cuts the cards three times with the left hand to the left and reassembles the pack.

The Reader then deals the cards, all of them to be viewed from the point of view of the Questioner (cards upside down are read as weakened or even reversed, and cards influence the reading of those near them), as follows:

One card in the center of the table (Present Influence).
One card across that left to right (Immediate Obstacles).
One card above that (Goal of the Present Question).
One card below (Past Foundations of the Current Situation).
One card to the right of the two crossed in the center (Past Foundations).
One card to the left of the two crossed in the center (Future Influences).
Four cards above the other, bottom to top on the right of all the cards previously laid out; these represent respectively (from bottom to top) the Questioner, the Environment of the Questioner, the Questioner's Inner Feelings or Thoughts, the Final Result of all the other cards.

The Reader interprets and relates the cards in relation to the question (which ought never to be spoken). You may not read your own fortune, ever. I know some people disagree with that, but they are wrong.

IT DEPENDS ON HOW YOU LOOK AT IT

The Greek augurs faced north for divining the future; signs on the east, at their right hand, were regarded as favorable. The Roman augurs faced south when operating, which put favorable signs in the west, on their right hands. Those in the east, at the left, were *sinister*.

FORTUNA

The Romans worshipped a goddess called Fortuna (Fortune), who had previously been a harvest deity and who therefore continued to be shown with a cornucopia of abundance. In her temple at Praeneste, Fortuna told fortunes with a pile of wooden tiles on which messages had been written; a child pulled out a tile at random, and the message was interpreted for the questioner. The same sort of thing goes on in the streets of big cities today where, for instance, a trained bird will pick a little piece of paper with your "fortune" on it from a collection placed in his trainer's tray.

A sobering thought: The Romans often portrayed Fortuna standing on a ball, not to show that she dominates the world but to suggest the instability of luck.

DEWEY-EYED INNOCENCE

American presidential elections are famous for their irrational qualities, but the unsuccessful campaign of Thomas E. Dewey in 1948 set some kind of record. For one thing, the *Chicago Tribune* jumped the gun and headlined its election story "Dewey Wins." For another, the candidate himself came up with a classic pronouncement: "You know that your future is still ahead of you."

May your future be full of what we turn to next—luck.

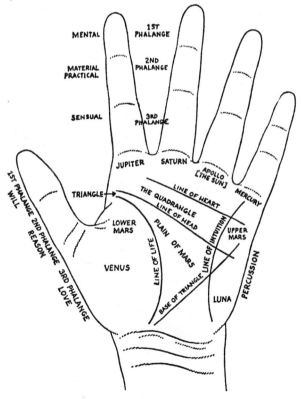

9

Luck

PICK A NUMBER

When asked to pick a number (between 1 and 10 or some such), more people will choose an odd number than an even. "Why do we all believe that odd numbers are best?" asked Pliny the Elder. Actually, Virgil had answered that question some forty years earlier in his Eighth Eclogue: "God delights in odd numbers." And Shakespeare agreed; "They say there is a divinity in odd numbers, either in nativity, chance or death."

Many superstitions are related to numbers, particularly 3 and 7. Consider the ban on three to a match. British investigators, trying to track down the antiquity of this superstition, have gotten as far back as the Crimean War, when, if you kept a match lighted long enough for three men to use it, you were giving the enemy something to fire at. (Matches don't go back much farther than the 1850s.) A more probable explanation is that British soldiers picked up the superstition from Russian prisoners of war. In Russia, altar candles were lighted in batches of three from one taper, and it was considered sacrilegious to light nonreligious items in threes.

SUPERSTITIOUS SCULPTOR

Michelangelo used to say that the figure was there already inside the block of marble just waiting for the sculptor to chip away the excess material imprisoning it; he spoke of freeing the sleeping statue. The British sculptor John Deare (1758–1798) had another theory. He believed that if he slept on top of a block of marble he would awake inspired to create masterpieces like Michelangelo's. All that happened is that he slept on some cold marble, caught a bad cold, and died.

8

The Chinese considered 8 a very lucky number. One Chinese in Hong Kong paid £2800 for the right to the car license number 8888.

TAKING A CHANCE

They cast lots to see who would take on Hector, how the Promised Land would be divvied up, to select the scapegoat of the Jews, to obtain possession of the garment Christ discarded at the foot of the Cross.

Jonah wound up in the belly of the whale because the sailors, terrified of a violent storm, cast lots to see who was the cause of it, and the choice fell on Jonah. He was thrown overboard to appease the Lord.

Out of lots came lotteries (which Voltaire rightly called "a tax on ignorance" but which give much hope to millions). One duke of Burgundy tried to recoup his losses to Italian bankers by taking a cut of lotteries, the king of France tried to finance bridges and wars by lotteries, Elizabeth I of England started a lottery to repair her ports (1566), and over the centuries rich and poor alike have had a "flyer" and hoped to repair their fortunes with One Big Win on something like a state lottery or the Irish Sweepstakes or the Mexican or Canadian lotteries, and so on.

That same Voltaire referred to a vapid portrait of the assembled ruling family of Spain as seeming to show "a butcher who had just won the National Lottery." Some nobodies did get really rich.

Ernie Eban in the *Village Voice* (June 26, 1978), in an entertaining survey of the lottery craze over the centuries, touches on something related to charms and spells when he notes that in Elizabethan England ticket buyers were identified not by name or number but by posies, brief verses they wrote on their tickets. Thus:

"I am a pore maiden
and fain would marry

And the lack of goods
is the cause I tarry"
or
"I was begotten in Calice [Calais] and born in Kent
God send me a good lot to pay my rent."

Then the buyers had to wait thirteen years until enough tickets were sold to justify distribution of the prizes. Today the results are on TV pretty quickly.

FRIDAY THE THIRTEENTH

When you put together the day of the Crucifixion and the number of Christ and the apostles (with the traitor Judas Iscariot included) you get a date which even some people who claim not to be superstitious at all find very uncomfortable. Ripley once constructed a remarkable list, however, of Fridays the thirteenth to show how lucky a date it was in American history.

Believe it or not, the thirteenth of the month falls on Friday more often than on any other day. Take a period of four hundred years, longer than you are going to have to worry about but a basic unit of the calendar, and you will find that, over that period, there will be 688 Fridays the thirteenth. Of Sundays and Wednesdays, the next most recurrent thirteenths, there will be 687.

MORE THIRTEENS

On the Great Seal of the United States there are thirteen stars, thirteen stripes, an eagle with thirteen feathers in each wing and thirteen feathers in its tail (it holds in one claw thirteen arrows and in the other a laurel branch with thirteen leaves and thirteen berries), thirteen letters in the motto beneath, thirteen clouds in the glory above. This is THE COAT OF ARMS OF THE UNITED STATES OF AMERICA. Count the letters—39, or 13 times 3. Which must make this the most unsuperstitious heraldic device in the world—no triskaidekaphobia here.

MONDAY NEED NOT BE BLUE

You will have good luck all week if you get pennies in change on a Monday. If you get one with the date of your birth on it, keep it for extra luck. The best thing is to find a penny with that date on it. But finding any kind of money is undoubtedly lucky.

OFF ON THE RIGHT FOOT

Britain's new National Theatre was opened in March 1976. That was the culmination of 128 years of bandying about the concept. Both houses of Parliament passed the necessary legislation without a division decades before, but still the project languished. Denys Lansdun, the architect, designed an aggressively ultramodern concrete monster in the Brutalist style and lived to see his design grow old-fashioned before it was built, for it took twelve years from drawing board to £16 million reality. There was only one piece of real stone in the concrete mass, the cornerstone—and that was one of four laid in different places at various times. It had been laid in 1951, on another site.

At the last minute the long-awaited building was not opened to the public on the date announced. It was not because the building was unfinished—they decided to open with only one of the three theaters in the building ready to go—but because someone pointed out that the chosen opening date was unlucky. It was the Ides of March.

RESULTS OF DOING UNLUCKY THINGS

American folklore says these results are to be expected if you ignorantly or foolishly do the following:

If you sneeze at the table,	a death in the family.
If you hear a dove mourn as the New Year breaks and you happen to be going downhill at the time,	bad luck for the coming year.
If you break a mirror,	seven years bad luck.

If you kill a frog,	the cow will die.
If you trim your nails on a Sunday,	you will fall sick by next Sunday.
If you sweep trash out the cabin door at night,	the slaveowner will sell you.
If you count graves,	bad luck.
If you drop a book and fail to step on it,	worse luck.
If he proposes to you in church,	the marriage will be unlucky.
Sneeze on Sunday,	Hell all the week.

JUST LUCKY?

"Some people have all the luck," you hear people say. But it could be that most people really make their own luck. As Benjamin Disraeli said, "We make our destinies and call them fate," and for some "luck" is actually careful foresight or the ability to take advantage of what comes along.

One man who made his own good fortune was architect Ranulf Flambard. He built the Tower of London and then was unlucky enough to be the first man to be imprisoned in that stout fortress. But he escaped, because as the architect, he knew a secret way out.

A LAMP UNTO MY FEET

Lamps shaped like a human foot were exchanged by the ancient Romans as a New Year gift. The belief was that they would prevent missteps in the coming year. (Romans were very superstitious and almost all their children wore amulets.)

COINCIDENCES

Coincidence is one of the most prolific origins of superstition. When a string of coincidences happens, people tend to seek far-out explanations, just as their judgment is affected by the coin that turns up heads ten times in a row. Actually the odds that it will turn up heads on the eleventh toss are still 50–50, but try to convince people of that. If you think of someone and the next instant the phone rings, that's odd. Is it any odder if this happens with ten phone calls in one day?

A lot of so-called magic is intricately tied up with coincidence, and there's nothing magical about it at all. But people have been willing to believe the strangest things.

For a remarkable string of coincidences, try this: Maximilian Joseph (1756–1825), king of Bavaria, celebrated not his actual birthday but the feast day of his patron saint, which fell on October 12. In the last six years of his reign there was no official celebration on that day. On October 12, 1820, the royal palace burned down. On October 12, 1821, his favorite servant died. On October 12, 1822, one of his ministers lost a hand in an explosion. On October 12, 1823, the queen suffered a severe hemorrhage. On October 12, 1824, several workmen were killed when a wall of the palace collapsed. On October 12, 1825, (or, perhaps, October 13) the king died.

Some people would say October 12 was Max Joseph's unlucky day, even that some kind of curse was put on it. What is your opinion?

LUCKY AT DOWSING

In the first half of this century, the Government of India hired Major C. A. Pogson as water diviner. In his three years of searching for water with the traditional forked stick, he chalked up a record of 93 percent accuracy.

You can even hold your dowsing or divining rod (preferably of hazel) over a map and find water, mines, buried treasure, and so on, by what is called radiesthesia, but some parapsychological powers, if not incantations, are said to be necessary to success. Not everyone can do it, and few can compete with the "gifted" diviners such as Major Pogson.

A MINISTERING ANGEL, THOU

Some people are lucky enough, they say, to get help from angels—not the theatrical kind, but the supernatural. Handel claimed he had seen the whole host of heaven before him when he dashed off the "Hallelujah Chorus" of *The Messiah*, a composition so stirring that it even got King George II to his feet (which is why audiences today traditionally stand for that particular chorus). Confined to a sanitorium during the final two years of his life, the composer Schumann made a similar astounding claim. He was lucky enough to have angels dictating music to him. Blake said an archangel appeared to him and taught him how to draw. Poet Allen Ginsberg claims Blake once appeared to him when he was a young student at Columbia University, but Ginsberg claims the figure was wearing "a toga," so it probably wasn't Blake at all.

BAD LUCK DEATHS

Fabius, "the Roman praetor," drank a glass of goat's milk containing one goat hair. He choked and died. The only English pope, Nicholas Breakspear, who reigned from 1154 to 1159 as Adrian IV, got into a tizzy cursing the Emperor Frederick I, took a drink from a fountain to refresh himself, choked on a fly, and died. William III (of Britain) died as a result of an accident: his horse tripped on a molehill. Clive of India (1725–1774) aimed a pistol at his own head and twice pulled the trigger. The pistol did not go off. When he asked his friend Maskelyne to come into the room and fire the pistol out the window, it did fire. "Well, I must be reserved for something," said Clive and went on to establish the British *raj* in India. Years later, he tried suicide again, because he thought his work was done and he was ill. The pistol fired without a hitch. Guy de Maupassant (1850–1893), in the last stages of syphilis, suffered many delusions (including the idea that his brain was leaking out through his nose) and cut his throat; they stitched him up and put him in a "sanitorium" in Paris, where he lived more than a year more. When Gamal Abdul Nasser (1918–1970) was a child he read in the Koran that anyone who died before the age of seven would not go to hell, so when he was six he attempted suicide by eating sealing wax.

THE VISIONS OF BLAISE PASCAL

He had something of a wild youth, or as wild a one as was consistent with devoting himself to mathematics, working out the geometrical theorems of Euclid independently for himself, and inventing the adding machine before he reached the age of ten. At about thirty Blaise Pascal underwent a religious conversion that suddenly made him an ascetic, a recluse, and a visionary. The last quarter of his life was spent in its shadow.

He moved into a sparsely furnished room and enjoyed no comforts he could do without, ignoring the servants of his wealthy household and taking care of himself in the simplest way. He spent most of his waking hours in prayer, reading the Bible, and writing down pious thoughts (*pensées*). He hardly ate.

He imagined that a yawning abyss opened up on one side of him wherever he went and "would never sit down till a chair was placed there to secure him from apprehended danger." He committed to paper another vision that he was unlucky (or lucky?) enough to have and then sewed the document into his coat lining so that it would accompany him everywhere he went. What was on the paper was a secret, and one that seems to have died with him.

An Italian mathematician of note, Jerome Cardan (the English form of his name), was convinced he was accompanied everywhere by "an aerial spirit, partly emanated from Saturn, and partly from Mercury." Cardan had delved deeply into the cabala and even black magic, but Pascal simply was "born again" and had a traumatic religious experience, a watershed vision of God in his life. Pascal did not have to turn to magic for happenings or hallucinations. Just reading the Scripture produced the most moving and terrifying visions for him. Some saints and many ordinary people have reported a great joy in religious ecstasy; others have felt a sense of being consumed in fire or a loss of self in ecstatic union with the eternal. But Pascal's vision was frightening, as crippling as Swedenborg's famous "fear and trembling." It haunted and darkened his life. Was it madness, or something even less understood?

HORSESHOES

People hang horseshoes up over a door for good luck but too few know that the superstition requires the shoes be nailed up with the ends upward. Otherwise "good luck drains out of the ends."

LUCKY 7

If your lucky number is 7 (and not everybody's is), not only is the seventh day of the month a propitious one for you, but so are the numbers that add up to 7. Expect good luck also on the sixteenth and the twenty-fifth.

RELIABLE SUPPORT

On February 23, 1895, John Lee mounted the scaffold in Exeter, England. He had been condemned to be hanged. They tried, but four times the trapdoor failed to open when the hangman threw the lever, though each time it had been inspected and tested and had worked fine. When the governor of the prison stood on it himself, sure it would stick again, it opened, and he fell through.

After four attempts to hang John Lee, prison officials gave up and consulted the Home Secretary. He granted a stay of execution and later commuted the death sentence to life imprisonment. Still later, the sentence was reduced to a few years. Lucky Mr. Lee!

"I have always had a feeling," said Mr. Lee, "that I had help from some power greater than gravity."

YOUR LUCKY DAY

A character in David Storey's play *Home* says: "My lucky day's the last Friday with an 'r' in it when the next month doesn't begin later than the following Monday."

What's *your* lucky day? How did you come to decide that?

"OH, WHAT A [LUCKY] FEELING!"

In Japanese, the family name *Toyoda* takes ten strokes to write. The trade name *Toyota* takes eight. In 1937, when the company was being formed, a numerologist advised that 8 was a luckier number than 10, so the world-famous name is now *Toyota*, not *Toyoda*.

"THE LUCK OF MUNCASTER"

"The Luck of Muncaster" is a green cup given by that embattled king of England, Henry VI, to his host, Sir John Pennington (died 1470), after the Battle of Hexham. Along with the gift, the king promised that the

Pennington family would prosper so long as they preserved that cup unbroken in Muncaster Castle.

In those days, when there was "a divinity" about a king, and when a monarch was the Lord's Anointed, such a promise was to be believed. The lucky cup is still preserved in Muncaster Castle. It is only one of hundreds of thousands of objects the world over to which special powers of "bringing luck" are attached.

SOME PROVERBS ABOUT LUCK

Throw a lucky man into the sea, and he will come up with a fish in his mouth. —Arabic

If a horse gets no wild grass, it never becomes fat; it a man gets no luck, he never becomes rich. —Chinese

Luck has but a slender anchorage. —Danish

The Devil's children have the Devil's luck. —English

He that has ill luck gets ill usage. —French

A lucky man always ends as a fool. —German

My right eye itches; some good luck is near. —Greek

There's luck in odd numbers. —Irish

Bad luck comes by pounds and goes away by ounces. —Italian

An ounce of good luck is better than a ton of brains. —Jugoslavian

Against a lucky man even a god has little power. —Latin

Luck is always borrowed, not owned. —Norwegian

If you were born lucky, even your rooster will lay eggs. —Russian

Better to be the lucky man than the lucky man's son. —Scottish

When good luck comes to you, invite her in. —Spanish

Luck never gives: it lends. —Swedish

Good luck comes to the saucy and the bold. —Welsh

And three more (for good luck) to make twenty:

He who is lucky in love should never play cards.   —Italian

It is better that the luck seek the man than that the man seek the luck.   —Yiddish

The only thing you have to worry about is bad luck. I never have bad luck.   —Harry S Truman

That last quotation was not a proverb. But may I wish that *you* will be able to say it for yourself?

10

Dreams

I'LL SEE YOU IN MY DREAMS

Many superstitious people believe that in dreams they are told of the future or are otherwise in touch with the occult.

This goes beyond the belief that one can compose poetry in dreams or get bright ideas of other sorts in sleep. (James Bovey, a seventeenth-century Englishman—whose descendants, like himself, have held the post of verderer of Exmoor forest—slept for more than forty years with a candle, pen, and paper by his bedside so he could wake up and jot down his thoughts.) Actually we all "process" the information of the day as the night goes by. Artists often use the dream state to get in touch with their unconscious and do some of their best work asleep. Architect Inigo Jones once claimed that he had designed the entrance hall of a manor house after the classical style by dreaming he was in a law court of ancient Rome and then waking up to sketch it quickly.

Ravanalona, queen of Madagascar, executed any of her subjects bold enough to appear uninvited in her dreams. Tippoo Sahib, the ferocious maharajah of Mysore, India, declared that his dreams were official acts of the government; while he ruled (1753–1799) he had each of them recorded in letters of gold. His most colorful superstition, however, may be enshrined in the statue of a tiger eating a British soldier, now in the Victoria and Albert Museum in London. It once had a machine inside that animated it and produced blood-curdling roars and screams. Perhaps it was a mere toy; perhaps it was intended by sympathetic magic to bring disaster on the

143

British troops. If so, it failed; they finally conquered his wonderful capital of
Seringapatam and destroyed its treasures—and him.

THE SHAPE OF THINGS TO COME

Beginning a year before the outbreak of World War I, Carl Jung began
to have premonitory dreams. An early one was of "a monstrous flood
covering all the northern and low-lying lands between the North Sea and the
Alps . . . a frightful catastrophe" and a sort of voice-over said: "Look at it
well; it is wholly real. . . ."

He continued with daydreams or "controlled hallucinations" that
revealed to him a terrible international warfare and (in a dream he shot
Wagner's hero Siegfried) even the enemy, Germany. He concluded that
"there are things in the psyche which I do not produce" and that in dreams
and visions we are spoken to by mysterious outside forces.

"IT CAME TO ME AS IN A DREAM. . . ."

Dreams have produced literary works (such as Coleridge's "Kubla
Khan" and Stevenson's *Dr. Jekyll and Mr. Hyde*), even scientific discoveries
(such as Watt's inspiration for making perfectly round shot pellets by
dropping molten lead from a considerable height into water).

One dream was less happy. A poor Cheshire plowboy named Robert
Nixon predicted the Battle of Bosworth Field and its history-changing
outcome. The victorious Henry VII heard of this and summoned Nixon to
court, entertained him, questioned him, and commanded that (since the lad
was illiterate) someone should follow him everywhere, ready at a moment's
notice to record any predictions Nixon should make.

One day Nixon predicted he would starve to death. He had had a vivid
dream; he was certain it was true.

The king pooh-poohed the idea. A special court officer was charged with
the responsibility for the boy's welfare. Now Nixon had nothing to worry
about.

When the king was off on business somewhere, the court official (fearing
what would happen to himself if any harm came to Nixon) had Nixon locked
in a secure room for safekeeping. He retained the only key. Then he was
called away on business and departed, taking the key with him.

Robert Nixon, locked in the room, could not be reached. He starved to death. It was as he had predicted.

ONE MAN'S MEDE IS ANOTHER MAN'S PERSIAN

The magi (from whose name comes our word *magic*) read the future for the Medes in astrology and in the livers of sacrificed animals.

When Astyages, the Median ruler, dreamed that his daughter (Mandane) urinated so great a flood that it engulfed all Asia, the wise men took this to mean that from her loins would come the new ruler of all the East. So Astyages married her off to Cambyses, king of Persia, whom he felt sure he could control as a satrap.

Then Astyages (who had a lot of dreams an analyst would welcome) dreamed that from the loins of Mandane a great vine spread to entwine all Asia. The magi decided this signified that the offspring of Mandane and Cambyses would conquer the Medes.

Legend says that therefore the child was (like Oedipus) rejected by his parents and given to a shepherd to be killed; the shepherd in both cases could not bring himself to do the dirty deed, and so the child grew up and made his way to the throne.

The child of Mandane and Cambyses was Cyrus the Great, founder of the Persian empire, who died, after a glorious reign, in 529 B.C.

Historical evidence convinces us now that Herodotus' story of Cyrus (and far different stories in Xenophon's *Cyropaediä*) are mere fantasy. But the ancients' reliance on dreams and oneiromancy was absolutely real.

THE NUMBERS

A great many people who "play the numbers" or want a "lucky number" for some other reason, rely upon their dreams to supply them.

Of course, if you dream of a number itself, you can use that. But be careful. We all know the story of the person whose dream was full of 7s, and so he ran out the next day and bet a bundle on the seventh horse in the seventh race. It came in seventh.

Whatever you dream of can be translated into a number. The method is a little complicated, so pay attention. First, look at this:

```
1  2  3  4  5  6  7  8  9
A  B  C  D  E  F  G  H  I
J  K  L  M  N  O  P  Q  R
S  T  U  V  W  X  Y  Z
```

Let's suppose the main feature of your dream was a car, specifically a Honda. You can work with the three-letter *car* or the five-letter *Honda*.

```
H   O   N   D   A
8   6   5   4   1
```

Add each pair of numbers: 8 + 6 = 14
                            6 + 5 = 11
                            5 + 4 = 9
                            4 + 1 = 5

With two digits, take only the last (*i.e.*, 14 gives you 4, 11 gives you 1). Now your five-letter word has given you a four-digit number: 4195. For a three-digit number, add pairs: 4 + 1 = 5, 1 + 9 = 10 (take second digit, 0), 9 + 5 = 14 (make this 4). Your three-digit number is 504. For a two-digit number you will have to regard the 0 as a 1. Thus, 5 + 1 = 6, 1 + 4 = 5, result 65. For a 1 digit number, 6 + 5 = 11, that is 1.

So your numbers are 4195, 504, 65 (some systems would make this 54— but you can always bet on both), and 1.

If you use *car*, you get 319, 41, and 5.

And if your numbers don't win, you may have chosen the wrong feature of your dream to emphasize.

BEAUTIFUL DREAMER, AWAKE UNTO YOURSELF

Virgil's *Aeneid*, in which a dream warned Aeneas of the imminent fall of Troy, is but one example from literature of what many claim to be true in life: that dreams give us "information" of use in the waking world.

Alfred Vierkandt, the German sociologist, contended that "dreams can reflect a sort of self-knowledge and unconscious estimation . . . a concentration and unification through which one may satisfy various hopes; a favorable attitude contributes towards success."

While dreams indicating anxiety or guilt are common (dreams of dying, flying, falling, pursuit, embarrassment at nudity, and so on), they can also bring premonitions. Most of us have numerous premonitions; the trouble is that few of them are correct. Some people claim to have a much better batting average than most of us.

Saint Augustine remarked that even a saint could not be responsible for his dreams. Saint Thomas Aquinas asserted that witches could have dreams sent by the Devil; today we might say they come from the darker side of our personalities, what Jung might call "the other face of God."

Dreaming is, after all, just another altered state, and in such states (trances, hallucinations, mystical visions, or drug-induced states) some people have found revelations. Witches used "magical ointments" to produce such states, in some of which they "flew to the sabbat," or had, or seemed to have, similar strange experiences.

Today scientific research into dreams is extensive and constantly revealing more to us about the nature and function of mind. But even unscientific analysis of your dreams, whether you use one of the common dream books (in which symbolism is explained, sometimes capriciously, sometimes with some accuracy) or not, may tell you more of your inner life.

WARNING

Whether, like a Hopi, you dance your way into *ahola* (possession by spirits of the dead), or like a dervish whirl yourself into ecstasy, whether you burn aconite and henbane or other hallucinogenic substances on your magic altar or ingest chemicals to open "the doors of perception" (as Aldous Huxley so aptly put it), whether you induce trance in yourself or hypnotize others— remember that in some languages *mind* and *soul* are the same and that you would be ill-advised to give up your sanity or your immortal soul. Whom the gods would destroy, they first make mad.

Charles Baudelaire was even leery of sleep, "that sinister adventure of all our nights," for "men go to bed daily with an audacity that would be incomprehensible if we did not know that it is the result of ignorance of the danger."

We forbear to mention what magicians believe about the dangers of sleep lest it keep you awake at night. Happy dreams!

"IN DREAMS BEGIN RESPONSIBILITIES"

In sleep every one of us, every night, experiences those "levels of consciousness" and "mind alteration" that have been so much the subject of interest of late, as we learn that the world's "reality" (as well as the human mind) has two hemispheres.

Experiments in sleep laboratories have shown that a dreamer can be influenced in what he dreams by telepathic transmission from another room. The "sender" stares at a picture, the dreamer somehow "picks it up" as a psychic suggestion. It is therefore not wholly beyond the bounds of possibility that, when we are asleep, we are somehow able to tune into strong signals from people in distress at a distance, able to "receive" veridical dreams.

Thomas King signed on as a member of the crew of the *Isidore* (out of Kennebunkport, Maine, 1847), but refused to sail, because in a dream he had "seen" the ship wrecked and seven of the crew lying dead on the deck. The ship actually was wrecked, and eight of its crew of fifteen disappeared; the remaining seven were corpses on the deck when it was found, which made King's story remarkable.

On the eve of the sailing of the *Amazon* from Port Talbot, Wales, in 1930, the captain had a premonition; he toasted his "last voyage." (Sailors *never* do that!) He sailed, the *Amazon* was hit by a cyclone, and that was the end of her and all who sailed in her. Perhaps, had the "warning" come in a vivid dream, the captain would have been dissuaded from sailing, and all would have been saved.

When one has a dream of disaster, has one seen what will be, or what must be, or what might be? What use is a warning if it cannot ward off calamity? On the other hand, if certain actions are taken to avoid the circumstances of the dream, thereby obviating the disaster, was the dream thus not a true one?

The files of the Society for Psychical Research in London and similar organizations around the world are full of testimony to dreams of prophecy, announcing the death of a loved one at a distance (in India, for example, in Victorian days). People claim they saw the departing person in their dreams or even "awoke" to find him in the room. How many such premonitions turned out to be groundless we shall never know, but we do have documentation for many cases in which the dreams, recorded on waking, eventually were "authenticated."

As some psychics can "see" lost persons in trance and lead police to the bodies, so some people can dream this sort of thing. Mrs. Rhoda Wheeler of La Pointe, Wisconsin, had a dream which guided rescuers to a remote island in Lake Superior on which her clergyman husband and two Indians had been wrecked, which suggests that when we are "dead to the world" we may, some of us, on occasion, be alive to Something Else.

John Chapman, a poor peddler of Swaffham, England, journeyed to London because a dream told him he would find buried treasure there. A stranger whom he stopped to ask directions scoffed at his story and, without knowing who the peddler was, added, "If I believed in dreams, I would be on my way to Swaffham because *I* dreamed there is a treasure buried there in the garden of a man named Chapman."

Chapman turned around, went home, dug up his garden, and found two crocks of treasure. Do you think, had he gone there, he might have found more or less in London?

Another true story. In 1845 Robert Barclay, laird of Urie, wanted to sell his ancestral estate. But he could not find the deed granted to his family by Charles II in 1679. An American Quaker, Joseph Hoag, sleeping in the laird's mansion, dreamed he saw an old man enter his bedchamber and place in a closet a title deed. The room, when he woke, had no closet. But on being told of the dream, Barclay stripped off the wallpaper of the bedchamber, pried loose some boards, and discovered an ancient hiding place in which the valuable deed to the estate had lain undisturbed for 166 years.

People are always claiming they bought just one ticket in a lottery, because the number came to them in a dream, and then won. In Scherin, Germany, there's a public fountain in honor of cigar-manufacturer Johannes Muhlenburg. It shows the donor and four seals. That's right, seals. He dreamed of four seals, consulted a "dream book," played the number in a lottery, and won. A recent winner of the New York State Lottery claimed to have picked the winning number in a dream.

But who or what is "sending" the messages, and how is it that only one person seems to "get" the winning number? Are we dealing with coincidence or communication, reception or deception?

THE MAN IN GREEN

It was the night of May 3, 1812, and John Williams, remotely secure in his manorhouse at Redruth in Cornwall, repeatedly dreamed that he saw a small man in a dark green coat shoot the British prime minister in the House of Commons in faraway London.

His dream was more vivid and persistent than any other he had ever had. The next morning he forced his wife and all his friends to listen to the details. He wanted to go to London and warn the prime minister, but everyone told him that would be folly.

On May 10 the prime minister, Spencer Perceval, had exactly the same dream. There he was, in his dream, in the House of Commons, and up came the small man in the dark green coat. When Perceval told *his* wife and friends all about it the next morning, he was able to add a detail that Williams seems to have missed. The little man's dark green coat sported bright brass buttons.

His family tried to dissuade Perceval from attending the House of Commons that day. His wife especially urged him to stay home. But, having told his dream, Perceval felt rather unburdened. Moreover, he was damned if he was going to miss an important sitting of the House just because of some silly dream, however vivid.

Perceval walked through the lobby of the House of Commons; a bushy-haired man he had never seen before leaped out from behind a pillar and shot him dead.

So it is not true at all, as American newspapers and magazines sometimes claim, that no British prime minister has ever been shot. And it is true that the assassin of Spencer Perceval was wearing a dark green coat with bright brass buttons.

A DREAM FROM SAN FRANCISCO

A woman living in London wrote in 1883 to the Society for Psychical Research to report a dream she had had many years before about a Danish teacher she had known who had gone to Mexico City "to improve his position." In the dream he was sitting in her father's San Francisco office and said to her, "You must not come near me. I am dying in Mexico of the sore throat, and I have come to tell your father."

The father did not have the dream, oddly. But on waking the woman told her family and friends about it. The Danish teacher did die in Mexico, it is reported, at the time indicated and of a *sore throat*.

What a pity the young woman did not record her dream with the SPR at the time, instead of years later. Then the "news" from far-off Mexico could have been measured against her report. What a story that would have made!

"I AM *FATED* TO GO"

A clergyman of Salisbury, England, told the SPR in 1884 of a dream he had had "between June, 1855, and June, 1856" that foretold the death of a friend.

In his dream, the man and a friend were "walking the cloisters of Westminster Abbey" when the friend suddenly said "he must go to a particular gravestone." Urged not to do so, he replied, "No, no, I must go, I am *fated* to go," and he "hurried to the stone, and sank through the floor."

On waking, the clergyman mentioned the strange dream to his landlady. Later he received a letter from his brother saying his friend had "died suddenly from a disease of the heart."

But why was the friend so anxious to get into *someone else's* grave?

IN SUMATRA

When the Bataks of Sumatra want camphor, they go to sleep in a special grove and dream where it is.

CHANNELING YOUR DREAMS

For thousands of years people have been trying to program their dreams. There are many rituals people follow even today to dream what they please. The Seroi of Malaysia have a whole system for producing the dreams they want, and tune them in at night almost like cable television.

WORKING IN YOUR SLEEP

People with a problem often say they will "sleep on it." Can we work in our sleep? The story of an English clergyman named Curnock suggests we can.

His problem was deciphering the *Journal* of John Wesley, the founder of Methodism. Like Pepys' diary, it was in code.

In a bookshop the Reverend Mr. Curnock found a Bible with annotations in the same complicated code. He bought the book and brooded over it for days. One night he dreamed he was reading not the code but what cryptographers call the "clear," and he memorized some of it. When he woke, he used what he recalled to break the code. He was then able to decipher the entire *Journal*, which he published in eight volumes (1909–1916).

That's what Curnock says happened. Do you doubt him?

But why did he dream an uncoded page and not the actual solution to the cipher? Here are questions not of magic but of the processing of information in the sleeping mind, for which, as storyteller H. P. Lovecraft writes in *Beyond the Walls of Sleep*, "one certainly ought not to underestimate the gigantic importance of dreams."

DREAMLAND

Goethe wrote that "the objects which had occupied my attention during the day often reappeared at night in connected dreams. On awakening, a new composition, or a portion of one I had already commenced, presented itself to my mind."

Lord Jeffrey (1773–1850) "had a fancy that though he went to bed with his head stuffed with the names, dates, and other details of various [legal] causes, they were all in order in the morning; which he accounted for," testified his biographer, "by saying that during sleep they all crystallized around their proper centres."

If sleep can permit us creative and organizing activities—that is that we "program" or "process" by night the information that comes to the conscious *and the unconscious* mind during the day—it may also permit us to get in touch with powers of the mind that are clairvoyant or to "tune in" with a greater sensitivity to "messages sent" by others.

Science has now established that certain persons with extrasensory powers can influence the thoughts of dreamers and communicate with them from a distance in the same way that receptivity to ESP is increased by hypnosis. Some people therefore believe that if there are "intelligences" around that are not human and alive—the spirits of the dead, for example, or demons—they may be able to "speak" to us in dreams of things beyond our time and place.

But it usually turns out that people say, "Oh, I had a dream that foretold that exactly" *after* the event. Let's see if we can't get some of these veridical dreams reliably on record. People have often trained themselves to wake up and jot down all the details of their dreams, and certain famous persons have been known to keep pencil and paper by their bedsides for this purpose. Why not write down all the "messages" you receive as "night letters" and see what percentage are accurate?

MERE COINCIDENCE?

G. N. M. Tyrrell in *The Personality of Man* (1947) relates two dreams with remarkable details in common:

> On the 7th October, 1938, Monsieur X (the real names are all known) attended a reception at the house of Madame Y in Brussels. He left at 10:30 pm. The same night Madame Y had the following dream: She is at the railway station with a gentleman (unknown); several friends see her off, including Monsieur X. Suddenly the train starts and Madame Y leaves without having time to take all her luggage. She calls through the open window to Monsieur X: 'Please bring my luggage and don't forget the yellow suitcase.' Arrived at her destination, she goes upstairs to the luggage depôt and finds all her luggage except the yellow suitcase. Monsieur X is there, too, and the lady severely rebukes him for his negligence.
>
> The next morning, 8th October, 1938, Madame Y related her dream to a witness, Monsieur Z: and an hour or so afterwards, while Monsieur Z was still present, Monsieur X arrived and before anything was said to him about Madame Y's dream, he recounted his own dream of the previous night, which was as follows: He finds himself at a station and in charge of Madame Y's luggage. A yellow suitcase is specially recommended to his care. He transports all this with great pains, but the yellow suitcase is somehow lost. He mounts the stairs to the luggage depôt and there meets Madame Y. She gives him a severe scolding for his bad behavior.

Your local gypsy would tell you (or you could ask your psychoanalyst) that the loss of something indicates frustration in love, just as walking up the stairs indicates a desire for sexual intercourse and the scolding dissatisfaction with a poor performance. Monsieur X seems to have been able to "deliver" everything but the yellow suitcase (Madame Y's orgasm). Both X and Y seem to have a one-track mind with a single train of thought running on it.

AND IF YOU DREAM ABOUT . . .

Your mind is running on sex if any or (God forbid) all of the following occur in your dreams: driving an automobile, boxes, caves, daggers, elephants, fires, goats, riding a horse, icicles, journeys, knives, locks, machine guns, nudity, orgies, peaches, angry queens, reptiles, snakes, torture, umbrellas, volcanoes, worms, X rays, yellow, zoos.

It is unlucky to dream about accidents, accordions, accusations, acrobats, alligators, altars, ants, fallen apples, automobile accidents, dull axes. . . . That's only the A's.

If you dream of bats, look out. If you dream of cherries, try to eat them. If you dream of a door, try to open it. If you dream of games, try to win. If you dream of paintings, don't buy them in your dream. If you dream of stairs, walk up and never down them. If you dream of water, wake up and get a drink; you are thirsty.

CHEMICAL REACTION

Friedrich August Kekulé von Stradonitz (1829–1896) made a major contribution to organic chemistry by working out the cyclic structure of benzene. In a dream "one of the snakes seized its own tail and the image whirled scornfully before my eyes. As though from a flash of lightning I awoke." By Jove, he had it! The benzene ring!

"PRINCE OF PHYSICIANS NEXT TO HIPPOCRATES"

That was the title given to Galen (c. 129–199), friend and physician to the Emperor Marcus Aurelius, a man so influential that he was still being quoted at the beginning of the Renaissance. He named many bones and muscles with names still used today, and some of his treatments are still in use, though we have given up some of his ideas about the Four Elements and discovered (in the Renaissance) that he was wrong in suggesting that the anatomy of the pig was so like man's that it was unnecessary to cut up human cadavers for study.

Strangely, though Galen was so skilled at diagnosing diseases that he preferred for the patient to remain silent and let him discover all symptoms himself, he liked people to describe their dreams to him in detail, for from that he could tell the future.

APOLLONIUS OF TYANA

The details of Apollonius' life (first century A.D.) are debatable because his biographers did not set to work until he was dead. But it is pretty clear that Apollonius was a miracle worker—he walked through closed doors, he cast out demons, he raised someone from the dead. According to his disciples, he also rose from the dead himself and ascended bodily into heaven.

Among his virtues were humility (he wanted to live simply, "have little and desire nothing") and simplicity (offered a great gift by a king, he chose "dried fruit and some bread"). He preached love of our fellow men, vegetarianism, and (according to his third-century biographer) communism. He gave away his wealth and wandered to India and many other places, preaching to every religion that there was but one God behind everything, that we should all be reincarnated, that we must love all God's creations and harm none.

He was by some later admirers said to have received all his wisdom by revelations in dreams and even to have appeared in their dreams after his departure for heaven to instruct and comfort them.

ONEIROMANCY

A brief study of divination by means of dreams was written by the patriarch of Constantinople, Saint Nicephorus, in ninth-century Greek, and among his interpretations were these:

An eagle means that your dream "whether happy or tragic, is a warning come from God."

A cock means "your dream will soon come true"; a fish means bad news for your plans.

Eating new-baked bread means "imminent misfortune"; a present means "imminent success."

Holding a bee means "your hopes will be disappointed"; a wasp means "danger, attacks."

Walking slowly means "success won with difficulty"; walking straight, "triumph."

Meeting a loved one means "a very hopeful augury," the same as eating grapes.

Talking with a king means "your plans will not mature"; kissed by a king means "you will enjoy the benevolence, favor and support of powerful persons."

Burning coals mean "harm at the hands of your enemies."

Flying means "a journey in a foreign land." If your feet are cut off it means a bad trip awaits you.

Holding a book means "you will rise in the world."

Thunder means "unexpected news."

Walking with back bent means "humiliation," on broken shells means "escape from the snares of your enemies."

Milk means "your enemies' plans for your downfall will fail"; a dog bite means the enemies will succeed in doing you some harm.

Eating something sweet means "bitter disappointment"; eating oranges means "illness."

Laughing means "you will cry when you awaken."

A marriage contract means "a change of abode."

Your house falling down means "loss of your worldly goods."

Meeting a eunuch means "success of an enterprise or the realization of a hope."

A wolf yawning means "beware of empty promises."

Saint Nicephorus has many other ideas. Follow his advice and don't dream of eating lettuce, drinking wine, enjoying figs, or cutting your hair. "If you dream you are sitting with no clothes on," he writes, "it means privation." Try to dream of seeing spilt wine or of washing your feet. Both mean "an end to your troubles." A house on fire or a serpent in your bed are "good signs," oddly. Finally, "If you see the skies or the stars are falling, it means great danger," and "If you see yourself dead, your troubles soon will be ended."

THE CABALA

The mystical writings of the Jews hold many secrets of the interpretation of dreams, very intricately worked out. Since every letter of the Hebrew alphabet has a numerological significance in this occult lore, dreams can give you symbols, numbers, predictions. As the stars are to the cabalists magical letters in the heavens, so people and objects in dreams also carry deep significance. The cabala (meaning "secret tradition") came to the West with the Jewish and Arabic scholars. Ever since then there have been commentaries, ranging from the creative to the crackpot. The basic works are the *seferim* (books) of *Yezira* (Creation), *Bahir* (Light), and *Zohar* (Splendor), and we have the authority of Eleazar of Worms (1176–1238) and Christian writers such as the thirteenth-century Raymond Lully of Catalonia, the fifteenth-century Pico della Mirandola of Italy, the sixteenth-century Paracelsus of Switzerland and Cornelius Agrippa of Germany, the sixteenth-century Robert Fludd and the seventeenth-century Henry More of Britain, and many others, for saying that the Cabala is of far greater interest than the Talmud. Certainly it has much more to say about matters mystical and the interpretation of dreams.

Ginsburg's classic of the midnineteenth century, *The Kabbalah*, has been reprinted in our time, and many scholars of the occult have shown extraordinary interest in the divining and other powers of cabalistic writings and commentaries. Give up your "gypsy dream books" and read the Cabala. Then go forth and enjoy wisdom without pride and power without selfishness.

RISE AND SHINE!

The *Brihadaranyaka Upanishad* of the Buddhists of India give this sage advice: "Let no one wake a man brusquely for it is a matter difficult of cure if the soul find not its way back to him."

Now, what happens when the soul leaves the body permanently and goes to "that undiscovered country" of afterlife? Read on.

11

The Undiscovered Country

GRAVE MATTERS

Here are some burial customs of the past, unfamiliar perhaps, but not more curious than those of today, which Jessica Mitford wittily derided in *The American Way of Death*.

Prehistoric people equipped their dead with weapons for use in the next life and gave evidence of trying to placate their dead, who frightened them. Ancient Britons placed stone hearts in the graves of misers and piled stones on graves to keep the dead from rising. But some tombs had doors.

The Visigoths buried their king Alaric (died 410) in the bed of a river, mounted on his favorite charger and equipped for battle in the spirit world. By diverting the river Busento in Italy, interring Alaric, and then permitting the river to flow once more in its old channel, they made certain that the grave and its treasures would not be disturbed by looters, a worry that Egyptians often had. The Visigoths took the precaution of killing all the slaves who had diverted the river; thus the burial place was kept a secret. In vampire and witch legends running water is supposed to defeat the evil one, and perhaps there was also some element of this superstition in Alaric's last resting place.

The funerary customs of the Egyptians, who were concerned to keep the body preserved so that it could be resurrected and the spirit and fame of the departed commemorated so that it would not die in human memory have produced lasting monuments in the great Pyramids. Most of them have been looted over the centuries, so that the discovery of an intact burial, even of a minor king such as Tutankhamen, is a great archaeological event. Bits of mummy were used in magical concoctions, and "Egyptian" rites have entered Western witchcraft and sorcery.

One lesser known Egyptian monument is the statue of Zedber, a physician, at Atribis where, for centuries, it was venerated by the Egyptians. Covered with magical inscriptions, it had water poured over it—water which the faithful drank as medicine, believing that some of the dead doctor's powers would somehow cure them still.

The Baganda tribe of Africa preserve the jawbones of all their dead kings, so that they may speak wisdom to succeeding rulers.

Roman Catholics preserve relics of saints and martyrs as aids to devotion. Actual pieces of the dead saint (the skull of Saint Catherine of Siena, still missing the two front teeth she knocked out when "the Devil pushed her down stairs," the arm of Saint Francis Xavier, the head of this or that saint in a portrait reliquary, a bit of this bone or hank of that hair) are "first-class relics." Something the saint owned (and preferably touched often, conferring some of his or her virtue on it) is a "second-class relic." Catholics venerate such objects, believing that the grace and favor of God may be obtained through the intercession of the saint so honored.

In witchcraft a piece of a person (fingernail clippings, a lock of hair, or whatever) can be used to work spells, and objects belonging to people enable "physical mediums" to "receive" information about them and sorcerers to work magic upon them. Even your name is a part of you and can be used in magic. The very names of the dead are invoked for magical power, and graves are robbed for pieces of corpses. Ghouls eat the brains of corpses, but magicians want all sorts of other bits and pieces for nefarious work. Even relics of saints can be used in black magic.

In places in Algeria, the graves of saints are sacrosanct, so secure from depredation that the natives pile all sorts of valuables outside the tombs, even precious firewood, sure that no one would dare steal from such a place.

To protect your grave from witches, plant a rowan tree nearby. To counteract necromancy, bury the dead with crucifixes in their hands. And you have heard that so strong is the old folklore of Charon, the ferryman across the River Styx in the Underworld, that even Christians are (or were) sometimes buried with pennies on their eyes, their fare for the last trip on the Underground. It is recalled in an old saying: "So mean he'd steal the pennies off a dead man's eyes." Maybe you'd better throw a few extra coins into the grave, for inflation.

CHILLING THOUGHT

They say that if you feel a sudden chill, someone is walking over your grave. Of course you can avoid this by arranging to be buried at sea, as one man did who wished to thwart a wife who said she would dance on his grave.

APPOINTMENT IN SAMARRA

In the end, we all wind up dead. I don't suppose you have given much thought this week to how and when you will die, but some people appear to have known, through magic or witchcraft or some other obscure means, when the Great Event was coming for them.

Witness these few examples.

Natalie von Hoyningen of Lechts, Esthonia, went to bed, wrote her will, took her pulse, announced that death was five minutes away, and died right on schedule. François de Moncriff, author of *Histoire des Chats*, told his friends, "Tomorrow morning I shall return your books," and died the next day. Many people in history have known exactly when they were going.

Moritz Arndt (1769–1860), German historian, reported to his publisher that in a dream he had seen his gravestone and on it was inscribed, "Died in his 91st Year." Some twenty-four years later he died; he was then in his ninety-first year.

Jane Garon (1705–1806), a widow of Rothwell, England, was warned in childhood that she would die on her birthday. Every year she spent her birthday anniversary in bed. She died in bed on her one-hundredth birthday.

Nothing like being prepared. Many people have ordered their tombs in advance, but few can have been as thoughtful as the wealthy Roman who had his constructed and decorated with four likenesses of himself: One as he appeared at twenty, one as he looked at forty, one as he looked at sixty, one showing him at eighty. He died in his eightieth year.

When he reached eighty, the Egyptian Amenothes carved a statue of himself and inscribed it: "I have attained the age of eighty and I shall endure until the age of 110." They say he died at 110.

Many people die of fright. Magic and witchcraft have capitalized on that. Isaac D'Israeli tells of a knight condemned to the scaffold. He was blindfolded at the block, but instead of having the ax fall, they threw a bucket of water on him, willing to let him off with disgrace rather than death. No use; he died of shock when the water hit him. People have been known to die of fright when they hear of a voodoo curse put upon them. Sophia, Lady Beresford, born February 23, 1666, dreamed she would die on her forty-seventh birthday. The day came, and she felt much relieved to find herself still around—until she realized that she had in error consulted the wrong calendar. She died of shock. It was February 23, 1713.

THE BRIDE WORE BLACK

In my family's papers of the last century, I have found many pieces of writing paper, calling cards, and such, edged in black. There were elaborate rules, too, about how long each member of the family had to wear full mourning or lesser black, gray, or violet. A great-grandmother of mine was in mourning when she got married, so of course her wedding gown was black. Of course it's bad luck to be married in black.

CHINESE FUNERALS

One of the most striking features of the extremely colorful funerals of the Chinese is the use of Hell Money. Scattered along the routes of funeral processions, Hell Money has the same purpose as the clashing gongs and other loud noises (such as firecrackers and music) that accompany these rites. It is hoped that the Hell Money will distract the nearby demons. If they stop to pick up the counterfeit cash, they will ignore the corpse. You can also burn counterfeit money; demons can't tell that your sacrifice is not real, and in this way the very poor can also afford to distract and dispel evil ones.

Those who die by misadventure or violence are watched with special care by the Chinese lest they rise from the grave on the seventh day for revenge.

POT LUCK

Among the Ashanti an *abusua kuruwa* ("family pot") is made when a person dies. Into it goes the hair shaved in mourning by all blood relatives;

then the pot is placed in a special "place of the pots" with cooking pots, hearthstone, and food. Only men are permitted to make these funeral pots and to decorate them with special anthropomorphic and zoomorphic designs. The women make all the other kinds of pots the tribe needs.

FOOD FOR THE DEAD

Some sorcery depends upon offering the dead something they want from the world of the living or performing some service they left undone. Among some African people, "soul pots" are made to resemble departed parents, which their children dutifully fill. In Britain it used to be a custom to leave food in graveyards, at crossroads, and other places for the dead. Hungry but live persons may well have eaten this food (though there were curses to fear if one did so), and this would strengthen the belief of the food givers that the dead were truly present.

THE END

Soldiers used to yearn to die not in bed but "with their boots on." Hindus are also not supposed to die in bed but on the ground, preferably by running water. The Hindus say that to die any other way is unlucky.

ZOMBIES

To most people zombies are powerful cocktails calculated to make you stagger around only partly aware of the world. But the name comes from the "dead" who are supposed to do that in Haiti.
. One expert writes:

The Zombie is a dead person whom a sorcerer has taken from the tomb in order to make him, by means of magical powers, seem a living person, making of him a walking cadaver, an automaton of flesh freed from putrefaction, a living dead man.

First, the zombie maker must make a pact with *bakas* (spirits) who serve Baron Saturday (as the Devil is called) to help him. Then he chooses his victim. Riding backward to the victim's house, the *houngan* (sorcerer) sucks out the soul of the victim through the keyhole of the door and breathes it into a bottle. The victim wastes away. The victim dies.

When the victim is buried, the *houngan* steals the corpse from the tomb, assisted by Baron Saturday himself in the guise of an old man with a long white beard. The Devil is conjured up with incantations and put back to rest with more spells (none of which I think you ought to have) and a shower of acacia leaves. It doesn't work, they report in Haiti, unless the body is taken from the grave with chants of *"Mortoo tombo mivi"* ("The dead in the tomb are mine").

Now you have the body obtained in the right way. You must take it past its former residence. If the corpse does not revive and recognize it, everything is going well. Then you can release the soul from the bottle and reinsert it in the body. A powerful drink, and the corpse will revive, now a living dead man, not an independent vampire but the slave of his zombie master.

In this you may perceive a mixture of medieval necromancy and Congolese witchcraft. In Haiti even to this day zombies are believed in, and there is hardly anyone who will not tell you he has seen a zombie or has a friend who has seen one.

What are they? Drugged workers? Or the Baron's *braceros?*

A MEMORY OF THE WIZARD

The zombies and the soul in a bottle reminds me of the souvenir of Thomas Alva Edison. When he died (1931) they did not want his death mask or a lock of his hair. They collected his dying breath in a bottle.

Had Edison not been in a coma, he would probably have had a good laugh over this. On his death his desk was sealed. About fifteen years later, while radio broadcast the great event, it was solemnly opened by his son and found to contain a few pieces of junk and a lot of jokes.

Edison's son had to pass over slip after slip of paper until he could find a joke suitable to be read on the air. Finally Charles Edison found one: "When down in the mouth, remember Jonah. He came out all right."

So much for the Wizard of Menlo Park's "last word."

GOOD INFLUENCE

Parents naturally want good influences on their children. Philip II of Spain stands out. His son Don Carlos was insane; he liked dwarfs, plotting, roasting rabbits alive. His viciousness and violence worried the old man so much that the king ordered that Don Carlos be put to bed with a pious cook. The hope was that some of the piety might rub off on him.

The cook, though pious, was dead, and the scheme failed miserably.

Ultimately the prince was imprisoned for plotting his father's death and died there, possibly murdered at age twenty-three.

IF YOU BELIEVE IN REINCARNATION,
DON'T BE NICE TO PEOPLE

Most people rather like the idea of reincarnation, but whether we come back to earth in some form or hover about out there somewhere is hotly debated, even in spiritualist circles. Do you want your own self to persist or would you prefer a whole new you?

"I expect to pass through the world but once," commented Quaker Stephen Grellet (1773–1855), whereas another philosophical mind has noted that once is enough if you play your cards right. But for some people once is not enough, and they are convinced that they have had a series of past lives. None seems to have been a medieval serf, only a knight or lady, not a housemaid in ancient Egypt, only Cleopatra. Didn't *anybody* work in the Renaissance equivalent of McDonald's? Or do people like that never come back?

J. J. Morse, a spiritualist, certainly believed in the Next World. He used to write "from dictation" the teachings of Tien Sien Tie, a Chinese sage who has not been around since the sixteenth century. But reincarnation? Silly, he said. Otherwise the doctrine of *karma* (reincarnation to atone for the mistakes made in a past life) would make it totally illogical for us to do anything to alleviate human suffering.

"A TIDE IN THE AFFAIRS OF MEN. . . ."

Tennyson dictated that when his poetry was published in collected form the volume should end with the poem "Crossing the Bar," in which he speaks of meeting his "Pilot face to face" and going "out to sea" at death. In Dickens's *David Copperfield*, Barkis at last dies: "And, it being low water, he went out with the tide."

Behind all this is an ancient British superstition that life goes out on the ebb tide, a superstition of which magical ceremonies make some use.

Others believe that most people die at about that dead hour which F. Scott Fitzgerald was fond of saying was "the dark night of the soul," about "three o'clock in the morning."

I had a great-aunt whose theory was that you don't die as long as you will to "hang on," and you go when you have "had enough" (she gave up cheerfully at the age of 106). If there is indeed a psychological factor in staying alive, you can see how strengthening a person's will or weakening a person's confidence can affect life and death.

So all of us, with faith and determination, may be able to summon up the strength to prolong the greatest miracle we know—being a live human being.

DEAD WRONG AND DEAD RIGHT

If a live human being is a miracle, a dead one is a mystery. A corpse makes every thinking person consider at least a little the great question that made Gautama into the Buddha ("the Enlightened One"). What is life and what is its purpose, what is death and what is its purpose?

The corpse of Nicholas L'Hoste, a French spy who drowned himself in the Marne when he saw escape was otherwise impossible, was embalmed, put on trial, convicted, and publicly quartered by being tied to four horses. The corpses of French kings were dug up and thrown around by Revolutionaries. Vindictive people, the French.

The corpses of Constantine the Great and Jeremy Bentham, however, prove that the French are not uniquely morbid.

Constantine the Great's corpse ruled the Roman empire for three months. It was preserved, sat on the throne, and was "consulted" daily by government officials until the emperor's son and successor got home from Constantinople.

Jeremy Bentham was an English expert on jurisprudence and ethics, one of the most able writers on utilitarianism. He was a rather long-winded stylist (Edward FitzGerald wondered "what would have happened to Christianity if Jeremy Bentham had been given the writing of the Parables") and has been, in a sort of way, a rather long-lived official of the University of London. Though he died in 1832, he still attends official meetings. He is recorded as "present but not voting." His preserved body is wheeled up to the conference table, hat and stick and all, gruesomely lifelike. When he is not attending meetings, they keep him in a sort of closet. You can see him to this day in London.

Those who live on, whether using a part of a corpse or the whole thing, often violate what may be called the privacy of the dead.

THE BLACK LACE PILLOW

In these days when doctors and relatives are empowered to "pull the plug" on brain-dead patients, it is probably not difficult to understand the feelings of our ancestors who, for selfish, practical, or humanitarian reasons, were moved to help the dying get there faster.

Many were the devices employed to speed up the inevitable. Some were thought magical. One of these was a pillow, covered in black lace, purported to have been made by a nun of Ely, England, and handed down from generation to generation to help bring quicker death to a suffering soul.

Placed beneath the head of a dying person, it was suddenly whipped out, giving him or her (it was hoped) a nasty shock, hastening them the way that they were going. Just seeing it arrive in the sickroom must have been less than fortifying.

In 1902 the last old lady who owned and operated this device passed on (without its assistance), and that was the end of the black lace pillow.

HEADS OF STATE

Because it contains the brain and hence the personality, the head has long been regarded as the most likely part of the body to retain some of the spirit of the deceased. Hence head hunters and shrinkers and scalp takers.

A severed head—I mentioned that of Saint Catherine of Siena earlier—
can be seen in many European collections of relics. You used to be able to
see the heads of traitors stuck up on London Bridge or Micklegate Bar in
York, left until they rotted to nothingness or were stolen.

There are two heads of Saint Thomas Aquinas, and a dispute has raged
for centuries over which is the real one. The same fate befell Button
Gwinnett (1735–77), signer of the Declaration for Georgia (whose chief claim
to fame is that his signature is the rarest of all Signers' signatures—he died so
young and so obscurely that he had few chances to sign anything). Sir
Thomas More's daughter treasured his severed head, as well she might. He
made a brave, even jaunty end, mounting the scaffold for his faith and telling
the headsman, "Assist me up, and in coming down, I will shift for myself."
The daughter subsequently carried the head with her everywhere. Like
Juana the Mad of Spain, who brought her dead husband entire wherever she
was invited, asking the young More daughter to a party put something of a
damper on jollity.

At the end of Shakespeare's play, Macbeth's head is supposed to be
brought on stage on a pole, but directors often omit this. The head of Oliver
Cromwell was dug up at the Restoration (1660) and used as a football by the
Royalists. Its exact place of burial is now a secret, to prevent further
outrages. Last seen officially on top of Westminster Hall, Cromwell's head
was blown down in a gale, picked up by a sentry, and sold, passing through
various hands (including those of "a drunken and dissolute actor called
Samuel Russell," a Canon Wilkinson, and Sidney Sussex College—Cromwell's own college—at Cambridge). When the head was reburied in 1960,
the memorial was not exactly placed, and the secret resting place is
presumably safe.

Few corpses have suffered the indignities of Cromwell's, which was
even tied to a hurdle, though largely decomposed, dragged to Tyburn, and
hanged. Before that it rested a night at the Red Lion inn in Holborn, giving
rise to a tradition that Cromwell's ghost haunts that spot.

A head, supposedly of the duke of Suffolk, father of the tragic "nine
days' queen," Lady Jane Grey, was found, 247 years after Suffolk's
beheading, in the vault of Holy Trinity Church in London; oak sawdust from
the scaffold, they said, had perfectly preserved it.

Head stealing was not unheard of in the heyday of sorcery. If
necromancers did not want to raise the whole body from the dead they might
try to make the head speak. To do this, one takes the head of a murdered
eldest son, opens it, applies ammonia and oil, and places an amulet of virgin

gold under the tongue. Charles IX of France, who in 1560 at the age of ten became king under the regency of his mother (the redoubtable Catherine de Médicis), had one of these made for him. He had "a young Jew" murdered for the purpose.

Several magicians, including the thirteenth-century Franciscan and alchemist Roger Bacon, were supposed to have made neater, more durable speaking heads out of brass.

TOWERS OF SILENCE

The Parsees (originally from Persia) in India have such respect for the sacredness of the earth that they shrink from defiling it even with the dead bodies of their loved ones. They take their dead to the Towers of Silence in Bombay. There they are exposed to the vultures, who pick the bones clean.

In Western tradition seldom or never does a ghost appear as a skeleton, while the ghosts of those cremated (an increasingly popular practice although forbidden by a number of religions) are practically never seen.

"I'M MY OWN GRANDPA!"

Jess Stern in *Yoga, Youth and Reincarnation* (1968) refers to the "regression" under hypnosis of a man in Wilmington, Delaware, who believed in reincarnation and who seemed to recall being in another body at the time of the Spanish-American War. He had other odd feelings. "He couldn't understand why he was so anxiously following the romance of his son and a pretty girl friend." And he heaved a sigh of relief when the son finally married the girl. Why? Because "he was slated to return as his own [great-]grandson, so he was in a sense waiting for his own father to materialize."

In magical circles people often claim to be the reincarnation of an earlier magician, say Paracelsus or Cornelius Agrippa (who, despite their classical-sounding names, were sixteenth-century physician/occultists), or even to have gone on living generation after generation (like the Comte de Saint-Germain). But I have never seen another case of one believing he was his own ancestor.

BAPTIZING THE DEAD

Joseph Smith said that the living could be baptized in the Mormon religion in the name of those who had died before that dispensation.

His authority was not so much the Angel Moroni (whom he encountered in New York) as I Peter 3:18–20, which speaks of Jesus preaching to the spirits of the dead, and I Corinthians 15:29, where Saint Paul writes of vicarious baptism for the departed. Other Christian sects have read these texts differently.

The Mormon desire to "seek out the dead" and posthumously bring relatives into the fold has led the Church of Latter-Day Saints to build up perhaps the most extensive genealogical archives in the history of the world and to baptize in the Mormon temple in Salt Lake City such non-Mormons as Abraham Lincoln.

One cannot say, of course, whether any of those offered this postmortem opportunity have availed themselves of it. In the end, the choice is theirs.

Baptism has been important in other religions, of course, and in witchcraft as well, where unbaptized infants were eagerly sought. The Devil's brood were baptized in his name. A baptized animal if sacrificed was supposed to grant certain powers of evil. But nobody ever thought of *un*baptizing the dead to bring them to the Devil's Party.

FUNERALS FOR THE LIVING

The Greek philosopher Diogenes one day told his followers that, when he died, he wished not to be buried with ceremony but to be left exposed to the sun and rain. That, he said, would consume his body.

But, they objected, the dogs would tear to pieces an unburied corpse.

"Then you must put a stick in my hands," replied Diogenes, "that I may drive them away."

"But when you are dead you will neither see nor feel anything."

"You see what fools you are," replied Diogenes; "for if that be the case, what matters it by what I am devoured, or what becomes of me when I shall be insensible to everything?"

Funerals cannot matter much to the dead; they are chiefly for the living. Faced with death, people need to mark and mourn the occasion, and even the most agnostic may want some comfort from ceremony or the most sophisticated some allaying of deep-seated old fears and superstitions.

Few of us can say with equanimity what Lt. Gen. Henry Hawley (died March 24, 1759) said: "My carcass may be put anywhere; it is equal to me, but I will have no more expense or ridiculous show, than if a poor soldier (who is as good a man) were to be buried. . . . The priest, I conclude, will have his fee—let the puppy have it. Pay the carpenter for the carcass-box."

Death, whether it is annihilation or entry into another kind of existence, is an occasion, and the feelings that have always struck the living at that time have provided a great deal of the impetus for occult beliefs and practices. Even a belief in demons is, in a way, comforting; if they exist, this is not "the be all and the end all here." Hardly anyone wants to be a ghost (certainly not immediately), but however frightening the idea of ghosts may be, it is also fundamentally a comfort.

CENOTAPH

Providing some sort of memorial for the dead so that a spirit may not be homeless in the afterlife has long been a concern of the living. Making some gesture to bury her brother (which her uncle has forbidden) is a strong motivation for Antigone in Sophocles' play of that title.

World wars have sentimentally but successfully provided graves for various "unknown soldiers," some nations choosing to erect cenotaphs (tombs in which no body is buried). France and America each chose an unidentified corpse and interred it in state in their respective capitals. At Runnymede, where King John sealed the Magna Carta, is a monument by Sir Edward Maufe to the air forces of the Commonwealth, remembering all those whose graves are unknown. Around the world are many monuments to persons lost at sea, and pagan custom is combined with modern sentiment when flowers are thrown into the water to memorialize deaths at sea.

REST IN PEACE

Flowers from the earliest times may have been placed on the bodies of the dead for sentimental as well as practical purposes (in days before embalming). Flowers are perfect symbols of beauty that perishes. They may also in a sense represent gifts to the dead, and it is impossible to say exactly to what extent gifts were offered to the dead to placate them, to protect the living against them. In magic and witchcraft we preserve our very ambiguous attitude toward the dead. We try to guard against them and, if possible, to use them for our benefit. We mourn them and we fear them. We give the dead homes to please them, to honor them, and to hold them.

We like to think of the dead as sleeping, and we do not like to think of what might happen if they are aroused from that "sleep." We are especially fearful and revolted in regard to grave robbers, but from the earliest times graves have been violated, generally to steal treasures entombed with the dead. Treasure hunters evaded all the ingenious protections provided by the Egyptian architects and desecrated the tombs of the pharaohs before archaeologists could get there to do likewise. In more recent times, "resurrectionists" stole bodies to sell to anatomists. The corpse of Laurence Sterne, for instance, was stolen only two days after his death (in 1768) by grave robbers, so a tombstone now marks the empty grave of the immortal author of *Tristram Shandy*. Mummies of pharaohs and kings have been unceremoniously dumped out of their coffins to be put on display in museums. Shakespeare has so far escaped this indignity. His epitaph contains a curse on anyone who dares disturb his "bones," and up to this day it has worked.

BODY OF KNOWLEDGE

Today death is hidden from us as much as possible. Family and friends seldom gather to watch a loved one die, as they used to. Today the "loved one" is quickly consigned to the "mortician," and the "cosmetician" begins his work (if the body is to be displayed, though increasingly the lid of the coffin is closed). At the funeral, the coffin is often covered with "floral tributes," so that funerals are getting perilously close to being flower shows. Try as we might to forget it, the dead body is there, in the box. However much we prettify, death is a fact. As faith wanes, we claim less and less knowledge of death's purpose, its nature, its mystery. And, as always, the less knowledge there is, the more fear, and the more fear, the more superstition.

It is alleged that if you touch a corpse, you will have nightmares about it. I do not find this true, but a friend of mine who "shook hands" with the mummified corpse of a "crusader," astoundingly preserved by the dry air in the vaults of St. Michan's, Dublin, had a terrible recurrent dream for a long while afterward. It was "set" in Ireland during the early nineteenth century, so that may not be a "crusader" after all. . . .

They say that if you kiss a corpse you will never be afraid of the dead. I think that probably has to happen in reverse order.

At the wake, drink up. The pallbearers must drink first. Each cup you quaff is supposed to contain some of the sins of the dead, so help the entrance into the next world as much as you can.

"POSSESSION BY GOOD OR EVIL SPIRITS . . ."

You might think that films, with all the photographic tricks available to them, would have brought many ghost stories to the screen, but cinema prefers to deal in more realistic surfaces. There has been a rash of movies about possession.

The popularity of a number of books, often made into movies, about multiple personalities (Eve with three, Sybil with five, others with dozens) prepared the public for what psychologists call "fragmented ego" and what demonologists called "possession," the inhabiting of a body by another intelligence from beyond the mundane world.

Ramona Stewart's novel *The Possession of Joel Delaney* (1972) was a case in point. Joel was possessed by the spirit of one Tonio Perez, a seventeen-year-old Puerto Rican maniac with a love of knives and a penchant for decapitating pretty girls. So his sister sought the help of Don Pedro, who ran the Botánica Santa Barbara and conducted a magical ceremony intended to drive out the evil spirit.

"All you have open is your eyes," he says to Joel's distraught sister. "Are you willing to believe and accept what you are told?" Well, the sister tries, attending a ritual that is a mixture of Christian exorcism and pagan rites. But Joel does not attend in person, and the attempt to drive the spirit of the dead Tonio into one of those at the ceremony (so that it can then be exorcised) apparently fails.

When Joel is shot by police at a beach house, his sister picks up his knife, and as the story ends she seems to have become the new residence of the evil spirit.

Like many other similar tales, *Joel Delaney* was made into a movie. Such films are long on violence and short on explanations, but they are clear evidence that the general public finds "possession" as gripping as did our medieval ancestors.

". . . ALIVE WITH THE SOUND OF MUSIC"

In my Shakespeare studies I have come across some books supposedly dictated by the Bard and his colleagues from Beyond. I have friends who "receive" poetry from Hart Crane and Walt Whitman, too, although death seems to have a deleterious effect upon talent.

Richard Strauss dedicated a wind serenade to the ghost of Mozart, implying that Wolfgang Amadeus himself had inspired him to compose it, perhaps even helped him from the grave.

Mrs. Rosemary Brown in Britain reported "receiving" compositions from Lizst and others, but an English musical authority describes them as "free association of sounds." If that's really what Lizst, Chopin, and the others are capable of these days, they are better off dead.

VIKINGS!

The many Viking invasions of Western Europe produced both new customs of magic and witchcraft and at the same time a suspicion that the dead in Valhalla might be having too good a time to bother with us.

In case they turned nasty, however, it was wise to propitiate them. Thietmar of Meresburg, a Danish chronicler of the eleventh century, records that in Lejre, Denmark, every nine years there was a Yule festival in January celebrated "by, among other things, sacrificing ninety-nine humans and as many horses to their gods, as well as dogs and cocks, and also hawks." In the sacred grove dedicated to Freya and Thor at Uppsala, Sweden, wrote Adam of Bremen in his chronicle, they also sacrificed every nine years: "Of all living things that are male and female, they offer nine heads." Then the corpses of men, women, and animals festooned the ash trees of the grove.

Peter Brent in *The Viking Saga* identifies sacrifice as "the basic act of worship" in Scandinavia. "What was offered heavenwards included the whole range of objects within mankind's control and gift, for the gods were greedy, capricious and powerful."

Someone should study the history of sacrifice, determine what has been offered to man's gods over the millenia of recorded history, and analyze what this shows about man's conception of his deities and himself. The gods of the Vikings were in their image: brave, proud, audacious, and rapacious.

The Vikings were avid collectors. They would take anything not nailed down. And they did not like the idea of "you can't take it with you." (Moreover, to leave easy riches to your children might make them soft.) When a Viking went, so did his wealth. It was a rule that a third of a man's estate must be spent on drink for those who attended the funeral.

At this grand affair the hero was buried with riches and honors. Sometimes the body was placed on a ship full of treasure and the ship was burned at sea. Sometimes the body was buried on land. Sometimes human sacrifices burned with the hero after they had been ritually murdered. Brent writes that "the killing of a companion for the dead certainly occurred in Norway, Sweden, Iceland and the Isle of Man" and chiefs were likely to be sent to the afterlife with a slave girl, perhaps with their horses.

RESERVED PLACE

The New Jerusalem (Revelations 21:16) is "twelve thousand furlongs," worked out by one authority as 497,793,088,000,000,000,000 cubic feet.

So don't worry about getting in. But if you want a special place the Yezidis, a group of Kurdish-speaking peoples with a religion of their own, will sell you one. Or you can check out with your local clergy about other offers in heavenly dwelling places. Uncertain about the prospects? Better be cautious. As Woody Allen says, "I don't believe in an afterlife, although I am bringing a change of underwear."

OMENS OF DEATH

The occult sciences have long concerned themselves with pulling aside the veil of the future, and astrology, necromancy, fortune-telling, and other superstitious practices have caused occultists to look for signs.

Saint Augustine warned that though all signs are things, not all things are signs. Where to look? Up into the sky or down into the entrails of animals?

Heavenly portents are said to have heralded the death of kings, and the star of Bethlehem announced the birth of the King of Kings. Even lesser mortals have omens to guide them. The bishops of Salisbury, England, keep an eye on the White Birds of Salisbury Plain; when they appear (as when owls bring similar unwelcome messages to the Wardour family of Arundel), death is near. The O'Neills, like many lesser Irish families, have their banshee. If you happen to hear a banshee (and you do not have to be an O'Neill), a sweet crooning sound means you will die peacefully. A malevolent howl means you are in for a much worse end.

YOU CAN GO TO HELL

Clergymen joke about the notice board outside a church: "Do You Know What HELL Is? Come In and Hear Our New Organist."

Whatever Hell is, whether alienation or a crowded prison, "other people" or private suffering, a state of mind or a place of fire and brimstone, the concept has long been with us and contributes much to our vision of the undiscovered country.

You can go to a real Hell (a town in Scandinavia) or Hell Bay (on Bryher, one of the Isles of Scilly). The ancient Greek Hell was entered at Cape Tenaris and Eleusis, the Italian Hell, through a cave at Cumae near Naples. The French said Hell was in the Alpes Maritimes.

In the parish register of St. Nicholas Within the Liberties, Dublin, there is an entry dated May 20, 1735: "Sarah Read from Hell."

"No," comments *Irish Times*, "poor Sarah was no witch, but a very respectable person indeed, and was buried with all Christian dignity. For Hell was the old name of Christ Church Lane, close to the old Law Courts." Similarly, an old street near Westminster Palace Yard was originally named Hell.

BODY AND SOUL

Tennyson rejoiced to think that at his death his spirit would not be a personality any longer but would become part of something larger, what Emerson called the oversoul. Others want to survive as individual personalities after death, freed of the body, and Christians believe in a resurrection of the body, but not necessarily the same body as in this life. "It is sown a natural body," says Paul in I Corinthians, 15:44; "it is raised a spiritual body." The Talmud mentions the Bone of Luz, from which the body was to be restored. For many centuries anatomists hunted in vain for this mystical bone. When they couldn't find it, they theorized that it vaporized at death. It was supposed to depart at death to begin its real work.

Can the spirit leave the body before death, to roam around the world or even just to float up to the ceiling? Some people who have been near death, even technically and momentarily dead, claim they have left their bodies in spirit and watched themselves "down there" for a while before resuming the intimate union.

After death, does the soul hang around or go elsewhere? Is it ill-disposed toward the living, as many people (not all of them primitive) believe? Is it reincarnated? Does it join God? Or what?

Too soon to know for certain.

Index

MAGIC &
WITCHCRAFT

Volume 2

In Memoriam

WALTER DENNIS WILLIAMS
called
MELBAS'SON
Entered Apprentice

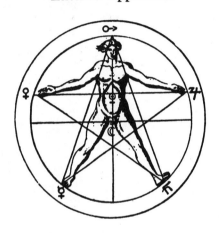

Contents

Preface

WRITING this book has taken me to some unattractive places, among "wizards that peep and mutter," among the petty and the potty, the diabolical and the desperate, the sacrilegious and the fanatical. The search for facts has spread before me an amazing documentation of human pride and arrogance, frailty and ignorance, deception and delusion.

The result is presented for your entertainment and enlightenment. I hope it will also make you think. For one man's cherished beliefs and obsessive ambitions may strike another—particularly if he lives in a later more superficially sophisticated age—as revolting, vain, silly, frightening. But one should translate the excesses of an earlier age—avarice and vainglory, bigotry and stupidity, malice and self-deception—into the terms of one's own time. There are lessons to be learned from seeing how ready man is to blame the Devil or some other supernatural entity for the more despicable, hateful, life-destroying, irrational aspects of human nature.

Exploring this mysterious land has many a shock and many a surprise, for there seems to be nothing so foolish or so vile that someone—somewhere, at some time or other—has not attempted it. The hideous and their wretched victims are here together. Here is a man who gruesomely murdered some two hundred children to tell fortunes and to please the Evil One. Here is a Hungarian noblewoman who murdered dozens of serving girls in order to bathe in their blood. Here is a witch hunter who preyed on deranged old women and innocent young people and collected twenty shillings a head for sending them to horrible deaths. Here is a judge who sentenced nine hundred poor souls to violent deaths for witchcraft, the evidence having been obtained by excruciating tortures. (The families or heirs of victims were charged the expenses of torture.) Here are primitive and harmless superstitions derived from ignorance and what Karl Marx called "the idiocy of rural life," and also terrifying crimes and persecutions perpetrated by educated persons in the name of faith. Here are saints and demons and frauds and wonders. Here are sincere believers in the Old Religion and on the other side men of zeal armed with a text that dictates "thou shalt not suffer a witch to live." Here are charlatans and dupes, magicians and alchemists, diviners and divines, men ready to destroy the mind to gain some diabolical power and men ready to destroy the body to save the soul.

"I am human," wrote Terence, in the second century before Christ, "and nothing human is alien to me," not even man's seeking to contact the inhuman, or man's inhumanity to man. The history of magic and witchcraft is a colorful part of the record of human behavior. Here is some of the humor and horror to be found in it.

1
Magic and Sorcery

MAGIC is difficult to define with precision, but in all its aspects it is concerned with making reality conform to one's will. It attempts to exercise power over events and to produce marvels by compelling the intervention of supernatural forces or bringing into operation the occult forces of nature. It rewards those who have penetrated the secrets by enpowering them to make spirits do their bidding.

Remember that "occult" means simply "hidden." Thus magic can also involve not necessarily the supernatural but also the arcane, the secrets not known to ordinary or unlearned men, the merely mysterious. In some people's view, modern computers perform "magical" operations. To others, the telephone and the television—indeed simple electricity—are deep, dark mysteries; average people believe in them, use them, but cannot explain them.

Right up to and through the Renaissance, magicians were classed among what we should today call intellectuals. They were learned men, familiar with ancient lore and languages, with the obscure symbolism of signs and numbers. They read the stars and dabbled in the mysticism that surrounded alchemy. They were respected. In the early centuries of Christianity, magic was not considered an evil thing. In the world thought to be inhabited by men and angels and devils, men also believed in spirits neither good nor bad, spirits of the air, of fire, of the sea, of the mountains, of

1

the woods, of the winds. It was believed that if a person was sufficiently learned in the art of magic, he could summon and control these powers, make them do his bidding. Ariel in *The Tempest* was such a spirit; Prospero was such a magician.

It was only at the very end of the Middle Ages and particularly in the Renaissance enlightenment that animism lost its hold on men's minds. Then religion preached that all spirits that were not angels, doing the bidding of God, must be evil, doing the bidding of His Adversary, Satan. The Church decided that men who worked magic through spells must also be in league with the Devil.

Even then—it is worth noting—few magicians were persecuted as witches were (unless they had committed sex crimes). Witches were chiefly the poor, the friendless, the impotent, whereas magicians were gentlemen and scholars and—whether in league with the Devil or not—entitled to all the privileges of rank.

THE MAGIC OF ABRAMELIN

Abraham the Jew (1362–1460), better known as Abramelin the Mage, lived chiefly at Würzburg, Germany, but he had important clients all over Europe. He was credited with having produced two thousand spirit cavalrymen to aid Frederick, elector of Saxony, and to have assisted Pope John XXIII. (Not the one you are thinking of but an antipope who reigned 1410–1415.) Abramelin was universally believed to have saved John—for a price—from the clutches of the Council of Constance, which had seized and deposed him. Abramelin is also supposed to have helped an earl of Warwick escape from jail.

Abramelin claimed angels told him how to harness devils, to make armed men appear, to raise thunder, to tame a demon as a personal servant, and so on. He left his magic recipes to one son and his knowledge of the cabala to another and wrote (probably in Hebrew) a book on magic. It was translated into English by S. L. MacGregor Mathers from a French version in the Bibliothèque Nationale in Paris. It has been very influential among modern magicians.

MAGIC IN CHRISTIAN FOLKLORE

Hrabanus Maurus, an encyclopedist of the ninth century, stressed that magicians could not overcome the set laws of the universe: "Not for that reason ought anyone to believe that certain men can perform magic operations without the permission of God."

As a brief example of magic in Christian folklore, apparently by "the permission of God," take the legend of the priory of Christchurch. The priory lies in Dorset, England. The legend is that the church was intended to be built on top of a hill, overlooking a valley site that dated back to Saxon times. Every morning materials were carted up to the top, and the following morning, they were found back at the bottom again. The builders eventually faced the inevitable and began to erect the church in the valley.

As they worked, they were joined by a helpful but silent carpenter, who took neither pay nor meals but labored beside them every day. One day they made a mistake and cut a beam just too short to reach from one wall to the other. They thought they had ruined it, but the next morning, they found that the beam had grown to be just long enough, and the mysterious carpenter had vanished forever. They named the place for him: Christchurch.

THE NAMES OF GOD

Some of my Jewish students persist in writing the title of a Eugene O'Neill play *The Great G-d Brown* and referring to "the pagan g-ds of the Greeks." Their action reflects the ancient fear of the name of God. A pious attitude, for God's name not only should not be taken in vain but also should not be consigned to a piece of paper that may be defaced or debased. God's name is power.

But they do not really have to worry, for *G*, *O*, and *D* do not add up to God's Name, any more than *D*, *O*, and *G* spell the name of my dog Wolfram. God simply told the Jews, "I am," which is where we got *Yahweh* and *Jehovah*, and left it safe at that.

The Jewish tradition developed words of reverence and respect to stand in place of the ineffable name of the deity. Here they are:

EHEDEH	EL	EL ADONAI TZABAOTH
IOD	ELOHIM GIBER	ELOHIM TZABAOTH
TETRAGRAMMATON ELOHIM	ELOAH VA-DAATH	SHADDAI

These have come to be used in magic. With the Nine Names of God, it is alleged, you can work wonders, that is, minor miracles. For truly magical effects involving the exercise of divine creative power, you would need the accurate name of God.

But the secret name of God is known to us cabalists. My own religion sees nothing wrong in setting it down, so if you are ready, here it is. (If you don't want to know, skip to the next paragraph.) The secret Name of God is *Emeth.*

GOLEMS

With that secret name, you can do wonders. You can make a golem if you like, an artificial man. Rabbi Judah Lowe did in the sixteenth century, and they were able to show me his grave—the rabbi's, not the golem's—when I visited Prague. The golem comes back, according to legend, every thirty-three years, even if you destroy it.

As early as the eleventh century one Eleazar of Worms gave instructions on how to put together spare parts of corpses to make a man. But his monster didn't come to life (because he did not have the essential name I just gave you). Elisse of Chelm in the sixteenth century did know the Name; his golem worked but had to be destroyed because it ran amok (like Dr. Frankenstein's monster). The Prague golem was known in Toledo and in all the other European capitals of sorcery. Prague was famous for Rabbi Lowe and other Jewish sorcerers but also had its Christian contingent of magicians; a column was pointed out as the place a priest got in big trouble when he tried to get out of his pact with the Devil. The Jews not only had a golem but also a dybbuk (a demon who was especially fond of preying on dedicated students of the Torah). Ansky and others have written famous plays about the dybbuk.

A dybbuk, unlike a golem, which is confined to thirty-three-year intervals, can come at any time.

HOW STRONG A FOUNDATION

People once believed that human blood mixed with the mortar made buildings stronger, and at the urging of magicians, human sacrifices were immured in fortresses. Geronimo of Oran was buried alive in the walls of the fort at Algiers (September 18, 1569); on December 27, 1853, they recovered his skeleton, now on view in the cathedral there.

S. Baring-Gould in *Strange Survivals* (1892) writes:

When, in 1842, the remains of the Romano-Batavian temple were explored at Stinvezand, near Rysbergen [Rijsbergen, Netherlands], a singular mummy-like object was found in the foundation. This was doubtless a substitute for the human victim.

Often, however, magicians used the real thing, even for Christian churches. The way that witches and such have pursued personal enmities under the name of magic, and caused the deaths of many people, is a history in itself.

THE MAGIC OF THE UNCONSCIOUS

Novelist Colin Wilson, who has a deep interest in the occult, wrote a foreword in 1978 to *Ritual Magic: An Occult Primer* by David Conway (a pen name). In it, he presents this theory of magic:

> "Magical powers" originate in the unconscious mind. And the reason that we are very naturally sceptical about their existence is that what you call "you" and I call "me" is our *conscious* egos. . . . In most of us, the unconscious has adjusted itself to the routine of everyday life, and sees no good reason to make unusual efforts. . . .

Many others attest to the powers that reside in us, unused, and that enable those who have made "unusual efforts" to perform astonishing feats. Yogi ascetics are only one kind.

SAINTLY MAGIC

Hagiography (idealizing biography of saints) is full of stories of "magic" attributed to saints. Most of these fanciful tales are legendary, pious inventions that became associated with various saints usually long after death. (Indeed many saints—including the beloved Nicholas, Christopher, and George—may have been pious inventions themselves.) It is interesting to note how similar some of the miracles attributed to saints are to feats of sorcery. That magic was real, Saint Thomas Aquinas himself attests to:

> Certain learned men have declared that magic does not exist except in the belief of men who impute to witchcraft the natural effects whose causes are obscure. But this is contrary to all the

authority of the saints, who say that demons have power over the bodies and imaginations of men, when they are permitted by God.

Saint Columba, the Irish missionary to the wild Picts of Scotland, is said to have obtained entry to the barred fort of a pagan king by merely making the sign of the cross. Saint Martin of Tours, a Roman soldier, gave half his cloak to a beggar and that evening had a dream in which Christ appeared to him, wearing the half cloak and saying, "Martin covered me with this garment." Saint Elizabeth of Hungary, carrying bread to the poor, one winter day (which she had been forbidden to do by her husband), was confronted by him unexpectedly. He demanded to know what she was carrying in her apron, and she lied: "Roses." But when he forced her to unfold her apron, out fell roses.

A number of saints have been reported to levitate spontaneously, usually during ecstatic prayer states. These include Ignatius Loyola, Teresa of Avila, John of the Cross, Alphonsus Liguori, and many more. Most remarkable of these was Joseph of Copertino (1603–1663); at Christmas Mass in 1627, he astounded the congregation by floating up into the air. He was accused of black magic, but he got off when he actually flew before Pope Urban VIII. Even on his deathbed in 1663, Joseph floated above his bed until ordered by his superior to desist.

One of the most curious magical phenomena associated with saints is the liquefaction of long-dried-up blood. This is said to happen to vials of the blood of several saints, always in southern Italy, the most famous of whom is Saint Januarius (died A.D. 305), or San Gennaro to Italians. Donald Attwater, in *The Penguin Dictionary of Saints* (1965), has this to say:

> There is preserved in the cathedral at Naples a glass phial containing a substance said to be the dried blood of St Januarius. This relic is shown in public eighteen times a year, when, after a varying interval of time, the substance liquefies. This phenomenon has been carefully examined and seems unquestionably to take place; so far no fully satisfactory explanation of it is forthcoming.

Italian-Americans in New York celebrate the feast of San Gennaro every year on September 19 with a famous street fair. The saint's statue is carried in procession, and food, games, and entertainment stretch out over a ten-block section of Mulberry Street. No blood liquefies, but the saint is considered sufficiently honored by the pleasure enjoyed by 300,000 visitors.

MAGIC AND SCIENCE

As easily as magic could be confused with murder (Mother Lakeland may have poisoned her husband at Ipswich in 1645 but she was burned for killing him by witchcraft), it could also be confused with natural philosophy. Learned men could be students of both magic and science at once.

Arnaldus Villanovanus (1235–1312), for instance, moved from distilling to alchemy and from medicine to magic. He distributed amulets and seals as serious treatment, even to the pope, and he added the black arts to his sound advice on hygiene. Dominicans denounced him as a heretic, and he was lucky to escape death by fire, a fate many of his precious papers did not escape. Feared, he rose high and had the ear of princes. He became counselor to Frederick II, Holy Roman Emperor and king of the Two Sicilies, and to Jaime of Aragon. He was personal physician to three popes: Boniface VIII, Benedict XI, and Clement V. None of his masters seemed to reject his magic.

Another such curious combiner of magic and learning was Raymond Lully (1235–1315), called *Doctor Illuminatus*. Born in Palma, Majorca, where he is now buried, he was educated at the best continental universities of his time: Montpellier (renowned for medicine), Paris, Rome, Naples, and Palermo. He was a noted alchemist, a magician, reputed to be able to turn himself into a red cock. At the age of seventy, he was prominent at the court of Edward II, for whom he is said to have turned twenty-two tons of base metal into gold. Fired with an ambition to convert Islam, he studied Arabic with a Moorish slave, and as an octogenarian, he set out on his mission, only to die within a year or two. The legend that he was stoned to death at Bougie (modern Bejaia, Algeria) cannot be substantiated.

Or consider Sir George Ripley, born in Ripley, Yorkshire, an Augustinian monk who in the fifteenth century was canon of Bridlington; he died in a priory near Boston (the English one) about 1490.

Ripley was universally believed to have made gold alchemically for the Knights of St. John of Jerusalem and was famous in his time. As late as 1678 "Eugenius Philalethes" (who was probably Thomas Vaughan, brother of the mystic poet Henry Vaughan) revived Ripley's published work.

Should a man purported to have made gold out of base metal be regarded as a magician or a scientist? Or put to death, as was Marc-Antoine Bragadin (a Venetian alchemist beheaded as a sorcerer by Wilhelm II, duke of Bavaria)? Should such men have been confined to the madhouse or promoted to the academy?

The early scientists in their laboratories and the magicians in their magic circles (wearing a seamless robe of black, a cap of lead engraved with symbols of the Moon and Venus and Saturn, with a magic wand and a sword and a grimoire) were much confused in the public mind. And, indeed, their roles often overlapped.

ELECTROMAGNETISM

T. C. Lethbridge, Cambridge archaeologist and author of a study of ancient gods entitled "Gogmagog," in *Ghost and Ghoul* (1961), concluded that magic was akin to electromagnetism:

> Magic is the application of resonance, whether it takes the form of thought-reading, projecting images, prophesying, faith-healing, or causing inexplicable death and disaster to an enemy. . . .
> There is one thing about all this magic which seems to be constant. There must at some stage be a link between two minds. It may take such forms as a letter to a psychometrist, a spot of blood to the faith-healer or black magician, a hazel twig to the water-diviner, or a fixed locality to the projector of a ghost . . . a link of some sort must be established before the current of resonance will pass.

PICO

At one point humanist Giovanni Pico della Mirandola (1463–1494) invited "all the scientists of the world" to visit him at Rome and to debate any one or all of his nine hundred theses, among them many concerned with magic and witchcraft. As an occultist who had served Lorenzo the Magnificent and others, Pico considered that "magic is the most notable part of natural sciences," so Pope Innocent VIII forbade the debates on the grounds of heresy, instead appointing a commission to examine his ideas. Pico was under a cloud until 1493 when Pope Alexander VI, the last of the Schoolmen and a philosopher renowned all over Europe, absolved him from charges of heresy.

Alexander VI was not only a Borgia pope of execrable personal and political maneuverings (father of Cesare and Lucretia Borgia) but rumored to be a magician himself. If so, his luck ran out; many think his death in 1503 was due to his having drunk poisoned wine intended for his host, Cardinal da Corneto. Ironically, Pico too was poisoned—by his secretary—but not by mistake.

SAINT-SECAIRE

In Gascony they celebrated a kind of travesty mass called The Mass of Saint-Secaire, in which a rogue priest (assisted by his mistress or minion as acolyte) parodied the mass, everything reversed. It was said at night rather than before noon, it used a triangular Host instead of a round one, water instead of wine, etc. The sign of the cross was made not with the right hand but the left foot. Thought to bring death to enemies, it was frequently offered (and so was a counterspell worked up by the Church) in Gascony where pride, easily bruised honor, and easily lost tempers were proverbial.

GHOST DANCE MAGIC

The American Plains Indian was dependent on the buffalo for food, clothes, even shelter. When the buffalo began to vanish from the plains, under the reckless assault of white men, the Indians faced widespread starvation and disaster. Then in January 1889, a Paiute shaman named Wovoka announced that he had died and visited the Christian God in heaven and had been told that the Indians would be saved from destruction by the Ghost Dance Religion. If they performed the dance and did "no harm to anyone," their plains world would be restored to them. The buffalo would come back to life, as would their ancestors slain in wars with whites, and there would be no more hunger or sickness.

The new cult spread like wildfire, but it was not until it reached the Sioux in Nebraska and Dakota that new prophets began to urge retaliation against the whites. Indians were promised a magical "ghost shirt" that would protect them from white men's bullets.

Instead of allowing the excitement to run its course, white agents sent for the cavalry, and on December 29, 1890, at Wounded Knee Creek, South Dakota, the shameful massacre of three hundred men, women, and children occurred. One of the first to be killed was the fiery old shaman Sitting Bull.

RIGHT-HAND PATH AND LEFT-HAND PATH

Dennis Wheatley, a member of the Secret Planning Committee of Churchill's War Cabinet, later turned to writing popular novels with backgrounds of witchcraft and magic, which sold over 30 million copies in thirty different languages. In *The Devil and All His Works* (a 1971 history of demonism) he defined magic like this:

> Magical operations undertaken for an unselfish purpose belong to white magic, and those who perform them are followers of the Right-hand Path. Operations undertaken for personal ends belong to black magic, and those who perform them are followers of the Left-hand Path.
>
> A considerable number of people are born with psychic gifts. In most cases, when they become aware of this, they use them in minor ways, more usually for the harmless amusement of fortune-telling. As they have not made a deliberate study of magic, their powers are very limited and not having "crossed the abyss," they are not fully committed either to the Right-hand or the Left-hand Path.
>
> To achieve real power is quite a different matter, and a most arduous undertaking. It entails many years of preparation and an almost exclusive preoccupation with the supernatural.

MAGIC WORKS

Éliphas Lévi, a nineteenth-century occultist, asserted that "when anyone invokes the Devil with intentional ceremonies, the Devil comes, and is seen."

If you try hard enough, that's true.

This is no more than to say that anyone who believes sufficiently will experience what he seeks. Whether what is subjectively produced has also an objective reality the true believer cannot tell and perhaps does not care. You have, after all, the power within you to make yourself see anything you can imagine. Whether you should fully use that power or not is up to you.

But the power is *there*, as surely as you are.

MAGIC AND WORDS OF POWER

Magic is full of ambition. It promises power. It says it can make a man a "mighty god." It challenges fate and the laws of nature, attempting to remake the world "nearer to the heart's desire." It dares.

It deals in secret knowledge and words of power. Elsewhere I mention the secret name of God. Also powerful is the word *AGLA*, from *Aieth Gadol Leolam Adonai* ("The Lord will forever be great"). To banish demons that came to devour human hearts, King Solomon is supposed to have chanted *Lofam Solomon Iyouel Iyosemacui*. The Spaniards still say *Ojala ojal oja ojo* to get a husband. Johann Wier in *De Praestigiis Daemonum et Incantionibus ac Veneficiis* (1568) recommended for a toothache *Galbes galbat galdes galdat* (which, my friends say, works; try it) and *Irioni khirioni effer khuder fere* for hydrophobia (which I beg to doubt).

The magic circle for calling up demons.

Used with sigils (seals) and talismans and amulets inscribed with zodiacal symbols or the Tetragrammaton (four letters signifying the "I am" of Jehovah), or even on a scapular or blessed medal of a saint or on parchment inside the mezuzah at the door of a Jewish home or inside a prayer wheel in Tibet, words of power carry the hopes of millions and always have. With this, now just a joke, people used to think they could work miracles:

```
A B R A C A D A B R A
  B R A C A D A B R
    R A C A D A B
      A C A D A
        C A D
          A
```

It was magical, like the "Open Sesame" in *Ali Baba and the Forty Thieves* or "Shazzam" in a comic book—or the device on a door that opens it to you when you speak your name (provided your voice-print is in the computer's memory).

MAGIC MIRROR

In the British Museum you can see an obsidian mirror with an incredible history. How it reached London is not known, but it was definitely brought to Europe after Cortés got it from the Aztec magicians at Tenochtitlán, the capital of the great empire he and his *conquistadores* destroyed in Mexico. The mirror may be fourteenth century or earlier.

It was used by the great English astrologer Dr. John Dee (1527–1608), who listed it among his precious curiosities as "the Devil's Looking-glasse, a Stone." Other owners of the mirror included a seventeenth-century earl of Peterborough, Lady Elizabeth Germain (who died in 1769), a duke of Argyle (who bought it at auction in 1770), Horace Walpole (author of Gothic novels, who received it as a present from Lord Frederick Campbell), John Hugh Smith-Pigott, Lord Londesborough, Hollingworth Magniac, and Prince Alexander Soltykoff. The provenance is clear. What they used it for is obscure.

Dee is said to have employed the black mirror to perform famous feats in the late sixteenth century, sometimes in association with his friend and medium, Edward Kelley. They seem to have used it in 1581 when they were at Walton-le-Dale, Lancashire, searching for buried treasure. You can see their pictures in a rare old print recalling that event; it shows them in a graveyard, confronting a corpse in its shroud, which they have "materialized."

The British Musuem has other souvenirs of Dr. Dee, including some of his books and a disk of pure gold involved with a "vision" Kelley had at Kraków in 1584. Also displayed are three wax disks inscribed with magical figures and names; they were used under Dr. Dee's "shew stone," a crystal ball, which is still extant.

You do not need an obsidian mirror, of course, to try what Dr. Dee did in "scrying," for the top of a black marble clock or even a bowl of water (they say) will do quite as well; but this black mirror seems to me to have an aura about it, seems somehow to be charged with the physic energy of all the outstanding lives it touched, to retain some of the "power" that Cortés and Dr. Dee and others claimed to be able to find in it.

IS MAGIC IMMORAL?

In his master's thesis, "Five Ceremonial Magicians of Tudor-Stuart Drama," Robert J. Goltra, Jr., dealt with magicians in Christopher Marlowe's *Doctor Faustus*, Robert Greene's *Friar Bacon and Friar Bungay*, Anthony Munday's *John à Kent and John à Cumber*, the anonymous *John of Bordeaux*—all plays of the 1580–1590 period in England—and Shakespeare's *The Tempest* (1611). He found "at least three views" concerned with the morality of magic. These were what had come to be the orthodox view (magic was witchcraft and therefore forbidden), the less orthodox but commonly held view (magic was moral or immoral depending on the magician's source of assistance), and the unorthodox view ("presumably held by the goetians [black magicians], that no form of magic was immoral").

What's your view? Or do you not believe in magic at all?

MIRACLES AND MAGIC

In *Legends of the Panjab* (1884–1900) Richard Carnac Temple tells of "counterparts of saints," distinguishing between the miracle workers and the creators of magic. Miracles were good, magic evil. He writes:

> Miracles may be defined as wonders legitimately performed, while magic embraces the class of illegitimate wonders. The actual deeds, whether the result of miraculous powers or magical arts, seem to be much the same. . . . It is good to work marvels miraculously, but very bad to arrive at the same result by magic.

This was the same way it was in Europe in the Age of Faith when saints were credited with and praised for miracles (usually performed for the benefit of others and principally the poor) while sorcerers were hated and feared for magic (usually performed for their own advantage).

STRANGE HERMETIC POWDER

Sir Kenelm Digby (1603–1665) traveled abroad both as naval commander in war and as diplomat in peace, and he brought home to England some great ideas from distinguished friends such as Descartes. He was one of the leading lights and a founding member of the Royal Society, but his undoubtedly important contribution to science—including the discovery that oxygen was essential to the life of plants—was accompanied by some very unscientific reasoning. Take his sympathetic powder, for example.

Sir Kenelm asserted that he had a wonderful recipe for an ointment that could cure wounds if applied not to the wound but to the weapon that made the wound. He also recommended a powder of "blue vitriol" that one applied not to the wounded person but to his bloodstained garments.

This imitative magic had a long history in the West but in this case was attributed to a mysterious Eastern source—and rotten wood:

> Strange Hermetic powder
> That wounds nine mile point blank would solder
> By skilful chemist at great cost
> Extracted from a rotten post. . . .

Perhaps the real source of the powder's "power" was that it left the wound alone, instead of applying the infection-breeding types of salve that were popular in Sir Kenelm's day.

ASTROLOGY AND HEAVENLY CAUSES

The most popular form of divination these days is astrology, in which it is popularly assumed that there is a *causal* connection between the stars and the lives of human beings—that is, that the stars and planets "influence" our actions. Not so. Not even the astrologers of ancient times argued for that. To them, as to every thinking person today, the idea that somehow distant heavenly bodies, reaching us across millions and billions of miles, could cause us to do this or that was incredible.

No, as Northrup Frye puts it, "Astrology is based on a conception of coincidence . . . a synchronic and acausal conception." Which means that the stars are arranged in such a way that there is a *pattern of coincidence* between them and human lives. Thus by studying those heavenly configurations and changes, we can understand more of terrestrial life and fate. Or so say astrologists.

MAGIC AND REALITY

Richard Cavendish suggests that magic is basically facing reality head-on:

> Magic is a power-hunger pursuit and the obvious problem, in theory and frequently in practice, is that finding a positive value in evil can put a seal of approval on the worst of evil impulses. All the same, the attitude has something to be said for it, not as a method of explaining evil away by pretending it is something else, which ultimately will not do, but as a method of trying to deal with it which goes far beyond the confines of magical practice into more elevated philosophies, and eventually into the simple, homely advice to make the best of things.

HOW TO BECOME A SATANIST

Francesco Maria Guazzo, author of the authoritative *Compendium Maleficarum* (1608), tells us exactly what is involved in becoming a Satanist. You must:

1. speak your denial of the Christian faith;

2. get rebaptized, taking a new personal name in the name of the Devil;

3. have the traces of Christian baptism symbolically removed by the Devil's touch;

4. deny your godparents (who are given to help you grow in the Christian faith) and select two new sponsors (who will guide you in the Devil's ways);

5. make a gift of clothing to the Devil, betokening submission;

6. pledge allegiance to the Devil, taking the oath in the magic circle;

16

7. inscribe your new name in the Book of Death;

8. promise to sacrifice children to the Devil;

9. promise to pay annual tribute (usually black clothes) to the Devil;

10. receive the Devil's Mark, creating a secret and insensitive place on your body;

11. vow to the Devil to destroy holy relics and not reveal secrets of the *sabbat.*

If any group offers to sell you a Satanic Bible or enroll you in an atheist or materialist organization for a fee or fails to demand any or all of these requirements of you, be assured you are not dealing with Satan but just with some Church of the Quick Buck or something of that sort. Remember: not all con games are of the Devil nor frauds in his name!

MIND BENDING

There is nothing magical about hypnosis, now an approved scientific tool and not the mysterious "animal magnetism" of the days of Mesmer; and Transcendental Meditation and other manipulations of mind are commonplace.

But the history of magic and witchcraft is replete with extremes of hypnosis and self-hypnosis, hallucination and the power of suggestion, delusion and deception, "altered states," not all of them attributable to fasting or sexual excess, narcotic or so-called mind-expanding drugs, states of trance or ecstasy.

The alchemists were on the right track: The key to the metamorphosis of the mundane is first to transform the mind, and the mind suffers severe strain when operating at or beyond the borders of sanity.

Magic is a dangerous occupation, even if one does not think a protective circle drawn on the ground is essential. "Do what thou wilt" imposes heavy obligations. So do orthodox pronouncements forbidding dabbling with the forbidden or serving "other gods." Even if you do not fear prohibitions, you must be concerned about whether you can handle possible discoveries, within and without, for which nothing has prepared you. Even Saint Theresa's warning about "answered prayers" should give us pause. She cautioned against asking for things—you might get what you really shouldn't have or do not really need.

In the words of an old Latin phrase, *verbum sat sapienti*: "A word to the wise is sufficient."

TO CAST SPELLS WITH KNOTS

One can cast spells by tying knots. The Incas used the quipu—a cord with dependant cords in various colors, knotted in certain ways—to keep records or convey messages. From Scandinavian sorcerers one could buy cords with three knots in them: untie one, slight breeze; untie two, violent wind; untie three, tempest. Very useful for Vikings and other seafaring people.

Mohammed's sûra (chapter) CXIII in the Koran calls magicians' activities "the evil of [women who] are blowers on knots," and at the time of his revelation (commentators suggest) the Prophet was suffering bewitchment from an evil man and his daughters who were "tying eleven knots in a cord which they hid in a well." Here is the story as told by Sir E. A. Wallis in *Amulets and Talismans* (1968):

> The result was that the Prophet fell seriously ill and would undoubtedly have died had not God interfered. He sent down these Sûrahs to him, and also instructed the Archangel Gabriel [who often accompanied Mohammed as a sort of guardian angel] to tell him how to use them, and where the cord was hidden. Muhammed sent Ali to fetch the cord, and when it was brought he recited over the eleven knots the eleven verses of the two Sûrahs, and as he recited each line one of the knots untied itself; as soon as the last knot was loosed Muhammed was freed of his bewitchment, and recovered his normal health.

WOULD YOU LIKE TO WRITE IN YOUR SPARE TIME FOR FUN, FAME, FORTUNE?

Writing is difficult. Many authors need curious stimuli. Some turn to drink. Thomas de Quincey, Wilkie Collins, Jean Cocteau, and others preferred opium. Byron found it helpful to keep a skull on his desk. Balzac wore a special robe when he was writing. Schopenhauer needed purple ink, or he could not write a line. One writer was helped by the smell of rotten apples, which he kept in his desk drawer. Ibsen stared at a picture of Strindberg over his desk and told himself: "He will be greater than I." Poverty has been a good goad.

In a mad book about Satanism, published in Grenoble in 1895, Domenico Margiotta alleges that Adriano Lemmi resorted to perhaps the most shocking stimulus of all. Lemmi (went the charge) "keeps constantly on his desk one of the hosts stolen from the Roman Catholic church and never writes a single line without having stabbed the Holy Eucharist with the pen called 'Calamus Transfigens' ["Piercing Reed"], which he maintains he received for this purpose from his familiar Sybacco, who appears to him with the horns of a bull and three eyes in his forehead."

ELDERBERRY WINE

Few people realize that the elderberry's name comes from Susannah and the Elders who spied on her while she bathed. The berries grow in a cluster upright until they begin to ripen; then the cluster reverses itself and hangs downward, as if in shame. Our forefathers said it hangs its head because it had given shelter to those prying elders.

With seven pounds of mashed elderberries and three gallons of water (plus a handful of raisins, several pounds of sugar, and some yeast) you can take the fruit of the tree and make elderberry wine, though it takes a year to do so and the result is not really worth the effort (in my view) unless you bolster it with brandy. On the other hand, with a wand of elder wood you can perform magic.

THE GIFT OF THE MAGI

The Magi were priests of the ancient Persian religion, which affirms that the supreme being Ahura Mazda (his name appears now mostly on light bulbs and rotary-motorized cars), created twins, reality and unreality. Magic bridges the two, complicating the religion of the Magi, which (Herodotus reported) had "no images of gods, no temples, no altars" and considered such things foolish. Later the Persians turned to the worship of Mithras (a god born of a virgin and resurrected after his death), and the astrologers and adepts gave way to more superstitious practitioners.

PETER OF ABANO

Peter of Abano (1250–1316) was the most famous magician of the very early fourteenth century, and also a famous physician, author of *Conciliator*

Differentium (1303). He argued that astrology was an essential part of the science of medicine, which the University of Paris and other august bodies of the time seemed to accept, and he brought into play a number of Arabic ideas from such doctors as ibn-Rushd (1126–1198), known as Averroës, that eventually were declared heresies by Pope Leo X.

One essentially heretical idea was astrology, for though Roger Bacon and many other scientists had accepted it completely, astrology was fatalistic, deprived man of his free will, and made him subject to the planetary influences. Whether it involved trafficking with demons or not, it put the emphasis not on God but on his creations, the stars and the planets. Saint Thomas Aquinas and many other influential teachers condemned astrology as leading to idolatry. The Church half believed in it and wholly feared it.

Peter of Abano himself (it is claimed) eventually abandoned belief in the stars. He may have been urged to this by having been twice hauled before the Inquisition on charges of practicing magic; he was acquitted at the first trial and died during the second. He is reported as having said that philosophy made him subtle, medicine made him rich, and astrology made him a charlatan.

He might have added that magic made him famous; to magic more than anything else he owed the reputation that caused him to have his statue erected in Padua and Urbino and his named recalled for long after his death.

RITUAL MAGIC

It is only possible here to suggest very briefly the incredible complexity of ritual magic, an art that requires long study and exact performance. But I can outline for you some of the things you need or must keep in mind to perform the ceremonies for some of the most common "intentions": namely achieving your ambition, success, or wealth; astral travel, divine reconciliation, or safe (ordinary) travel; studying for examination or safeguarding the home; disrupting friendship or attaining victory at arms.

To achieve your ambitions as described, you need the rite of Jupiter, auspicious stars (determined by study of astrology), blue hangings and garments, the help of Bethor, Chasmalim (as guardian angel), and the Archangel Zadkiel—and a number of symbols (unicorn, eagle, lion, dragon), metals (especially tin), gems (amethyst and sapphire), plants (oak, poplar, narcissus, agrimony), and perfumes (nutmeg, cinnamon, cloves, aloes, balm). You need incantations and magic implements and maybe sacrifices.

For astral travel, turn to the Moon, violet trappings, silver, crystal, pearl, quartz, hazel, almond, peony, dogs, geese, elephants, Phul and Gabriel, camphor, jasmine, white sandalwood (red is more common but useless here), and frankincense. The guardian angel needed here is Ishim.

For exams, try Saturn, and assemble indigo, civet, musk, crocodiles, crows, ash, yew, cypress, hemlock, lead, onyx, sapphire, a woman, Aratron the planetary spirit, Zaphael the archangel, and Aralim as guardian angel. There is a disagreement about colors. You could try yellow. Indigo may work better for you, though.

Causing discord or war is very serious indeed and needs the rite of Mars, with scarlet trappings, horses, wolves, bears, stags, a basilisk, rue, absinthe, a magic sword, lamb's tongue, iron implements, rubies, and Phaleg, Chamael, and the Seraphim.

So, if you and your friends, or just people you have heard about, are not getting truly magical results, maybe the proper tools are lacking—and, of course, the *timing* of magic and the *state of mind* of the magician and the *vibes* (as we might call them these says) must all be right. Ritual magic you may think is only for the credulous; most certainly it is not for the careless.

"DRAW A CIRCLE ROUND HIM THRICE"

Medieval magicians performed their rites within a magic circle (symbolic of protection, perfection, involvement, infinity) nine feet in diameter. This yielded the magical three times three and plenty of space to write Names of Power (in a band a foot wide) and place necessary bowls of water, herbs, crosses, the name of God anagrammatized, apt Biblical quotations, etc. The circle can be painted (ideally with paint containing elements of the philosopher's stone such as mercury and sulfur), made of a magnetized iron chain or (best of all) drawn with a magic sword.

This is convenient for me—I happen to live in a house with round towers nine feet in diameter inside—but inconvenient in a small apartment.

You do not need other circles outside the one I describe, despite what modern witches seem to think, unless you have assistants who need protection from the demon(s) to be summoned. Why not handle the work with no help? Demons are often easier to manage than assistants.

According to Éliphas Lévi, the circle drawn for evil magic (in that case absolutely drawn in the direction opposite the sun's movement) *must* be drawn with a magic sword. But there is really little use telling you how to make that useful object. Even if you had a magic sword, where would you get such other necessary supplies as strips of parchment (you could use goat's skin) nailed down with four nails from a criminal's coffin (the *Grand Grimoire* specifies a baby's coffin nails), vervain, chains from a gibbet, and candles of human fat in black wooden candlesticks?

THE RUNES

Runes were invented by Teutonic people as a crude way of writing messages, but they came in time to be considered powerful magic. They were thought to be able to keep the dead in their graves or to resurrect them, and each one had its name and its power.

The Saga of Egil, probably by Snorri Sturluson in the thirteenth century, tells how Egil, presented with an alehorn of poison drink, cut the ale runes on it, rubbed the runes with a drop of his own blood while he recited the magic incantation, and the horn "sprang asunder, and the drink spilled down into the straw."

At Björketorp in Sweden the runes that in Iceland protected Egil in Sweden protected a monument with the inscription:

I hid here magic runes, undisturbed by evil witchcraft. He shall die who destroys this monument.

The Swedes gave up the runes in the Middle Ages. The Icelanders passed a law in 1639 that anyone using the runes would be burned as a witch. But—in Germany in recent times—less civilized persons continued to attempt to use their magic. In the early twenties Adam Glauer (1875–1945), who liked to be called the Freiherr Rudolf von Sebottendorf, started a short-lived and virulently anti-Semitic organization called the German Orden, and Teutonic runes were part of their secret foolishness. This seems to have affected Heinrich Himmler, who chose *Sig* (the rune for "S") doubled as the symbol of his SS organization.

THE CRYSTAL BALL

If only from jokes and slang expressions, the average person knows that a crystal ball is used by some people to "see" the future. I think its so-called magic is in its ability to concentrate the mind of the "seer" (a bowl of water or any bright object or a number of other things would do as well) and permit him or her to look into his subconscious mind or even (some people think) to pick up "vibrations" from the "sitter" who is there to have a fortune told. To avoid the latter, some people have their fortunes read by proxies.

The holder for the ball is often inscribed with various magical symbols and names. Devotees treat the ball itself carefully, will let no one touch it lest they "charge" it wrong, and fortify it before they use it by making magical passes over it with the hands: with the right hand to render it stronger and more powerful, with the left hand to render it more sensitive. A good deal of this gesturing goes on before the ball is looked into.

Then in the ball, or in a kind of haze that comes between the "seer" and the ball after intense watching, one may see "clouds" of various hues and motions, and these are to be interpreted as follows:

white	favorable, auspicious
black	unfavorable, inauspicious
violet green blue }	excellent, coming joy
red crimson }	danger, trouble, illness
orange	deception, betrayal, slander
yellow	loss, trickery, unpleasant surprises

If the clouds are ascending, that is an affirmative answer to the question asked; if the clouds are descending, that is a negative response.

The basic book on this is John Melville's *Crystal-Gazing and the Wonder of Clairvoyance* (1920).

BLEEDING HOSTS MATERIALIZED?

Consecrated Hosts used in sorcery are usually stolen, but a man named Vintras used to materialize them, people claimed.

Pierre-Michel Vintras (1807–1875) was born Eugène Vintras and later was called Strathaniel ("Herald of God"). He was the author of an important *Oeuvre de la Miséricorde* ("Work of Compassion") and was well known for conducting magical ceremonies. The "fact" that at some of these ceremonies he used to materialize *bleeding* Hosts, in full view of everyone present, was often reported.

That people believed this was done, that they testified it was done before their very eyes and was not sleight of hand, is remarkable; and it is even more remarkable (I think) that the debates I have found in the literature of magic in France in the last century are not about whether he did that or not; they argue about whether he *ought* to have done that or not. His enemies call him not a trickster but a blasphemer; he is not accused of fakery but of evil magic.

Vintras with his shocking ceremonies surely was blaspheming in at least one way, for as early as Origen (185–255), who wrote in his *Homilies* that "scripture rightly prohibits the use of magic," the Church was moving ever farther away from exorcisms ("In My Name shall they cast out devils," Mark 16:17) and connecting magic only with the Evil One. "No good spirit obeys a magician," Origen warned.

EXURGENT MORTUI ET AD ME VENIUNT

"The dead arise and come to me," chants the necromancer. Incredible as it may seem, people once generally believed that the dead could be brought physically from their graves by magic, not the spirits (as in spiritualism) but the bodies. The artist and autobiographer Benvenuto Cellini claims soberly that a necromancer brought to him his dead mistress Angelica "for several minutes, materialized."

Just as Saul consulted the dead Samuel, in the *Epic of Gilgamesh* the hero evokes the ghost of his friend Enkidu. In the *Odyssey* the hero consults the dead soothsayer Tiresias. In Aeschylus' *The Persians* Atossa's calling up of the ghost of Darius the Great is regarded as perfectly possible and credible. The ghost of Constantine the Great (Michael Glycas wrote) appeared to his father, summoned by the magic of Santabarenus. Macbeth has the witches call up people yet unborn, the line of kings to be descended from Banquo (whom Macbeth has had murdered), including James VI of Scotland and I of England, sitting in Shakespeare's audience at a royal performance of the play.

As one of its tasks, the Society for Psychical Research has energetically weeded out fraudulent practitioners. But contemporary mediums have a self-serving rule: Touch a "manifestation," and the medium in a trance will die.

My favorite medium story involves a man invited to quiz the spirits at a séance. He asked if he could see his grandfather. After some impressive mumbo jumbo, the luminous figure hovered near. The young man was told, "I am your grandfather." He then asked if he could pose a question. Granted permission, he solemnly asked: "Grandfather, what are you *doing* here; you aren't dead!"

That was the end of that little séance.

2
Witchcraft

WITCHCRAFT differs from magic in two particulars. First, it is, above all, the people's magic. The witch did not pore over cabalistic screeds or ancient grimoires (magicians' manuals), draw on the ground elaborate circles filled with Hebraic inscriptions, or chant the many names of gods and devils. Usually she could not read or write at all. She had her little charms and spells, her amulets and fetishes, her herbal cures and secret potions, but essentially her magic was performed on a small scale. She could cure your headache, but she did not raise spirit armies.

Second, witchcraft—unlike magic, which was one of the learned arts— is considered the survival of an ancient form of worship, tens of thousands of years old. This "Old Religion," or worship of a Horned God, is said to have existed side by side with Christianity. (Not all historians agree on this theory, and even those who do have not worked out the connection between this "worship" and the village wise woman with her charmed herbal cures.) The great feasts of this supposed Horned God were four, all celebrated at midnight: February 1–2 (Candlemas); April 31–May 1 (May Day, Beltane, or Walpurgis); July 31–August 1 (Lammas); and October 31–November 1 (the eve of All Saints Day, or All Hallows Eve). The last of these has, of course, survived as the children's holiday, Halloween.

On these four nights, witches were said to leave their village homes by stealth, repair to the meeting place where they held their sabbat, or assembly, presided over by a man wearing the mask and skins of a goat and representing the Horned God. It was these meetings that Christian leaders interpreted as Satan worship.

In the early Middle Ages, sabbats were either not known to the authorities or were quietly overlooked. A woman charged with witchcraft—for casting a murrain (sickness) on a neighbor's cattle, say—was usually fined, reprimanded, and released. It was not until the fifteenth century, when the tensions of the highly charged Renaissance galvanized a sleeping Europe into activities of all sorts, that the really savage persecutions began. They were to continue for nearly three hundred years.

WITCH MASK OF DORSET

If anyone has an ooser for sale, I'd like to know. There were a great many of them around at one time, or so it is claimed. I suspect a few examples are still to be found somewhere.

An ooser was a horned mask, with a boss on the forehead where some people would locate the psychic "third eye," and was used to give the wearer the appearance of a devil or a heathen god. In seventh-century England, Theodore, archbishop of Canterbury (688–690), tried to root out their use:

> Whoever at the Kalends of January [Christmas season] goes about as a stag or bull; that is making himself into a wild animal and dressing in the skin of a herd animal, and putting on the heads of beasts; those who in such wise transform themselves into the appearance of a wild animal, penance for three years because this is devilish.

Doreen Valiente in *An ABC of Witchcraft Past & Present* (1973) draws our attention to *os* (god) in names such as Oswald (God-power), Osmund (God-protection), and so on. So the ooser may have been worn in imitation of *os*, or a heathen god.

The mask certainly suggests the Horned God of the witches. One of his titles, *Hu*, meaning "everywhere," explains the "Har, har, hou, hou" cries reported of witches dancing on the "goat field"—that is, the sabbat meeting place. His horns and cloven feet and tail are the probable origin of our modern concept of the Devil. The costume of the dancer who wore the ooser is similar to that seen in the most ancient cave paintings, where men are depicted cavorting in the skins of animals.

Valiente reports:

> As late as 1911, a Dorset newspaper carried a report of a man being charged with frightening some girls by chasing them when he was "dressed in a bullock's skin and wearing an ooser."

If you see another of those horned and horrible masks, let me know; I'd like to make sure it goes to those in Dorset to whose supposedly long tradition it belongs and does not simply hang on someone's wall as decoration.

APPLES

As one example of how ordinary things are related to sorcery, take the apple. Throughout history, apples have been thought of as having magical properties.

Remembering pre-Christian customs, English countrymen still "wassail" their apple trees and have many folk customs related to apples. Without any idea of the origin of the "game," children bob for apples on Halloween or tell the initial of the one they will marry by throwing apple peels.

One of the most terrifying moments of my childhood was when, in Walt Disney's *Snow White*, I saw the horrible old witch offer a shiny apple to our heroine. If you saw this cartoon as an impressionable child, I'll bet it scared you too.

Even more frightening, when seen through our eyes, is this report by one of the earliest good writers on witchcraft in England, Joseph Glanvill, author of *Sadducismus Triumphatus* (1681). He was Charles II's chaplain and a leading scientific mind of the period. He wrote:

> On Sunday, the 15th of November, 1657, about Three of the Clock in the Afternoon, Richard Jones, then a sprightly youth about twelve years old, Son of Henry Jones of Shepton Mallet in the County of Somerset, being in his Father's house alone, and perceiving one looking in at the Windows, went to the Door,

where one Jane Brooks of the same Town (but then by name unknown to this Boy) came to him. She desired him to give her a piece of close Bread, and gave him an Apple.

Soon after the boy suffered from fits and neighbors said he flew over the garden wall. He became the center of controversy: Was he bewitched? Jane Brooks's sister (who had once said "How do ye, my honey?" to the boy) escaped after close questioning, but Jane Brooks herself was sentenced to death by the Chard Assizes and hanged on March 26, 1658.

ALEX SANDERS

Seduced by his seventy-four-year-old grandmother in his teens, Alex Sanders says this started him off as a witch. His biography was called *King of the Witches*. He is credited with founding 107 covens.

NICHOLAS TROTT

Judge Trott told a Charleston, South Carolina, jury in 1703:

They that have given good proof of apparitions and witches have done service to the common cause of religion, for if there be such creatures as witches, then there are certainly spirits by whose aid and assistance they act, and by consequence there is another invisible world of spirits. . . . That there are creatures [such] as witches I make no doubt, neither do I think that they can be denied, without denying the truth of the Holy Scriptures, or most grossly perverting the sense of them.

If you believe in God, you believe in Satan, in angels, in devils—or so claimed such seventeenth-century experts as the clergyman Cotton Mather and King James I.

BABA YAGA

One of the most gruesome of European folktales involves the hideous Russian witch named Baba Yaga, who is said to live in a ramshackle cottage that moves around on chicken legs. It is surrounded by the skulls and bones of her victims, many of the children like those of the hag in Hansel and Gretel.

Baba Yaga is said not only to be a cannibal but also to have the power to turn you to stone with a glance. She secretly sucks the breasts of beautiful women while they sleep, rendering them shriveled and ugly. She eats children and consumes the souls of the dead. And at night Baba Yaga rides through the air not on a broom but on a blazing mortar.

"GIMME THAT OL' TIME RELIGION"

There are more survivals of paganism than you imagine, just disguised a little for Christian consumption. In medieval times, old statues of Venus and Cupid were sometimes equipped with halos and dubbed "Madonna and Child." Zoroastrianism gave us Easter eggs, and Teutonic animism produced Christmas trees.

In the United States many old customs still flourish and superstitions persist, even if not one person in a million who refuses to walk under a ladder knows that the bad luck is supposed to come from violating the Trinity or that the black cat who crosses your path may be a witch's familiar.

Some of the American customs came from England, and there they also still flourish. I have attended celebrations of the goddess Flora (turned into the Queen of the May) and "clipped a church" (the congregation stands around in a ring of power, holding hands, as the Romans did on the Feast of Lupercalia) and attended many harvest festivals (blessing the plow, decorating the church, strewing the church floors with hay, rush bearing). Our pagan ancestors would find it very familiar if they dropped in today. The rising from the dead in mummers' plays and the antics of morris dancers have very distant pagan origins. "Pace egging" (rolling Easter eggs) goes back to rolling the stone away from the tomb of Jesus.

I have seen the bonfires not only on Guy Fawkes' Day (November 5— when one of the conspirators who tried to blow up the houses of Parliament more than three hundred years ago is burned in effigy) but on Midsummer Eve (June 23). A string of bonfires—"good" fires? bone fires?—stretches across Cornwall's ancient duchy that night, and people jump over the flames for fertility, throwing in the "simples" and herbs of witches' concoctions.

London has not seen a maypole since the last century (and I believe they are still illegal in Massachusetts) but you can still dance around one in Devon. These days the garlands of Garland Day (in Abbotsbury, Dorset) wind up on the war memorial, but the pagan origins are still visible. In certain Yorkshire towns, the Devil's Knell is tolled each Christmas Eve—but some of the age-old customs are very much alive.

TO KEEP AWAY WITCHES

To keep witches out of your house, Hispanics in Texas suggest you kneel and recite this prayer three times in a low voice:

> *Cuatro esquinas tiene mi casa*
> *Cuatro angeles que la adoran,*
> *Lucas, Marcos, Juan, y Mateo.*
> *Ni brujas, ni hechiceras,*
> *Ni hombre malchechor.*
> *En el Nombre del Padre,*
> *Y del Hijo, y del Espiritu Santo.*

> Four corners has my house.
> Four angels adore it,
> Luke, Mark, John, and Matthew.
> Neither witches, nor charmers,
> Nor maleficent man [can harm me].
> In the Name of the Father,
> And of the Son, and of the Holy Ghost.

HOODOO

A hoodoo bag contains certain herbs, dirt (most effective if from a grave), maybe a piece of cloth (preferably red), even hair or fingernail clippings of the person to be hoodooed. To gain the power to hoodoo, a person has to sell his or her soul to the Devil, who appears for the purpose as a black bird at midnight on the darkest possible night.

Look around your house or apartment to be sure you have not been hoodooed. If there is a snake bone in your pillow or "wreathes" or "knots" in a feather pillow or a little bag tied to the tester of your bed, you have been hoodooed. Look for cards stacked over the door or a little doll with a pin in it or a loaf of bread with pitch on it or salt and pepper on your doorstep. Look for peculiar marks on your body, wounds that will not heal, a *gris-gris* (talisman) made of feathers or horsehair and other materials tied up with a red thread, or unusual knots in your horse's tail or mane, or pains in the wrists (if your wrists "open," you can "close" them by wearing bits of red flannel around your wrists). If you open your front door and there is a tiny coffin, with or without a hoodoo doll in it, you are in extremely bad trouble: This (in case you missed the other two) is your third and last warning that you have had the curse put upon you, and you are going to die.

You are not powerless, of course. You can get another hoodoo woman (other than the one who laid the curse) to take it off you—even to send it back whence it came. You can let a little blood or have teeth drawn (hoodoo often enters the teeth) or burn special candles (any color but red—red is the color of candle that brings down the curse on people) or say special prayers or destroy the hoodoo doll or bag with fire or running water. You can discover if people who have visited and have expressed sympathy with the trouble you have suffered are the actual cause of it or not. Just melt lead and cool it soon after their visit. If it cools smooth, they are friends; if it cools rough, they are "bad mouth" enemies.

Wear a silver coin on a string around your neck or get some other charm against falling victim to a hoodooer in future. Or become a hoodoo adept yourself, for protection!

TRANSVECTION

Goya's *Caprichios* shows witches on brooms sailing through the air. Many people used to think witches really did fly, and they testified to it under oath and under torture. Some learned men said it was impossible, but added that if witches thought they could fly, then that was proof enough that they had sold their souls to the Devil. Burn them anyway, said seventeenth-century Scots.

The earliest picture I can find of witches depicted as flying is by Ulrich Molitor, dated 1489, and shows them mounted on forked branches, rather like dowsing rods, not the brooms you see in pictures of Halloween witches. Soon popular art depicted witches aloft on sticks, tree trunks, pokers—anything phallic, in fact—but broomsticks predominated, since the broom was a symbol for a woman. Italian witches (*stregas*) traveled on mules. There are stories of the parking lot at sabbats containing he-goats (always black), dogs (black), and these days Rolls-Royces (also black).

The broomsticks were anointed with a special unguent. Witches on trial were always being asked for the recipe. The ointments usually would have excited the sexual organs, numbed the feet and hands, and made the witches

"high," if not on their broomsticks, then on drugs. Hallucinogenic incense could also have had an effect.

Some people were just not buying the story. Gian Francesco Ponzinibio's *Tractatus Subtilis et Elegans de Lamiis* (the Lamia being a predatory witch that turns up frequently in Romantic literature) published in Venice in 1563 was neither subtle nor elegant in its dismissal of the whole idea of witches flying.

Martin Luther introduced a healthy Protestant skepticism. Of course witches did not fly to their sabbats, their *souls* were transported there, he said. Had he taken one step more and said they went there *in their minds*, I think he would have hit upon the truth.

Luther, however, was up against equally argumentative, dogmatic, and learned Biblical scholars ready to cite him chapter and verse. Did not Satan transport Jesus to the pinnacle of the Temple? Had not Christ gone straight up to Heaven on the day of the Ascension? Saints were occasionally levitated. So why not witches?

Witches kept confessing they flew, proof of a pact with the Devil. One seventeen-century verdict I like was: "Not guilty. No flying." Bishop François Sadoval in *Historie de Charles V* states that a witch was kind enough to give him a demonstration of flying, right in court. Taking her helpfulness into account, he pardoned her on the charge of witchcraft.

Today we talk more of teleportation and astral projection.

SWINGING WITCHES

Magic and witchcraft often demand highly excited states in the participants. Medieval witches sometimes used to be put into sacks and swung from trees to bring on ecstatic visions.

I know a New York wizard who used one of the rides at Coney Island for exactly this purpose. But the Cyclone and roller coasters in general made it "impossible to concentrate."

BLACK MASS

Over the centuries, black masses, travesties of Christian ritual, have been said for patrons as different as the fifteenth-century soldier Gilles de Retz and the eccentric nineteenth-century novelist William Beckford. The black mass, often undertaken by some renegade priest, has been recorded as early as the seventh century and is regarded by French historian Jules Michelet as a "peasant revolt against the church." Other scholars believe, as we have said elsewhere, that it was in reality a survival of ancient pagan religious forms.

It was usually practiced at night and in secret out of fear of Christian reprisal. Some members of the "congregation," called a coven, rubbed themselves with the juice of belladonna or deadly nightshade (the source of the modern drugs atropine and hyoscine), which is said to have given them the illusion of flying through the air to the rendezvous. This was always a lonely spot, preferably a ruined or deconsecrated church. There, torches and braziers of pitch burned balefully, adding to the smoky confusion.

Roman Catholic ritual is turned upside down, into sacrilege and blasphemy. In place of aspersion with holy water, the coven is sprinkled with urine. The kiss of peace, a ceremonial embrace among the officiating clergy at high mass, becomes a kiss on the posterior. The body of a nude woman is the "altar." Everything is black: the vestments, the hangings, the garments of the participants. Black bread and black wine (like the heather beer of the Picts) can be used, but a stolen Host is considered the most efficacious. Sometimes a toad is elevated and broken instead of the Host. Some authorities recommend a slice of black or red turnip. Often a goat or other animal is sacrificed.

Early in the fourteenth century, in an effort to free himself of money troubles, Philip IV of France attacked the rich and powerful Knights Templars with charges of witchcraft, sodomy (acts of homosexuality), and cannibalism. Under torture, the Grand Master, Jacques de Molay, and 140 knights confessed to such abominations as substituting the nude body of a young boy for that of a nude woman at the "altar" of a black mass, and on March 18, 1314, de Molay was burned at the stake. Since that day, the toad used at black masses has been called a "philippe," after the king.

Today a black mass in honor of the Horned God is most likely to be held in a suburban house or a city apartment. A pungent incense from the local "head shop" replaces the urine, subdued electric light illuminates the scene, and if a sacrifice is made, it is presumably carried out with neatness and decorum. The performance, however, is often expected to end in a sex party, much like the original.

WOMEN'S LIBERATION

Jules Michelet claimed the black mass was "the redemption of Eve from the curse Christianity had laid upon her," a liberation because "at the Sabbath woman fulfills every office," while women still cannot be ordained priests in many Christian churches.

But at the sabbat, Michelet points out, woman "is priest, and altar, and consecrated host, whereof all people communicate. In the last resort, is she not the very God of the Sacrifice as well?"

WITCH TREE

An example (which can stand for many) of how corruption of a word can give birth to a folk belief is to be found in the case of "witch hazel" or "witch wood," names for the mountain ash or rowan, long believed to have magical powers to defend against witchcraft.

But, as dialect shows us with the name "wick wood," these trees are not connected with witches but simply "alive." The Anglo-Saxon was *cwic-beám*, and that *cwic* ("alive") we still have, though you may never have noticed it, in expressions such as "cut to the quick" and "the quick and the dead."

The great Elizabethan herbalist Gerard (1597) refers to this: "This *Ornus* or great Ash is named . . . in English wilde Ash, *Quicken tree*, Quickbeame tree, and *Whicken tree*."

But the sacred grove of the Druids and other tree worshippers combined with the corruption of the language in English to make a witch tree out of an "alive tree," and in German also now magic is connected with the witch hazel, called *Zauberstrauch* ("magic shrub").

FASCINATING AND EVIL GLANCES

From the time before history, throughout the world, men have believed that witches and similar malefactors can injure with a glance. They call this the Evil Eye. In England women were burned at the stake for it. In Ireland witches with "eye-biting" powers were said to harm cattle. In Cornwall, as recently as a century ago, people bought "witch powders" to protect children or cattle that had been "overlooked" by someone possessed of the Evil Eye. A writer in *The Graphic* (December 1882) said that such witchcraft was more common in the West of Britain then that it was in Africa.

Fear of the Evil Eye is noted in many phallic and other amulets worn by Italian-Americans (and others) and is part and parcel of life in such places as southern Italy and Sicily. Montague Summers writes:

> Throughout Italy nobody is so feared as he who has this baleful influence, *mal d'occhio*. In the South *jettatura* [sic] is the common term. At the appearance of a person having this reputation the most crowded street in Naples will empty in a moment. The cry *Jettatore!* is heard. Everyone vanishes, rushing into shops, into churches, up entries, down side-alleys, helter-skelter, anywhere.

In Italian thinking, anyone can be born with this destructive gaze. The *jettatore*, writes Lawrence Di Stassi in 1981, "through no apparent fault of his own . . . is said to be born with eyes that damage whatever they see. Wherever he goes, he is feared." F. T. Elworthy in *The Evil Eye* (1895) tells of a hapless Polish father who believed that he possessed this unconscious power; he blinded himself rather than do harm to his children with his glance.

In popular belief, not even popes were spared the Evil Eye. Giovanni Maria Mastai-Ferrett (1792–1878), who reigned as Pope Pius IX, *Pio Nino*, was widely believed to have the *mal d'occhio*. In his last years, wherever he went in procession, the streets emptied; people who could not avoid his presence averted their eyes, crossed themselves (or their fingers), made the defensive sign by extending the first and fourth fingers and holding back the second and third and the thumb. Actually Pius IX was a devout prelate, much involved in the bitter battles in Italy between Church and State, and it was in his papacy that the doctrine of papal infallibility was declared. But infallible or not, Italians (and others) were terrified to look him in the eye.

THOSE SATANISTS DON'T COMMIT SACRILEGE

And they won't say a black mass. Gordon Wellesley in *Sex and the Occult* (1975) points out that "to the true follower of Lucifer the Host or the Crucifix means nothing, so to him there would be no point in violating them or committing sacrilege." A true Satanist has no interest in outraging Christians, Jews, or Muslims; he has his own "god" to serve.

But, you say, to *me* they are committing a sacrilege. However, it's God who is concerned in matters of that sort, and any good theologian will tell you without intention there can be no sin.

NAMES

You can do witchcraft using names; it's connected with numerology. In covens people often use just first names or adopted names. In some magical organizations, one is baptized in the name of the Devil (by some thought essential if one has previously been baptized a Christian) and given a new name. In others people take new names as, for example, people do upon entering certain religious orders.

Familiars usually have names, as you may have noted from the witches' scenes in *Macbeth* (where Greymalkin and others turn up), from the play *Bell, Book, and Candle* (where the cat has the old-fashioned name of Pyewacket), and so on, if not from the grimoire handbooks where cats are to be called Greedigut, Howffbacket, and such.

Other ceremonies require Egyptian or the ability to use the alphabets of the Rosicrucians or Masons, runes, the Ogham scratches (named after the Gaulish god of speech), even the Malachim alphabet or Celestial script.

BANISHING WITCHES

The Scots waved firebrands at Halloween and chanted:

This is the night of Halloween.
All the witches to be seen,

> Some of them black, and some of them green,
> And some of them like a randy quean [prostitute].
> Halloween we fear will come.
> Witchcraft will be done by some.
> Burn your brand and let us see
> Confusion to the witches be!

Cleansing by fire is an old practice but be careful: Certain candles can attract spirits.

SATAN'S MEMBER

Marguerite de Sare, aged seventeen, of Labourd, France, told inquisitor Pierre de Lancre, a famous expert on witchcraft, that the Devil's penis was "like a mule's, [he] having chosen to imitate that animal as best endowed by nature; that it was as long and thick as an arm." De Lancre commented:

> Quite the opposite is told by [Henri] Bouget, who says that the witches he was prosecuting in the Franche-Comté have never seen one longer than a finger and correspondingly thin. All that can be said is that Satan serves the witches of Labourd better than he does the witches of Franche-Comté.

Sylvester Pierias wrote in 1521 that evidence was plentiful to suggest that the Devil's penis was bifurcated. Many witches spoke of this under torture and added that the Devil's semen was cold, his foreplay was clumsy, and his performance was painful.

De Lancre's *Tableau de l'Inconstance des Mauvais Anges* (1612) recorded this "eye-witness account" of a sabbat's orgiastic conclusion:

> The Devil in the form of a goat, having his member in the rear, had intercourse with women by jiggling and shoving that thing against their belly. Marie de Marigrane, aged 15 years, resident of Biarritz, testified that she had often seen the Devil copulate with a group of women, whom she knew by forename and surname, and that it was the custom of the Devil to have intercourse with the beautiful women from the front and the ugly from the rear.

BATTLE DRESS

The Mau-Mau in Kenya and the blacks revolting against the Tshombe government of the Congo in midtwentieth century underwent witchcraft ceremonies to make them invulvernable to the bullets of the enemy. Then they ran berserk.

That old word "berserk" goes back to the Vikings who in "bear shirts" ran amok, also considering themselves impervious, invincible. Their mad eyes and terrifying screams as they attacked in a state of frenzy frightened their opponents.

Some British regiments still wear bearskin busbies, but the old British habit of painting soldiers blue to scare the enemy (that so shocked the invading Romans) has now been abandoned. It is impossible to say when the British stopped painting themselves to strike horror into their enemies, but we all know that warpaint (which also had a magical component) was used by the Amerindians.

SURFING WITCH

At Newbury in 1643 during the early days of the Civil War in England the Roundheads of Cromwell got a shock from a surfing witch. She was "taken by some of the Parliament Forces, as she was standing on a small planckboard and sayling on it over the River of Newbury."

GOOD WITCH

"Witch" originally meant a good witch. The Anglo-Saxon *wicca* means "a magician who weakens the power of evil." All witchcraft means to do good; the bad use of these powers is sorcery.

THE LEGACY OF WITCHCRAFT

Guazzo's influential *Compendium Maleficarum* (1608), an encyclopedia of witchcraft, spoke of "the contagion to children by their sinful parents" and the fact that witches introduced their offspring into the evil rites; indeed it was suggested that witchcraft was almost hereditary. Certainly many seventeenth-century documents attest to women dedicating their children to the Devil, or so they confessed.

Many people claim that witchcraft has run in their families for generations, and in America it is often believed that powers such as "second sight" are inherited. Of course, though most of the witches accused in England between 1556 and 1712 were women and children, the word "witch" can also mean a man; some fathers handed on the tradition and maybe even the talents to their sons.

In Africa it is generally believed that magical powers are inherited but only through the mother. Most American witches and even warlocks claim to derive their powers, if they believe them to have been "gifts," from their mothers.

The Rental of Sir Edward Moore (1677) tells us he had two tenants who were witches, Margaret Ley and her sister, the Widow Bridges. Their mother "who died thirty years agone," it is said, "was poor." When she died "she had nothing to leave" the girls but "her two spirits," familiars who assisted the daughters all through their lives. "God bless me," commented one writer, "and all mine from such legacies. Amen."

It is interesting to note that the executioners who put the witches to death were also in a trade handed down in families. Members of the famed Famille Samson served as Monsieur de Paris (official executioner and torturer) for seven consecutive generations, 1635–1889.

MACBETH'S NIGHT

Now o'er the one half world
Nature seems dead, and wicked dreams abuse
The curtain'd sleep; witchcraft celebrates
Pale Hecate's offerings; and wither'd murder,
Alarum'd by his sentinel the wolf,
Whose howl's his watch, thus with his stealthy pace,
With Tarquin's ravishing strides, towards his design
Moves like a ghost.
                    —William Shakespeare

AKHELARRE

The above is the Basque word for sabbat which means "goat pasture." That's where these assemblages of witches were supposed to be held.

WELSH RABBITS

The eminent historian and naturalist Giraldus Cambrensis (Gerald de Barri, 1147–1223) recounts many marvels with a straight face, among them how witches turned into hares and, in this form, drank milk from the cattle.

URBAN BLIGHT

The sixteenth-century diary of Giancinto Gigli in the library of the Vatican tells an incredible story of machinations involved in the struggle for the papacy. It was a chancy time to be pope anyway; between 1590 and 1592, three different men wore the tiara.

Gigli was the nephew of Cardinal d'Ascensio, believed by some to have a good chance at the throne of Peter—if and when Urban VII should vacate it. Other people were anxious to hasten that along, too—by witchcraft if necessary.

Now, trying to encompass the death of a pope by witchcraft was tricky. But Urban VII seemed vulnerable, so it was worth a try.

They did a sort of dry run with the wax image of a woman. The woman died. Encouraged, they made one of the pope. But it would not melt. They tried again but realized they needed a stronger spell, one that used human blood.

The conspirators drew lots to see whose blood they would use. Gigli lost. He demurred. And he pointed out that Cardinal d'Ascensio was *his* uncle and that later on the conspirators might find themselves in a position where it would be useful to have him to intercede for them. Seeing the wisdom of this argument, all the conspirators could do was to draw lots a second time.

The intended blood-supply then proved no more willing than Gigli had been. In fact, he ran right off to the Holy Office (the Inquisition) and spilled the beans, naming all the conspirators.

They were immediately rounded up, quickly tried, condemned, and burned alive in the Campo dei Fiori for trying to bring about the death of the Vicar of Christ.

Urban died shortly afterward anyway. His successor was *not* Cardinal d'Ascensio.

QUALIFIED M.D.

The witch doctor in the New Hebrides is not considered fully prepared until he has captured a wild boar whose tusks have grown in a spiral. He then wears a tusk on a cord around his neck, much the way your doctor puts his diplomas on the wall. It inspires confidence.

THE WITCH OF ENDOR

The Witch of Endor was acceptable for King Samuel to visit, despite the law that "thou shalt not suffer a witch to live," because she was not a witch; she was a diviner.

The Scriptures call her *ba'alath ob* (mistress of a talisman), not *kashaph* (sorceress). The Hebrew words hint at her practice of cutting herself and using the blood ("the life itself") in the worship of Baal.

In *The Discoverie of Witchcraft* hard-headed Reginald Scot suggests the Biblical word meant simply "poisoner," not witch, an idea some later scholars have embraced.

SAINT PATRICK AND THE WITCHES

A fanciful story is recorded in Charles Kirkpatrick Sharpe's *A Historical Account of the Belief in Witchcraft in Scotland* (1884):

About the year 338, the singular piety of St. Patrick, according to tradition, became so offensive to the devil, that he incensed the whole body of witches in Scotland against him. In a band they assailed the astonished saint, who fled toward the river Clyde, near the mouth of which he found a little boat, wherein he immediately leapt, and set off for Ireland. It is well known that witches cannot cross a running stream in pursuit of their prey; but these tore a huge fragment of rock from an neighboring hill and hurled it after Patrick, taking, however, so bad an aim, that the mass fell harmless to the ground. . . .

It became, "with some additions from art," the fortress of Dumbarton.

A CAVEAT TO IRISH WITCHES

I pass along this warning to the half dozen Irish witches I happen to know personally.

So far as I can determine, the statute of the Irish Parliament of 1586 (passed to bring Irish law into line with that of the English) has never been repealed. Now, the English have given up punishing witches, but this Irish law threatens the pillory or imprisonment or both for the first offense and death as a felon for the second.

It also provides that the government can confiscate the witch's property, long a powerful encouragement in the rest of Europe to witch hunting.

GAY WITCHES

In the 1970s homosexuality, with sadomasochistic overtones, was combined in the published works of a New York "gay witch," Dr. Leo Martello, who claimed to come from a long line of Sicilian witches. He wrote several books publicized in *Gay* magazine, and rumors were rife that there were gay covens of witches dedicated to the androgynous god Baphomet. Other such covens were said to base their sex-magic rituals on what they could find out about the Knights Templars, whose Grand Master was burned for "abominable practices" in 1314.

Sybil Leek devotes a long chapter in one of her entertaining books on witchcraft to "Homosexuality and Witchcraft." In the 1980s the gay witch cult appears to be more active on the West Coast, especially in Los Angeles and San Francisco, somewhat dampened by fears of AIDS.

The Greeks (and some later peoples) believed that in the sex act, through the semen, "the virtues of the lover were transferred to the beloved." That quotation is from Gordon Wellesley's *Sex and the Occult* (1975) and he continues:

> It was believed that this happened physically through the trans-
> mission of the semen which contained the essence of the soul,
> at least in part, for which the copulative act was necessary. This
> allegedly metaphysical explanation lent, in the eyes of the Greeks,
> a dignity to the homosexual act never ascribed to it by the prud-
> ery of later centuries. It refutes the suggestion that to the Greeks
> it [paederasty] was solely a form of sexual self-indulgence.

Today the slang vocabulary of child molesters—or at least of the minority of them who are gay—indicates that the concept of transfer of qualities (especially the desired ones of youth and beauty) are somehow still at the back of the minds of men who refer to boys as comestibles: "chicken," "twinkies," etc. As some Amerindians ate the heart of a brave enemy in an attempt to acquire, by sympathetic magic, some of the dead enemy's courage, so some men appear to be trying to "consume" the youth of their boyish companions. *Having* another person takes on quite a magical significance, and the term "sexual communion" an extraordinary and to many very offensive connotation.

INEXPENSIVE ROOM PURIFIER

Common salt sprinkled on the fire, they say, will drive evil spirits and witches right out of the room.

TEARS

Don't expect a witch to shed salt tears. First, witches are supposed to be very afraid of salt. Second, witches can never weep more than three tears at a time, the old books assert.

THE WITCH OF EDMONTON

In the seventeenth-century play *The Witch of Edmonton*, based on the true story of Elizabeth Sawyer, hanged for witchcraft in 1621, the witch character is made to describe herself as "poor, deformed, and ignorant," and to sell her soul to the Devil (who appears to her in the form of a dog) in order to get back at the locals who persecute her:

> Some call me witch;
> And being ignorant of myself, they go
> About to teach me how to be one.

The authors—Thomas Dekker, John Ford, and William Rowley—may have put their finger on an important truth here. For many of the despised hags who eventually "confessed" to being witches and trying to work evil on their neighbors may well have gotten the idea in the first place just because they were described in malicious rumors as crones in league with the Devil. "Poor, deformed, and ignorant," they may have hoped that witchcraft would enable them to get their own back.

GOSSIPS

Talk about male chauvinist pigs! One of the earliest books on European witchcraft explains why there are more female than male witches: Women can't keep a secret; they tell each other what they have learned. For every sorcerer, 10,000 sorceresses, they said.

COMMITTED TO MEMORY

Julius Caesar in *De Bello Gallico* mentions that the Druids in Britain were forbidden to write down the mysteries of their religion but had to retain them in memory and hand them down from one generation to another by word of mouth. Thus the ancient magical lore would be preserved pure, they thought.

Some of magic and witchcraft today reaches us just like that. Much may have been lost, but much is remembered as well.

WITCHES AND MAGIC IN ENGLAND

Witchcraft has a long history in England. Saint Augustine rapidly converted some British kings in the seventh century (and hence, in those feudal times, all their vassals), but he could not stamp out the Old Religion completely. As many claim, it's not dead yet.

In 685 Theodore, archbishop of Canterbury, felt it necessary to point out that it was un-Christian to sacrifice to demons. He also took exception to frequenting pagan temples and participating in pagan ceremonies. So Withraed, king of Kent in 690, fined subjects who sacrificed to demons. In 750 it was necessary for the archbishop of York to reiterate that. Also, the animists were still sacrificing to trees, and there was too much praying at wells.

Eventually holy wells were incorporated into Christianity, just as all those wild hermits of the West Country became "saints," and wells and annual well dressing and all that became as Christian as holy water.

King Alfred then arrived, and knowing his Bible, he condemned witches to death. By the tenth century, though, only fines were imposed. Then in 959 King Edgar condemned worship at wells, stone circles, and trees (especially oaks, alders, and rowans). Later King Canute tried a little to do away with *walcyries* ("choosers of the dead"). No success.

By then it was a thousand years since the birth of Christ. In 1008 King Aethelred forbade magic. But it kept on, especially in hard times; peril and pestilence drove people back to the old ways.

Nor did the arrival of William the Bastard from Normandy in 1066 by any means bring an end to Anglo-Saxon magic and witchcraft. *Au contraire*, it reinforced it with continental strains. William the Conqueror's son, William Rufus, may well have perished as a knowing sacrifice to the ancient "the king must die" tradition to ensure the continuance of his people. (But then again he may simply have fallen victim to a hunting accident. Historians differ.) Some claim Rufus was of the Old Religion, and mystery certainly surrounds his death. Ask why he is not buried in his tomb.

It was a distinguished Englishwoman, Dr. Margaret Murray, who theorized in *The Witch-Cult in Western Europe* (1921) and *The God of the Witches* (1933) about the vast extent of pagan survivals. It was she who first argued that witchcraft was simply *la vecchia religione* (as the Italians say) conceived of as the Devil's work by pious Christians. English scholars such as Mathers, Summers, Waite, and Gardner, to name a very few, have been fascinated by the occult, as have novelist Colin Wilson and the late Dame Frances Yates.

Finally, in this too brief survey, there were the notable French magician Alphonse Louis Constant (who went by the name "Éliphas Lévi") in the last century, and in the twentieth an Englishman, Aleister Crowley—or "The Great Beast," as he preferred to call himself after the beast mentioned in Revelations 13:18.

A BREATH OF MAGIC

Babies sometimes have oral moniliasis, or candidiosis, a fungus infection. Some people believe that they can be cured by taking them to a man who has the Power, who then simply breathes into the baby's mouth. (Presumably the disease then runs its course, and the baby is "cured.") The Power comes only to men who have never seen their fathers, the folk say.

FOLK CURE FOR ERYSIPELAS

In 1902 the *Journal of American Folklore* had an interesting article about the mountain folk's cures for burns, bruises, bleeding, and so on, some of which involved magical incantations. Afraid of being thought to be witches, or ridiculed by the unbelieving, the folk kept their incantations mostly to themselves, but the folklore collector did find out this:

> Erysipelas can be cured by taking a red hot brand from the fire, and passing it three times over the person's face, saying the words. ["clear out, brand, but never in. Be thou cold or hot, thou must cease to burn. May God guard thy blood, thy flesh, thy marrow, and thy bones, and every artery, great and small. They shall all be guarded and protected in the name of the Father, the Son, and the Holy Ghost."] This ordeal by fire was not fancied by some of the patients, so my witch told me; she sometimes put coals on a shovel, and waved it over the face, saying,

Three holy men went out walking,
They did bless the heat and the burning,
They blessed it that it might not increase,
They blessed it that it might quickly cease,
And guard against inflammation and mortification
In the name of the Father, the Son, and the Holy Ghost.

Their witch also claimed to be able to stop hemorrhaging, and she claimed "it was not necessary for her to see the patients; they might be far away. Only the first name must be known and pronounced exactly, also the side of the body from which the blood came, the right or left side; this was essential."

WITCHES' GARDENS

In another book of mine you will find many long-held and curious folk beliefs, and elsewhere in this present book I mention the idea that witches' gardens are bordered by red flowers. Like old English soldiers in their red coats, these red flowers "guard" the powerful herbs and botanicals the witches cultivate for their brews.

A SABBAT EVERY DAY

Popular belief has always been that the witches fly off on their broom sticks to their meeting (sabbat) only four times a year, but if we are to believe Sister Madeleine de Demandoulx de la Palud, whose alleged possession in 1611 in France was the subject of a detailed *Admirable History*, "there is a sabbat every day. . . . The witches are gathered together by the sound of a cornet which is blown by a devil."

WITCH WORDS

The words for witches and their activities are many, in English, German, Italian, Latin, and other languages. For example, the hex signs of our Pennsylvania Dutch go back to *Hexen* in German. Some of the strangest words are those given to us by Jordanes de Bergamo in 1470 in a work in which he listed: *bacularia* (because witches rode on broomsticks), *fascinatrix* (because witches had the Evil Eye), *herberia* (because witches used strange herbs in their potions), *maliarda* (because witches were maleficers, workers of evil), and *pixidaria* (because witches made magical ointment, which they kept in a little box similar to that in which the consecrated Host is kept, called a pyx).

THE BIBLE AND WITCHCRAFT

In addition to its poetry and piety and history and philosophy, the Bible has also been consulted in fortune-telling and magic. Bibliomancy used to be quite common, and people really believed that sticking a pin or a finger into the Bible at random would get them the Word of God like a fortune in a Chinese cookie. Designed to explain history and foster truth, the Bible has been used also to darken history and spawn superstition.

You would think that not only Exodus but antiwitchcraft texts in such books as Leviticus and Deuteronomy would put them off, but witches and magicians have sought power in the book, even in antiwitchcraft stories in I Samuel, II Kings, in Isaiah, and so on. They simply turned the message to their needs. Occultists have especially been interested in using the Book of Moses (the first five books of the Bible) and have added other books allegedly by the same author. They use Ezekiel and the Revelation of Saint John pretty much as found and feel free to interpret the rest.

Witches and magicians both are at once confused and stimulated by the Bible. The Old Testament seems at once to deny the existence of Hell and to be the basis of misinterpretations that have led worshippers into Satanism. The New Testament seems to approve of certain types of magic and has been used to condemn other types of heresies.

A *Canon Episcopi* ("Bishop's Rule") of the tenth century asserts that the belief in witches "who profess that in the dead of night . . . ride upon certain beasts with the pagan goddess Diana, and fly over vast tracts of country" is both stupid and heretical and then turns and says that such persons do indeed exist and not to believe in witches flying is to join them in their heresy. Likewise what is written in the Bible has been advanced as both the empowerment of witches and magicians and at the very same time embraced as our justification for destroying them, even one of our most potent weapons (the book of "bell, book, and candle") for doing so.

3

Magic and Witchcraft Around the World

AMONG the Arunta tribe (studied by Spencer and Gillen, 1927) evil spirits (*erintja* or *eruncha*) appear "when the victim is *alone in the dark.*" In all cultures, people to some extent are verily alone and in the dark about a great many things; magic is therefore called in to help protect them and to counter the threat of the Unknown.

Even societies that prohibit magic have it practiced by their rebels. We have seen that Origen very early in Christianity asserted that "no good spirit obeys a magician" and went so far as to argue that "scripture rightly prohibits the use of magic" and such traffic with "apostate and evil spirits and foul demons." But from the time Christ Himself said, "In My Name shall they cast out devils," some Christians performed magic in the service of the Good, and some took an adversarial Left-Hand Path, unwilling to deprive

49

themselves of magical powers. In non-Christian societies the prohibitions and the practices were more or less similar.

Here now are a few items to suggest a broader scope than this present book can encompass, a few items that will remind us that magic exists all around the world, in all societies.

FIRE WALKING

You have heard before of people who could walk on fire without getting burned. You can even take courses on it now right here in America.

In the late eighteenth and early nineteenth centuries playing with fire was a major entertainment. There was Robert Powell, "the Fire King," who claimed to have mediumistic powers and "ate" hot coals "as natural as bread." There was Signora Josephina Giradelli, who walked barefoot on red-hot metal for the delectation of London audiences in 1814, and J. Xavier Chabert and his talented sister who walked on red-hot coals, put searing shovels to their tongues, and amazed London audiences of 1819 by entering an oven with a leg of lamb and not coming out until the leg of lamb was done to a turn.

In primitive societies walking on hot coals has been widely reported by anthropologists as part of native religious ceremonies and tests of bravery.

In connection with magic, some who have mastered the arts of playing with fire use them to impress audiences and gain greater belief in supposedly even more amazing spiritual powers. At the sabbat of Voodoo rites, says Pennethorne Hughes in *Witchcraft* (1952), adepts "can juggle with white-hot iron, dance in flames, smell ammonia, eat broken glass, and stir boiling water with their hands, without apparent pain or after-effects."

WORK CLOTHES

Sorcerers of Tibet, when appearing in public, comb their hair to cover their faces and wear aprons made of human bones over their magical robes.

"WE FEAR THE EVIL SPIRITS OF LIFE"

On his fifth expedition to Thule, Greenland, famed Danish explorer and ethnologist Knud Johan Viktor Rasmussen (1879–1933) was told this by an Iglulik Eskimo:

We explain nothing, we believe nothing, but in what I have just shown you lies our answer to all you ask.

We fear the weather spirit of earth, that we must fight against to wrest our food from land and sea. We fear Sila.

We fear death and hunger in the cold snow huts.

We fear Takananagapsaluk, the great woman down at the bottom of the sea, that rules over all the beasts of the sea.

We fear the sickness that we meet with daily all around us; not death, but the suffering. We fear the evil spirits of life, those of the air, of the sea and the earth, that can help wicked shamans to harm their fellow men.

We fear the souls of dead human beings and of the animals we have killed.

AZANDE WITCHES

Among the Azande tribe of Africa it is believed that one does not have to curse or cast spells or do anything at all to be a witch. They say a person may create witchcraft quite unwillingly, just because he or she has it in him.

BALEFUL BALOR

Balor, a giant warlock of Irish legend, was famed for being a cyclops. His one eye was an Evil Eye. He opened it only to scare the enemy, at which time it took four men on the battlefield to lift his eyelid. Like the glance of the mythical basilisk, Balor's glance froze you, rendered you paralyzed.

According to Celtic myth, this is what happened to this seemingly invincible giant. The god Lugh (still celebrated in Celtic lands at Lughnasa, a harvest festival) danced around Balor, chanting insulting remarks. Balor's curiosity was aroused, and he opened his big eye to see who could be so foolhardy. Instantly, avoiding Balor's glance, Lugh let go with his slingshot and got the warlock smack in the eye.

VOODOO AND TABOO

The explorer Soares de Souza in his description of Brazil reported in 1587 a number of deaths among the Tupinambás Indians we can attribute only to Voodoo. Merolla saw evidence of the same kind of thing in the Congo in the following century. In the eighteenth century the explorers in dark corners of the world constantly reported cases of what we might call Voodoo. In New Zealand, in the nineteenth century investigators commented on its prevalence, and similar reports came out of Africa, Haiti, and elsewhere.

Yet we had to wait until Walter Bradford Cannon brought out his book *Traumatic Shock* (1923) before we had a grasp on the physiology and psychology of Voodoo and the force of taboo. Fear can kill; belief that others can kill you by magic gives them the power to do so.

AZTEC MAGIC

The Aztecs lived in a world dominated by astrology; they believed that only magic could prevent the end of the world at the conclusion of the fifty-two-year cycles of their elaborate and surprisingly accurate calendar.

In addition to a crowded pantheon of fierce dieties, they also believed in ghosts (such as the *ciuapipiltin*, women who had died in childbirth and who haunted crossroads, able to paralyze any child who viewed them).

Their magic and their medicine were intricately mingled. A sick child might be held over a bowl of water, used somewhat like the magic mirror Merlin is credited with having introduced into Britain. If the face of the child reflected in the water appeared dark or shadowy, the soul had been stolen away.

The Aztecs knew a great deal about herbs and other medicines, but according to Warwick Bray in *Everyday Life of the Aztecs* (1968), a lot of their cures worked as much on magic as on a scientific basis: "Many of the remedies (like the morning dew dropped into the nostrils of children who snuffled) had a purely magical value."

MASKIM

In the complex demonology of the Sumerians, the *maskim* ("Ensnarers") were the worst of all the classes of demons. They disrupted nature even to the extent of putting the stars out of their courses, and they were implacable toward mankind:

They are neither male nor female, those who stretch themselves out like chains, they do not take wives; they do not beget children; they are strangers to benevolence and heed neither prayers nor entreaties.

". . . AND NEVER THE TWAIN SHALL MEET"

Moses saw God in a burning bush and was able to strike water from the stone with his magic staff. In the "Great Miracle of Shrāvasti," the Buddha (to confound six heretical leaders who opposed him) caused fire to spring from his head (rather like the tongues of fire that descended upon the apostles in the upper room at Pentecost) and water to flow from his feet.

East and West, after all, are reachable one from the other, and if you go west far enough you wind up in the East, east far enough and you reach the West. Some ways, particularly in religion and magic, we are very much alike.

Our Western exorcisms require bell, book, and candle. In Tibet and Nepal they would call for a book (the Verbal Plane), a statue or a painting (the Physical Plane), and a *stupa* (relic mound, representing the Spiritual Plane). On our altars we burn candles; the Tibetans burn butter on theirs.

Maybe the East and the West are not so irreconcilable as Kipling thought. These days we are studying everything from each other's philosophies to each other's technologies and management systems.

AFRICAN SCULPTURE

For almost a century Western collectors have appreciated and acquired African sculpture. What they were encouraging Africans to sell—or stealing for them—were often religious objects, masks from magical dances, fetishes, carved idols. A tribe's principal god wound up in a New York gallery. Of course this is true of many artifacts now found in museums.

We have made off with the bronzes of Benin and the little gold weights of the Ashanti and a great deal of whatever was portable. One carving too large to be taken was made from a single tree and depicted three monkeys, twenty-two feet high. They guard the palace of the Sultan of Fumban. They were commissioned in the army and entered on the royal payroll as bodyguards.

In the Congo witch doctors treat patients suffering from stomach aches by putting medicine into a hole in a carved statue. We have even taken some of those. And figurines pierced with nails. You will see a number of magical figurines in musuem collections of ethnology as well as in art museums and galleries and private collections. A childless couple I know have a fertility god on their mantel, but they bought it without knowing what it was.

Even furniture can bear magical symbols or have magical uses. Idols of the Hamileke tribe are constructed in the form of chairs; you can sit in the arms of the protective spirit. I own a pair of ceremonial stools, originally provided for visitors; I gather the tribe didn't want to encourage them to get too comfortable and overstay their welcome.

The symbolism seen is often beautiful and speaks volumes to the initiated. Outsiders cannot fathom things like the keyhole-shaped doorways of the Mogroom tribe in Chad. The keyhole shape is supposed to keep out unwelcome visitors. My Chinese desk is heavily carved with dragons and good-luck symbols (including swastikas, which disturb my Jewish friends).

Next time you see native art, be respectful. That may be somebody's god.

MURDER FOR THE POWER

Occasionally the Satanist promises the Devil to sacrifice children to him. In some primitive societies it is believed that in order to become a witch one must murder a close relative. The Navaho witches had to kill a brother or a sister to get their power, the natives of the Marquesas Islands a father or grandfather.

DOWN-UNDER JUSTICE

The *kaidiche* (emu-feathered slippers) worn by witch doctors among the aborigines of Australia really work: Criminals see the footprints and die of fright.

PIGEON FANCIER

We are more likely to call "magic" the actions of those not of our faith. Mohammed is said to have had a familiar in the form of a pigeon that sat on his shoulder and whispered in his ear. Probably it was only a pet, or a symbol like the lion of Saint Jerome and the other animals associated with Christian saints and holy men. But legend says Mohammed's pigeon was the Archangel Gabriel.

My favorite legend about the Prophet (a wonderful man whose life you ought to read some time) concerns a cat that fell asleep on the sleeve of his garment as Mohammed sat at a table. Mohammed cut off the sleeve of the garment rather than disturb its rest. A similar story is told of Saint Malo.

AUTOPSY FINDING

"I once had the pleasure of interviewing Bokane, an African pygmy from the Ituri forest," wrote R. R. Marett in *Psychology and Folk-Lore* (1920), "and he told me how his people were wont to cut up a dead man in order to find out what had killed him. If in the course of this veritable post-mortem they lighted upon an arrow-head or a thorn, well, that had done it. If, however, nothing was found, then it must have been done by *oudah*, 'the mysterious.'"

Our Western doctors occasionally mark a chart "GOK," for "God Only Knows," which sometimes seems to be the only reasonable diagnosis.

MAGIC IN MEXICO

In the Florentine Codex, one of the few Mayan manuscripts that escaped the fire of the destructive first bishop of Oaxaca, a *nahualli* is mentioned: "He is a sorcerer, possesses seeds, and knows magnificent herbs; a witch doctor, he prophesies with cords."

The descendants of the Maya still have their medicines and their magic. The botanicals are spread out, often on bits of newspaper on the ground, at markets, and many are the powers attributed to the dried flowers and leaves and powders and twigs and what tourists regard as unrecognizable bits of nature. The magic is harder to find, but still there.

Among the Aztecs, Tezcatlipoca the creator god was also the god of the witches. He ruled the heavens, came by night, brought fire, could change himself into a jaguar, overthrew a rival god and (temporarily) ruled the universe. A perfect patron for witches, most of whom among the Aztecs were men. All were said to have been born with the gift, and some were believed to be able to transform themselves into animal form as Texcatlipoca did. They were called *nagual*. It was believed they could fly, enchant, cast spells, cure or cause death by sucking out the soul or introducing worms or stones into the victim's body. Today the descendants of the Aztecs still deal in herbs and hexes.

When the *conquistadores* came, they brought witchcraft and magic: What had been religion before became heresy, the old gods became devils. The Spanish also brought their lively tradition of *brujos* (witches) and black arts and added such concepts as that of the Evil Eye to the local repertoire.

The early missionaries saw witchcraft and demons everywhere and were certain that the old ways were superstitious, bloody, dealing with the Devil. What they failed to grasp was that in New World thinking, good and evil were not closed in some Manichean battle but intertwined, interdependent: Every god could be baleful or beneficent, everything fitted together.

The *indios* assimilated the new ideas and mixed them with the old; they would have father confessors and *curanderos* (witch doctors). I have seen copal burned as incense to pagan gods on the steps of the Church of Santo Tomás in Chichicastenango, Guatemala, while the Roman Catholic rites were going on inside. I have seen the *curanderos* operating in the church itself, before statues of *santos* and the Virgin. In religious processions in Mexico and farther south I have seen the Blessed Sacrament and Christian images carried in processions whose tail ends contained natives dressed as the ancient corn deities and others.

The old and the new, magic and Christianity, have simply been combined; and this is true, too, of the Christianity of Puerto Rico and Trinidad, Haiti and the Dominican Republic, and all the rest of Hispanic America.

The sabbats that were such a feature of the early colonial history of such provinces as Yucatán have gone underground, but a good deal of the Old Religion is there for anyone to see.

Today in Mexico the descendants of the Zapotecs have *hechiceras* who send out little *chizos* (stones, thorns, or other cursed particles) to trouble the bodies of their enemies. Or you can hire them to do it against your enemies, who will then have to turn to a *curandero* to break the spell.

The Tzotzils pray to Pukuj, the Mayan god of death, to harass their foes. Elsewhere there are evil *aires* to be combated with age-old prayers and ceremonies and the *tabayuku* (a sort of succubus) and *vampiros*.

Adivinas can make you a doll of *jonute de hule* (rubber tree bark), but at the same time evil magicians are manufacturing their dolls and sticking pins in them, tying red cords around their necks, and so on.

In both cases there is a liberal sprinkling with blood, albeit chicken blood, for both the *indígenes* and the Spanish have long traditions of gory gods and bloodletting.

Certain places such as Tepepán are known all over the country for their wondrous *brujos de naturaleza* (natural-born witches, as opposed to those of the Spanish tradition who sought their calling). Slightly more sophisticated centers have their spiritualist circles and dabblers in the occult arts. Before Francisco I. Madero became president of Mexico, he was commissioner for the First Spiritist Conference (1906) there, and spiritualist temples and curers abound both in places where foreigners have gathered (such as Guadalajara) and in more Mexican cities. Ever since Madero was assassinated (1913) he has been, like others who have died violent deaths—from Cuahtemoc, the last Aztec emperor, to less noble souls—available (Mexicans believe) as a "dark spirit" or guide to mediums.

William and Claudia Madsen in their highly recommended *Guide to Mexican Witchcraft* (1972) report interviews with a wide variety of practitioners and in a do-it-yourself section give recipes and instructions. Want to seduce a girl? Carry a dead hummingbird in your pocket. Or, if you can't get powdered human skull, put the leg of a beetle in her soda pop: guaranteed to drive her *loca*. Where to buy *piedra iman* (loadstone)? Try Puebla and Torreón. To keep a husband from running away, bury a live horned toad in a sealed jar under the house, or tie two large *chiles pasillas* together with a red ribbon and put them under his pillow. How to drive him *loco*? Put some of your dried menstrual blood in his coffee.

Here is one the Madsens do not guarantee:

A man who wants to kill his woman can bury the tooth of a
rattlesnake at the spot where she urinates in the morning. That
is supposed to make her dry up and die.

As for herbs and drugs, there are many books—and much that has never found its way into a book. The Mexicans gave us chocolate and chilis, which we now know affect the mind (chocolate contains a chemical that gives you a *high* when you are "in love") and the body in "magical" ways. Californian hippies (*jipes* in Mexico) discovered the hallucinations the Mexicans had been getting for a long time from morning-glory seeds and certain mushrooms that can (as Aldous Huxley put it) open the "doors of perception."

In New York, at least one pharmacy has for generations been selling such items as are used in European folklore and magic; now it has added a whole range of Hispanic herbs. In Hispanic neighborhoods the folklore of Puerto Rico and other places produces some exotic items, including the blue chalk you can apply before you sleep to protect you from the creatures of the night. *Botánicas* here offer a wide range of goods.

The *botánicas* of Mexico may be more informal but they offer *coatl xoxouhqui* ("green serpent," good for both gout and bewitching), *mixitl* (to crack the tongue to silence an enemy, to deaden the testicles), *tochtetepen* ("rabbit's leg," another paralyzer), and *tlapatl* (one of the daturas so prominent in European witchcraft).

MAORI MAGIC

The Maoris believe that *kaiwhatu* (a charm) defends you against witchcraft. They say that Rongo-mai and Ihenga, two legendary characters, brought it back from a journey to the underworld, along with some songs and the *whai* (what we call a "cat's-cradle").

OBEAH

There is no "white magic" or herbal cures in Obeah, witchcraft devoted entirely to getting back at your enemies. Obeah still flourishes in the Caribbean and elsewhere, despite a 1760 law defining it as a "Wicked Art of Negroes going under the Appelation of obeah-men and obeah-women pretending to have Communication with the Devil and other Evil Spirits."

A law against *pretending* to work evil!

THE IRNA

Among the Arunta tribe of Australia, the *irna* (pointing stick or bone) is used to bring evil and death upon a victim selected by the magician. First the magician has to take the stick or bone away into the bush, crouch over it, and charge it with curses. "May your heart be rent asunder," he repeats over and over.

He then hides the *irna* back home until he can creep out at night and, getting near enough to his victim to be able to discern his or her features, he repeatedly jerks the stick or bone over his shoulder and hurls curses under his breath. *Arungquiltha* (evil magic) is then supposed to strike the victim, who will sicken and die unless he suspects some such attack and calls in another magician to counter it. Meanwhile, the evil magician must hide the *irna*, because if others see him with an *irna* they will put him to death as a murderer.

CHINESE MAGIC

As I noted earlier, we in the West have put people into the foundations of buildings to give them strength; so the Chinese strengthened the Great Wall with the bodies of slaves. But the most striking example of this magical belief in practice was involved with the great bell of the temple of Ta Chung Su, which the emperor Yung Lo is said to have demanded be "strong" enough to be heard one hundred *li* (about thirty-seven miles) away. The tale goes that the bellmaker's own daughter, Ko Ai, was thrown or jumped into the molten metal to make the iron and brass and gold and silver fuse properly.

UNFROZEN CORPSES

This, from Ross Nichols, in Paul Christian's *History and Practice of Magic* (1963):

> In Tibet the object of reviving the corpse in a rite called *rolang* is to bite off its tongue whilst it is leaping in a violent dance. If this is not done the corpse kills the sorcerer who has revived it. This process must be distinguished from the animation of a corpse by a wandering spirit seeking embodiment, a process said to be accomplished by the *trong jug* rite in Tibet. The *jibbuk* [dybbuk] of Hebrew folk-belief is such a re-inhabited corpse; in this case it usually seems to be acting as a kind of medium for the re-establishment of communications with this world by a departed human spirit. More horribly, West Africa, together with the other Voodoo regions of Haiti, Jamaica, British Guiana, Cuba and parts of South America, has its *zombies*, revived corpses acting as servants and slaves of the living.

STONE MAGIC

With the old Cornish language now extinct, place names that had ordinary meanings in Cornish have been given fanciful English form: Mousehole, Penny Come Quick, St. Just in Roseland. And to explain quite simple words, folklore comes up with odd stories: *The Merry Maidens* (*maen* for "stone") are nineteen stones about four feet high each, squatting in a field, but the legend has been invented that they were Cornish maidens turned to stone when they danced on a Sunday. Nearby are fifteen more stones called *The Pipers*, who supposedly played for those irreverent revels. The belief in magic, however, is enshrined in that tale.

In another area of Cornwall, where there are moors, *Men-an-Tol* is a five-foot stone with a hole in it, standing between two large boulders. (Christians came to call it the Devil's Eye.) In ancient times, sick children were "brackened" here to cure them by passing them nine times through the stone against the sun.

Elsewhere ancient people passed people through holes in trees for similar purposes. For example, the Bhil tribe in India passes a sick child seven times through a hole in a *palas* tree to effect an instant cure.

DEATH WISH

From M. Laird and R. A. K. Oldfield's *Expedition into the Interior of Africa* (1837):

Yesterday there was a procession of the wives of the late son of the king. . . . The women came down to the water-side. . . . They proceeded to drink poison, from a belief that they had *wished* their husband's death. . . . Out of sixty of these poor infatuated wretches, thirty-one of them died; while others, who vomited immediately, escaped death.

The belief that one can be guilty of another's death just by wishing the death to occur is also common in the West, and August Strindberg's *Brott och Brott* (*Crimes and Crimes*) is a play that reflects his own deeply held belief that one can be guilty of another person's death just by hoping for it.

MAGICAL FASTING

When people believed that there were demons resident in trees and streams, they also believed that certain foods contained such spirits. They attempted to purify themselves by fasting, refusing such foods as contained demons. They fasted also to placate the gods, to sacrifice to them, to earn credits by denying the human needs for sustenance, as it were, and thus approach the angels and demons (who never ate).

They were also aware that fasting could, in the long run, produce visions, and by what was called in Latin the *jejunium propheticum,* they sought to produce the ability to prophesy. In the early days of Christianity, some of the strangest visions, in which magic and religion were inextricably mixed, occurred to hermits and anchorites fasting in the desert, mortifying the body and attempting to strengthen the spiritual part of man. But the "prophetic fast" and the purification rites of shamans were calculated to increase power, not to weaken the individual.

FORBIDDING HEATHENISM

From the Laws of Canute, king of England (1017–1035), comes this:

> We earnestly forbid every heathenism: Heathenism is, that men
> worship idols; that is, that they worship heathen gods, and the
> sun and the moon, fire or rivers, water-wells or stones, or forest
> trees of any kind; or love witchcraft, or promote *morth-work* in
> any wise.

THE MAGIC CIRCLE

The Crowthers in *The Secrets of Ancient Witchcraft* (1974) write:

> The circle represents the borderland between this world and the
> domains of the gods. Since it [magic] is a fertility cult, it also
> represents the womb of Mother Earth.

The Crowthers worry about the dimensions of the magic circle—only nine feet across—but conclude that it is large enough to accommodate the thirteen members of a coven and speculate that for more people one might use a multiple of nine. Ceremonies in circles occur all around the world.

BIBLIOGRAPHY

For Western witchcraft you will need *The Book of Shadows*. It is not in print. Someone will give you a manuscript copy if you get to be a magician. Without a copy, you cannot work magic in the ancient tradition.

You may also have great trouble acquiring the following highly recommended and rare volumes: the *Sixth, Seventh, Eighth, Ninth, Tenth, Eleventh, Twelfth,* and *Thirteenth Book of Moses; The Little Book of Romanus; The Black Raven; The Spring Book; The Spiritual Shield; The Blessing of the Saints.* If you find *The Fiery Dragon,* be certain it is *The Authentic Fiery Dragon.* There are several grimoires (magicians' manuals) that tell you how to get demons to bring you books you will need, but these grimoires (never printed) are hard to find.

Eastern guide books are sometimes surprisingly similar.

REPTILE MAGIC

E. E. Evans-Pritchard lived right in the center of Africa from 1926 to 1930. He wrote *Witchcraft, Oracles and Magic Among the Azande,* which reports that it is *kere* (a bad omen) to see a certain kind of lizard, because this will foretell the death of a relative: "If you see the skin it has shed (or a python's slough) you will die."

In Central America, iguana meat is used in several potent magic recipes, and snakeskins are sometimes employed in magic as well. W. H. Goldie wrote of native New Zealand life in *Maori Medical Lore*:

> If a traveler should see a lizard in the path before him, he would know that the creature had not come there of its own accord, but had been sent by an enemy as an *aitua* (evil omen) to cause his death. He therefore at once kills the reptile, and craves a woman to step over it as it lies in the path. By this means the evil omen is averted.

REVERSE PSYCHOLOGY

If magic is the reverse of religion, understandably things work backward.

Many spells depend on reciting formulas backward. The authors of the *Malleus Maleficarum*, whom we will encounter in the next chapter, made it a point to stress that it was witchcraft if one put emphasis on the *manner* in which a spell was said. In some ritual magic one walks backward or otherwise reverses things.

The witch doctors of Africa's Kaguru tribe walk around on their hands. Among the Amba people witch doctors stand on their heads when not otherwise occupied or hang, naked, upside down from trees. They quench their thirst with salt. In fact, they do whatever they can backward. If you are going to try to reverse natural law, it only seems sensible to work backward.

SWEDISH MAGIC

From my very learned friend Erik Gunnemark in Sweden, some magic of West Gothia:

To understand all languages, catch a young swallow, roast it in honey, and eat it. Also . . .

To make dirty linen white, say I SAW A SWAN when you open the door to the laundry. (If you wanted it to remain dirty, you'd say I SAW A RAVEN.)

To banish the ague, say KULUMARIS KULUMARI KULUMAR KULUMA KULUM KULU KUL KU K.

He warns against whistling: "As a child I never whistled; it wasn't done—only godless people whistled. If I had whistled I would have 'called up the Devil!'" Singing early in the morning is also taboo. "The eagle will take you before the sun is down," Russians warned him. Erik quotes his father-in-law: "*E skata ska du inte hata*," ("You shall not hate a magpie!") to the effect that you must never bother a magpie or destroy its nest ("If you do, expect to be dead within the year"), for magpies are "sacred birds in the Swedish countryside."

From southwestern Sweden (and apparently nowhere else) he reports that *tvesulning* is "a mortal sin," which means that one must not put two kinds of thing on one's bread. A ham open-faced sandwich, yes; a cheese open-faced sandwich, yes; but never ham and cheese. And he and his family and friends have revived an ancient custom of "running Gregor" on March 12.

> The trouble is that we must run barefoot when the ground is still frozen, sometimes covered with snow and ice—not pleasant at all. But if we run *three times* around the house or the compost heap we will get a good harvest and won't suffer from lice for the rest of the year.

He has all sorts of other folk beliefs to tell about, including one that seems to combine the pre-Christian and the Christian: All knives and scissors must be hidden and not used on Good Friday. Some superstitions far older than that persist in Sweden to this day, and some have been brought to America by Swedish immigrants of the nineteenth century.

"GET THEE BEHIND ME, SATAN!"

The Gialo "ghost women" of Kufara in the Libyan desert dress in heavy black robes to keep out the heat—an odd custom since the color black is supposed to absorb heat. Even odder, the "ghost women" drag six-foot trains behind them. Why? The trains obliterate the women's footprints, making it impossible for the Devil to creep up and tempt them into sin.

NATIVE GUILE

In Malaivi—or Nyasaland as it was then called (about 1934)—bands of *bamucapi* (witch finders) in Western suits and with Western methods of soft-soap and threat went around detecting black magicians by their reflections in mirrors. They forced witch doctors to give up their bloody robes, lizard skins, horns, and fetishes—and they used magic to keep them from returning to practice.

Each suspect was compelled to drink a soapy, reddish liquid which (he was assured) would, the moment he returned to practicing magic, cause him to swell up horribly and become so heavy that the people could not carry him to his grave.

Then the *bamucapi* moved on to the next villages, after selling the locals charms and magic powders—to protect them against evil magic, of course. The most expensive charms promised to assist the owner to cope with government officials (to whom, at last, the *bamucapi* themselves fell victim).

SJØNHVERFING

That Scandinavian word means "deceiving the eyes," and Scandinavian witches were supposed to have that power. In the Icelandic *Eyrbyggja Saga*, for instance, we find the tale of the witch Katla who protected her son Odd from men who wanted to revenge the fact that he had cut off the head of a woman.

When the men, including the bold Arnkell, arrived at Katla's house, all they could see was the old woman sitting on a dais, spinning. Odd, sitting beside her, she made invisible. The men went away, returned, and still could not see Odd; this time she was combing Odd's hair, but they saw only an old woman combing a goat. On a third trip the determined men thought they saw only a boar, but it was Odd asleep.

Arnkell was sure that they had had "a goatskin waved around our heads" but he could not conquer the magic of Katla until he found another witch, Geirrid, who was her match. As soon as Katla saw the blue cloak of Geirrid as she arrived with the men, Katla realized that her "deceiving the eyes" would not work on the second witch. Katla hid Odd under a dais, but as soon as Geirrid entered the house, she slipped a sealskin bag over Katla's head, rendering her powerless, and unerringly directed Arnkell and his friends to where Odd was hidden. Katla was stoned to death, and Odd was hanged.

LAPPLAND DRUMS

Lapps used to make magic drums from trees found in remote spots where the sun never shone. The heads were of reindeer hide painted with pictures of what Amerindians called the spirit animal, with the blood-red extract of alder bark used for paint. Decorated with bones and other objects, the drums were kept in a part of every Lapp's dwelling where women were never permitted to enter.

To tell what the future held, the male Lapp would place a brass ring or a little brass frog on top of the drum and watch how the object moved over the painted pictures as the drum was solemnly beaten. Though the conversion of

Lappland to Christianity led to the destruction of most of the old drums (a few remain in museums), new ones were made and used by every Lapp household down to nearly modern times.

In many other cultures the drum is used in magic to induce a trancelike state in which a shaman or priest may be able to get in touch with higher powers, but perhaps only in Lappland were drums ever beaten to watch magic little frogs hop to symbols in which the future could be divined.

LIKE PRODUCES LIKE

That is the basic principle of sympathetic magic, like Sir Kenelm Digby's wound ointment. It's what lies behind the practice of sticking pins in figures created to represent enemies and hoping thereby to injure or slay them.

If you make your image with something that has come in contact with the enemy or (even better) some part of the enemy himself (hair, nail clippings, even excrement), the magic will be that much more effective. Or employ contiguous magic, which attempts to injure the man through something he has touched, as when Australian aborigines put sharp pebbles or ground glass in the footprints left by an enemy.

The Ojibwa employ sympathetic magic to drive away evil from a community. When someone has a dream that some disaster—usually illness—is about to strike his village, he sends out messages to all the families involved, inviting them to assemble at a certain place and a certain time, usually his own house. A short distance away, a human-shaped figure of straw has been set up, dressed in male costume, to represent the impending trouble. The people eat, smoke tobacco to ask for a spiritual blessing on the enterprise, and at a signal from the dreamer, rush out at the straw man. First the men shoot it, then the women rush up and club it to bits, and finally the remains are heaped up and burned. This is believed to ward off the disease and thus save the health of the community.

CLOSE TO HOME

And lest you think that modern, learned, scientific societies are immune . . .

At a conference on geolinguistics in 1985, my colleague John Allee produced and handed around the audience a small figure from Greenland, carved from a tusk. The grotesque little image was a *tupalak*, he told us, and was used by the Greenlanders to cast a spell or place a curse. I noticed that the majority of my learned colleagues in linguistics, few or none of whom had any concern with magic or witchcraft, superstitiously gazed at the *tupalak* but resolutely refused to touch it.

HOW TO KEEP WITCHES AWAY

In New Mexico they say that if you will burn red pepper cores on a Friday you will keep witches out of your house.

The people of northern Italy seem to have had a different method. Rachel Harriet Busk in *The Folk-Lore of Rome* (1874) reports the following from a religious Roman woman with a highly superstitious husband:

> "He always kept a bag of particular herbs," I heard from her another time, "hung up over the door, all shred into the finest bits. As he was very angry if I touched them, I one day said, 'Why *do* you want that bundle of herbs kept just there?' and then he told me that it was because no witch could pass under them without having to count all the minute bits, and that though it was true she might do so by her arts without taking them down and handling them, it was yet so difficult when they were shred into such an infinite number that it was the best preservative possible against evil influences."

HAWAIIAN IDEAS

Until the last century there was a kingdom of Hawaii and in that society a system of taboos operated, hedging the royal family, the nobles, the priests with a magical circle of protection.

It was taboo to bathe in streams and springs set aside for the royal family or the priests or to touch pigs marked for sacrifice in the temples. It was taboo to stand in the presence of the king without permission, to approach him any way except on the knees, to step upon his shadow. Only royalty could wear yellow, only the priests red. Only royalty wore the exquisite mantles made from *oo* and *mamo* feathers.

Only the royal family and the nobility could eat turtle or squid or certain kinds of birds. No women could eat plantains, bananas, or coconuts, pork or certain kinds of fish. Never could men and women eat together.

At certain sacred times no food could be eaten at all, no canoe shoved off from the shore, no pigs or fowls utter a sound, and nobody but priests walk around in plain sight.

In this world of strict regulation, however, certain persons were thought to be able to work magic that could disrupt everything, and these persons were greatly feared. A kahuna anaana (one who prays his victims to death) was thought to be able to work magic against anyone provided only that he had a bit of something from the person, such as a lock of hair, a nail paring, even a drop of his spittle (sympathetic magic again). For this reason the king's spittoon-bearer was, in ancient Hawaii, a high-ranking and extremely trusted nobleman, assigned the vital job of safeguarding the king's spit.

Even in more recent times Hawaiians believed in *kilos* or sorcerers who were thought to be able to call up the spirits of the dead and sometimes to steal a living man's spirit from him while he was asleep.

HOW PEOPLE GET CONJURED

An informant told the *Journal of American Folklore* in 1900 how he was "conjured in May 1898, while hoeing cotton" with "some yaller dirt, and knew it was graveyard dirt." Searching his house in panic, he found "a bag under my door-step. I opened the bag and found some small roots about an inch long, some black hair, a piece of snake skin, and some graveyard dirt, dark-yaller, right off some coffin. . . ." He threw some red pepper around to purify the place and went right off to a "root-doctor" to have the spell removed, because "one root-doctor often works against another."

The informant was certain that professional help was needed to counter any spell that employed material as powerful as graveyard dirt, of which he said:

> Only root-doctors can git the graveyard dirt, they know what kind
> to git and when, the hants [ghosts] won't let everybody git it,
> they must git it through some kind of spell, for the graveyard dirt
> works trouble 'til it gits back inter the ground, and then [the
> spell] wears off. It must git down to the same depth it was took
> from, that is as deep as the coffin lid was from the surface of the
> ground.

TREES

Trees are associated with a great many magical beliefs and customs, some of which are carried down to our day. Here are just a few of the English folk beliefs about trees:

Apples. It's bad luck to pick all the apples in the orchard; some must be left on the trees for the fairies. It's called "the pixies' harvest." To go out and take the apples left for the pixies is called griggling or scraggling. Children who engage in such pranks then call at the farmer's house for some "goodies" or a penny, much like American children trick-or-treating on Halloween.

Ash. Want to know whether it will be a wet spring? Here's the old English rhyme; it refers to the leafing of the trees:

> If the oak's before the ash,
> You will only get a splash.
> If the ash preceeds the oak,
> You will surely get a soak.

Sap from the ash was used as an ointment on the newborn, a protection against witchcraft. The ash was closely connected with the Old Religion, and it was in a sacred grove of ash trees that the Druids conducted their religious ceremonies, so the ash became a part of many survivals of *wicca*, the ancient knowledge.

Bay. Tradition or superstition said that if you moved, you ought to take your bay tree with you, unless you wanted to leave behind your luck and your protection against witches.

Birch. A birch branch over the door advises a witch to visit elsewhere.

Blackthorn. To bring the blossoms of blackthorn indoors was thought to invite evil into one's house. The blossoms of mountain laurel are even more fraught with danger.

Cherry. Cherry trees in blossom may attract evil spirits, so it is best to have them blessed when they are in full bloom.

Elder. Some people advise elder wood for magic wands, and it used to be a common British practice to carry a cross-shaped elder bud in the pocket to ward off evil. But the elder bud had to be from a churchyard tree, or it didn't work. If you were a horseman, you carried a twig of elder to guard against saddle sores.

Hawthorn. There are many superstitions attached to the hawthorn and its blossoms, but one that seems to have disappeared entirely in Britain is the formerly widespread habit of making whistles for the children to blow (driving away evil spirits) at May Day celebrations, a time when witches were thought to be especially virulent.

Hazel. Hazel sticks used to drive the cattle were likely, people once thought, to guarantee that they would be fat and content. Willow was thought to hurt them.

Holly. Holly could keep away witches, and the English traditions of the Holly Boy and Ivy Girl—holly was a symbol of masculinity, ivy of clinging feminity—have gone, but we still use holly and ivy as Christmas decorations, even though we seldom or never recall their significance in the Old Religion.

It might be useful to remember, however, that holly may not be brought into the house any earlier than Christmas Eve (or bad luck will follow), and if you do not observe the ancient practice of keeping a piece of the yule log to start the next year's yuletide fire, then perhaps you have room even in a modern apartment for storing a few of Christmas' holly leaves. Tradition says they are to be saved and burned under the next year's Christmas pudding. It may not keep evil spirits away, but it does provide a charming bit of continuity from one year to the next.

With the more or less familiar holly, we will cut short what otherwise could be an extremely long list of superstitious beliefs in the magical powers of trees. Today you do not see the Dutch in New York horsewhipping their peach trees on Good Friday morning or yews and rowans in graveyards or even ash logs in the Christmas fireplace for protection against evil. Even with the few old customs we honor, we do not always get things right, forgetting such details as that hawthorn twigs have little power unless cut on Ascension Day.

AMERINDIAN MAGIC

Algonquian young men went through a sort of initiation ceremony just before attaining adulthood which was also seen, in one form or another, in many other Amerindian nations.

The young man retired to a specially built hut in an isolated place and there prayed and fasted until he was so purified the "spirits could see through him." At that point he was granted a dream in which a spirit guide appeared to him, bringing the secrets of hunting and curing disease, invulnerability to the weapons of enemies, and much more wisdom. Thereafter, awake, the young brave could use the wisdom and power to run his adult life and was expected to honor his guardian spirit throughout life.

THE OLDEST MAGICAL INSTRUCTIONS IN THE LIBRARY

The British Library has some two hundred tablets inscribed with the essence of Chaldean magic, charms, amulets, incantations, and more, all copied from the original texts set down for King Asurbanipal (884–860 B.C.) in Assyrian and Akkadian languages.

4

Witchcraft Trials

IT took very little for someone to be accused of witchcraft. Perhaps he had walked past a neighbor's field the day before the cattle took sick of some ailment. Perhaps she had a soured and crabby nature, and people of her village did not like her. Perhaps a couple had prospered more than others in their town, and fellow townsmen were jealous.

But once the accusation was lodged, the whole process of condemnation seemed to roll forward of its own accord. The suspect was jailed and a watch kept on her—it was usually a her. She was questioned—and questioned and questioned and questioned. If the business took place in England or an English colony, no torture could be used (except pressing and then only if the accused refused to plead either guilty or not guilty), but she could be ducked in the village pond, or "swum" to see if she sank, and there was no law against keeping her awake for days on end. If she had been arrested anywhere on the continent of Europe, there were no restrictions at all; she could be broken on the wheel (which meant being strapped to a wheel and beaten systematically with an iron rod), racked, thumb-screwed, eye-gouged, burned, scourged until she confessed. What she had to confess to was not only her own guilt but that of other witches. And soon the persons she was named were arrested, too, and tortured to confess still other names.

It is from the confessions of these tormented wretches that most stories of black masses, Satan worship, broomstick flying, magic spells, soul selling, covens, and so on come. Much of what they "admitted" had been suggested to them by their interrogators.

Having "confessed" to witchcraft, the accused was then put through a travesty of a trial. Occasionally (not often) a confessed and repentant "witch" was allowed to go free, but only with a verdict of "not proven"—"innocent" was not allowed after such efforts. More often than not she was hanged, burned alive, drowned, or put to death in some other unspeakable way.

SATAN MIGHT SMILE

Henry Charles Lea in *The Inquisition of the Middle Ages* (reissued 1961) wrote of the persecution of witches:

> Satan might well smile at the tribute to his power seen in the endless smoke of the holocausts. . . . Protestant and Catholic rivalled each other in the madness of the hour. A bishop of Geneva is said to have burned 500 witches within three months, a bishop of Bamburg 600, a bishop of Würzburg 900. The Inquisition evidently had worthy pupils. Paramo boasts that in a century and a half from the commencement of the sect, in 1404, the Holy Office had burned at least 30,000 witches who, if they had been left unpunished, would easily have brought the whole world to destruction.

THE SHAME OF SALEM

Superstition and stupidity, hand in hand with Puritan virtues of fortitude and piety, led to the shame of Salem in the spring of 1692.

The Salem witchcraft story, as we have stated elsewhere, is far from the goriest in the annals of witchcraft persecutions, but it has received a great deal of attention because, as an isolated colonial incident, it stood out starkly. And, of course, because parallels can be aptly drawn between the performances of our Puritan ancestors and our political and social contemporaries.

It all began in the home of a clergyman, the Rev. Samuel Parris. Some silly girls, no more or less superstitious than others of the time, were dropping egg whites into water, hoping to foretell thereby the occupation of their future husbands. (The idea was that the shapes formed would hint at the trades.) One egg white shaped up like a coffin, and the girl got hysterical.

The hysteria spread to other adolescents, girls developed false pregnancies, and eventually the whole town was in an uproar. Realizing that their antics were getting them attention, the girls began to make accusations of witchcraft.

The first charge was leveled at a Caribbean slave, Tituba. She had, in fact, filled the impressionable children with her own superstitious tales, but she was no witch. Unfortunately, she was a "heathen," and everyone "knew" that black slaves dabbled in all sorts of "hoodoo" and charms. Tituba had little defense against the testimony of the preacher's overwrought daughter, Elizabeth, and young Abigail Williams and their friends.

Pleased with their success and basking in the limelight, the girls denounced others. The girls claimed that they could detect witches simply by touching them. Arrest followed arrest. In this rigidly theocratic society one could not deny belief in the supernatural; that would be tantamount to denying the existence of God. So, people believed in the accusations—or said they did. The accusations broadened. Soon a kindly pastor, the Rev. George Burroughs, was executed for witchcraft, and the mania spread to nearby towns.

Incredibly, more than 150 people were arrested on serious charges, while the public—the superstitious and the sincere, the silly and the sadistic—allowed it to happen. The execution of Bridget Bishop in June 1692 was followed by the death of twenty others, three victims dying in prison before they could be killed. But unlike similar outbreaks of hysteria in Europe, those who confessed went free, among them Tituba the slave.

Then the witch hunters overreached themselves. They presumed to accuse the governor's wife. That caused the whole hideous structure to collapse.

It is only fair to note that even at the time some distinguished men, such as Thomas Battle and Increase Mather, thought the courts and the people were acting irrationally, and bravely said so. But Increase's son Cotton testified at the trial as an "expert witness" and the following year published his own book on witchcraft, *Wonders of the Invisible World*.

In 1697, the witch hunters began to regret their rashness, and Samuel Sewall, one of the presiding judges, posted a notice in his own meeting house: "Sensible . . . as to the Guilt contracted . . . at Salem . . . he

. . . Desires to take the Blame. . . ." Any relatives of the victims still around in 1711 received £600 in compensation. It was not really possible to make amends for the horror, but the witch hunters at least wanted to.

In more recent times the history of the dark days in Salem has been reexamined and reevaluated in the light of other forms of hysteria. In 1953 Arthur Miller produced his play *The Crucible,* using the Salem experience to examine guilt by association in the age of McCarthyism.

INNOCENT VIII AND THE INNOCENTS UNDER THE HAMMER OF THE WITCHES

The witch-hunting mania really began in 1484 with the issuance of the papal bull *Summis desiderantes* by Pope Innocent VIII. (Innocent may have been hoping to distract public attention from his own scandalous personal life and disastrous dabbling in Mediterranean politics, for he was anything but a pious and high-minded man.) The bull empowered two Dominican professors of theology, already at work in northern Germany hunting out "wretches [who] afflict and torment men and women," to

> proceed, according to the regulations of the Inquisition, against any persons of whatever rank and high estate, correcting, mulcting, imprisoning, punishing, as their crimes merit, those whom they have found guilty, the penalty being adapted to the offence.

The theologians were Fathers Jakob Sprenger and Heinrich Kramer, and the result of Innocent's bull was the publication of their notorious work on the nature of witchcraft and how its adherents were to be ferreted out: *Malleus Maleficarum, Hammer of the Witches.* It was to become the inspiration and guide for one of the ghastliest persecutions in history.

Summis desiderantes did not impose belief in witchcraft as dogma of the Church, but it certainly made disbelief in it more perilous. In Germany, many witchcraft trials began instantly, but there were repercussions in Italy as well; by 1510, 140 had been burned at Brescia, three hundred at Como. In France, suspected witches were questioned under torture—the soles of their feet were burned, and they were forced to swallow burning oil; eventually an eleven-year-old girl was burned to death. Backup directives were issued by Julius II and Paul III.

Soon the mania spread to England, where as a French writer says, "Henry VIII and Elizabeth persecuted sorcerers with extreme vigour, and we must not forget the sinister James I, who took the trouble to write with his own royal hand the treatise entitled *Daemonologia.*"

In the latter, the character Epistemon speaks for the King's point of view of mercy for innocents:

> EPISTEMON. The death by flames of fire is that most often laid upon them [witches and sorcerers]. . . .
>
> PHILOMATHUS. Think you that exception should be made or consideration taken in that they be, namely, male or female, of ripe or tender age, or by reason of their state, dignity, or degree, base or exalted?
>
> EPISTEMON. I adjudge that there must be no exception.

HOW'S THAT FOR GRATITUDE?

In the first secular witchcraft trial in France, in 1390, Jehane de Brigue was accused by a man named Ruilly—of having *saved his life* by the use of charms. A Paris court imprisoned her, tortured her into confession of witchcraft, and burned her, along with Ruilly's wife.

SADDUCISMUS TRIUMPHATUS

The Rev. Joseph Glanvill (1636–1680) was one of the original scientists in the Royal Society and one of the most important of seventeenth-century English writers on witchcraft. In his work *Sadducismus Triumphatus* (published 1681), we find stories like this sad tale:

> . . . at Stockholme a young woman accused her own Mother of being a Witch, and swore positively that she carried her away at night; whereupon both the Judges and Ministers of the Town exhorted her to Confession and Repentance. But she stiffly denied the Allegations, pleaded Innocence, and though they burnt another Witch before her face and lighted the Fire she herself was to burn in before her, yet she still justified her self, and continued to do so to the last, and continuing to do so, was burnt.
>
> She had indeed been a very bad Woman, but it seems this crime she was free from, for within a fortnight or three weeks

after, her Daughter which had accused her came to the Judges in open Court, weeping and howling, and confessed that she had wronged her Mother, and unjustly out of spleen she had against her for not gratifying her in a thing she desired, had charged her with that Crime which she was innocent of as the Child unborn. Whereupon the Judges gave order for her execution too.

GIVING THE DEVIL HIS DUE

"Whatever is not normal," wrote Nicholas Remy (1530–1612) in his much-consulted volume *Demonolatreiae* (1595), "is due to the Devil." With that excuse, Remy, a judge in Nancy, France, condemned to death an old beggar woman who had been angry when he refused her alms, for soon after that Remy's son died.

In a period of about ten years, Remy was personally responsible for—and boasted of—the deaths of some nine hundred other witches, an average of one a week. At his disposal there were nearly as many laws (one authority says eight hundred) against witches and very little protection for anyone accused of witchcraft. It was a world in which the majority of people were truly terrified of what a prayer after mass described vividly as "Satan and all the other wicked spirits who roam through the world seeking the ruin of souls."

THE SIGN OF THE BEAST

It is believed that Satanism is the reverse, a sort of mirror image, of Christianity.

Just as the baptism of a Christian was supposed to cleanse the body (and leave a indelible mark on the soul), so initiation into the Devil's Party would mark, or befoul, the body and the soul.

To find a witch, then, you looked for the Devil's mark. Perhaps the Devil had put a brand (a birthmark? a scar?) on the witch; perhaps where he touched the witch there would be an insensitive spot, detectable with a probing needle.

So suspects were shaved (removing all the hair also prevented amulets and such from being hidden on the body) and examined with great care. Every mole or imperfection was scrutinized.

Jacques Fontaine in 1611 wrote a treatise "on the marks of witches and actual possession taken by the Devil of men's bodies" and warned that examiners should be suspicious of ordinary things. "Those who say that it is difficult to distinguish marks of the Devil from natural imperfections, from boils or impetigo, show quite clearly that they are not competent doctors."

Sadistic clergymen and prying lawyers jabbed the suspects (often senile old women) with pins, probing for a spot that could not feel pain, often in areas where the victims felt the most embarrassment. On some witches examiners found marks they regarded as extra nipples; were these used to suckle familiars?

Even in England, where the judicial system ordinarily treated the accused as innocent until proved guilty, people suspected of witchcraft found themselves in the difficult position of having to prove their innocence. When you were "swum" as a test you were often tied, right thumb to left big toe and left thumb to right big toe, and then thrown into the water. If you *floated*, it proved that the Devil was buoying you up.

Speedy trial by prejudiced courts was followed too often by horrible death: You could be hanged, beheaded, burned alive, drowned, whatever was in fashion. Persons of high rank were sometimes hanged first and burned afterward, in consideration of their station. Gilles de Retz enjoyed this last privilege, despite his appalling crimes.

The Renaissance was the time of the Iron Maiden and other ingenious devices of torture. Or they could just ask you to pull a blessed ring out of a vat of boiling water; if the bandaged hand then healed in three days, you were a witch. Or they might hand you a bar of red-hot iron and ask you to carry it nine, or twelve, paces. . . . In an earlier day, they did that for ordinary crimes, too.

The connection between witch hunting and sadistic psychopathology needs more study. It is a vile record of human ferocity.

ELIZABETH DUNLOP'S CASE

Sir Walter Scott tells the story of Elizabeth Dunlop of Scotland. On November 8, 1576, she was tried for witchcraft and told the court that she dealt with a familiar who was really Thomas Reid (killed at the Battle of Pinkie, September 10, 1547, when an officer to the Laird of Blair).

She claimed, and all her neighbors agreed, that she only did petty sorcery and never anything but good deeds for the benefit of her friends. Whereupon she was "convict and burned" forthwith.

EVIDENCE

Jules Michelet's monumental study of medieval superstition, *Satanism and Witchcraft*, is full of incredible reports. Here is one in the translation of A. R. Allinson (1939):

> The procedure is of the simplest. To begin with, apply torture to the witnesses, and build up a travesty, a caricature of evidence, by dint of pain and terror. Then drag a confession from the accused by excruciating agonies, and believe this confession against the direct evidence of facts. For instance, a Sorceress confesses she had recently dug up a child's dead body from the churchyard, to use it in her magical compounds. Her husband says, 'Go to the churchyard and look; the child is there now.' The grave is opened, and the body found intact in its coffin. Yet the judge decides, against the testimony of his own eyes, that it is only an *appearance*, an illusion of Satan. He credits the woman's confession in preference to the actual fact,—and the poor creature is burned.

Why this judicial insanity? A hint from the first sentence of Michelet's chapter: "The Church always granted the judge and the accuser a right to the confiscated property of those condemned for Sorcery."

Behind the urge to be a witch is very often an insane desire for power and sheer greed; behind the persecution of witches, lie ecclesiastical and civil power gone mad—and greater greed.

THE EYES HAVE IT

Elizabeth Device was hanged as a witch in 1612 in Rochdale, England, on no other evidence except that she could look up with one eye and down with the other.

Isadore of Seville, the erudite medieval encyclopedist, solemnly wrote that you could easily spot a witch, because they have two pupils in each eye. No, that's not a mistranslation of his clumsy Latin; he really believed it.

THIRSTY WORK

Elspeth McEwen was burned to death in a tar barrel as a witch in 1697 at Kirkcudbright in Scotland. An old bill survives:

Payed to Robert Creighton . . . 8 shill[ings] Scots for beating the drum at Elspet[h] M'Queen's funeral, and to James Carsson his wife [James Carson's wife] thirteen shillings drunken by Elspet[h]s executioner at sev[er]all times.

A FEW FIRSTS

The Bible is the first significant book to suggest killing witches.

Tacitus was the first major historian to take ghosts seriously.

Agnes Ode was the first Englishwoman to be tried for sorcery (thirteenth century), and after she passed the carrying-a-hot-poker test, she was acquitted.

Angela de la Barthe was the first Frenchwoman to be tried as a witch. She was burned in 1274.

Agnes Waterhouse, the first woman to be hanged as a witch in England, was executed at Chelmsford, Essex, in 1566.

Alice Young was the first woman to die for witchcraft in the bloody assizes of Connecticut in 1647.

FRENCH JUSTICE

Henri Bouget, author of the *Discours des sorciers* (1602)—for a generation, it was *the* handbook for witchcraft trials—is credited with having condemned more than six hundred wretches in Burgundy, though the number may have been exaggerated because of the judicial eminence of the writer.

The book that supplanted the *Discours* was by Le Sieur de Bouvet, provost-marshal of the French army. The title translates as *Admirable Ways and Means of Investigating All Sorts of Crimes and Witchcraft* and appeared in 1659. Where Benedikt Carpzov gave Augustus of Saxony a mere seventeen methods of torture, Bouvet was far more inventive. The book is a sadist's dream.

It was Bouget who established the rule that the more the prisoner denied his guilt, the more he was to be punished. To Bouget, denial of guilt "was an especially good reason to continue the torture."

QUAKER JUSTICE

Leave it to sensible Quakers to distinguish between public opinion and fact. The 1684 verdict of a Pennsylvania jury on an old woman accused of witchcraft was that "the prisoner is guilty of the common fame of being a witch but not guilty as she stands indicted."

SPANISH LOGIC

Pedro Sanchez Cirvelo (1475–1560) was canon of Salamanca at a time when that university was drawing students from far and wide. In 1521 he published *Opus de Magica Superstitione* and in 1539 *Reproof of Superstitions and Witchcraft*, the first really important Spanish work on that subject. In this he maintained the odd contention that, although sorcery is *not* a heresy, the Inquisition ought to punish it as if it were.

But perhaps the Inquisition had enough on its hands with heresy, for witchcraft persecutions did not flourish in Spain—the one country in Europe that refused to be panicked into such mindless folly. In *Witchcraft* (1958) Geoffrey Parrinder writes:

> When the secular authorities stimulated a witch-craze in Navarre in 1526, a congregation of the [Spanish] Inquisition seriously debated the root question of the reality of witchcraft, and the punishment to be applied. . . . They agreed that confession was not proof enough, and that in any case the witch should be dealt with by the Inquisition which would impose penance.
>
> The Inquisition in Spain checked the popular and civil efforts to destroy witches and it protected their lives.

THE LAST WITCH EXECUTED IN SCOTLAND

The last Scottish witch to be executed was an old woman of the parish of Loth, condemned by Captain David Ross, "sheriff-depute," who believed that she had ridden upon her own daughter, transformed into a pony, and shod by the devil, which made the girl ever after lame."

The accused was asked to give the Lord's Prayer (in Gaelic), and when she got *one word wrong*, they burned her. The Witch's Stone still marks the spot where she died.

HOW MANY DIED?

It is curious that Salem, Massachusetts, should be so famous for witchcraft persecutions. Twenty-one persons died in the months the hysteria lasted. The total figures for all witchcraft executions during the entire colonial period for all thirteen American colonies was thirty-two.

During the same period in Germany, estimates of the deaths from witchcraft accusations have run as high as 300,000 (far too high, say modern authorities—even 100,000 is overgenerous), many from drowning, burning, or from torture to which the accused were routinely subjected. Even England, where torture was not permitted as punishment, the most conservative modern estimates run to 1,000 dead, and in Scotland the figure may have been three or four times that many. But what community is famous for witchhunts? Why, Salem, Massachusetts, of course.

SPECIAL TREATMENT

If you were a woman who had murdered her husband, or a counterfeiter, heretic, or one of a few other special groups who were condemned, you could be burned at the stake. Witches were burned at the stake partly because that was a purification for heresy and partly because of the fear that, if their bodies were buried, they would come out of their graves to hurt the living—like vampires.

DAME ALICE AND THE BISHOP

The history of Ireland includes a number of sensational trials for witchcraft, the most famous being that of Dame Alice Kyteler in the fourteenth century. It is the only Irish one in which torture was used in a prosecution for witchcraft.

Dame Alice came from a wealthy Norman family long settled in Kilkenny, and her money gained her a succession of husbands. The first was a banker, William Outlawe. He died—they said of poison—but that did not discourage Adam le Blund and Richard de Valle, both of whom also died after marrying her—also with poison suspected. Her fourth husband was Sir John le Poer, and the rumors flew that she had caught him by means of love philter and by other evil potions had deprived him of his senses.

Finally in 1324 the bishop of Ossory investigated, and a commission in Kilkenny reported that Dame Alice was reputed to be a member of a local group of sorcerers. These wizards denied the Christian faith and absented themselves from its sacraments, sacrificing animals to demons and distributing pieces of the animals' bodies at crossroads to a low-ranking demon they called the Son of Art. The demons in exchange gave them powers. They met nightly to conduct their ceremonies (some of them blasphemous parodies of Christian rituals) and to bring evil on their neighbors by the use of a witches' brew. The brew contained, among other ingredients, entrails of animals sacrificed to demons, herbs, bits of the shrouds of unbaptized infants or the brains and hair and nails of men's corpses, and other horrible things, all cooked up in the skull of a decapitated thief.

They put curses and spells even on their own husbands, it was alleged. The children of Dame Alice's first three husbands accused her of murdering their fathers by witchcraft and depriving them of their rightful inheritances. They said her present husband, Sir John, had lost all his hair and his strength and would have died had not a maidservant alerted him to his wife's witchcraft and showed him where he could find, locked away in her private chests, some of the ingredients of the witches' brew.

The hideous things found there were turned over to the authorities, but the accusers were unable to produce the incubus (named Art or Robin) with whom, they claimed, Dame Alice had sexual relations, or the big black dog, called Aethiops, an incubus and her familiar. Some witnesses did swear they saw her in the streets "between compline and twilight" sweeping up all the dirt toward her son William Outlawe's front door and chanting:

> "To the house of William, my son,
> Hie all the wealth of Kilkenny town."

A complicated power struggle ensued between the bishop and Dame Alice's powerful relatives, which the bishop ultimately won. But Alice fled to England, her son William, her accomplice in witchcraft, was too powerful to punish except by a brief imprisonment, and the full brunt of the law fell on Dame Alice's servant Petronilla.

The bishop had the girl flogged six times, forcing her to confess the details of Alice's and William's obscene magical rites. She directed the authorities to where, she said, Dame Alice kept her magical flying ointment ("wherewith she greased a staffe, upon which she ambled and galloped through thick and thin, when and in what name she listed") and a desecrated Host, on which the name of the Devil had replaced that of Jesus Christ.

This proof against Dame Alice served only to destroy Petronilla. When it was added to her confessions, she was burned at the stake in Kilkenny on November 3, 1324, the first instance of burning for heresy in Ireland.

The rest of the members, "the other heretics and sorcerers who belonged to the pestilential Society of Robin, Son of Art," were (according to an old report) rounded up and punished:

> the order of law being preserved, some of them were publicly burnt to death; others, confessing their crimes in the presence of all the people, in an upper garment are marked back and front with a cross after they had abjured the heresy, which is the custom; others were solemnly whipped through the town and the market place; others were banished from the city and diocese; others, who evaded the jurisdiction of the Church, were excommunicated; while others again fled in fear and were never heard of after.

This tale of Dame Alice and her son amply illustrates the way that the witchcraft laws were weighted against the poor.

WITCHCRAFT BANNED IN BOSTON

The four children of John Godwin said to be possessed by the Devil in Boston in 1688 were the subject of Cotton Mather's *Memorable Providences* published the next year. There were two boys (aged five and eleven) and two girls (aged seven and thirteen), and they alarmed the whole populace of Boston when they fell into "strange fits, beyond those that attend an epilepsy, or a catalepsy, or those that they call the diseases of astonishment." Whenever anyone wanted to get the children up in the morning, or put them to bed at night, or dress them, all Hell broke loose. They contorted their bodies so that they could not be dressed, they screamed and roared, they seem to go deaf and dumb or blind, and they twisted their heads "almost round."

Modern parents with obstreperous children might well suspect mere acting up or hyperactivity, but in seventeenth-century Boston there was only one explanation: "Nothing but a hellish witchcraft could be the origin of these maladies."

The cause was suspected to be Goody Glover, described as "a scandalous old woman," accused of having laid an "enchantment" on the children, having cursed them in her bad temper. She was just an old Irishwoman who could speak little English, but the fact that she could not say the Lord's Prayer in English was considered a sinister sign. When they searched her house, authorities produced "several small images, or puppets, or babies, made of rags and stuffed with goat's hair and other such ingredients." They said she confessed to hurting the children by wetting her finger and applying it to various places on the dolls. She apologized for being unable to say prayers in English; she said them, she explained, in Irish and—horrors! a Catholic?—in Latin.

Goody Glover was condemned to death by Judge Stoughton, deputy governor of Massachusetts, a figure who was to be more prominent later at the Salem witchcraft trials. After a second old woman was also condemned, things quieted down in Boston.

But Cotton Mather (1663–1728) was not content with that, and one of the most influential of his nearly four hundred books soon appeared as *Memorable Providences, Relating to Witchcraft and Possession* (1689). "I am resolved," Cotton Mather wrote, "after this [Boston incident] never to use but just one grain of patience with any man that shall go to impose upon me a denial of devils or of witches."

THE KING JAMES VERSION

James I of England is famous for the King James Version of the Bible. He ordered that translation, but of course it was not his work. He did write *Daemonologia*, a blast against Reginald Scot's *Discoverie of Witchcraft*, which called the black arts a mere "artful imposture." James defended the reality of witchcraft, because he was sure he knew, from personal experience, its widespread dangers.

In 1591, twelve years before he came to the English throne (he was then James VI of Scotland), a witchcraft conspiracy had come to light in the town of North Berwick. The women and men rounded up confessed to bizarre acts—going to sea in a sieve, causing a violent storm on the sea by drowning a baptised cat, and similar claims—and confessed that their purpose was to kill the king by causing his ship (he was returning from Denmark at the time with his new queen) to founder. At their trial, they swore that their leader was Francis Stewart, earl of Bothwell, son of a bastard son of James V (and thus the king's half first cousin).

James had always suspected his cousin of having designs on the throne, and the witches' confessions may have been an attempt to curry favor. If so, they did not know their James, for he had the group subjected to mangling and death, torturing one Dr. Fian until he was "less a man than a bleeding mass," and ordered a woman "burned in ashes quick [alive] to death."

Bothwell himself escaped being tried by fleeing to England, but at Christmastime the following year, he reappeared in Edinburgh and tried to get into Holyrood Palace, the king's residence, to demand a hearing. James cowered inside in terror and refused to admit his cousin, who eventually gave up and, fearful the king would have him secretly murdered, fled to Normandy and then Naples, where he remained for the rest of his life.

James meanwhile wrote *Daemonologia* and became king of England.

RADICAL VIEWS

The rule used to be that you couldn't take a valid confession actually on the rack. But five minutes before or after the rack was technically not under duress. Clever?

Peter Binsfield (1540–1603), author of a seminal Latin treatise on "malificers and sorcerers" of 1589, was willing to believe evidence obtained under duress, but despite "confessions" begged leave to doubt the reality of ailuranthropy (changing into a cat), cynanthropy (changing into a dog), and lepanthropy (changing into a hare). This position was regarded by other authorities of the time as wrongheaded and dangerous.

SWEDISH WITCHES

The Swedes were usually calmer than the French or the Germans when it came to witchcraft, but in 1670 at Mohra seventy women and fifteen children were executed for witchcraft and 136 children (aged nine to sixteen) were sentenced to "run the gauntlet and be whipped on their hands at the church door," some as often as once a week for a year. Later in that decade, between 1674 and 1677 some seventy persons were burned or beheaded in Sweden for witchcraft.

The severe sentences of the earlier part of the century in the reign of Gustavus Adolphus (1618) seem to have been aimed more at poisoners than witches. Queen Christina put a stop to sorcery trials. Still accusations spread, and executions at Mohra, just mentioned, led to forty-seven cases at Fallun, more in Upsalla (an old stronghold of witchcraft), and Stockholm. The death sentence for witchcraft was abolished in Sweden in 1799.

Today, witchcraft is hardly active at all in Sweden (compared to Britain, for example) but the folk remedies and customs smack quite a bit of the pagan past.

MORE ON THE NORTH BERWICK WITCHES

At the trial of the witches in North Berwick, already mentioned, King James attended in person. At one point he was moved to yell at Agnes Simpson that she was lying in the dock.

She asked to talk with him privately and repeated word for word what James and his queen had said in bed on their wedding night. That convinced King James that she was a witch after all. So all the defendants, including Alice Simpson, were executed.

REALLY LAYING AN EGG

At the beginning and the end of the sixteenth century the normally placid Swiss had wild outbreaks of witch-burning: five hundred executed in Geneva in 1515 and three hundred executed in Bern 1591–1600, for instance. In 1474 in Basel, a fowl was sentenced to death for laying an egg. You see, it was a rooster.

A HIGH SCORE

In the quiet little Protestant town of Quedlinburg in Saxony in the year 1589, the population of 12,000 burned 133 witches on one single day. It would have been 137 witches, but four of the condemned were pretty young girls, and the executioner saved them, giving out that the Devil had spirited them away.

THE LAWGIVER

Benedikt Carpzov II (1595–1666), called the Lawgiver of Saxony, had two proud boasts: (1) that he had read the Bible fifty-three times and (2) that he had caused to be burned at the stake a total of twenty thousand witches.

Modern historians tend to be skeptical of such figures, even when not given as boasts. But plainly Carpzov gave it his best shot.

THE LAST

One of the most stringent laws ever enacted against "witchcraft, enchantments and sorceries" were Henry VIII's statute of 1542. Yet under that law only one single person was actually convicted, and he was pardoned. Under other laws, however, the accusations and killing continued, and in 1604 James I managed to get a law passed that made accusation of witchcraft virtually tantamount to conviction.

Under this law, one authority claims, over a period of some two hundred years, a total of 30,000 "judicial murders" for witchcraft were carried out. King James I once condemned a whole assizes for daring to acquit a woman accused of witchcraft.

About a dozen witches were executed in Northamptonshire in the first few years of the eighteenth century, and in 1716 a Mrs. Hicks and her daughter (aged nine) were hanged for witchcraft in Huntingdonshire. The laws against witchcraft were then repealed in the tenth year of the reign of George II (1736) when, according to Joseph Hayden's *Dictionary of Dates* (1841), "an ignorant person attempting to revive them" instituted a "bill against a poor old woman in Surrey for the practice of witchcraft."

The last execution for witchcraft in Scotland was in 1722, as we have described elsewhere. That did not end the persecution in the British Isles, however, for much hounding and torment went on clandestinely. In the 1750s in Hampshire, two oldsters were accidentally killed while their interrogators were "swimming" them in the village pond.

In the American colonies, trials for witchcraft were not confined to New England—although that is where they flourished—but Maryland is the only other mainland colony that actually executed a witch. In 1685, Rebecca Fowler was hanged for practicing "diabolical arts." Maryland was also the scene of the colonies' last witchcraft trial, in 1712, when a certain Virtue Violl was found not guilty of sorcery. The last execution for witchcraft in the British colonies was in Bermuda in 1730, when Sarah Bassett, a slave, was hanged for killing her master by spells.

In the Spanish-speaking parts of the Americas the persecution of witches continued much longer than in Europe, and the last person burned as a witch seems to have been a woman put to death in Peru in 1888.

In Germany in the seventeenth century, the bishop of Bamberg burned more than a hundred people for sorcery and perhaps as many as two hundred (accounts vary). Philip Adolf von Ehrenberg, a prince-bishop, and his cousin Johann Georg II Fuchs von Dornheim (the Axe Bishop) between them accounted for fifteen hundred dead. In 1627, the Germans built a big *Hexenhaus* to hold the accused until they could be tortured into confessions of witchcraft. The end of the eighteenth century saw the last important accusations of witchcraft. The age when Wolfenbüttel—and all too many other German cities—was "a forest of stakes" was finally over.

THE GUILT OF WITCHES

In times when a scapegoat was needed or when religion felt threatened, witchcraft became an abomination and a heresy, and toward it was directed all the righteous violence of the society. But was there really such a thing as a compact with the Devil?

Wallace Notestein's *History of Witchcraft in England from 1558 to 1718* (1911), leaning heavily on the court records, tends to agree with Reginald Scot's Elizabethan opinion (then unorthodox) that witchcraft is a delusion and that "witches" are more senile than Satanic. But such a viewpoint has been mocked as late as 1926. In that year Montague Summers published *History of Witchcraft and Demonology*, in which he says:

> A few authors have painted the mediaeval witch in pretty colours on satin. She has become a somewhat eccentric but kindly old lady, shrewd and perspicacious, with a knowledge of healing herbs and simples, ready to advise and aid her neighbors. . . . And so for no very definite reason she fell an easy prey to fanatic judges and ravening inquisitors, notoriously the most ignorant and stupid of mortals, who caught her, swum her in a river, tried her, tortured her, and finally burned her at the stake. . . .

Surely the truth is that some witches were decidedly antisocial, lawless, vengeful, murderers for hire, poisoners, terrorists, heretics, and some were indeed kindly old ladies with some old country recipes for healing. In either case, their treatment by the law was barbaric.

5

Amulets, Talismans, and Charms

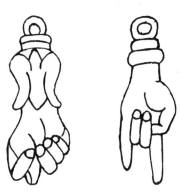

TALISMANIC magic is one kind that most people have practiced at some time or other. Have you ever had a rabbit's foot or a "lucky coin" or any other object you carried around "just for luck"? Have you known anyone else who did?

Actually, many of the things we will be discussing are not talismans but amulets. Amulets ward off evil, whereas talismans attract good results. Just "knowing" one has something working for him helps to alleviate worry, creates confidence, and thus enhances the wearer's performance.

If you believe, as have many occultists such as Paracelsus and Colin Wilson, that magic is in the mind, then the wearer's personal attitude is the most important thing. But magicians believe that a true astral force or some other supernatural power can literally be put into an amulet or talisman and that it can function even if the wearer is wholly unaware of it.

Many people employ amulets and talismans as integral parts of orthodox religion: phylacteries and mezuzahs, crosses and medals. The Egyptians used scarabs and ankhs, the Africans use fetishes, the Mohammedans the Hand of Fatima and other devices.

Here are just a few examples of magical and ritual objects.

GRIS-GRIS

The African practice of making small idols or images of protecting spirits arrived in the Western Hemisphere along with slavery. Today, often still used in Voodoo and similar cults, they are worn as charms.

A.M.S.G.

The practice of the Society of Jesus is to put at the top of documents *A.M.D.G.*, which stands for *Ad Maiorem Dei Gloriam*, "To the Greater Glory of God." Others used *J.M.J.* ("Jesus, Mary, and Joseph") and similar devices.

Satanists use *A.M.S.G.* (*Ad Maiorem Satanae Gloriam*, "To the Greater Glory of Satan") on documents, in pentacles, on amulets and talismans, and so on. Sometimes *D.V.* (*Dei veri*, "The True God") is added.

FREE SERVICE

Occult tradition dictates that the maker of amulets and talismans must receive no fee for his services, though it is allowable for him who is to wear the amulet or talisman to provide the metal (usually silver or gold).

Thus getting your own metal disk and sending it out to be engraved by your local jeweler does not work, because you must pay him. Moreover, you will not know the precise moment when he gets to the work, and that is essential if you are to meditate on your intention and so help "charge" the amulet or talisman.

A CHRISTIAN CHARM

The *Malleus Maleficarum* allowed charms to Christians provided that no unknown names were used (lest these be of pagan gods or demons), no pact with the Devil, no belief in any power other than the power of God, nothing untrue or pagan (only the sign of the Cross for "passes"), and only Biblical phrases.

NOTHING BUT THE TOOTH

When you were a child, and lost a tooth, did you put it under your pillow to get a coin from the Tooth Fairy?

There are other strange superstitions about teeth, about babies born with a full set (who will be vampires or worse), about the order in which baby teeth are cut, about "wisdom" teeth, about horses' teeth hung around a child's neck to make the child's teeth strong (an old Scandinavian idea), and so on.

Did you know that the gypsies recommend that the first tooth a child loses must be thrown into a hollow tree? Clearly a tribute to the gods in the trees we used to worship.

Teeth that fall out after the age of seven should be saved; they can come in handy. If a child then has a severe toothache, a discarded tooth can be thrown into a stream. This recalls our ancient worship of the spirits in water.

Saved teeth come in handy when you have something to sell and no customers. Keep them in a little bag, along with the bones of a tree frog or toad or an ash twig. On market day, you simply rub the bag and wish and customers will then appear—if you believe strongly and if the bag has been properly prepared. (The main problem is getting the small bones clean. Bury them in a perforated container in an anthill; the ants will pick them quite clean.)

I have only once seen this ancient superstition alive in the modern world. At Caledonian Market, the outdoors antiques market at Bermondsey (part of London) in 1969, I saw an old man with his little bag and a deserted stall. He needed all the help he could get. His few goods looked a bit ratty, and it was very early on a very wet Friday.

I popped up behind him and asked, "Are there teeth and bones in your little bag?" He was startled, doubly so when I confessed that I got my information out of books.

"I didn't know things like that were in books," he said. "Perhaps a gypsy wrote that book, but he oughtn't to have done it."

I chatted awhile and eventually bought an old painting from under the stall that cleaned up fine and proved to be a fair copy of an original portrait of Lord Byron. The old man wrapped my purchase carefully in some old newspaper, and as I paid him, I jokingly remarked that one must never conclude a bargain on a Friday, for Friday (when Christ died) is unlucky.

"That's all very true, Guv," he responded, "but Caledonian Market is only open on a Friday, so what can a man do?"

What indeed? Well, a man can stick to his superstitions. In a way, his little magic bag did work. It brought me right over to his stall, and I was his first customer. As for me, I have my Byron portrait with a good story thrown in—not a bad bargain for £3.

THE LONDON CURSE

On a site in Princes Street, London, a piece of lead, perhaps once nailed to a door, was excavated. It read:

T[ITUS] EGNATIUS TYRANUS DEFIC [T]US EST ET P[UBLIUS] CICEREIUS
FELIX DEFICTUS E[S]T

It put a curse on Titus Egnatius Tyranus and Publius Cicereius Felix. One wonders whatever happened to them. If they *saw* the curse, it may well have had its effect.

LINES (AND CIRCLES) FROM CHRISTOPHER MARLOWE

These metaphysics of magicians
And necromantic books are heavenly:
Lines, circles, scenes, letters and characters:
Ay, these are those that Faustus most desires.
O, what a world of profit and delight,
Of power, of honour, of omnipotence
Is promised to the studious artisan!
      —*The Tragical History of Doctor Faustus*

A TALISMAN

In the will of Napoleon III (1808–1873), that emperor of the French left to his son "as a talisman the seal I used to wear attached to my watch."

THE PRIEST'S HAND

Eric Maple, active in the Society for Psychical Research and the author of numerous books and radio talks, writes in *The Complete Book of Witchcraft and Demonology* (1966):

> During the Protestant ascendancy, no sport was more popular, if we except witch hunting, than hounding to death those Jesuit priests who attempted to keep alight the candle of Roman Catholic faith in Britain. These priests were usually to be found in the homes of the old Catholic families, often hidden in secret rooms ["priest holes"] and passages. When caught they were often tortured and condemned to the dreadful punishment reserved for male traitors: partial hanging, castration, disembowelling and finally decapitation.
>
> In the reign of Charles I, Father Edward Arrowsmith [1585–1628], a Jesuit, was tried and executed for the mere fact of being a Romish priest, but before dying, asked those nearest to him, to sever his hand after death, declaring that with the aid of this talisman, they would have the power to work miracles.

The hand did, in fact, get credit for many curses and "miracles" over the next three hundred years and the *Dictionary of National Biography* noted that it "is preserved as a relic" in Newton-le-Willows, Yorkshire.

COSMETICS

In the sense that cosmetics are supposed to "draw" people to you, by making you look more beautiful, they are rather talismanic, and some ancient recipes mix magic with their ingredients, charms with charm.

Cosmetics are said to have been invented (along with astronomy and astrology, metal workng and armaments, magic and witchcraft) by "the Watchers," two hundred angels under the command of Azazel who descended to earth (at Mount Hermon) and married the daughters of men, according to the apocryplial Book of Enoch (first century B.C.). What they taught of magic cosmetics is among the most closely guarded secrets of the adepts in magical arts. Few covens, in fact, know of the powers attributed to body painting and perfuming for magical ceremonies.

Magical cosmetics are supposed to be a sort of warpaint in the battle the Satanists wage. If these "recipes" are indeed of ancient origin, then early adepts were well aware of the exact chemicals that cause human sexual excitement, for that seems to be the principle result of using them. (They also affect animals; it is reliably reported that when Aleister Crowley wore his perfumed ointment, the horses started and neighed as he walked by them in the street.)

CURSES

Superstitious people feared the curses of witches and magicians, and maleficers risked the curses of Church authorities. Plato, however, wrote in his *Laws* that the most effective of all curses was that of the parent on the child. "The curses of parents," you may care to remind your obstreperous offspring, "are mighty against their children as no others are."

GAINING THE FAVOR OF A JUDGE

When MacGregor Mathers obtained a court order to prevent Aleister Crowley from publishing the secrets of the Order of the Golden Dawn (1910), "The Beast" appealed the decision, and this is the talisman he used— borrowed from Chapter 19 of Mathers' own translation of *The Sacred Magic of Abramelin*—to get a judge to reverse the order of the court:

```
A L M A N A H
L
M A R E
A A L B E H A
N
A R E H A I L
H             A
```

If you are ever on trial, try writing these letters on parchment. They worked for Crowley—at least, he did get the order reversed.

BASMALA

The *basmala* is the Arabic formula for "In the Name of Allah, the Merciful, the Compassionate." In Arabic that is nineteen letters, equal to the *zabaniah* (company of angels under Malik).

Write it sixty-one times and wear it, and if you are barren, you will become fruitful. Write it six hundred times and wear it, and you will gain great honor among men. Or so it is claimed.

FETISH

The word *fetish* these days, as casually used by Europeans, generally refers to something with sexual significance, but it came originally from an old Portuguese word for "false" and is related to the current word for sorcerer: *feiticeiro*. It's primary meaning is still occult: any artifact or natural object held by its owner to possess supernatural powers.

ANTIDOTE

Secretum Secretorum ("Secret of Secrets") was a medieval magic book falsely attributed to Aristotle. It says that a bezoar stone prevents epilepsy in children. A bezoar is a mineral lump or concretion, like a gallstone, found in the stomachs of ruminants, particularly goats and deer. Epilepsy was only one of its uses. Ground up, it was prescribed as a cure for leprosy and fever, and carried about (preferably in a gold box) it was regarded as a preventive for plague—a true amulet.

But by far the commonest use of the bezoar was as a universal antidote for poison. When a Spanish nobleman tried to sell one to Charles IX of France, the king summoned his court physician, who happened to be Ambroise Paré, "the father of surgery," and asked if it really worked. Paré, a man famed for his common sense, said it wasn't possible for any single substance to be an antidote to all poisons, so the king tried an experiment. One of his cooks was about to be executed for theft; Charles offered to let the man go free if he would subject himself to a trial of the bezoar, and when the condemned man eagerly agreed, he was given the poison (corrosive sublimate) to swallow followed by some of the ground-up stone. The poor man died seven hours later "with great torment and exclamation," bleeding from every opening of the body. Charles burned the rest of the bezoar.

A CHARM IS A SIN

The Greek fishermen who seek for sponges around Tarpon Springs, Florida, know that their deeply held Christian faith forbids such superstitions as they have inherited from a pre-Christian past, but they manage to combine the old and the new. For example, they will not set out to sea on a Tuesday (Tuesday is an ill-fated day to begin any enterprise) nor begin the fishing season before Epiphany. They believe that if a storm is brewing at sea, they can protect themselves from its fury by carving a cross on the mast of the ship and sticking the knife into it.

Folklore in America (selected by T. P. Coffin and Hennig Cohen) adds:

This saves them from the fury of the storm. The person who performs this charm is committing a sin and must do some form of penance. The fishermen do not hesitate, however, to resort to this charm when in danger.

Anthropologists all over the world notice that fishermen may not use magic in unthreatening situations (like fishing in a lagoon) but resort to magic in danger.

KNIVES TO MEND

Among many people, knives are considered potent devices to use with charms. The Greek seamen above stick one in the mast to cause a high wind to die down. English seamen do the very same thing for the opposite purpose—to call up a wind when they are becalmed, or to change a foul wind to a fair one.

The Scots are particularly fond of knife superstitions. Carrying one in your pocket will prevent the fairies from abducting you at night. (Fairies are afraid of cold iron.) A recently killed deer must be stored overnight with a knife stuck into it, or the fairies will carry *it* off. When you enter the house of a fairy or a witch, you must stick a knife in the door, which will prevent the owner from closing it; once you are safely outside again, you remove the knife and go your way. If, on an otherwise calm day, you see an eddy of wind whisking up dust and straw, that means the fairies are carrying people off, and you must throw a knife at the eddy; that will force them to release their captives.

THE MUMMY'S CURSE?

Ancient Egyptians considered the pharaoh's person sacred and tried hard to protect it in death as in life. Their priests were clever, and they were vengeful; they used to put a picture of their enemies on the soles of their sandals, so that they could tread on them at every step. It was believed that the priests laid a curse on anyone who disturbed the sacred bones of a dead king.

If so, such curses did not work very well, for one after another, the tombs of pharaohs, no matter how carefully sealed and guarded, were broken into by grave robbers and rifled. Only one pharaonic tomb came down to the twentieth century intact.

On November 4, 1922, after seven years of searching, archaeologist Howard Carter discovered and opened the tomb of Tutankhamen, who had lived in the fourteenth century B.C. It was overwhelming. There was the mummy of the boy-god-king, adorned with about a hundred pieces of fabulous jewelry and (a poignant touch) a wreath of faded flowers, perhaps a last token from his young wife. The rest was a storehouse of treasures. The discovery made "King Tut," an obscure boy who had reigned ineffectually for only a few years, the best-known pharaoh in history.

But when Lord Carnarvon (1866–1923), Carter's patron, died of pneumonia during the excavation of the tomb, rumors started that he had been a victim of a pharaoh's curse. Subsequently, other members of the expedition died from various causes, mostly natural. Out of these unlikely ingredients—for no one could even point to a curse inscribed on the tomb— sensation-mongering newspapers created the myth of an ancient curse against anyone who disturbed the bones of the dead king.

It's hard to see why, if there was a curse, it didn't take Howard Carter first. He lived until 1939 and was sixty-six at the time of his death.

WANT TO TRY YOUR HAND?

A talismanic ring of the ninth century in the British Museum bears this inscription in runes:

AERKRIUFLTKRIURIPONGLAESTAEPON

Nobody has ever been able to interpret it.

TEMPLE OF THE TOOTH

Kandy was once the capital of a separate kingdom but is now the jewel of Sri Lanka, formerly Ceylon.

Among its many marvels is the Temple of the Tooth, one of the most sacred shrines of Buddhism. It is said to contain one tooth of Gautama himself, smuggled into the country by a princess who hid the relic in her elaborate hairdo.

At one time the Christians desecrated the temple, burned the relic, and threw the ashes into the sea. But Buddhists asserted that the tooth the Christians destroyed was a fake, that the real tooth of the founder of one of the world's great religions had been secretly saved.

Today, in a replacement temple the tooth is on display at the heart of a magnificent shrine.

I have seen the cloak of Mohammed in the treasures of Topkapi, palace of the Ottoman emperors, now a museum in Istanbul. I have seen relics of Jesus Christ, such as the Shroud of Turin. But these are "second-class" relics, simply associated with those men; the tooth is a "first-class" relic, a part of the Buddha himself.

If there can be magical power in things "charged" or blessed or touched by holy men, it is natural to believe that a piece of the person himself will have great power. Think of the blood of saints, for example, and, on a secular level, even the awe with which one regards the bloodstained shirt of Charles I, a lock of Napoleon's hair, a star's autograph.

THE SORCERER'S CURSE

Poussinière, sentenced to be burned at the stake in Fougères, France, said just before he died that the steeple of the church of St. Sulpice, nearby, would tilt that very day. It did, and for hundreds of years it has stood with its tip a foot and a half out of plumb.

INCANTATION AGAINST NIGHTMARES

Hang over your bed a crucifix or a stone with a natural hole in it. Before lying down to sleep recite these verses:

> St. George, St. George, Our Lady's knight,
> He walked by day, so he did by night:
> Until such times as he her found,
> He her beat and he her bound,
> Until her troth to him he plight,
> He would not come to her that night.

TREES AND STONES

Tree worship was denounced in Aelfric's "Homily on the Passion of St. Bartholomew the Apostle":

> It is not allowed to any Christian man to fetch his health from
> any stone, nor from any tree.

Note Aelfric doesn't say you *can't* do that—just that you *must* not. The English were a long time giving up the worship of trees.

In *Ancient Laws and Institutes of England*, Thorpe quotes the *Canones Edgari* to the effect that "tree-worshiping and stone-worshipping and that devil's craft hereby children are drawn through the earth" are expressly forbidden.

That last requires some explanation. Ancient custom had a child crawl three Fridays (the day of the Crucifixion, a nice tie-in of the New Religion with the Old) successively, silently, through an arch of brambles. Until fairly recent times Swedish women in labor were passed through *elfenlöcher*, holes in trees.

But we no longer worship trees, knock on wood.

THE CROSS

The Cross is of course a common symbol in post-Christian amulets, etc. The sign of the Cross has substituted for a number of the "passes" magicians used to make with their hands. Appearing often in missals and other religious books, it once convinced the ignorant that magical symbols were used in Roman Catholic rituals. Even Satanists use the symbol, though it ought to be neutral for them.

The cross surmounts many churches, including St. Paul's Cathedral in London. But the architect Sir Christopher Wren wanted a pineapple there.

SACRED STONES

Throughout history certain precious and semiprecious stones have been thought to have magical powers.

In Iceland jet, or black amber, is carried as a protection. In Africa, certain stones often form part of the pack buried under an enemy's threshold to put a curse on him. In medieval Europe, jet was used to test virginity (I am uncertain how) and burned to drive away evil spirits.

The breastplate of the High Priest of the Jews was composed of a number of precious and semiprecious stones, each believed to have its own special power. (I discussed these in *The Wonderful World of Superstition, Prophecy, and Luck* [1984], so I will not repeat their meanings here.)

It was inevitable that heavenly powers should be attributed to such stones as fell from the "pavement of Heaven" to earth. Tondriau and Villeneuve in their *Dictionary of Devils and Demons* stray a little from their subject to discuss aerolite, defined as a "piece of a star which has fallen to earth." But meteorites and such have been less used in magic than stones mined from the earth.

Among stones believed to protect the wearer are amber (against poison), amethyst (against drunkenness), coral (against violence), jade (against nightmares), topaz (against injury), turquoise (against assassination), and zircon (for many uses).

To bring or retain love people have worn beryl, emerald and lapis. Moonstones, onyx, and opal are unlucky for most people, though opal (it is said) will warn the unlucky wearer by becoming cloudy.

Millions of people still concern themselves with birthstones, and in my book on superstition, prophecy, and luck, of course, I gave a list of them. Here let me amplify it a little by commenting on each of the stones.

January	**garnet**	gives constancy, sincerity, friendliness, frankness, generosity.
February	**amethyst**	cures alcoholism, creates contentment, draws favor of superiors.
March	**aquamarine**	gives hope and confidence, cheers up the unhappy.
April	**diamond**	reconciles lovers, gives constancy, fidelity, innocence.
May	**emerald**	strenthens love and intelligence, eloquence, popularity.
June	**pearl**	gives purity, fidelity, gentleness, tears of joy or sorrow.
July	**ruby**	gives boldness, anger, loyalty, charity, cruelty, courage, misery.
August	**sardonyx**	gives intellectual power, can be used in magical rites.
September	**sapphire**	gives loyalty, justice, truth, peace, contentment, humility.
October	**tourmaline**	gives vitality, potency, vigor, exhilaration, excitement.
November	**topaz**	gives sobriety, fidelity, love, draws honor or wealth, cures anger.
December	**turquoise**	prevents assassinations or accidental death, brings safety.

If you think pearls are unlucky, (as many people do), you can wear alexandrite. This variety of beryl changes color and so seems in some people's minds to combine the advantages of other stones it can resemble: sapphire, emerald, amethyst. The reason that ruby's characteristics seem at odds with each other is that rubies are believed to alter their appearance, and when they do, they bring on the negative: the cruel and uncontrolled side of the individual comes out.

It is considered unlucky to wear a stone of a month other than one's birth month, but jade or crystal are reckoned as exceptions. Anyone can gain luck by wearing jade or crystal. Jade is for persons of the highest morality; crystal is likelier to create a better morality in a person by sharpening the intellect, directing it toward a better harmony. Anyone can wear beryl to attract the opposite sex, jet to protect against fears and apparitions, zircon to promote sound sleep and good health and to protect on journeys.

Opal, once thought unlucky for anyone not born in October, is now passed by very often even by them, tourmaline being chosen instead, but October people can wear opal safely if they will just discard it should it grow dull (unlucky).

Probably the most revered stone in the world is the "black stone," set in silver, and built into the Ka'abah at Mecca. A pilgrimage to that site is the dream of every Muslim in the world, and every year a great many people of the Islamic world make their way there. Some say that this black stone was once part of the Temple of Solomon.

HERESY

The Inquisition sitting at Saragossa, Spain, in 1585 solemnly declared that keeping a dead man's finger as a good luck charm was a heresy.

SWEDISH CUSTOM

Besides keeping on or near one's self certain things to bring good luck or protection, there is also the matter of sacrificing material to God or the Devil.

Sacha Segal Scarlet in a *Key to Stockholm* (1960) says that "a tradition that is dying out is at Christmas for the children to carry a bowl of rice porridge to the attic for the Robin Goodfellow [Devil] or goblin of the dwelling. Possibly the family cats regret that this custom is now so little observed."

From the earliest times people sacrificed animals. The Germans used to offer reindeer, their most valuable livestock. The Greeks poured wine on the ground. Melchizedech, king of Salem and priest of the Most High God, substituted bread and wine for animal sacrifice and set the tradition now followed by the Christians. This custom of offering human food to the gods is seen in many religions around the world, and the "rice porridge" offered to Swedish goblins is part of this.

WHAT'S IN A NAME?

Names play an important part on amulets and talismans, and many have an inscription beginning "in the Name of" followed by names or *Shemoth* (substitute names) of God or demons or archangels.

A name in magic is regarded as a part of the person who bears it and is often used just as a lock of hair or some nail clipping would be. Magicians were believed to exert power over spirits and demons by knowing their names; once they had drawn their magic circle (containing the names of God) to protect themselves, they would summon up the supernatural beings and force them, by the use of their names, to do the bidding of mortals.

In black magic, many names are reversed or anagrammatized.

Never put your own name or an amulet or talisman, but put as much of "yourself" as possible into its manufacture and keep it with you continually to increase and derive the most benefit from its power—even if you are not sure you believe in its efficacy.

SPIT

Baseball pitchers spit on the ball. Laborers spit on their hands. People spit on the ground to seal a bargain. Enemies spit at you in derision or contempt.

Spit is magical. Voodoo magicians spit on their little effigies to "give them life." Christ used spit to work miracles of healing.

A Dr. Gregory, lecturing to the British Association (Oxford, 1894), explained how he and the chief of the warlike Masai tribe of Africa made peace after a disagreement: "We spat on each other."

Spitting is messier than shaking hands (which comes from the old custom of showing you were holding no weapon) but better in that it transfers a part of yourself to the other. Blood brothers the easy and painless way!

People also spit on money "for luck" and on charms, kiss "good luck" pieces, and so on. Did you ever wonder why? Now you know.

THE STAR THAT ISN'T DAVID'S

Common on amulets and talismans, as in pentagrams, etc., is the six-pointed "star of David," honored by the Jews and dishonored by Hitler who tried to make it a badge of inferiority.

It was King Solomon, not King David, however, who had a seal ring with this ancient star on it; engraved with "the real Name of God," it was supposed to give him power over demons. It's lost; he was buried with it.

Cabalists adopted the six-pointed star because it incorporated the symbol for fire, a triangle resting on its base, and that for water, a triangle on its point.

They called it the Seal of Solomon and used it for talismans and put it on their equipment, such as their magic robes. It is found as a sign of power in the magical books ascribed in the Middle Ages to Solomon himself. These have been "adapted" and reprinted. Useless. Magicians insist they must be in manuscript.

This "Jewish" symbol is seen in Christian churches (sometimes combined with the Greek *alpha* and *omega*, suggesting the beginning and the end) and on magicians' hats from places as far apart as Wales and Algeria, Nepal (where it is combined with a sword as an insignia of the king) and Mexico.

NIGHT MAGIC

Lenormant's *Chaldean Magic* (1877) and similar historical studies of the Sumerians and the Babylonians and Assyrians, demonstrate something of the age-old nature of magic.

A Chaldean magical tablet yields a talisman to keep demons out of your house. It translates thus:

Talisman, Talisman,
Boundary that cannot be taken away,
Boundary that the gods cannot pass,
Barrier immovable,
Which is opposed to malevolence
Whether it be a wicked *utuq*,

A wicked *alal*, a wicked *gilgum*,
A wicked god, a wicked *maskim*,
A phantom, a spector,
A vampire, an incubus,
A succubus, a nightmare,
May the barrier of the god Ea
Stop him.

Perhaps a little more translation will help. *Utuq*, *alal*, and *gilgum* are kinds of demons; *maskim* are seven subterranean demons. You know the others. As I say elsewhere, a vampire is not really a demon (being undead) but is in some manner related to demons associated with the bloodthirsty Moloch. The nightmare used to be thought of as a kind of animal demon or hag who tormented people during their sleep, as did incubi and succubi. Ea was the god of wisdom.

"Now I lay me down to sleep. . . ." The night has always held terrors for people and is the Devil's time of day, as it were. Chaldean demons also appeared at night. Against them they used such a *teletē* (Greek for "rite"), while an amulet gave passive protection.

Today people use a four-leaf clover, the pompom from a European sailor's hat, the *fascinum* (winged phallus, some of which were found in the ruins of Pompeii and seemed to have done little good there), and so on.

As O. Henry said on his deathbed, we do not want to go home in the dark.

MORE STONES

Precious and semiprecious stones were thought to have medicinal as well as magical powers; medicine and magic were closely intertwined anyway, like the snakes on the *caduceus*. One Roman emperor drank up a fortune in crushed rubies and other precious gems in a futile effort to cure a fatal disease. In Shakespeare rulers dissolve pearls in wine, another expensive drink.

But any odd-shaped stone found on or in the ground or fallen from heaven could be put to use, and was. Islan had the Seal of the Snake, a stone handy for love charms. The *quirin*, or "traitor's stone" (found in the nest of a lapwing), was a primitive sodium pentathol: Place it on the forehead of a sleeping man, and he will tell the truth, confess secrets.

Don't forget the larger stones: the rune stones of Scandinavia, the ogham-inscribed stones of Ireland, the massive monuments of the Druids, the Stone of Scone (on which all British monarchs have been crowned since it was stolen from the Scots in 1306). The Stone of Scone is Scottish sandstone and not from the Holy Land, but many believed it was Jacob's Pillow, the stone on which he rested his head as he dreamed of the angels ascending the stairs into heaven. No amount of argument could convince people that other stones were not also full of magic and had, in a sense which Shakespeare did not intend, "sermons" in them.

CHARMING FACTS

It was characteristic of magicians to associate charms with astrological matters. In fact, charms can only be effectively made at certain astrologically correct times. Here in brief is a good deal of the "correspondence":

Aries	Diamond	Axe	Iron	Mars	1987, 1994, 2001, 2008
Taurus	Emerald	Owl	Silver	Moon	1984, 1991, 1998, 2005
Gemini	Agate	Caduceus	Silver	Mercury	1983, 1990, 1997, 2004
Cancer	Ruby	Anchor	Silver	Moon	1984, 1991, 1998, 2005
Leo	Sardonyx	Heart	Gold	Sun	1981, 1988, 1995, 2002
Virgo	Sapphire	Spider	Silver	Mercury	1983, 1990, 1997, 2004
Libra	Opal	Scales	Copper	Venus	1982, 1989, 1996, 2003
Scorpio	Topaz	Tau	Iron	Mars	1987, 1994, 2001, 2008
Sagittarius	Turquoise	Arrowhead	Tin	Jupiter	1986, 1993, 2000, 2007
Capricorn	Garnet	Cat	Lead	Saturn	1985, 1992, 1999, 2006
Aquarius	Amethyst	Key	Lead	Saturn	1985, 1992, 1999, 2006
Pisces	Bloodstone	Fish	Tin	Jupiter	1986, 1993, 2000, 2007

There you have your birth signs, with their birthstones and symbols, metals and planets, and the years in the current cycle (of the sun 1981–2016), in which "your" planet will be most influential.

You can use general charms, such as a cross or acorn (the latter in tin and copper is supposed to maintain vigor or regain a wayward lover) or a silver skull (but ruby eyes are vulgar) but you are promised most "power" and "protection" if you wear the appropriately made and appropriate charms listed above. It is considered very bad luck to wear the charm of another astrological sign; Gemini's caduceus is really bad news for anyone else, as is Libra's opal, and so on. Most people, if they wear charms at all, wear silver or gold, but less than half the people will benefit from this. Tell your loved one that cheaper tin or lead may be best for you.

An amulet or talisman must be made or bought (if you have to) on the appropriate day. Otherwise, forget it. Here are the planets that rule the days of the week:

Sun	Sunday	Leo
Moon	Monday	Cancer
Mars	Tuesday	Aries, Scorpio
Mercury	Wednesday	Gemini, Virgo
Jupiter	Thursday	Sagittarius, Pisces
Venus	Friday	Libra, Taurus
Saturn	Saturday	Capricorn, Aquarius

You can choose your sign by the day of the year on which you were born (mine is Sagittarius) or the day of the week on which you were born (mine would still be Sagittarius, or Pisces). Every day of the week has both "positive (even-numbered) and "negative" (odd-numbered) hours. If you know the exact time of your birth and the latitude and longitude of the place you were born, astrologers promise your horoscope will be more accurate.

Once you have chosen the right sign and charm, and you have decided to be a little fancier than just carrying a coin with your date of birth on it (be sure it's really copper, silver, or gold)—to make assurance doubly sure make or buy your amulet, talisman, or charm at one of these hours (when the planet of the day is most influential): 1 A.M., 8 A.M., 3 P.M., 10 P.M.

Never wear a ring that has belonged to a dead person without having the stone reset, not even on a chain around your neck. Women can make broaches out of old rings.

Now, all this sounds very complicated. It is. But if you are going to wear something, whether is be an Egyptian ankh, a religious medal, a cross, a gris-gris, an amulet, a talisman, or whatever, consider this: If you are superstitious enough to wear it with magic in mind, you ought to be scrupulous enough to do it right.

TO HAVE PROPHETIC DREAMS

Get up between 3 and 4 A.M. any morning in June, go out silently, and pick one full-blown red rose. Take it back to your room and "fumigate" it over a brazier in which you are burning sulfur and brimstone; let it have at least five full minutes of this. Write the name of the person you love and your own name on a clean sheet of paper and fold the rose in it. Seal the paper with three wax seals and bury it under the tree from which the rose was gathered. Over the spot trace the letter A (for *Amor*, "love").

On July 6 at midnight, dig up the rose wrapped in paper, take it to your room, and put it under your pillow. Sleep on it for three successive nights. "You will enjoy dreams of great portent."

HOW TO RUIN A DINNER PARTY

"Take the four feet of a mole and slip them under the tablecloth without being seen. The guests will not fail to come to blows." The magician who called himself Paul Christian offers this "as a joke."

HOW TO WIN AT GAMBLING

In *The History and Practice of Magic* by the above author, this hope is held out to habitual losers:

Would you like to *win at gambling*? . . . On the first Thursday of the new moon, at the hour of Jupiter, before the sun rises, write these words [in dog Latin] on virgin parchment: "*Non licet ponare in egarbona quia pretium sanguinis.*" Then take a viper's head, and put it in the middle of the writing; fold the four corners of the parchment over the head and, whenever you wish to gamble, attach the whole to your left arm with a red silk ribbon, and no one else but you will win.

If you don't wish to put all your eggs in this basket, Paul Christian has eight more to suggest. He adds: "Whichever of these methods you choose, never forget to keep a tenth part of what you win for the poor. If you forget this precept, instead of winning you will lose."

PASS IT ON

An extremely nasty and (one hopes) now abandoned practice was to "get rid" of venereal disease by having sex with another person and "passing it on." This kind of magical idea is to be found in many cultures. In Haiti, for example, if you are ill, you leave food at a crossroad; anyone who finds and eats your food gets your illness, taking it away from you.

RELICS

The Roman Catholic Church has long recognized the use of relics as devotionals—objects which, because of their physical connection with a saint or someone of great piety or inspirational conduct, increase in Christians a sense of veneration. Devotion to a particular saint—which does not mean worship anymore than devotion to the memory of some personal acquaintance does—can be aided by viewing or touching a relic of that saint. Relics give a sense of closeness.

Relics fall into three classes. First-class relics are actual remains of a person: the skull of Saint Catherine of Siena (with two front teeth missing as a result of the Devil having pushed her down a flight of stone steps), the arm of Saint Francis Xavier that was sent to Rome after the rest of him was buried in Goa, the tiny bits of bone that are placed in an altar when one is consecrated. Second-class relics are objects that were used by the saint in life: clothing, crucifixes, books. A third-class relic is one that has merely been touched by one of the other relics.

Over the authenticity of relics there has been a great deal of dispute. Relic faking was an old art even in the Middle Ages, but in the Age of Faith, people set great store by the fragment of the True Cross that was exhibited in their local church or by a reliquary containing the Crown of Thorns, and so on. A nail purportedly from the True Cross was built into the jewel-encrusted crown of the Hapsburgs. Pieces of the True Cross itself (found, according to tradition, by Saint Helena, mother of Constantine the Great) were to be seen in many Western churches.

People made hazardous pilgrimages to pray at shrines where relics of famous saints were on display or where the saints were buried—the tombs provided with apertures so that the faithful could reach inside and touch the corpse. Wealthy persons gladly bought bones or tattered garments that were sworn to as "genuine relics" of this martyr or that renowned bishop and had bejeweled reliquaries made to contain them. The cathedral at Chartres once housed garments supposed to have been worn by the Blesed Virgin at the hour of Christ's birth; brought from Constantinople, they survived an accidental fire in the Middle Ages, only to be destroyed on purpose during the French Revolution.

Frenchman Roger Peyrefitte discussed the relic problem in his satiric novel *The Keys of Saint Peter* (1957). The urbane but saintly Cardinal Bellaro is speaking:

> "A great many *outré* relics were destroyed during the religious wars or the French Revolution. Thus, for example, a sneeze of the Holy Ghost, a sigh uttered by St. Joseph while he was sawing wood, the bones of the fish that Christ multiplied, the tail of His ass, the rays of the Star of the Three Magi, a feather of the Angel Gabriel, the candle of Arras which burned without ever being consumed. Some equally curious relics still exist in Italy, but . . . the march of enlightenment is beginning to be felt; St. John the Baptist has sixty fingers, but formerly he had more than a coral reef; St. Giulia has forty heads but once had more than the hydra of Lerna; St. Agatha has five breasts, but used to have almost as many as Diana of Ephesus. A few more centuries and our saints will have one head, two hands and two arms, like the rest of us."

Whatever the intentions of the Church authorities in encouraging the veneration of relics, there is no doubt that some people misused them. Instead of making them devotional aids, they regarded the relics as having magic power in their own right. Relics were often stolen to be used in magical incantations or midnight orgies, to prophesy by or to raise spirits of the dead. Many genuinely devout—but simple—people misunderstood the idea of veneration and felt that if they simply touched the relic, the object itself would miraculously do what they wanted done.

In all too many cases, the relic of a holy man became an amulet, a talisman, or a charm.

ABRAXAS STONES

Certain pre-Christian and early Christian cults believed in gnosis, spiritual truth obtainable by faith alone. Gnostic sects used the term "abraxas" to denote the hierarchy of spirits collectively that emanated from a supreme being.

The letters of the word "abraxas" in Greek add up to the number 365, and thus it was believed that there were 365 orders of these spirits. "Abraxas" has frequently been found on ancient talismanic stones, which were thus called abraxas stones. It is thought that the word "abraxas" may have been the origin of the talismanic formula "abracadabra"—although some cabalists claim that it is made up of the Hebrew *Ab* (Father), *Ben* (Son), and *Ruach Acadsch* (Holy Spirit).

THE EVIL EYE

The famous author W. Somerset Maugham used on the cover of his books and on the gates of his fabulous Villa Mauresque on the French Riviera a symbol from the East designed to ward off the Evil Eye.

Did you notice it on the door of one of the buildings in the long-running TV comedy *M*A*S*H*?

On the cover of his books Rudyard Kipling used an ancient symbol for good luck employed by peoples as different as the Indians in America and the Indians in India. Later, the old symbol acquired a tragic new meaning. It was the swastika.

SKULLS

The skull (thought to contain the "personality") has become more than any other part of the body associated with the spirit of the departed. A skull above two crossed bones represents the dead. When the Gravedigger unearthed Yorick's skull in *Hamlet*, he brought back to Hamlet a rush of memories of that jester and his own youth.

The Vikings drank from the skulls of their enemies. Necromancers used them in their black ceremonies.

Some Christian chapels, as *memento mori*, are entirely "decorated" with skulls and bones. They have a peculiar fascination for Hispanics, but in France and Germany also bones are gruesomely displayed; in Hallstadt, Austria, bodies are disinterred after ten years and the skulls bleached and arranged in rows with identifying inscriptions. In Ireland, an oath taken on a skull was considered inviolate.

Headhunters of the Amazon and Africa place their collections of skulls both outside and inside their houses. In Taiwan human skulls were lined up to indicate position and were regarded as wealth. In Sarawak the government, after banning headhunting as barbarous, had to set up a kind of lending library of skulls; headhunters could "check out" an old skull instead of acquiring a new one, renting it for age-old ceremonial rites.

The witch doctors of Africa wear necklaces of skulls. The chief of the Sanem tribe of Papua sleeps with the skull of an enemy as a pillow, to acquire the bravery of the dead. In Tibet skulls are frequently used in magic.

In the West we display the skulls of heroes and saints. The skull of Saint Valentine is shown on Valentine's Day each year in the Church of Santa Maria Cosmedin in Rome—and some believe that if you gaze on it you will keep the brow of your loved one free of frowns for a year.

We used to keep skulls on our desks to remind us of death. Mary Queen of Scots had a watch in the form of a skull; she carried it around in her hand to keep her mind on the passing of time and the inevitability of death. A few people kept the skulls of their departed love ones, and in the Azera tribe of New Guinea, widows can wear no adornments but the skulls of their dead husbands. Mourning rings and Victorian jewelry made of human hair are a milder Western version of the same custom.

The bush people of Maleluka, New Hebrides, use human skulls to make memorial scupltures; they entertain them with spirit-puppets in their funeral ceremonies. The natives of the Nicobar Islands, in the Bay of Bengal, annually dig up the skulls of their dead relatives and, dressing them in colorful rugs, invite them to a four-day feast at which they are the guests of honor. These customs seek to propitiate the dead. Where the New Hebrideans seek to induce the dead to do them favors, the Nicobar Islanders merely hope to get the dead relatives into such a good, relaxed mood that they will not trouble the living for another year.

In some old illustrations you will see skulls used as candlesticks. No serious magician would use so powerful a thing in such a way nor depict such a thing on an amulet or talisman.

MAGIC MUSIC

I have always thought of Wagner's *Parsifal* as "Mounted Boredom and the Holy Grail," although it is full of cabalistic lore and symbolism. So is the charming *Magic Flute* of Mozart (he and his librettist, the actor Emmanuel Schikaneder, were Freemasons).

TO BRING MONEY

A necktie with small portraits of Adam Smith on it is beginning to be seen worn by economists of the more conservative stripe. They might try this talisman instead: a ring with a piece of red chalcedony in it engraved with the picture of a man holding a scepter. The ancients swore it brought wealth.

RESTIVE PERSON

French novelist Nicholas Edmé Réstif de la Bretonne (1734–1806) recalled in his autobiography a conjuring incident of his youth. A boy named François Courtcou found an old almanac in which there was a description of how "a Shepherd may call up the Devil." He talked young Nicholas into trying it. When the Devil appeared, Nicholas was shaking so hard he could not write down the "pact" that Courtcou kept shouting he was "getting" from the hoarse voice that was heard. Forty years later, Nicholas still remembered the occasion vividly, but by that time he had come to the conclusion that François was drunk and engaging in a little ventriloquism. Or perhaps, as the credulous Montague Summers believed, Courtcou may just have "attracted some of the very lowest of spirits."

WORKING EVIL WITH A TALISMAN

The amulet is supposed to ward off bad forces, the talisman, to attract good forces. But Francis Barrett in his confused but presumably authoritative book *The Magus, or Celestial Intelligencer* (1801), argues that a talisman can draw bad forces and so can be used to work evil against someone.

As a talisman of silver (made of the Moon's favorite metal and in the right phase of the Moon) can bring health and respect, so a talisman of lead (the metal associated with the maleficent planet Saturn) if engraved with messages of power at the right aspect of the planet and buried near an enemy's house, can bring evil upon him.

CURE FOR HYDROPHOBIA

Write HAX, PAX, MAX, DEUS ADMAX on a slice of apple and eat it. *Deus* ("god") and *pax* ("peace") are real Latin words but the rest are nonsense syllables.

CHARM AGAINST SCORPION BITES

Try pinning forget-me-nots to your clothes.

CURE FOR A DISLOCATED JOINT

As we have noted elsewhere, magical formulas were frequently attributed to famous persons, from Vergil to Agrippa and Paracelsus. Here is a set of nonsense syllables said to be from "Cato," which could mean Cato the Elder (234–149 B.C.), his famous great-grandson, Cato the Younger (95–46 B.C.), or even "Dionysius Cato," whose name is attached to 164 moral precepts of the fourth century A.D.

Whoever this "Cato" was, he advises victims of dislocation to step within the pentacle and chant:

"HUAT HANAT HUAT, ISTA PISTA SISTA, DOMINABO DAMNAUSTRATA."

CONCLUSION

Whether you wear a bracelet of elephant's hair or an asofetida bag or (as Honoré de Balzac did all his life) a talisman of a square of numbers that add up to fifteen in all directions, good luck!

Charlemagne's talisman was a large sapphire said to contain bits of the

True Cross and to have been given to the emperor by Harun al-Rashid, famed caliph of Bagdad. It was supposed to protect the wearer and symbolized the Protectorship of Jerusalem and the Holy Sepulcher.

Charlemagne always wore it, and when he was buried, sitting upright on his throne in full imperial regalia, it went to the grave with him. Then 186 years later Otto III opened the tomb. He placed the head of Charlemagne in a jewel-encrusted golden reliquary (now in the cathedral at Aachen, Germany), and the talisman went into a church treasury. Napoleon got his hands on it in 1804, and after his death it reached the cathedral treasury at Rheims. It remains there to this day, though Kaiser Wilhelm II did try to buy it.

Harun died of apoplexy (809) very soon after having given Charlemagne this nice present, and the caliph's successors repudiated what the gift was said to represent politically. From the disagreement eventually arose the Crusades.

HOW TO SPOT A THIEF

There are amulets against being robbed, but among the Tome tribe of Africa you hardly need them, for thieves can be spotted easily. They wear talismans to give them good luck in their burglaries.

COUNTRY MATTERS

Witches were supposed to be kept from cattle if one put around the cattle's horns or necks wreaths of rowan tied with red threads. (The witches were especially deterred by braids: They supposedly had to count the threads before attempting to harm the animals.) Witches were also to be put off by farm machinery and carts painted in bright colors—once again red was a favorite.

These precautions, with rowan in the barns and perhaps "spectacles" or "butterfly wings" designs painted on the wagons (actually magical symbols to ward off the Evil Eye) pretty much protected the cattle in England. The horse brasses that Americans today so avidly collect in Britain (and which are being imitated at a great rate today) often had symbols on them, which suggested that they might be amulets against evil, and bells on the harness were certainly aimed at annoying any spirits that might want to injure the teams.

"Collars of holly and bittersweet saved horses from witchcraft, and whips with holly-wood handles were favoured by Fenland coachmen after dark," writes Margaret Baker, an authority on *Folklore and Customs of Rural England*.

WALL STREET REPORT

If civilization lasts long enough for people to look back at our time as a distant past, some of the things we do casually they may consider bizarre.

In Iceland in ancient times a falcon's claw was hung over the fireplace to protect homes from disaster. Do we not have some equally strange ideas?

A friend of mine, a very successful executive in a big, no-nonsense corporation, has for years kept a "lucky tie." He says it got him through his early important job interviews, and he has worn it at similar occasions ever since.

"A security blanket," readers of psychoanalytical works (or Charles Schulz's *Peanuts*) will say. The tie gave him the confidence to make a good impression; his self-assurance helped to get him the jobs.

But now that my friend has reached the top, he still keeps the tie. He does not, I suppose, have to face any more interviews: then why the tie? He says he keeps it "out of gratitude" and because "I wouldn't feel right throwing it away; and who knows what would happen?" Would someone else pick it up and take over his company?

He laughed at the foolishness of his skyscraper not admitting it had a thirteenth floor, but I think my friend believes in magic.

Have we changed so much from the American Indians who ate the hearts of their enemies, hoping to gain their courage? Are we, in the age of "smart missiles," much different from the ancient Britons who rubbed the stones for their slingshots in the brains of slain foes, to make the missiles "smarter"?

A PRECIOUS OPAL

Pliny the Elder (A.D. 23–79) in his *Natural History* recorded 20,000 facts that he considered worth noting. From this mine of information, one gem: Rather than let his precious opal fall into the hands of Mark Antony, the senator Nonius chose exile from Rome.

From the earliest times opals were valuable but risky to own. The Norse *Edda* tells of gems made from the eyes of children, probably opals, and it has always been the gem associated with the eyes. In Venice during the great plagues of the Middle Ages, those who wore the opals were said to see them grow bright when they caught the dread disease, only to fade with the death of the wearer.

George Stimpson, in *A Book About a Thousand Things*, says that "much of the modern superstition no doubt owes its origin to Sir Walter Scott's story entitled *Anne of Geierstein*, published in 1829, where the opal is represented as an unlucky stone, inviting misfortune and unhappiness to the possessor."

Albertus Magnus, great thirteenth century saint, theologian (Thomas Aquinas was his pupil), and eventually bishop of Ratisbon, was a firm believer in the power of opals. According to *The Book of Secrets* (supposedly compiled by one of his students):

> Take the stone which is called *Ophthalamus* [opal], and wrap it in the leaf of the laurel, or Bay tree; and it is called *Lapis Obtalmicus*, whose colour is not named for it is of many colours. And it is of such virtue that it blindeth the sights of them that stand about. Constantius [an eleventh century monk] carrying this in his hand was made invisible by it.

The sixteenth century writer Stephen Bateman agreed with Albertus about this quality of the opal: It "dimmeth other men's eyes so that in a manner it maketh them blind, so that they may not see what is done before them, so that it is said to be the patron of thieves."

THE TALISMAN

In Sir Walter Scott's *The Talisman* (1825), Saladin saves the life of Richard the Lion-Hearted with a snakestone or madstone that draws the poison out of a wound, the "talisman" of the title.

Perhaps Scott got the idea from the Lockhart family in Lanarkshire, which preserves such a good-luck talisman called a "Lee penny" brought back by their ancestor, Sir Simon Lockhart, from the Crusades.

Belief in the efficacy of snakestones to draw out the poison was common in early America, too. Some Amerindian peoples were said to use them as antivenins, and Abraham Lincoln himself took his oldest son, Robert, from Springfield to Terre Haute, Indiana, to have a madstone applied for snakebite. Robert at least survived.

THE MIRACLE OF HOLY CROSS ABBEY

Holy Cross Abbey, in Tipperary County, Ireland, was so named because it boasted a piece of the True Cross. The story is told of a certain woman who, "tortured by magical spells," was cured by wrapping around her stomach a scarf that had touched the relic.

"Suddenly she vomited small pieces of cloth and wood," wrote Patrick Byrne in *Witchcraft in Ireland* (1967), "and for a whole month she spat out from her body such things. . . . This he [the abbot] took care to set down in writing."

"YE OF LITTLE FAITH . . ."

Some say that all power of amulets and talismans, including the power to make you well, comes from faith. So, throw away Blue Cross, Medicare, pills and potions, and think straight! Cancel your insurance policies and get a few amulets.

To be on the safe side, get a talisman of the Sun (engraved on a plaque of very pure gold), made on a Sunday at the proper time, and consecrated with the fumes of cinnamon, frankincense, saffron, and red laurel, burned with laurel and heliotrope stalks in an earthen vessel. That protects against fires.

But if you dream of a purple cloth, get ready to see a doctor; you are going to be very ill.

LONGEVITY

For a long life, why not try a talisman on a disk of wood from a macrozamia tree? These trees grow in the Tambourine Mountains of Queensland, Australia, and are among the oldest living things on earth.

TRAIN YOUR MEMORY

Many magicians complain that though, in complicated rituals, one can consult a sort of manual as one goes along, one is not supposed to keep a drawing of an amulet or tailsman to copy. One is supposed to re-create it from memory—"alphabet of the Magi," Hebrew letters, and all! You must not copy amulets out of books!

IT FIGURES

There's one cabalistic amulet that you should never see anyone wearing. Hung around the neck, if donned before sunrise on Sunday, it is supposed to make the wearer invisible.

6

Recipes and Formulas

FOLKLORE tells us of many strange recipes and remedies. Some of
these concoctions really do work, because they contain useful medicines
that our forefathers discovered. Aspirin (in the form of willow bark), digitalis
(foxglove extract), atropine and hyoscine (belladonna) are all ancient
medicines. Some of these discoveries were aided by magical beliefs, such as
the belief in signatures, which suggested that a plant with, say, a heart-
shaped leaf or flower might be good for heart disease. And some worked only
because the remedies were administered with magical incantations, and the
recipients were convinced of their efficacy.

In addition to taking the medicine—often bitter or disgusting to
convince you it really was doing you some good—you could also transfer the
trouble to some other person or animal, or even a tree or a stone. It was just
a matter of knowing what magical words to say.

Some people, especially "wise women," specialized in folk medicine,
including the magical. If they used their "powers" for good and took no
recompense for cures, they were "white witches." If they dealt in poisons
and love philters and such and did evil, they were "black witches." At one
time *wicca* meant both wisdom and magic.

Wicca it was that told you that this or that mysterious potion had to be made up only when the astrological aspects were right for it, that this or that ointment had to be applied with appropriate chanting and only at the correct time—and never with the "poison finger," the forefinger. *Wicca* it was that claimed to have inherited wisdom of herbs and botanicals, charms and curses, and that its practitioners were powerful because of birth order or "gifted" ancestors or other special circumstances. These wise men or women could tell you that, since the house leek was a potent charm against your house catching fire, its creamy juice was also (naturally) good to soothe burns. They it was who, taking no chances, applied their remedies with a combination of mysterious mumbo jumbo from the Old Religion and also the potent "in the Name of the Father, the Son, and the Holy Ghost" of the New Religion.

Folk medicine drifted into folk magic. When one drew three rushes (not two) through the mouth of a child suffering from thrush (because *rush* sounds like *thrush*) and then threw the rushes into a stream so that the disease would be washed away with them, then that was magic. Similarly, when goose grease was thought not to be worth applying to the chest of a child suffering from a cold unless the grease was on a *heart-shaped* piece of paper, or a poultice was considered not worth trying unless it was tied on with a *red* rag, or a bitter draft had to be taken only after uttering an incantation, then one had superstition, not just medicine.

If the flowers of eyebright were used to make a medieval Murine, if the patient had to eat food given to him or her only by a woman whose name had not changed when she married, if you had to keep the sharp instrument that had cut you bright and shiny until your wound healed (rust would lead to the wound "going bad"), there you had sympathetic magic and superstition.

"WHITE WITCH" REMEDIES

As we have just said, much of the pharmacopoeia of the witches or "wise women" was based on sympathetic magic and the doctrine of signatures. Some of the witches' remedies were eventually recognized as very beneficial; comfrey root, used in casts for broken bones (hence its alternate names "knitback" and "boneset"), now turns out to contain allantoin, a crystalline substitute that promotes bone growth. Some still sound merely superstitious to us. And some ideas have caused regettable damage, such as the recommendation that alabaster chips be used in certain compounds, which caused large chunks of alabaster to be whacked off church monuments—the most convenient supply.

Naturally belief in the efficacy of the medicine or the powers of the physician has always been a major factor in recovery. A framed diploma or a necklace of skulls helps a great deal. Being the seventh son of a seventh son doesn't hurt either, because belief in the natural powers of such a person is widespread. Crones are popular too.

A sick person can hang up a kind of "magnet" to attract away his disease—a stone with a hole in it, a peeled onion, a doll woven of straw—or sprinkle a little holy water around or ride a piebald horse or say a charm.

Or he can take his bed to the cow loft and breathe in its ammoniac odors of dung. (Dung was also considered good in various poultices—King Charles II on his deathbed was smeared with pigeon dung and God knows what else.) To staunch bleeding, he can get the blacksmith to touch him or wrap the wound in cobwebs. For virility he can eat some mandrake root (don't let them pass off bryony on you), or adopt any one of the many rural remedies entertainingly described by Margaret Baker in her *Folklore and Customs of Rural England* (1974).

Here are a few of the ways of country magic:

Warts: Prick each wart with a new pin and then drive the pin into an ash tree (transferring the disease to the tree) as you say:

> Ashen tree, ashen tree,
> Pray buy these warts of me.

Or you can cut as many notches in a stick of elder as you have warts and bury it. As the stick decays, the warts vanish.

Jaundice. Eat nine lice on a piece of bread and butter.

Tuberculosis. Before modern methods were adopted, "an emulsion of snails dissolved in salt was taken with cream and sugar, or the patient made to sleep over the cowhouse. . . . 'Hetherd-broth' of adder-flesh and chicken was taken in Lancashire," reports Ms. Baker. Other sufferers employed "lungs of oak," the lichen *Sticta pulmonaria*, found on the oak trees. Or—sympathetic magic again—the lungs of a healthy sheep were bound to the patient's feet.

Arthritis and rheumatism. The skin of an eel or snake, worn as a garter, keeps you supple and prevents cramp; a stolen dried potato or a cross-shaped bud from a churchyard elder helps. Beekeepers attribute their freedom from rheumatism to the stings they receive (another remedy that has received scientific imprimation). Beating with a holly spray has been tried or carrying the dried front feet of a mole in the pocket nearest the afflicted limb. Of course, aspirin is often recommended; we don't know exactly how that works, either—but it was first synthesized (by an unknown chemist at Friedrich Bayer and Company, Elberfeld, Germany, in 1899) from willow bark, an old "wise woman's" remedy.

BLOODY GOOD MEDICINE

Baths in human blood were recommended by ancient witches as cures for numerous illnesses from leprosy to epilepsy. Blood baths were also supposed to keep one from aging. The Countess Elizabeth Bathory (d. 1614) is reputed to have taken such baths to preserve her good looks. Her agents lured young peasant girls to her castle with the promise of well-paid jobs, only to turn them over to the countess to be "milked" of blood until they died. Estimates of the number of her victims run from thirty-seven to six hundred. She died in prison and entered Hungarian vampire legend as one of the "undead."

MAGICAL POISON

One of the most powerful (and peculiar) magical poisons calls for, among its ingredients, the finger whorls from twins.

MAGICAL FLYING OINTMENT PRESCRIPTIONS

With tongue in check, Reginald Scot (1538–1599) wrote the *Discoverie of Witchcraft*; from Scot's book are recipes for which many sought in his time. Take . . .

the fat of yoong children, and seeth it with water in a brasen vessell, reserving the thickest of that which remaineth boiled in the bottome, which they laie up and keep until occasion serveth to use it. They put hereunto [add] Eleeoselinum, Aconitum, Frondes populeas and Soote.

sium, acarum vulgare, pentaphyllon, the blood of a flitter mouse [bat], solanum somniferum and oleum. They stampe all these togither, and then they rubbe all parts of their bodys exceedinglie till they look red and be verie hot, so as the pores may be opened and their flesh soluble and loose. They joine herewithall either fat, or oil in steed thereof, that the force of the ointment maie the rather pearse inwardly and so be more effectuall.

Scot goes on to say that on a moonlight night then "they seeme to be carried in the aire to feasting, singing, dansing, kissing culling and other acts of venerie with such youthes as they love and desire most" but attributes it not to magic but to the drugs' actions on their imaginations "so vehement that almost all that part of the braine wherein the memorie consisteth is full of such conceipts."

Another traditional English recipe for flying ointment undoubtedly "worked," considering that the first and principal of its nine ingredients was *Cannabis indica*.

ALL-PURPOSE INCANTATION AGAINST DISEASE

These words are from Albertus Magnus himself. Step within the pentacle (five-pointed star) and recite: OFANO, OBLAMO, OSPERGO. HOLA NOA MASSA. LUX, BEFF, CLEMATI, ADONAI. CLEONA, FLORIT. PAX, SAX, SARAX. AFA AFACA NOSTRA. CERUM, HEAIUM, LADA FRIUM. (A mixture of real and nonsense Latin.)

OLD MEASUREMENTS

In making up old magical cures, you may need to know that a noggin is a quarter of a pint and that two kilderkins are a firkin and a runlet a scant kilderkin and that four firkins make a tun. Also, a cubit is 18 inches (or twice a span), a pace is exactly two and a half feet, se'nnight is a week and a fortnight (a word still in use in Britain) is two weeks.

The British still weigh in stones but Americans need to be told that's 14 pounds, and everyone needs to be told that a clove is a half a stone, a burthen is one stone more than a firkin, a kip is half a ton (not tun), a pennyweight is 24 grains, and a hundredweight—in a nation where public schools are private schools—is not 100 pounds but 112 pounds.

Add to that some Scots forms. Two mutchkins of liquid equal a chopin, two chopins equal a Scots pint (about nine-tenths of an English pint), and eight Scots pints equal a Scots gallon. In dry measurements, four lippies (or forpits) equal a peck, four pecks to the firlot, four firlots to the boll, and sixteen bolls to the chalder. A chalder is equal to about ninety-six American bushels, which of course differ slightly from English bushels. In Scotland heavy loads were weighed at the public weighing machine called a trone; trone weight was based on a pound that equaled anything between 21 and 28 ounces, and therefore 3,000 trones weight was the nearest Scots equivalent to the ton.

STAR CHILD

Star Child, a firm in Whitby, Yorkshire—a kind of modern day John Wellington Wells—conducted a mail-order business in magicians' supplies; ash wands (hazel wands were too hard to dry "in this coastal climate"), herbs, resins, balsams, oils, spices, incenses, Solomonic swords, Athame (black-hilted) and white-hilted daggers, tridents and burins, and other "Magical tools." Their catalog announced that they could not undertake to "consecrate Magical tools for you," but they provided virgin parchments (for talismans and other things), beeswax (for candles and *fifth-fath* dolls), Chinese wash (for purifying the threshold and magic circle), and an anointing oil based on an old recipe.

The catalogs and sales of Star Child were evidence of a lively interest in witchcraft in Britain and overseas, especially among young people.

Here is Star Child's recipe for Elfin Incense. Whereas Aztec Incense is "powerful . . . slightly dark . . . useful in works of sacrifice and sex magic, not for the weak-hearted," and Incense of Saturn "may bring unpleasant surprises," Elfin Incense "conjures up the dark wooded country-side and the folk tales of the Elves and Fairies who peopled our land in the distant past." Here's how to make Elfin Incense:

Break up 2 parts of *Rhus aromatica* (fragrant sumac) and grind together with 1 part juniper berries, mix in 2 parts willow bark, 2 parts red sandalwood, and as much honey as you like.

For Ruthvah, the Perfume of Immortality, the most famous of occult perfumes (also called Satyr and Perfume of the Eternal Triad) you need more expensive ingredients, but you may think it worth the money. Mix 1 part real ambergris (*Kether*), 2 parts real musk (*Chokmah*), 3 parts real civet oil (*Binah*). But some people swear by its effectiveness. This perfume was supposed to have been used not only by the beauties of ancient Arabia but by Aleister Crowley. Crowley wrote:

It must be rubbed on the body, particularly at the roots of the hair, where the skin is not too tightly stretched, so thoroughly that the subtle perfume [!] is not detected, or even suspected, of others. The user is thus armed with a most powerful weapon, the more potent for being secret, against the deepest elements in the nature of those whom it is wished to attract. They obey, and they are all the more certainly compelled to obey, because they do not know they are being commanded.

Worth a try? Crowley's own success with women and men was astounding, but I must tell you that a friend in New Orleans to whom I gave the recipe, at his request, was soon after murdered.

RHEUMATISM CURE

For rheumatism, patients are seated in St. Fillan's chair, a stone seat in Renfrewshire, Scotland, and dragged down the hill by their heels.

MODERNIZING MEDICINE

In *The Lost Gods of England* (1957), Bruce Branston demonstrates how physicians in the Middle Ages took the ancient magical formulas and adapted them to Christianity for use in whispering them into the patient's ear. Here's the Old High German charm for a sprain from the tenth century:

Balder and Woden rode to the wood where Balder's foal wrenched its foot when Woden charmed as he well knew how: as for bone-wrench so for blood-wrench so for limb-wrench: Bone to bone, blood to blood, limb to limbs as if they were glued.

For Christian consumption this becomes:

Our Lord rode his foal's foot slade [slipped] down he lighted: bone to bone, sinue to sinue, blood to blood, flesh to flesh, in the name of the Father, Son, and Holy Ghost.

The old Germans also used phylacteries; Orthodox Jews still strap on these little boxes every day to pray. Inside are little bits of parchment on which Old Testament verses are written. The Germans employed an odd combination of heathen charms and Biblical texts, and the use of medical amulets along with the potions and powders is as old as the Assyrians.

A CUSTOM FROM CUMBERLAND

Cumberland has always been a little strange; it did not become a part of England until 1157 and is still rather offbeat, strongly northern, slightly Scots. Its people proudly cling to their ancient traditions.

Here's one that ought to be more widely adopted: Cumberland Rum Butter. Just melt half a pound of butter (the goodness of life) with a pound of brown sugar (the sweetness of life), a generous amount of rum (the spirit). On top sprinkle nutmeg (the spice of life).

Now you are ready for the birth of a baby. When visitors come to see the new infant, give each a taste of the Rum Butter, preferably on a homemade oatcake. The visitor then leaves a coin for the child. When the Rum Butter is all gone, the coins are put into the dish, which is never cleaned out (thus money will *stick* to the baby, and it will never be poor).

"THE FLAGON WITH THE DRAGON HOLDS THE BREW THAT IS TRUE"

One piece of witch's paraphernalia that must never be bought is the cup. The chalice must always be a present from another member of the craft.

FOLLOW THE SCRIPT

Hugh Dalziel Duncan, *Communication and Social Order* (1962), reminds us that, if not used exactly right, the sacred, powerful words of magic can fail to produce the desired effect—worse, they can turn the tables on the magician and bring harm to him who would harm others. Duncan writes:

Magic spells must be handed down, without change. The slightest alteration from the original pattern would be fatal.

DEFENSE AGAINST WITCHES

If you can draw even one drop of a witch's blood, her spells are rendered harmless. "For the time being," the instructions add.

CHARM AGAINST AGUE, FEVER, OR WITCHCRAFT

The *Transactions of the Devonshire Association* (1899) offer this old incantation from the West Country of England:

When Jesus saw the Cross thare to be crucified Pilate said unto him "what aileth thee? Why shakest thou/ hast thou fever, ague or witchcraft?" Jesus said unto him "I have neither fever, ague nor witchcraft but shake for thy sins. Whosoever carryeth this in his mind or in writing shall never have neither fever, ague nor witch-craft. In the name of the father and of the Son and of the holy ghost. Amen Amen."

ANOTHER CURE FOR DISEASE

"Diseases can be cured by wearing a girdle of ferns gathered on St. John's Eve, at midnight, and arranged in such a way as to form the magic character HVTY." This is from Jacques Collin de Plancy (1793–1887), *Dictionary of Witchcraft.*

HOW TO LOCATE THE GUILTY PARTY

Cornelius Agrippa in one of his books describes how to detect a thief or other criminal from a group of innocent people. The diviner takes a sieve (in the fifteenth century these were flat circular utensils), grips it with a pair of pincers or tongs, which in turn are held in place by the middle fingers of two assistants—that is, it is suspended in air by a very slight grip. The diviner then says these six words:

"DIES, MIES, JESCHET, BENEDOEFET, DOWIMA, FNITEMAUS."

The conjuration is followed by the reading of the names of the suspects. When the guilty party's name is read, the sieve—"by the help of the demon," says Agrippa—will turn.

MOTHER DEMDIKE'S METHOD

From the *Wonderful Discovery of Witches in the County of Lancaster* (1613), here is the standard sympathetic-magic way of attacking an enemy as described by a woman burned as a witch for using it:

The speediest way to take a man's life away by witchcraft is to make a picture [figurine] of clay, like unto the shape of the person whom they mean to kill, and dry it thoroughly. And when you would have them to be ill in any one place more than another, then take a thorn or pin and prick it in that part of the picture you would so have to be ill. And when you would have any part of the body to consume away, then take that part of the picture and burn it. And so thereupon by that means the body shall die.

THE BASIC CAKES RECIPE AND ITS USE

In one of Shakespeare's plays a merry group replies to the puritanical Malvolio that just because he is dour and depressed there is no reason there should be no cakes and ale.

Cakes and ale are features of the *esabat* (frequent meeting of witches, more informal and less infrequent than a sabbat). They are also in evidence in the Cakes and Wine ceremony, which the coven conducts somewhat along the lines of Holy Communion of the Christians.

The wine is usually sweet (often sherry or white), and the cakes are made of whole meal, salt, honey, wine, oil and (sometimes) blood. They are crescent-shaped, in honor of the Moon Goddess, the Great Mother, the female principle.

When making the cakes, the witch recites this incantation:

I do not bake the meal nor the salt, nor do I cook the honey and the oil with the wine. I bake the blood and the body and the soul of the Great Aradia that she shall know neither rest nor peace and ever be in cruel suffering till she grant the fulfillment

of my innermost desires. If the grace be granted, O Aradia, in
honor of thee I will hold a feast. We will drain the goblet deep,
    We will wildly dance and leap.
And if thou grantest the grace which I desire, then, when the
dance is wildest, we shall extinguish the lamps and love freely,
caring neither for age nor kin.

It is worth noting that where religion propitiates, magic threatens and
compels.

A LOVE POTION

William Butler Yeats was a great student of the occult and of Irish
folklore, and in a book on Irish fairy tales and folk tales he says that lovers

can make love-potions by drying and grinding into powder the
liver of a black cat. Mixed with tea, and poured from a black
teapot, it is infallible.

LOVE MAGIC

In Malaysia they take sand from the footprint of a beloved and fry it.
This is supposed to make him or her itch with desire.

The Arabs write certain characters in oil on the palm of their hands,
then rub the hand furtively on the face in the presence of the beloved.
Irresistible.

American girls recite the alphabet while twisting the stem of an apple;
when the stem comes off, the initial of the beloved is revealed. (Boys named
Zachary don't have much of a chance.) Or you can peel an apple in one long
continuous strip and throw the peel over your left shoulder; whatever letter
it forms should be the initial of your future lover's name. Or you can jump
rope while reciting the alphabet:

> Ice-cream soda, cream on top,
> Tell me the name of my sweetheart.
> A, B, C, D, . . .

You will miss on the letter of your lover's name. If you reach Z, start over.

Mary and Herbert Knapp in their charming book on the folklore of
American children, *One Potato, Two Potato* (1976), give instructions for

what they call the "wiggle-waggle" paper predictor and many other American children's devices for telling fortunes. The most frequently asked question is "Does he/she love me?" or something about dating or marriage.

If you want something more complex than "loves me, loves me not" plucking of the daisy's petals, try this chant, quoted by the Knapps, of a Mississippi girl counting the seeds from her apple:

> One I love, two I love, three I love, I say.
> Four I love with all my heart,
> Five I'll cast away.
> Six he loves, seven she loves,
> Eight they both love.
> Nine he comes, ten he tarries,
> Eleven he courts, twelve he marries.

ANOTHER LOVE RECIPE

On a Friday sew into a green silk bag a mixture of vervain, southernwood, and orris root, crushed between sandstones. Wear the bag pinned to your undergarments, next to the skin.

CHINESE RECIPE

The Chinese say, "Respect spiritual beings—but keep aloof from them." If you decide to ignore this sage advice, here's a good trick: Collect as many scorpions as you can find and put them in a jar. Screw the lid on tight and leave them for a year. (Well, a long time.) The scorpions will eat each other until there is only one left. Thus you get a really terrific poisonous creature to set on an enemy.

This is *ku*, reverse magic. *Ku* also means rubbing out an enemy by making a straw effigy and pouring water over it (to drown him), sticking pins in it, and so on.

HOW TO DIG UP THE INGREDIENTS

Iris foetidissima, or stinking gladdon, is called for in many recipes. Like a mandrake (whose "shriek" when pulled up was supposed to drive men

134

crazy), it is difficult to collect. If you cannot tie it to a dog's tail and have him pull it up when you are out of earshot, draw a circle round it three times with a double-edged sword (which bears some resemblance to a crucifix) and be sure to leave in place of the pulled-up plant a flat wheat cake (the kind King Alfred let burn). This is payment to the forces of nature—not a replacement for gladdon but a kind of real-estate tax.

MAGIC OF THE BOOK

Christians used to (many still do) use their Bibles for fortune-telling. Open it at random and put your finger on a message. In Islam the superstitious eat the ink in which certain texts of the Koran are written, hoping thereby to absorb the message.

HOW LONG WILL YOU LIVE?

You can get a good horoscope. You can summon a demon and ask him. You can make a pact with the Devil for a stated period, at the end of which you can count on going—dragged off like Faust, if necessary. You can use any one of a number of methods to get an answer to this important question, provided you are sure you want to know. Think about it.

Here are two methods, one Mexican, one Muslim.

The Mexicans used to put their arms around a certain pillar in the temple at Mitla and measure the distance between their fingertips. That indicates how long they will live. I have tried this and was pleased to discover that, in exchange for having arms so short that I always have to have my shirtsleeves shortened an inch, I am going to live to a ripe old age.

The Muslim system is more complicated and varies with the time of year.

In the first month, close your eyes at midnight, say "God is One" (in Arabic) ten times; then open your eyes quickly and look immediately at the moon. If it looks black, you will die soon. In the fifth and sixth months you can only ask the question fruitfully on Wednesday nights, and you must use a lamp, not the moon. In all other months, gaze at a cloudless sky or at water in a bowl. If they have a reddish tinge, you will die soon.

The Muslims have no system (besides astrology) for long-range forecasting; you have to keep checking.

FOR THE CRAMP

The Devil is tying a knot in my leg.
Mark, Luke, and John, unloose it, I beg.
Crosses three we make to ease us:
Two for thieves and one for Jesus.

CURE FOR DRUNKENNESS

Wear on a piece of paper or parchment, hung from a string around the neck: IAEO, IEALO, IOELET, SABAOTH, ITHOTH BAE. (Mostly nonsense syllables.)

MAGICAL DEFENSE

Write on a parchment and carry with you everywhere this:

DULLIX, IX, UX.
YEA, YOU CAN'T COME OVER PONTIO.
PONTIO IS ABOVE PILATO.

No, I can't figure it out, either!

HOUSE PROTECTION CHARM FROM LANCASHIRE

Lancashire folklore preserves this potent charm against all harm. Over the door write:

Sun, Moon, Mars, Mercury, Jupiter, Venus, Saturn, trine, sextile, dragon's head, dragon's tail, I charge ye all to gard this house from all evil spirits whatever, and gard it from all desorders, and from aney thing being taken wrangasly, and give this famaly good ealth and welth.

INCONCEIVABLE

Fron an ancient grimoire, here is a recipe for curing barrenness:

If a woman may not conceive. Take an Harts horne, turned into powder, and let it be mixed with a cows gall; let the woman keepe it about her . . . and she shall conceive.

It might be classed as folk medicine if the user were expected to swallow it, but since she is enjoined to "keepe it about her," it is clearly magic.

AN ANCIENT CHARM AGAINST MARSH FEVER

Nail three horseshoes to your bedpost with a heavy crucifix (Holy Crok, formerly the Hammer of Thor) and you have the Christian God, Wod (Wotan), and Lok (Loki) all working to protect you if you chant as you do so:

FATHER, SON AND HOLY GHOST
NAIL THE DEVIL TO THIS POST.
THRICE I SMITE WITH HOLY CROK,
WITH THIS MELL I THRICE DO KNOCK,
ONE FOR GOD, AND ONE FOR WOD, AND ONE FOR LOK.

HELP FOR THE AFFLICTED

Remember Sax Rohmer, creator of the improbable Dr. Fu Manchu? He found this in a seventeenth-century chapbook and copied it out. I hand it on to you:

To help a Person under an ill Tongue, and make the Witch appear, or the Effect cease:
Cut off some of the Party's Hair, just at the Nape of the Neck, clip it small and burn it to a Powder, put the Powder in Sal-Armoniack, write the Party's Name you suspect [that is, of casting the spell] backwards, and put the Paper, dipt in *Aqua Vitæ*

[brandy], into the other two, then set it over a gentle Fire; let the Party afflicted sit by it, and dilligently watch that it run not over to catch flame, speaking no Word, whatsoever Noise is heard, but take Notice of what Voice or Roaring is heard in the Chimney, or any part of the Room, and then write how often you hear it, and fix before each writing this Character [he shows a crescent moon]—and if the Party who afflicts you appear not Visible, though you may know the Voice, repeat it again, and if she appear in no visible Shape, it may make her Charm impotent, and give relief to the afflicted Party.

KILLING OINTMENT

On the subject of witchcraft, Johann Wier (1516–1588) was extraordinarily reasonable for his time, pressing for medical examinations of the accused. As a pupil of Cornelius Agrippa, he had been initiated into the healing arts, but he knew their darker side as well. Here, from him, is potent medicine indeed:

> Hemlock, juice of aconite,
> Poplar leaves and roots bind tight.
> Watercress and add to oil
> Baby's fat and let it boil.
> Bat's blood, belladonna too
> Will kill off those who bother you.

ANY WEDNESDAY

Some people have been pestering me for the formula for invisibility. If I give it to you, will you promise to—disappear?

The *Grimoire Verum* is an eighteenth-century fake purporting to be the work of Alibeck the Egyptian, 1517. It's based on *The Key of Solomon* (very ancient already by the time it got on the list of books banned by the Inquisition, in 1559), but itself not prohibited. Here are its instructions:

Take the head of a dead man and put a black bean in its mouth, one up each nostril, one in each ear, one in each eye. That's seven. Then trace a magic pattern of your own devising on the dead man's head with your fingers. Bury the head in the ground, face up. Each day before sunrise, water the place with good brandy. On the eighth day a spirit will interrupt and ask what you are doing. Reply: "I am watering my plant." Do not permit the spirit to water it, though it will ask to do so.

It will show you the pattern you have traced on the head, proving it is a spirit and a good one. *Then* you can permit it to water the place.

On the ninth day the plants will sprout. When the beans finally appear, pick them and place one in your mouth. When you look in the mirror you will not see yourself, for the beans "carry the invisibility of the dead and buried head." *Do not, in your surprise, swallow the beans*; you can only become visible again by removing them from your mouth.

If this fails to make you invisible, it may be because you did not plant at the right time. That's any Wednesday, Mercury's day, before sunrise.

ITCHING POWDER

In Haiti a powerful itching powder is made from the plant called creeping cowage. When "baptized" with an incantation, it is said to irritate the eyes and skin so much it will drive a person crazy.

GARLIC

I'm a garlic freak, and I have good company. Homer called garlic a god, the Chinese have revered it for 4,000 years, and the Egyptians were so sure it gave strength that they fed it to their pyramid-builders.

Garlic occurs often in recipes for invisibility, but I insist on heliotrope, instead. What's the use of being invisible if people can detect you by the garlic on your breath?

TAKE A TRIP

In *Ingoldsby Legends* R. H. Barham (1788–1845) gives a lighthearted description of witches flying off to the sabbat.

> Hey Cockalorum! my Broomstick gay!
> We must rush back ere the dawn of the day,
> Hey up the chimney! away! away!
> Old Goody Price mounts in a trice,

> In showing her legs she is not very nice;
> Old Goody Jones, all skin and bones,
> Follows 'like winking.'—Away go the crones.

Sound like fun? Here, according to a grimoire, is how to get the same results: "Into a well-covered receptacle place the following:

> 100 grams of lard
> 5 grams of superior hashish
> a pinch of hellebore root
> a pinch of crushed sunflower seeds."

Then: "Fill the container with flowers, hemp, and poppy. Let it simmer over water for about two hours. Remove from the heat and uncover."

Before retiring one is supposed to smear this stuff all over, including under the armpits. Then—presumably in sleep—one "flies."

HOW TO GET TO THE OTHER SIDE

From *De Mirabilis Naturae* (1730), translated for your convenience:

Communication with the other world is easy . . . all that you need is a bell made from an alloy of lead, tin, iron, copper, mercury, silver, and gold. Inscribe on it: ADONAI, JESUS, TET-RAGRAMMATON. Then place it for seven days in the middle of a ditch in a cemetery.

THE HAND OF GLORY

Possibly the most famous charm in the history of magic is the Hand of Glory, which, if properly made, is supposed to paralyze all spectators, so that the possessor of the Hand can rob them freely or do whatever he wants to them.

The process begins when the would-be sorcerer obtains either the right or left hand of a criminal who has been gibbeted—that is, left hanging on the gallows to rot. It is then wrapped in a piece of winding sheet, pickled in an earthenware pot, and dried in the sun. Finally the grease extracted from it is combined with virgin wax and Lapland sesame to make a candle, which is placed in the mummified hand (as in a candlestick), and lighted. As long as the candle flame burns, the spell operates.

Burglars, supposedly protected by the Hand, have been caught in the act of robbing a house. So the spell seems to be more famous than efficacious.

SIMPLE CURSES

Perhaps the simplest curses are those effected by sticking a candle or an onion with pins. The Italian witches claim to get good results with *la ghirlanda delle streghe*: the "witches' garland" is simply a piece of rope in which knots are tied, each accompanied by the repetition of the curse and the sticking of a black feather into the knot. For best results, the witches' garland should then be hidden in the victim's mattress.

THE CURSE OF BREADALBANE

At a Scottish site at Killin, on Loch Tay, stood a castle where the earl of Breadalbane had a witch put to death. She, in her last throes, cursed the earldom, vowing that the title would not pass from father to son for seven generations.

On May 18, 1923, a correspondent wrote to the editor of the London *Times* to point out that the curse had been fulfilled: For seven generations the earldom had not passed from father to son, and the latest earl, whose obituary had recently appeared in the paper, was succeeded by a distant cousin.

The curse seems to have run its course. The present earl (born 1919) succeeded his father (born 1889) in 1959.

THE LORD MAYOR'S CURSE

Daniel Cohen in *Curses, Hexes and Spells* (1974) notes: "In 1521 the Mayor of Lincoln published a formal curse against those who had taken the records and books of the Common Council."

We are not informed what the result of the curse was.

MAGIC STONE

Considered "the food of the Immortals," green jade is also said to be good for you, if you powder it and eat it.

SOMETHING ABOUT PLANTS

Out in the witch's garden (with its white circle in the center to honor the Moon Goddess) there are a lot of plants, some nice, some nasty. Angelica's name suggests the former, and indeed it is worn around the neck to protect children from spells, much as asafetida or camphor used to be worn to protect against disease. Daffodils bring gold, and ginseng, as a tonic, is almost worth its weight in gold; it is reputed to aid digestion, improve the mind, tone up the system, and on and on—but make sure the root you take is seven years old exactly.

Anything with spikes or thorns on it (briar, holly, thistle, thorn) belongs to the Devil. Anything that smells good is good.

An oak was sacred to a Druid. Rowan trees drive off evil spirits. Hazel wands are good for dowsing. Plant a juniper to keep the witches away and a conifer for a Teutonic god to live in.

To be on the safe side, apologize to a tree before you cut it down. Never ever bring an "insulted" tree in for Christmas.

Dillweed, mallow flowers, and horehound keep evil at bay. Bay is unlucky. Hemlock, chestnut, and hawthorn are also unlucky.

The "promethean plant," when mixed with the gall of four animals makes a great "beverage of hate" to use against enemies.

There are two plants called the devil's eye—one for each eye, perhaps. There's also devil's milk, devil's oatmeal, devil's beard, etc. Devil's bit is mandrake, a sovereign remedy.

Place the roots of wild carrots (Queen Anne's lace) under your pillow, and you will dream of your future.

Four-leaf clovers are lucky; everyone knows that. But did you know that fern seed can make you invisible and that mustard seed can protect the front and back doors against unwelcome and unlucky visitors, or that barberry plants (my house has a hedge of them) are supposed to ward off demons?

Low John the Conqueror is a good luck plant used in Voodoo. High John the Conqueror is used for good luck charms in Mexico.

Put belladonna on your horse to make him strong, but only on *Walpurgisnacht* (the evening preceding May Day), or there will be trouble. When you cut belladonna, let a black hen loose to distract the devil; no other color will do. Cut hazel wands for divining on the first night of the full moon, but never cut them from the east side of the plant.

Peas should be eaten only on Thursday (in honor of Thor), but at any time you can rub pea vines on jilted lovers to console them. If you should find nine peas in one pod, put it on the windowsill, and if, when you hear footsteps, you hold your breath, your future husband will appear.

And then there's "the primrose path." Never bring fewer than thirteen primroses into your house. (Never bring in flowering hawthorn at all, never.) But better still, leave the primroses outside to ward off witches. Also good for this are all evil-smelling weeds (except a few dedicated to the Devil) and such things as flax in flower. Burn juniper berries to keep out witches.

Anemones tell witches when people are coming. Witches plant clumps of purple (violets, sorcerer's periwinkle, lilac) to bring money, grow morning glories to protect them (the seeds are also hallucinogenic), and lay in St. John's wort (good boiled in wine to stop vomiting of blood) for the neighbors. They need lots of herbs; recipes like them to be combined in groups of as many as seven or nine, always odd numbers. Sun worshippers like yellow flowers on Mondays. . . .

There are, of course, also appropriate times for gathering simples and herbs: the waxing or waning of the moon, and so on. Any farmer's almanac will tell you the auspicious times for planting, whether you practice witchcraft or not.

CLASSIC RECIPE

From those famous witches, in Shakespeare's *Macbeth*:

> Double, double toil and trouble;
> Fire burn, and cauldron bubble. . . .
> Eye of newt and toe of frog,
> Wool of bat and tongue of dog. . . .
> Finger of birth-strangled babe,
> Ditch-deliver'd by a drab,
> Make the gruel thick and slab. . . .

SOME OLD UN-RELIABLES

Henbane poisoning (a witch's standby) is supposedly cured by the juice of purslane mixed with white wine. If a fishbone sticks in your throat, put your feet in a bath of cold water. Painless childbirth is obtained by fumigating the house with dried eagles' droppings thrown on burning embers. To make your hair grow, mix mouse droppings with roasted bees, burned chestnuts, or beans burned to ashes, held together with attar of roses. To cure shingles and other skin eruptions, eat leeks cooked with barley flour and oil.

If you hold a stalk of nettle and another of millefoil in your hand, you will be "impervious to fear," but they must be picked when the Sun is in Leo (July 19 to August 23). Agnus castus (an ornamental shrub of the verbena family) protects virginity and when added to "smallage [wild celery] and sage in salt water" makes a liniment which, applied to the back of the head, brings people out of comas.

If you want to know how a sick person is going to make out, simply approach his bed with a sprig of verbena *in your left hand*. When you ask him how he feels, if he says "unwell," he will get better; if he says "well," he is in danger of death. If he says, "What are you doing with a sprig of verbena?" the whole thing is best forgotten.

CALCAREOUS AGGREGATED SKELETONS OF DEFUNCT CORALLIGENOUS ZOOPHYTES

That's coral, venerated in ancient India, worn (says Pliny) on the war helmets and weapons of the Gauls, put around the neck of Roman children to protect them (and later used on teething rings and rattles for babies), perfect material for an Italian amulet against the Evil Eye, considered for that purpose (by the Persians) even better than the eye of a sheep whose throat has been cut. Like jade, it can (it is said) detect poison in food or drink. It can cure bleeding and defend you against losing your virility, being struck by lightning, many other misfortunes.

It's just what the doctor ordered, if the doctor is John Schroeder (1660), for purifying the blood: Crush it to a powder and ingest it. Also good (except the black kind) for making you merry, curing fluxes of the belly and malfunctions of the womb, runny eyes, ulcers, fits and convulsions, among other things. Albertus Magnus added, "It stemmeth anon blood, putteth away the foolishness of him that beareth it, and giveth wisdom. . . . And it is good against tempests, and perils of floods."

SORCERERS IN THE SOUK

Edward Mace, writing of a holiday in Rabat, Morocco, in 1975:

If you are out of snake skins, dead bats or rats' tails, the sorcerers in the souk [suq, the marketplace] in the Spanish quarter is the place to go. . . . We bought kurin [cummin?] and saffron there and nutmegs, pine nuts and musk, weighed out for us on a chemist's balance from huge, conical mounds. The sorcerer, sitting among bowls of dried rose petals, produced from an astonishingly questionable jar a black raisin which, placed on the tongue for half an hour, induces a deep drunkenness from which few recover.

I have seen similar "pharmacies" in other countries. In one place I asked the seller, "Will this work if I take it but do not say the *words*?" "I do not know, señor," he replied. "I have never taken it without the words."

We must respect these "crude native remedies." One of them was "Jesuit's bark"—quinine. But I never would patronize the lady in Jalisco, Mexico, who can, by all local accounts, put more hair on your head. I was afraid the witch would shrink my head to fit the hair I already have.

GETTING BACK AT THE WITCH

Robert Herrick tells us how to revenge ourselves on the hag who has taken some hair or nail clippings of us and cast a spell to hurt us:

> To House the Hag, you must doe this:
> Commix with Meale a little Pisse
> Of him bewitcht: then forthwith make
> A little Wafer or a Cake;
> And this rawly bak't will bring
> The old Hag in. No surer thing.

"IT'S LOVE THAT MAKES THE WORLD GO ROUND. . . ."

Suppose you have added up the numerological values of your first name and your birth date (don't forget to add 3, the magic number) and you "know" therefore the "number" of the boy or girl who is just right for you. Now you have the number. How are you going to attract him or her?

You could make a wax figure and go through a lot of burying and unburying of it, and many other—often disgusting—actions. You could pray to Venus. You could tie a wryneck (a variety of woodpecker) to a wheel and turn it, "turning the affections" of your intended. You could sneak your fingernail parings—or a few drops of your bathwater—into his or her food.

You could slip the object of your affections a maddening drug, from datura to laurel, or something more subtle, such as lettuce or cinnamon. You might dare to call on the devil Asmodeus, but that's very risky.

It used to be a crime to "provoke another to unlawful love" by magic, as bad as ruining people's sex lives by tying knots in cords and all that. First offense (under laws of 1563 and 1604 in England) you got a year in jail. Second offense? The law of 1563 got you life and in 1604 they made it death. The crime was increasing.

TYING THE KNOT: HOW TO MAKE A LOVE KNOT
AND HOW TO UNDO A HATE KNOT

From a magical papyrus of ancient Egypt:

You take a band of linen of 16 threads, 4 of white, 4 of green, 4 of blue, 4 of red, and make them into one band, and stain them with the blood of a hoopoe [a European bird, often used in magic perhaps because of its eye-catching crest], and you bind it with a scarab in its attitude of the sun-god, drowned, being wrapped in byssus [a fine-woolen cloth], and you bind it to the body of the boy who has the vessel and it will work quickly.

Later and simpler methods were developed to make people fall in love. There was even an antilove (or at least anticopulation) black magic trick called knotting the cord.

You attend a marriage ceremony and hang around at the back, rather like the bad fairy not invited to the christening in "Sleeping Beauty." While the couple are taking their vows, you secretly tie knots in a cord. Virgil's *Eighth Eclogue* suggests "three colors in three knots," which sounds good, if a little difficult to do surreptitiously.

Roman Emperor Theodosius the Great (346–395) and King Philip Augustus of France (1165–1223) are but two of the many personages unmanned for marriage (they said) by knots. Arranged marriages for political purposes may have accounted for other impotence among the high-born.

Pliny was sure it was a danger, but he told how to break the spell: Rub the threshold of the marriage chamber with wolf fat. Sounds slippery, but you are *not* to step on the threshold when you carry the bride over it anyway.

Or you can make yourself immune to knots by filling your pockets with salt and urinating just before you enter the church (not in the graveyard, though—you might make a dangerous enemy). Or while you are picking out the bride's wedding ring, get one for the groom, too. Make sure it is gold and "contains the right eye of a weasel."

RAISING THE DEVIL

Here is the German formula for raising the Devil, who arrives in the form of a he-goat. This conjuration takes a loud voice that rises to a terrific scream on the final commands for the "King, King" to come.

> *Lalle, Bachea, Magotte, Baphia, Dajam,*
> *Vagoth Henech Ammi Nagaz, Adomator*
> *Raphael Immanuel Christus Tetragrammaton*
> *Agra Jod Loi. König. König!*

Once again, Haining's *The Necromancers* is helpful. If this doesn't work, he has a second one "to be read backward except the last two words," which are "*Komm! Komm!*" That should do it. The formula given to dismiss the Devil, Haining says, "would evidently make almost anybody go away."

ALCHEMICAL FORMULAS

Strictly speaking, alchemists were the research scientists of their day, exploring the properties of various minerals and chemicals, mastering the art of changing matter by combination, distillation, calcination (reducing a mineral to powder), fixation, and other techniques.

The ultimate goal of alchemy was to make or discover the philosopher's stone, sometimes called the elixir, a substance that was believed capable of turning base metals (lead, tin, mercury, iron, copper) into gold or silver. "The belief that it could be obtained only by divine grace and favour," writes E. J. Holmyard in *Alchemy* (1957), "led to the development of esoteric or mystical alchemy, and this gradually developed into a devotional system where the mundane transmutation of metals became merely symbolic of the transformation of sinful man into a perfect being through prayer and submission to the will of God."

It was all too easy for this mystic aspect of alchemy to become tainted with sorcery, for astrology to replace trust in God, for prayer to turn into incantation and ritual magic—especially when the alchemist's patron was impatient. Gilles de Retz turned first to alchemy to recoup his squandered fortune; then when the transmutation did not occur, he hurried on to a particularly vile form of black magic. The same impatience beset Augustus the Strong of Saxony, as we will see below, but with happier outcome.

One of the objects of the alchemist's search was the alkahest, a universal solvent, which was said to exist. (Old joke: If it dissolves everything, what do you keep it in?)

The alkahest could be made from sweat, spit, worms, and so on, but the best raw material was blood. A true magic formula, for blood represents life itself, and spitting is in widespread use in spells.

Many formulas for making the philosopher's stone were developed over the centuries, all immensely complicated and tiresome to read about. Here is one, much simplified. You start by purging the original material (not specified) with water from the Black Sea, distilling the result into what is known as mercurial water, and dividing that into five portions, two of which are set aside. The other three portions of mercurial water are added to one twelfth of their weight in virgin gold (gold that has never been used for mundane purposes), put through another distilling process in an alembic (a primitive pot still), and when they have formed a solid amalgam, one of the reserved two portions is added to the mixture, followed by the other, in seven installments. The container is then sealed and kept warm for forty-seven days, and at the end of that time—if all has gone well—the result should be the long-sought substance, of a beautiful purple color. In theory the alchemist could then set about turning base metal into gold. Other formulas are even longer and more tedious.

Here is a recipe for making gold that does not require the elixir. It is from the magical Sanskrit *Atherao Veda*, but there is more of metallurgy about it than of magic:

Take the following ingredients: twenty parts of platinum, the same amount of silver, plus 240 parts of brass, and obtain also 120 parts of nickel. Melt these separately in different crucibles. They are then to be combined when in the molten condition. This alloy is then poured into moulds to cool. Then use the metal.

Alchemy had many sources: ancient Egypt, where men were said to have made some mysterious oxide to use in the worship of Osiris, which effected wonderful cures and transmuted metals; China, where they studied the chemical and mystic properties of gold, cinnabar, and other materials; Babylon; Arabia, where learned scholars discovered caustic alkalis; Spain, where Christians had their closest contact with Arabic and Jewish lore.

By the late Middle Ages, when alchemy was flirting with magic, it began to get a bad name, and yet it hung on. Henry V banned it from England in 1404, but his son granted licenses to various alchemists to practice their craft and actually employed one himself. So, it is said, did Elizabeth I. James IV of Scotland (1473–1513) was interested in alchemy, as was Holy Roman Emperor Rudolf II (1552–1612). Charles II, according to Holmyard, "had an alchemical laboratory built under the royal bedchamber with access by a private staircase." Learned men found it attractive, too: Roger Bacon, Saint Thomas Aquinas, Sir Thomas Browne, John Evelyn, and even Sir Isaac Newton.

The elixir has been reported found on a number of occasions. In 1648, one Johann Richthausen demonstrated the art of transmuting metals in the presence of his emperor, Ferdinand III (1608–1657); with one grain of his magic powder, he changed two and a half pounds of mercury into gold, which the emperor had struck into medals. (They no longer exist, but see illustration of what one looked like.) In 1676, during the reign of Ferdinand's son, Leopold I, a monk named Wenzel Seyler—again in the imperial presence—changed both tin and copper into gold. Leopold made Seyler a baron and had a medal struck from the "gold" that carried Leopold's image on one side and on the other a bit of verse: *Aus Wenzel Seylers Pulvers Macht/Bin ich von Zinn zu Gold gemacht* ("By the power of Wenzel Seyler's powder, I have been changed from tin to gold").

That medal too disappeared, but the result of a later "transmutation" by Seyler, a medallion, survived until 1888, when it was examined by a chemist. Unfortunately for believers in alchemy—if any still existed—the medallion turned out to be decidedly brassy in color and to have a specific gravity of only 12.67—6.63 short of the specific gravity of gold.

This medal was minted in 1648 in honor of an alchemical demonstration in Prague before Emperor Ferdinand III—supposedly of the gold that, everyone was convinced, had been created out of base metal.

There were other "successful" alchemists, including a number of learned men, but after the 1780s, when the Royal Society sent chemist Joseph Black to investigate the claims of a certain James Price, interest languished. Price had reportedly changed mercury into gold by adding a white powder to it, mixing it in a flux of borax and niter, and heating the results in a crucible, which he stirred with an iron rod. The results assayed out as the purest silver. Price later performed the same "transmutation" with different quantities and produced gold. But when Black arrived to test out the process in person, Price swallowed prussic acid and died before the chemist's eyes. It turned out that Price was not only a fraud, but a little mad into the bargain.

And then we come to the case of Frederick Augustus I (1670–1733), called the Strong, elector of Saxony and off-again-on-again king of Poland. Augustus had luxurious tastes and no urge to stint his personal pleasures. He caused his capital city, Dresden, to erect many gorgeous (and expensive) baroque buildings, and founded a famed art collection. He was particularly fond of porcelain, then obtainable only from China at enormous expense, and indulged himself lavishly in buying it. (He also conducted some expensive wars, chiefly in his efforts to retain the Polish crown.) Inevitably he ran out of funds. To recoup, he hired a young alchemist, one Johann

Friedrich Böttger (1682–1719), to find the philosopher's stone and make gold.

Böttger was kept virtually a prisoner and nagged regularly by the impatient Augustus. But the great discovery remained elusive as ever. One evening, as the story goes, when the harassed Böttger was entertaining a friend in his quarters, he poured out the tale of his troubles. The friend was sympathetic, but he thought Böttger was going at things the wrong way. "Even if you find the elixir," he pointed out to the alchemist, "Augustus will simply take the gold and spend it on porcelain. I say, forget about learning how to make gold. Learn how to make porcelain."

Böttger thought it over and decided that was a good idea. Abandoning the alchemical search, he learned how to make porcelain. In 1710, in partnership with Count Ehrenfried Walter von Tschirnhaus and under the patronage of Augustus, he established the Royal Saxon Porcelain Manufactory at Meissen. In a few short years the names "Meissen" and "Dresden china" were synonymous with exquisite ceramics. Over the centuries the manufacture of fine porcelain has brought Saxony more wealth than it could have acquired with a thousand philosopher's stones.

KILLING RECIPE

Get a specimen of your victim's urine. Buy a hen's egg without haggling over the price, and on some Tuesday or Saturday night take the egg to some deserted place where you will not be disturbed. With a circular incision at the broad end, extract the white only. Add the urine to the yolk in the eggshell and, saying the name of the victim, close up the end of the shell with a small piece of virgin parchment. Bury the egg in the ground and leave without looking back.

The only thing then that can prevent the victim from dying of jaundice is the discovery and destruction of the egg, burned by the same hand that buried it. If the egg is allowed to rot in the ground, the victim will die within the year.

SOVEREIGN CURES FOR EVERYTHING

Remember the fad for copper bracelets "for rheumatism"? Magic? In fact, the copper bracelets worked because people thought they would. Earlier copper bracelets "cured" cholera, typhoid, and other ills, and guarded against the dangers of impure water. Faith can move mountains!

In case you'd like to be the first on your block with a new fad, note that silver is supposed to cure or relieve epilepsy, platinum keeps you from being constipated, tin is recommended for worms, lead improves the complexion (but don't ingest it—it killed off the Roman patrician class, which used lead pots, and threatens our poor infants who eat leaded paint in tenements), iron builds the blood, and gold can help you to sleep at nights (keep it in Swiss banks).

Whoever said that "diamonds are a girl's best friend" dwelt too much in the world of practicality. Diamonds are "unconquerable" (Greek: *adamas*) and impart courage and faith. They are connected in arcane lore with Aries and in the popular mind only with buxom blonds having "more fun."

INCENSE FOR SUCCESS

Mix together these ingredients (powdered if necessary) by weight:

sandalwood	30 percent
myrrh	10 percent
patchouli leaf	5 percent
orris root	5 percent
cinnamon	10 percent
frankincense	40 percent

Add a dash of saltpeter. Burn with incantations for your desire.

THE ELIXIR

And even the search for the philosopher's stone was intimately connected with the search for the elixir of life, for youth, a search that continues today with "life extension" plans using procaine and other drugs. The count of St.-Germain (supposed to have lived hundreds of years under a series of names) suggested an extract of senna, "St.-Germain tea," the vitamin C of its day. Arnaldus Villanovanus recommended alcohol (our word *whiskey* means "water of life"). Our grandparents liked patent medicine, of which alcohol was always a main ingredient (even those labeled "temperence beverages"), and tonics and cordials of various sorts. The Irish philosopher Bishop Berkeley praised tar-water as a panacea. Sir Francis Bacon recommended smelling freshly turned earth, the very clay of which God made us. The Countess Bathory (as I say elsewhere) bathed in the blood of countless maidens. Others swallowed blood, urine, gold.

In *The Alchemists*, F. S. Taylor gives the recipe for Dr. Stevens' Water, a seventeenth-century potion guaranteed to preserve life and make a man "seem young in his old age."

To a gallon of "Good Gascon Wine" (red), add a dram each of ginger, cinnamon, nutmeg, cloves, fennel seed, caraway seed, oregano, and galingale. Then throw in a generous handful each of sage, mint, wild marjoram, wild thyme, thyme, pellitory (a southern European herb), rosemary, red rose petals, pennyroyal, mint, camomile, and lavender. The herbs are bruised, the spices ground, and the liquid (once the solid ingredients have been allowed to soak in it for twelve hours or more) is thrice distilled. The distillate should be taken in small but very regular doses.

This certainly sounds more healthful than the "eye of newt" preparations we are usually offered. And don't be like the Scottish clergyman who is said to have concocted in his youth an elixir of life, but was afraid to swallow it. Thirty years later, he felt he was old enough and brave enough to try it. But by then it had evaporated.

RULERSHIP

A rule of magic is "as above, so below." From the most ancient times, the planets were said to rule terrestrial destinies and powers. Days of the week were named for the seven "planets" then known: Sun Day, Moon Day, Mars Day, Mercury Day, Jove Day, Venus Day, and Saturn Day. We can still see the remnants of these in the English Sunday, Monday, and Saturday and in the French Mardi (Tuesday), Mercredi (Wednesday), Jeudi (Thursday), and Vendredi (Friday). The magician learned and exploited celestial rulership over people, plants, metals, and minerals—everything.

Magic rituals must be conducted at astrologically correct times and with instruments, incenses, and plants correct for the ruling planet. For example, a love potion demands herbs controlled by Venus. Periwinkle's blue flower is described in the book attributed to Albertus Magnus as the best ingredient for a love potion, but it must be gathered at a date and day and hour dictated by astrology. It is ignorance of rulership and such arcane matters, say magicians, that render totally useless the concoctions thrown together by amateurs.

7

"All Manner of Folk"

WITCHES and magicians both tend to be people who are a little set apart from the rest of us—bolder, more learned, more restless, more confident, sometimes more wicked, but always imbued with a strong sense of self and a belief that the rules that govern ordinary people do not apply to them. The great English jurist Lord Coke hit on their basic quality when he legally defined witchcraft. Sorcerers, he said, are *determined* to work their will.

French historian Grillot de Givry writes in *Witchcraft, Magic and Alchemy* (first published in America in 1931):

> Some skillfull sorcerers knew the art of calling up the Devil or
> the subordinate demons of the vast infernal army. . . . Other
> sorcerers, known as necromancers, could call up apparitions of the
> dead. . . . There were sorcerers whom we should now class as
> "intellectuals." They were called sorcerers because what we mean

by "learned man" did not then exist. . . . There were monks, even, to whom the name of sorcerer was applied, both Roger Bacon and Albertus Magnus. . . . There were also sorcerer-monarchs like Henry III [of France] and his mother, Catherine de Médicis, and, strangest of all, sorcerer-Popes, Pope Honorius in the seventh century, and Pope Silvester II in the eleventh century, were considered, rightly or wrongly, to be sorcerers. . . .

In this chapter we shall meet some of these strange people, who considered themselves, or were considered by others, or laid claim to being, magicians and witches. And some others, who preyed on them.

DOUBLE GLOUCESTER

Humphrey, duke of Gloucester, brother of the ill-fated Henry VI, had a wife who was very curious about when the king would die. Some people said she was trying to hasten that event and that she had a wax figure of the king by her fireplace, hoping that, as it melted, the life of the king would drain away.

The duchess of Gloucester was tried and on flimsy evidence, she and her "accomplices" were all convicted. One woman from the town of Ely was burned. A canon of Westminster was confined to the Tower, where he died. Another "accomplice" was hanged, drawn, and quartered at Tyburn. Of course you couldn't treat the wife of "Good Duke Humphrey" in that way, so her punishment was this: On three successive days she carried a tall wax candle to the high altars of St. Paul's, Christ Church, and St. Michael's, three London parish churches. There, in the presence of the lord mayor and aldermen of London, she did her penance. Then she was sent off to the worst place they could think of, the Isle of Man.

The locals there believe that she haunts the Isle of Man to this day.

SIMON PURE AND SIMON NOT SO PURE

In Acts 8:9–12 and 8:18–24 the Bible tells the story of Simon, a magician, who in former times had "bewitched" the people of Samaria and had paraded himself as "some great one." Simon was baptized a Christian and became a follower of Philip, but when Peter and John arrived in Samaria and began to heal by the power of the Holy Ghost, Simon was so impressed that he offered them money if they would confer on him the same gifts. Peter rebuked him, saying, "Thy money perish with thee, because thou has thought that the gift of God may be purchased with money." Simon thereupon repented and asked Peter to pray for him. From this incident we have our word "simony," for the buying or selling of church offices.

That is all that the Bible itself says about this Simon, but some later works, especially the apocryphal *Acts of Saint Peter*, tell us of a certain Simon Magus, who supposedly appeared in Rome during the reign of the Emperor Claudius (A.D. 41–54), and these two Simons may—or may not—have been the same person.

Simon Magus was an evil sorcerer, who won many followers by performing acts of magic. He survived into the reign of Nero (54–68) and when Peter arrived in Rome, they became rivals. As the story goes, Nero demanded that Simon demonstrate his vaunted powers at high noon before a gathering of Roman citizens, and the magician agreed.

When a great crowd, among them Peter himself, had gathered in the imperial forum, Simon took center stage, magic staff in hand. His first act was to stand the staff upright and tell it to wait for him. It remained where he had placed it, erect. Then, having bowed to the emperor and his court, Simon stretched out his arms and began to rise into the air.

Higher and higher he rose until he was level with the top of the shrine of Juno Moneta (where Roman money was coined). At that point, Peter knelt down and made the sign of the cross in the air, and the spell was broken. The magician's staff toppled over, and Simon's body came crashing to earth.

Since Peter's original name was Simon, this can be said to be the magical duel of the two Simons. And Peter himself was martyred shortly afterward, during the Neronian persecutions.

PARACELSUS

His real name is impressive enough: Theophrastus Philippus Aurealus Bombastus von Hohenheim. But for this sixteenth-century physician and occultist, it was not enough. Considering himself equal in greatness to the ancient Roman writer on medicine, Aulus Cornelius Celsus, he named himself Paracelsus ("alongside Celsus").

Paracelsus was one of the most multitalented men of his time (1493–1541), a universal scientist, discover of zinc, a man deeply involved in very ancient magic and in the most advanced science of his time, alchemist and chemist, magician and physician, mystic and pioneer in medicine, metallurgy, pharmacy, and just about everything else.

His was a brilliant but not at all a humble personality. He went to the University of Basel at sixteen, became a physician and town doctor of the city, and outraged all the other medical professors by advocating new methods and attacking the old-fashioned, even superstitious beliefs of the great doctors of the past, such as Galen and Avicenna. It was time, he said, to observe rather than to believe, to experiment (as he did) very boldly with new compounds and new concepts, and, of course, to recognize genius (his).

They drove him out of Basel in 1529, and thereafter he led a life of wandering and conflict. He published a long list of works on subjects ranging from mineralogy (which he had early studied in the Tyrol) to magic. He died in Salzburg in 1541.

Quite apart from his innovations in pharmacy and medicine, he believed in an earth peopled below and above with gnomes and spirits. He forged some strange kind of link between the scientific emphasis on observable fact and the magical stress on the invisible world. Thus this extraordinary mind, one of the most advanced of the Renaissance, not only launched medical treatment and research on their way to modern empirical science, but fostered the most ancient mystical and magical beliefs.

A SCOTS SORCERER

Thomas Weir, born sometime around 1600, was the chief officer of the town guard of Edinburgh and one of its most respected citizens. A pillar of the Establishment, a "saint" of the very strict and upstanding sect known as the Bowhead Saints, Weir had served as a soldier on the side of Parliament in the Civil War, where he was distinguished for his cruelty toward Royalists and was known far and wide for his devout Presbyterian piety and his extraordinary gifts for moving extempore prayer. Thus, when Weir, at the age of seventy, suddenly and voluntarily confessed that he practiced the black arts as a magician, owned a magic staff, and was full of "blackness and darkness, brimstone and burning to the bottom of Hell," the provost (mayor) of Edinburgh was embarrassed and astonished.

And yet this "pillar" proceeded to add that he had for years committed incest with his sister—from the time she was in her teens until she reached fifty, at which point he was disgusted with her age and wrinkles—and had had carnal knowledge of Margaret Bourdon (the daughter of his dead wife), Bessie Weems (a serving girl, over a period of twenty years), and had "polluted himself" with various sheep, cows, and his own mare. When doctors and ministers tried to help the old man, he cursed their efforts to save his soul from perdition.

On April 29, 1670, Thomas and his sister appeared before the court, charged with sexual offenses. Weir was convicted of four—incest (two counts), fornication, and bestiality. He was sentenced to be strangled to death and his body to be burned, his black sorcerer's staff along with him. Jane offered the court a free confession that she was guilty of incest with her brother and "most especially [of] consulting witches, necromancers, and devils," keeping a familiar that not only assisted her in evil but also spun extraordinary quantities of wool for her. She was more helpful to the court than it wanted her to be, for the details were frightening. She was sentenced to be hanged in the Grassmarket, a street in central Edinburgh.

But despite her cooperation at the trial, when the day of execution arrived, Jane put up a battle royal. She struggled with her guards, threatened to remove all her clothes and shock the spectators, stuck her head between two steps of the scaffold, and was very difficult to pry loose. Worse, she said she had no remorse for her sins. They hanged her anyway.

As long as the two lived, some people were willing to dismiss the confessions as the results of madness or senile decay, but once the Weirs were dead, their reputation as sorcerers grew and spread. Thomas Weir's house, called Bow Head, stayed uninhabited for a century or more, while rumors of hauntings pervaded the city. It was said that other inhabitants of the street often heard, at night, the sound of a spinning wheel. . . .

ACCORDING TO RULE

Margaret Rule (whose story is vividly recounted by Cotton Mather) was prosecuted as a witch in Boston in 1693.

She reported that the Devil forced her to swear fealty on a big red book, by which she must have meant the lettering. It was not uncommon for grimoires to be printed in red—they were said to burn the eyes if gazed at too long—but they were always bound in black.

BOULLAN'S ATROCITIES

The abbé Boullan (born in France in 1824) claimed to be John the Baptist "returned to earth" and the "reincarnation of the prophet Elijah." He was, in fact, one of the most despicable of nineteenth-century magicians.

Jean-Antoine Boullan took holy orders at the age of twenty-five and almost immediately set out to "exorcize the Roman Catholic Church." As part of this campaign he performed the black mass (for which he was briefly jailed in Rome) and committed other sacriliges.

Early in his pastoral work, Father Boullan became the confessor of a nun named Sister Adele Chevalier. She became his mistress, and they had several children, at least one of which he was widely believed to have sacrificed in a demonic ceremony. With his mistress the nun, he founded a Society for the Reparation of Souls and engaged in blasphemous rites, offering to exorcise demons from nuns by administering the consecrated Host smeared with human excrement. Later he headed the Church of Carmel, and some people who were taken in by his apparent piety flocked to his "services," among them famed French novelist Joris Karl Huysmans (1848–1907).

A couple of Rosicrucians showed him up as a Satanist. Stanislaus de Guita and Oswald Wirth infiltrated the Church of Carmel and learned what Father Boullan was doing. They wrote a book, *The Temple of Satan*, which exposed his attempts to call up incubi and succubi, to practice sex magic, to exorcise with excrement and to practice Satanism. They labeled Father Boullan as a "pontiff of infamy, a base idol of the mystical Sodom . . . an evil sorcerer." This ended Boullan's career, and he died in disgrace.

AGRIPPA, THE CABALISTIC PHILOSOPHER

It is very difficult for moderns to understand a man like Heinrich Cornelius Agrippa von Nettesheim (1486–1535), philosopher, physician, magician, and more. Although he spent time in exile and even in jail for debt, his ideas influenced the study of the occult for generations.

His life was remarkable. Born in Cologne without good prospects, by the age of twenty he was well launched on a career in diplomacy and was sent on a secret mission to Paris by the Emperor Maximilian I. Then suddenly we find him entering the academic profession, lecturing on theology and occultism. His opinions so angered the church that he found himself right out of a job. He returned to diplomacy for a while, then acquired a medical degree from the University of Pavia. But soon he was in trouble again for his beliefs, this time for daring to defend a woman accused of witchcraft.

In Fribourg, Switzerland, he became so famous as a physician that the Queen Mother summoned him to France to be her personal doctor. When she wouldn't pay his salary, he went to Antwerp as historiographer to Charles

V, but soon the salary there was refused too. After more adventures—including being arrested as he passed through France for complaining about how badly the Queen Mother had treated him earlier—he found his way to Grenoble, where he died on February 18, 1535.

Agrippa gained a reputation as a magician for his *De occulta philosophia* (1531). He owned a black dog named Monsieur to which he was much attached; the animal ate at his table and slept on his bed, and though friends testified that it was a perfectly ordinary dog and could be walked on a leash, gossip said that Monsieur was Agrippa's familiar demon.

Agrippa believed in magic as a way of gaining deeper knowledge of God and nature. His ideas combined the ancient mysteries and the new Lutheranism, science and superstition, the cabala and Catholicism, and many other elements, and his influence was to prove greater in later times than during his exciting life.

AUGUST STRINDBERG

"Strindberg still remains," wrote Eugene O'Neill in 1924, "the most modern of moderns," but this great Scandinavian playwright (with Ibsen, a founder of the modern drama) had some very old-fashioned ideas, too, among them alchemy and black magic. Dabbling in the latter poisoned his later life.

Strindberg believed he could will things to happen and felt deep remorse when he reconsidered willing his child ill, not ill enough to die but problem enough to reconcile the parents.

He wrote that "there are crimes and crimes," some of which the law cannot punish but which nonetheless bring guilt, and in one play Strindberg traces the fate of a man who wills the death of his only child. Like all the fifty volumes of his work, this is partly autobiographical.

In the mad, mystical mind of this modern dramatist and old-fashioned alchemist were mingled the most advanced ideas and some of the oldest superstitions.

PAPAL SORCERERS

A number of popes have, at one time or another, been accused of practicing sorcery. Benedict XIII (1394–1423, actually an antipope, not to be confused with the real Benedict XIII, 1724–1730) was said to hold "continuous traffic with spirits" and to keep "two demons . . . in a little bag" for personal use and to search "everywhere for books on magic." Gregory VII (1081–1084) was pronounced a sorcerer by the Synod of Bressanone, June 25, 1080. Honorius I (d.638) was anathematized (formally cursed) forty-two years after his death. Benedict IX (1032–1048) bought his way to the papacy at the age of twenty, was twice deposed for profligacy, and ended up as antipope to Clement II. Antipope John XXIII (as I have said elsewhere) was reputed to have employed Abramelin to save him from the Council of Constance (1414–1417). Alexander VI (1492–1503), one of the two Borgia popes, bought his way to the papacy, fathered Cesare and Lucretia Borgia, and devoted himself entirely to expanding the temporal power of the papacy and the wealth of his own family.

But all the above men were involved in political clashes. Honorius and Gregory VII were austere reformers, opposed by worldly cardinals (Gregory was canonized in 1606); antipopes were the result of disputed papal elections; and pontiffs who lived scandalous private lives eventually shocked even people who had adopted lascivious life-styles of their own. In the struggles to control the papacy, charges of sorcery were freely employed— much as charges of "communist" and "pinko" were freely employed during the Senator McCarthy era. Usually there was nothing back of them except a desire to get rid of the accused.

But the label "sorcerer" has been pasted on others, less political, too. Leo III (795–816) is supposed to have authored a manual of magic called *Enchiridion*, which he sent to Charlemagne. Honorius III (1216–1227) also has a book of magic attributed to him, a new version of the *Black Book*, but it might also have been the work of antipope Honorius II (1061–1064) or of some Honorius who was not a pope at all.

But the pope about whom the most fanciful tales are told was Sylvester II (999–1003). Prior to his election, he had been known as Gerbert, and he was the foremost scholar in Europe. He invented an elaborate abacus and celestial and terrestrial globes for the teaching of mathematics and astronomy. He is credited with construction of a remarkable sundial at Magdeburg and several pipe organs. A devoted bibliophile, he collected manuscripts from all over Europe, especially of classical (secular) Latin authors, and created one of the great libraries of the Middle Ages. He devoted his short papacy to diplomacy, reconciling quarreling prelates and advancing old rivals and confirming their appointments.

But genuine achievements were not enough apparently, for after his death, fabulous tales began to circulate about Sylvester. He was supposed to have been a powerful magician and to have won the papacy by his spells. (He did have pull; his former pupil, later Holy Roman Emperor Otto III, obtained the See for him.) He was supposed to have had a love adventure in Spain. It was claimed that he had sold his soul to the devil and received in return a magic statue that made prophecies, one of them being that Sylvester himself should not die, "except at Jerusalem."

As the story goes, he was saying Mass one day in Rome and was taken ill. He remembered the prophecy and asked for the name of the church he was in; he was told "Holy Cross of Jerusalem." He knew then that he was going to die, and he did.

MAGICIANS AND SCIENTISTS

Johannes Heidenberg (1462–1516) was abbot of the Benedictine monastery of Trittenheim, West Germany. He was a theologian, and since magic was then regarded as one of the learned arts, he drifted into the study of it. He maintained that there were three kinds of magic—natural, cabalistic, and black—and pored over the works of the great Dominican, Albertus Magnus (1193–1280), who had also dabbled in magic.

His fellow monks were impressed at first by Heidenberg's writings; then (perhaps because witchcraft persecutions were then beginning to rage throughout southern Germany) they became uneasy and burned their abbot's books. Heidenberg left for Würzburg and continued his arcane studies. In *Stenography* he taught not shorthand but the art of raising demons, and he greatly influenced such magician-scientists as Agrippa and Paracelsus.

"In magic," wrote Heidenberg, "it is the practice that is dangerous, not the knowledge," and the great Albertus is said to have agreed with him:

> Every science is good in itself, but its operation is good or evil
> according to the end to which it is directed. . . . Magic is neith-
> er forbidden nor evil, since through knowledge of it, one can
> avoid evil and do good. . . . Magic . . . is useful knowledge,
> but very dangerous when one gets to know nature in depth.

However they did it, Heidenberg and his cohorts delved into pharmacy and psychology, magic and mesmerism, physics and medicine, philosophy and the occult. And along the way they laid the foundations for any number of later sciences.

WILLIAM JAMES

The great American psychologist (*Principles of Psychology* and *The Varieties of Religious Experience*) and philosopher (*The Will to Believe* and *Some Problems of Philosophy*) said every hallucination was "as good, and true a sensation as if there were a real object there. The object happens *not* to be there, that is all."

SAINT ALFONSO MARIA DE' LIGUORI'S ADVICE

The founder of the Congregation of the Most Holy Redeemer, known as the Redemptorists (1696–1787), says that in breaking a pact in which you sold your soul to the Devil you must repent and make restitution to any persons you have injured, adding in his *Moral Theology*, Book III (one of seventy volumes on his works), that if the Devil has given you any books, amulets, talismans, or what-have-you, you must burn them but, if he holds the document of your deed of gift of the soul—Bishop Liguori had been a prominent trial lawyer before he entered the priesthood—you don't need to get it back to burn it; just tell the Devil ; ou recant.

But for all the sophistry in such reasoning, Liguori was best known for the simplicity and dignity of his sermons, understandable by the least sophisticated of his peasant flock.

ROGER BACON

Roger Bacon (1214?–1294?) was famous as a student of the occult, though he was, in fact, a scientist. (Even as late as Shakespeare's time, Bacon was portrayed by dramatist Robert Greene as a magician.) A Franciscan, he was the author of a *Treatise on the Secret Works of Nature and Art*; his experiments (detailed in his *Mirror of Alchemy*) laid some foundations for chemistry and physics, including studies of the rainbow and magnets.

It was widely believed that he had created some sort of golem, or Frankenstein's monster, and a brazen head that could speak. Pope Clement IV asked to read his work, and Bacon sent him his *Opus Majus*, a kind of encyclopedia, but it only seems to have got Bacon in trouble, for the head of the Franciscan order denounced him for "suspect novelties," put him under house arrest, and forbade the reading of the *Opus*. What could you do with a man who was inventing the magnifying glass, fiddling around with gunpowder, studying astrology as well as astronomy, and working on an elixir of life, except to throw him in jail and ban his books? His ideas about a lighter-than-air flying machine alone were enough to show he was in league with the Devil.

DOCTOR FAUSTUS

Faust is so widely known as a legendary figure, the subject of drama, epic verse, and opera, that most people assume he was a figment of someone's imagination. But a magician named Georg (later Johann) Faust actually did live from about 1480 to 1541.

He was born probably in Knittlingen in Baden-Württemberg, southwestern Germany. He learned the black arts in Kraków, then led the life of a wandering magician, traveling to various cities in Germany accompanied by a performing horse and dog. He called himself Magister (Master) Georgius Sabellicus (Sabine) Faustus (lucky) Junior. He told fortunes and cast horoscopes. He laid claim to occult knowledge and power, such as the ability to restore lost works of Plato and Aristotle and to perform the same miracles as Jesus.

Some of his contemporaries denounced him as a charlatan and mountebank, notably Johann Wier, who called Faust a drunken vagabond of "unspeakable deceit, many lies, and great effect." But the religious reformers of the day took the magician seriously. Melanchthon feared him as "a disgraceful beast and sewer of many devils" and considered the horse and dog his familiars. Johann Gast, a well-known divine, claims to have taken a meal with Faust at which these creatures were attendants. Luther himself declared that Faust had worked sorceries against him, which he only overcame by God's help.

One morning in 1541, at Staufen in his native Württemberg, Faust was found in his room, lying on his face, dead. His neck had been wrung as if by superhuman force. It is said that the corpse, though repeatedly laid out on its bier face up, was five times discovered to have been turned face down.

Out of this material, men's imagination constructed the story of a learned man who sold his soul to the devil Mephistopheles (or Mephisto) in return for youth, love, and universal knowledge, then was claimed by Mephistopheles and carried off to Hell. The first book to carry the story was printed in Frankfurt in 1587, and from there it became Marlowe's play *Doctor Faustus* (1588), Goethe's great dramatic poem *Faust* (1808 and 1832), a drawing by Rembrandt, and countless operas, symphonies, tone poems, overtures, and other musical pieces.

For a drunken mountebank, it was quite an apotheosis.

THE PRINCE OF SORCERERS

The title, common in his lifetime, was really too grand for Louis Gaufridi, a handsome priest of Provence, whose real offenses were chiefly sexual. He fell in love with a twelve-year-old nun, seduced her with the help of a charm which he carried in a walnut, and "married" her in the name of the Devil (because he couldn't marry her in the name of God).

But he ran into an accusation of witchcraft by a fellow resident of his mistress' convent, a hysterical woman named Louise Capeau, and was brought to trial by Church authorities. They assigned an exorcist to his mistress (Madeleine de Mandols de La Palud), and he claimed to have driven 666 devils out of her. They forced Gaufridi to confess in court to a story of obscenities, blasphemies, and heresies. Madeleine, now "unpossessed" of the Devil, gave evidence that Gaufridi had said black masses, and Capeau testified that she could see the Devil, in the shape of a toad, sitting on the priest's shoulder.

Father Gaufridi was burned at the stake on April 30, 1611, at Aix-les-Bains. They put Madeleine away safely, lest she bring more embarrassment to Church and civil authorities; first she was set to chopping wood for charity, later (1653) they feared her more and put her in perpetual cloister. Louise Capeau went free. She accused a lot more people and managed to get another person burned at the stake. That victim was a little blind girl named Honorée.

MACDUFF

Shakespeare's *Macbeth* is not only full of witches, prophecies, spells, incantations, and ghosts. It also contains the brave Macduff who, in revenge for Macbeth's many crimes, including the murder of Macduff's wife and children, kills Macbeth. Macduff, having had a Cesarean birth, was considered "not of woman born" and thus of mystic origin. In Scotland to this day, Macduff figures in occult lore.

In Fifeshire there is the base of what used to be a Celtic cross named for the Macduffs. The cross itself has long since disappeared, demolished in the Reformation as papistical, but the site remains haunted to this day.

In medieval times Macduff's Cross had been a place of sanctuary. Anyone could run to it, hold onto it, and be safe from retribution for murder, provided he arranged to pay blood money to the relatives; some say the price of a life was nine bulls and a heifer.

The story goes that the relatives of one murdered man were too angry to respect this tradition or accept this payment. They chased the murderer to the cross, dragged him off it, and killed him on the spot. At a place called Nine Wells (the 3 times 3 is interesting), they washed the blood off their hands. The site of the cross is said to be haunted by the ghost of the murderer, who was entitled to sanctuary and got only vengefulness.

THE MONKS OF MEDMENHAM

Near West Wycombe, not far from London, stood a Cistercian abbey which, by the eighteenth century, had fallen into ruins; by then it belonged to young Francis Duffield, who had come under the influence of the madcap Sir Francis Dashwood (1708–1781).

Sir Francis inherited great wealth in his teens and was devoting himself to a life of aesthetic debauchery. He founded the Friars of St. Francis with himself as prior and Duffield, several poets (Whitehead, Selwyn, Potter), politicians (John Wilkes and the Earl of Sandwich), and others as rollicking members. They staged orgies in a specially designed cave, had black masses said in a Satanic chapel, and were generally known as the Hell-Fire Club.

Over the doorway the "monks" inscribed *Fay ce que voudras* ("Do what thou wilt"), the motto of the Abbey of Thelema in Rabelais' *Gargantua*. Later Aleister Crowley, who tried as hard to be wicked as Dashwood and Duffield did, picked up the motto and the name of the abbey for his own orgiastic organization.

In time Sir Francis succeeded his uncle as Lord le Despencer (1762) and became postmaster general and chancellor of the Exchequer. The "monks" broke up, having scandalized all England.

At one point Lord Sandwich found himself arguing in the Lords for the impeachment of Wilkes (who had been Lord Mayor of London and held other political offices) on the grounds of blasphemies at the abbey, outrages of which Sandwich was especially knowledgeable because he himself had participated in them.

THE WITCH-FINDER GENERAL

During the turmoil of the Civil War in England, Matthew Hopkins of Ipswich appeared in Essex (1645–1647) as a witch finder. He did what Americans call a land-office business, at 20 shillings for every witch he identified to the authorities.

He looked for "a mark whereof no evident Reason in Nature can be given," and he often found one. (Looking for the devil's mark like this was common; in Scotland "common prickers," as they were called, were numerous enough to form a kind of union.) Thus the fact of witchcraft was considered proved if the suspect had a mole on her back or under the armpits or lip or on her private parts. Some said the mark was red like a flea bite, some said brown like a mole, some said blue like a nip, and *The Highland Papers* report that at the trial of one Kate Moore a white spot was found. It was "the devil's mark" if, probed with a pin, it was insensible. The pins could be up to three inches long and some had pins that retracted into the handles so that "pricking" could be faked.

With this "pricking" method, Hopkins found hundreds of witches in Chelmsford and Bury St. Edmunds in July and August 1645. He also used interrogation; English inquisitors were not permitted to torture suspects with instruments, but they could keep them awake for several nights in a row, and this worked perfectly well. They could also test to see if a bound suspect would float if thrown into water. If you did not sink, you were a witch—the Devil kept you afloat; the water would not receive you.

Hopkins operated with great success for about four years but then fell under suspicion himself, so cleverly had he made the populace aware of witchcraft. He was tied up and given the water test. He either floated (in which case he was executed as a witch) or sank (and was drowned). Nobody is quite sure which, but he died. And that was the ironic end of the witch-finder general.

GERALD B. GARDNER

One of the most knowledgeable and respected of modern witches was Gerald B. Gardner (1884–1964). After some years in the East, Gardner retired as a wealthy man and began to devote himself to the occult—

theosophy, Rosicrucianism, and particularly a coven of witches in the New Forest. The group called itself the Craft of the Wise. When witchcraft laws were repealed in England, the group, which had hitherto been secret, surfaced and in the ensuing publicity, drew many would-be witches and magicians to their organization.

Gardner impressed a great deal of his strong personality on British witchcraft. His *Witchcraft Today* (1954) is a refreshingly rational attempt to divorce the reputation of the Old Religion from that of Satanism, black arts, and blood sacrifices, devil worship and malicious acts.

> If I were permitted to disclose all their rituals, I think it would
> be easy to prove that witches are not diabolists; but the oaths
> are solemn and the witches are my friends. I would not hurt their
> feelings. They have secrets which to them are sacred. They have
> good reason for this secrecy.

The press called him Britain's Chief Witch, and occasionally he referred to himself as King of the Witches. He founded the Witchcraft Museum at Castletown on the Isle of Man, and he was unquestionably more knowledgeable about witchcraft than many self-proclaimed wizards who had been taken up by the popular press.

TWO INQUISITORS

Pierre de Lancre was a relative of the great Montaigne. In 1608 King Henry IV of France appointed Lancre to investigate the outbreak of witchcraft among the Basques, and he promtly sent six hundred people to their deaths for sorcery. He thus became a recognized expert on the sabbat, lycanthropy (werewolves), and similar matters, and he published a big book in Paris in 1612, disagreeing with those who urged moderation. Lancre claimed to have found *une Royne du Sabbat* in *chasque village*—"a Queen of the Sabbat" in "every village."

At the same time, Alonzo Salazar de Frias, sent to quell an outbreak of witchcraft in Cigarramundi, reported to the Inquisition in Spain that he had examined the evidence of 1,800 people (including 1,384 children) and after eight months of investigation decided that there was no evidence whatever of dealing with the Devil.

He had experimented by alternately sending word that he was coming (to investigate witchcraft in a certain village) and arriving unannounced. In the former case, there were always ample accusations ready when he reached the village in question, and in the latter, none. He concluded therefore, and so reported to the Inquisition, that "there were neither witches nor bewitched until they were talked and written about." The Holy Office did not go so far as to deny the existence of witchcraft, but it followed Salazar's council in insisting on adequate evidence of evil actions (such as out-and-out poisoning) before it allowed a suspect to be condemned.

MELMOTH THE WANDERER

The apex of the Gothic novel is often considered to be *Melmoth the Wanderer* (1820), written by an eccentric and mysterious Irish clergyman named Charles Robert Maturin (1782–1824).

Melmoth is a gruesomely horripilative tale of an Irish gentleman who has sold his soul to the Devil for a long life and, wearying of it, dejectedly wanders among the ruined men whom fate has cast down, vainly hoping that one of them may be foolish enough to take over Melmoth's pact and free him from the terrible burden.

Balzac ventured to rank the novel with the works of Molière, Goethe, and Byron (creators of *Don Juan*, *Faust*, and *Manfred*) as contributing authentic and enduring allegorical figures to modern literature. (People tended to lose their literary judgment in those days when horror was involved.)

In the story, the term of the agreement with the Devil runs out, and the Wanderer disappears; all that is left is his scarf, caught on a crag some distance from the brink of a great cliff that juts out into the tumultuous ocean. But in Balzac's continuation, *Melmoth Reconciled*, the Wanderer finds a villain willing to assume his fearful responsibility and goes to his own death without fear of eternal damnation.

As the century closed, a descendant of Maturin, Oscar Fingal O'Flahertie Wills Wilde, found himself in jail, his brilliant writing career blasted by homosexual scandal and disgrace. When he was released from Reading Gaol, Wilde fled to Paris, where, to hide his identity and shame, he took the name "Sebastian Melmoth." As Sebastian Melmoth, Wilde lived out his last few years.

HENRY III OF FRANCE

The third son of Henry II and Catherine de Médicis, Henry (reigned 1574–1589) was widely reputed during his lifetime to be a sorcerer—as was his formidable mother. At his castle of Vincennes, in a wood east of Paris, he studied the black arts under various magicians, who had been summoned there for that purpose.

His reign was a bloody one. Two years before he came to the throne, he had helped instistigate the infamous St. Bartholomew's Day massacre of French Protestants, and in the religious wars that followed his ascension, many Frenchmen died for one faith or the other. And despite his personal inclinations, he allowed 30,000 people to be executed for witchcraft.

After his assassination at the hands of a Dominican priest, his retreat at Vincennes was examined. In the keep servants found "the dressed skin of a child."

HEARTS

Mention of Henry III, whose heart was buried separately from the rest of him, reminds us of some of the others whose hearts were connected with superstition.

Take Blanche Parry (1507–1589), governess of Elizabeth I. She was buried in St. Margaret's Church, Westminster, in two pieces. Her heart was separated lest it burst with "love of the queen."

King Robert Bruce (1274–1329) died of leprosy in Scotland, but his henchman Sir James Douglas, called the Black Douglas (1286–1330), undertook to carry his embalmed heart to Palestine to be buried in Jerusalem. He died fighting the Moors in Spain, so Bruce's heart went back to Scotland and was buried in Melrose Abbey. Bruce's body was buried in Dunfermline Abbey.

The old idea that the heart was the seat of emotions (still recalled on valentines) led to many superstitions and occasional use in witchcraft. A pig's or sheep's heart, stuck full of pins or thorns, served the same purpose as a wax image—brought a curse on one's enemy.

SWEDENBORG

Emmanuel Swedenborg was born in Stockholm in 1688. He died in London on March 29, 1772—as he had predicted he would.

In 1743 he had a vision of a magician in a purple robe—a vision that was repeated the next year. From this apparition and from necromancy (he called up the spirits of men such as Virgil and Martin Luther), he claimed to have derived a rich store of occult information.

He turned to spititualism and pneumatology (hypnotism) and added a reputation as clairvoyant and prophet to one as scientist (his interests ranged from anatomy and astronomy to zoology). He had visions of historical events and of the end of history, the Last Judgment. He lived in an "illuminated" world, peopled with visible angels and informed by visions.

He never preached or attempted to establish a church, but after his death his followers founded the Church of the New Jerusalem, thus fulfilling another of his prophecies, that his influence would long outlast his life.

THE ROSY CROSS

Johann Valentin Andreä (1586–1654) published *Fama Fraternitatis* ("Report of Brotherhood," 1614) under the pseudonym of Christian Rosenkreuz, and there may possibly have been a person of this name (1378–1484?) who is often credited with founding the Rosicrucians. It is alleged that he returned to his native Germany with the wisdom of the East, recruited eight disciples, and sent them to eight different countries to spread the secret lore. More than a century after the death of the first Rosenkreuz, his body was said to have been found uncorrupted in a mysterious octagonal tomb and accompanied by occult papers that are the basis of modern secret societies.

Other Rosicrucian organizations claim even more ancient origins, tracing them all the way back to pharaonic Egypt and asserting that over the centuries many of the world's greatest sages have owed their knowledge to the occult symbols of the rose and the cross, the pyramid, and the swastika.

If the *Fama Fraternitatis* and the book published the next year by the same author, *Confessio Rosae Crucis* ("Testimony of the Rosy Cross"), are to be believed, then Rosicrucianism did derive its symbolism and lore from the East, especially from Arab lands, but probably not from Egyptian mysteries.

There is some sort of connection between the Rosicrucians (variously called Brothers of the Rosy Cross, Knights of the Rosy Cross, and Philosophers of the Rosy Cross) and another secret society that claims very ancient origins, Freemasonry. Even the authoritative A. E. Waite (*Real History of the Rosicrucians*, 1887) and H. S. Lewis' respected *Rosicrucian Questions and Answers* (1929) have by no means answered all the questions or convinced everyone of the true history.

Complicating the matter still further, the European Rosicrucians, who were known as the Illuminati, have only very vague connections with the theosophical teachings of the American AMORC (Ancient and Mystical Order of the Rosy Cross). The latter group is not really ancient at all, having been founded in California in 1915 by H. S. Lewis, author of books on such matters as Atlantis and the so-called secrets of the pyramids. It is not really very mystical either, certainly not secret, since it advertises itself widely in magazines.

A competing American organization, *Fraternitas Rosae Crucis*, was founded by R. Swinburne Clymer and is advertised not as the modern inheritor of the secrets of the pyramids but of the clandestine brotherhood that (they claim) numbered among its members such well-known names as Plato, Jesus Christ, and Benjamin Franklin.

Competing with Lewis and Clymer is the society of Rosicrucians founded in New York by G. E. S. De Witow, author of *The Temple in the Clouds*, and the Rosicrucian Fellowship. The fellowship, the richest Rosicrucian group, headquartered at Oceanside, California, was founded by Max Heindel, a former ship's engineer. Directed by astral orders, he said, he wrote *The Rosicrucian Cosmo-Conception* (1908), and his brand of esoterica, combining astrology, Christianity, vegetarianism, and faith healing has many attractions for American occultists. When the founders of some of these groups died, their families continued their work—and often their lawsuits.

At the moment Rosicrucians of all groups seem to be doing very well, whether they are teaching the authentic doctrines of ancient Rosicrucian masters or just pretending to have learned secrets from the magic of Tibet, from aliens visiting from other planets, or whatever. Meanwhile, the John Birch Society is said to fear that the Illuminati are still with us and plotting—with four hundred members sworn to the deepest secrecy—to take over the world by black magic.

MIRIAM

Maria Prophetissa (also known as Mary the Jewess) of the fourth century was thought by her contemporaries in Alexandria to be none other than Miriam, the sister of Moses. Cooks of today will be amused to hear that her alchemical pots and pans are supposed to have given rise to the *bain-marie* ("bath of Mary"), the very useful double boiler.

GEORGE GIFFORD

In *Dialogue Concerning Witches* (1593) George Gifford, a clergyman who died in 1620, condemned *white* magic!

"These cunning men and women with charms, seeming to do good," he wrote, "ought to be rooted out."

ABRAMELIN

Abramelin, also called Abraham the Jew, as I said earlier, is supposed to have been a fifteenth-century magician, the author of *The Book of Sacred Magic* (1458), said to have been delivered to his son Lamech. The modern edition (translated by S. L. M. Mathers) is *The Sacred Magic of Abramelin the Mage.*

In this book, Abramelin recounts many journeys he took about the then known world in search of magical enlightenment: Egypt, Arabia, Greece, Hungary, Austria, Constantinople. In Prague, he encountered "a wicked man named Antony," who rendered himself invisible, flew through the air, entered rooms through the keyhole, knew everyone's secrets "and once he told me things that God alone could know." In Lintz a young woman anointed "the principle pulses of my feet and hands" with an unguent that was supposed to enable him to fly, and he did indeed have the sensation of flying through the air and seeing wonders, but he woke up depressed and with a headache.

Later, this same young woman, at Abramelin's request, rubbed herself with the same unguent in order to travel two hundred miles to visit a friend of his and bring back news. She fell to the ground and lay insensible for three hours, then woke up and told him what she had learned of the friend. Alas, when he checked with the friend, her story was "entirely contrary to his profession." He therefore concluded that "what she had told me was a simple dream, and that this unguent was a causer of phantastic sleep." Thus, though Abramelin was a believer in magic and demonology, he was no fool.

His book offers readers cabalistic magic squares that will purportedly perform such feats as raising tempests, causing spirits to appear, changing men into animals and vice versa, procuring visions, raising the dead, rousing love or hate, demolishing buildings, walking under water, and even making stage performances appear.

COUNT OF ST.-GERMAIN

When a man calling himself the count of St.-Germain turned up in Paris in 1748, looking about thirty, he claimed he was two thousand years old. Was he an Alsatian Jew or a Portuguese with a whale of a good line? Or was he a man who had discovered the elixir of life? Did he die in 1784 in Schleswig, or was he the "Major Fraser" who appeared in the 1850s claiming to be St.-Germain? Or perhaps he was the gentleman who turned up on top of Mount Shasta, California, in this century making the same claim? Many people insist they have met him, including Madame Elena Blavatsky (1831–1891) and Annie Besant (1847–1933).

He told eighteenth-century Parisians that he had known Henry IV (1553–1610). If that was true, then perhaps he was also the man who scared Catherine de Médicis to death in 1589, for she was Henry's mother-in-law. An astrologer had told Catherine (1519–1589) "to beware of St.-Germain," so the queen carefully avoided the Faubourg St.-Germain, a district of Paris. Then she fell ill and sent for a priest to hear her confession. He appeared and announced that his name was St.-Germain, and she dropped dead.

But back to our St.-Germain. When he arrived in France, it was probably from Germany. But was he a Jew? A Jesuit? The heir or illegitimate son of Frederick II Rákóczky of Hungary? Nobody knew much except that he was mysterious and liked it that way.

He told the court that he had developed an elixir to keep him thirty forever. He graced many dinner tables, but would never eat; he said he never touched food but lived on his magic elixir. He did add that he had partaken of one wedding dinner—the one that Christ attended at Cana. He opened a scientific laboratory outside St.-Antoine to various society visitors, but no one could figure out what he was doing. Even when the king of

France gave him laboratory space at Versailles, they were no wiser. Nor Charles of Hesse-Cassel later.

St.-Germain became a confidant of Louis XV and a favorite of the king's mistress, Madame de Pompadour. In a society in which gossip was the leading indoor sport, he heard much and repeated nothing. He never invited anyone to his home, took nobody into his confidence. He said he was a Mason but had forgotten the signs.

He got involved in diplomatic intrigues and went on several confidential missions for the French king, journeying mysteriously to Vienna, Constantinople, Moscow, and other exotic capitals. In Paris, he made lots of friends, mostly ladies. They kept him so busy (he told Casanova, also an agent of Louis XV) that he didn't have time to invent the steamboat, but he would get to that in the next century. Meanwhile, he distributed to them a wash that took away wrinkles and warned Marie Antoinette of the impending revolution (she didn't believe him).

In 1760, a spell of unpopularity caught up with him, and he moved to London for two years, perhaps serving as a spy for the English government. From there he traveled to Russia, where he served in the army of Catherine the Great as "General Welldone." In 1770 he was back in Paris for four years, until his final move to Schleswig, where he went into the magic business with Landgrave Charles of Hesse-Cassel. In 1784 he died.

Or did he? Not according to "Major Fraser," Madame Blavatsky, Annie Besant, and some others.

THE QUEEN OF VOODOO

Marie Laveau, a mulatto born in New Orleans near the end of the eighteenth century, was the most colorful of the Voodoo queens of that fascinating city. She was living in a rickety shanty on Lake Pontchartrain when a rich white family appealed to her to save their son from being convicted of a crime. Marie put three peppers in her mouth and prayed in the cathedral for a while, then placed the peppers under the judge's bench. The young man, despite all the testimony against him, got off scot-free. The grateful white family gave her a cottage on St. Ann Street, between Rampart and Burgundy streets in the Old Quarter.

For more difficult cases she had a "magic" shawl (which she claimed the Emperor of China had sent to her) and innumerable gris-gris charms, African fetishes, and Catholic religious articles. She could make people fall in and out of love. She could tell fortunes. She gave spiritual advice and material help. She was even said (having failed to get him out of jail on a charge of murder) to have poisoned Antoine Cambre, the bouncer at the Louisiana Ballroom, at his request, to prevent him from having to face hanging; she used a bowl of the gumbo she frequently brought along when she made her regular charitable visitations to the city prison.

On June 7, 1869, when she was over seventy, Marie Laveau was replaced as Voodoo queen of New Orleans by Malvina Latour, who performed such astounding public exorcisms as that of the chaplain of the Louisiana legislature, who coughed up a live black mouse and was thereafter wholly cured. But never again was anyone to be so relied upon or so feared as was Marie Laveau in her prime. She died about 1875, but is still remembered as one of the most outstanding characters in the checkered history of the French Quarter.

BERNARDO DI COMO

When the inquisitor Bernardo di Como came along at the very beginning of the sixteenth century, he argued that witchcraft had flourished in Como, Italy, for as much as 150 years and something drastic had to be done about it. To accomplish this, he was prepared to write his own rules and to act as he pleased, whatever the advice of lay experts and councils.

One of his problems was that learned opinion of the time often tended to the belief that the sabbat was a delusion: Witches did not really fly off to these obscene orgies but, under the influence of drugs or delusions, just thought that they did so. If the sabbat was not real, how could the witches be punished for attending it?

In his magisterial history, *The Inquisition of the Middle Ages* (1887), Henry Charles Lea writes that Bernardo di Como "triumphantly adduced the fact that numerous persons had been burned for attending the Sabbat, which could not have been done without the assent of the pope, and this was sufficient proof that the heresy was real, for the Church punishes only manifest crimes." So, Bernardo burned hundreds more.

"THE BLACK POPE"

Anton Szandor LaVey is the head of the Church of Satan. He believes that the mass proper desexualizes and dehumanizes true pagan beliefs, and thus is a parody—hence the black mass is only a parody of a parody. He complains that "all of the books about the Devil have been written by the agents of God," whereas real Satanists refuse to be defined by the Church.

In the manifesto of his Church of Satan he writes:

> It would be an over-simplification to say that every successful man and woman on earth is, without knowing it, a practicing Satanist, but the thirst for earthly success and its ensuing realization are certainly grounds for Saint Peter turning thumbs down. . . . If the love of money is the root of all evil; then we must at least assume the most powerful men on earth to be the most Satanic. . . .

APOLLONIUS OF TYANA, MAGICIAN EXTRAORDINAIRE

One of the most famous magicians of the ancient world was Apollonius of Tyana (in Cappadocia, now part of Turkey), the date of whose birth is unknown but which may have been in the reign of the Roman emperor Caligula (37 A.D.–41). In any case, he enters history with a vengeance in the reign of the emperor Nerva (96–98), with a terrific reputation as Pythagorean philosopher and miracle worker. In his biography, written by Flavius Philostratus, a third-century philosopher and literary man, Apollonius is said to have arrived in Rome heralded by word that he had rid Antioch of scorpions by imitative magic (he buried a bronze scorpion in the city), rid Ephesus of plague (by encouraging the inhabitants to stone the spirits who brought it), and rid Corinth of a vampire.

In *Anatomy of Melancholy*, author Robert Burton featured the vampire tale in the English tradition, and John Keats picked it up for his poem *Lamia*. The story goes that Menippus, a young student of Apollonius, was irresistably drawn to a very beautiful woman in Corinth. They married, but on the wedding night Apollonius entered Menippus' house, revealed to him that she was a *lamia* (vampiric serpent woman of Greek folklore), and caused her to vanish.

Apollonius in Rome became a part of the literary circle around Julia Domna, the wife of the emperor Septimus Severus and mother of Caracalla. It is said that Apollonius annoyed the emperor by being called *deus* (god) and was brought to trial. As a preparation for that, it is reported, they cut his hair (attempting to diminish his power, as Delilah did with Samson), but his magic seems to have remained unaffected, for legend asserts that he vanished from the courtroom, never to be seen again.

THE MAHDI

Mohammed Ahmed ibn-Seyyid Abdallah (1843–1885), a member of the mystic Sufi sect of Islam, moved from the civil service to the slave trade and eventually proclaimed himself the Mahdi (Messiah).

In the 1880s he and his dervishes battled the Egyptians and the British for control of the Sudan. On November 4, 1883, he defeated an Egyptian army led by a British general named William Hicks, known as Hicks Pasha. On January 26, 1885, the Mahdi captured Khartoum, and his men (though orders were to take the British general alive) killed Charles George "Chinese" Gordon and delivered his head to the Mahdi.

This helped to fulfill the prophecy that the Mahdi and Gordon would meet "face to face." Gordon's face "bore a cheerful smile," it was reported. The Mahdi was impressed that Gordon had a space between his two front teeth such as was prophesied that the Muslim Messiah would have.

Four months later, on June 22, the Mahdi himself died. When the British army under Kitchener finally retook Khartoum in 1898, they looted for days and blew up the tomb of the Mahdi, having first thrown his body into the Nile and shipped off his head to Cairo. The head (or skull) was eventually buried at Wadi Halfa, Sudan.

Kitchener, who was responsible for this indignity inflicted on the self-proclaimed Messiah of Islam, was told that he would be punished by being drowned at sea and yet his body would be consumed in flames. Some eighteen years later Kitchener was drowned in the sinking of H.M.S. *Hampshire* off the Orkneys on June 5, 1916. There is some question about whether the body was recovered and cremated.

Harold T. Wilkins in *Strange Mysteries of Time and Space* (1959) reports: "The Mahdi's formerly blown-up house, rebuilt, is one no Sudanese, *today*, will stay in. It is haunted by *afreets*, and a British Commissioner went mad in it."

Is the Madhi, a Sufi magician, still at work?

IAMBLICHUS

Anyone who has tried to carry the nuances of one language over to another recognizes the seed of truth in the Italian proverb "A translator is a traitor," which equates "translator" (*traduttore*) with "traitor" (*traditore*).

Greek philosopher Iamblichus argued that this is especially true of magic formulas and incantations.

Iamblichus (250–325), the founder of the Syrian Neoplatonism (which he tried to reconcile with Chaldean magic and pagan religions), was himself a magician of no mean talents. But even he, he said, could not translate his spells into other tongues, because translation alters the letters and hence the numerology; the magic words lose their power.

CALVIN

John Calvin fulminated against relics, mocking the French king who built Sainte-Chapelle to contain the Crown of Thorns. Or one of them. There were so many "real" Crowns in existence, Calvin scoffed that "it must have been a hedge." Bits of the True Cross, he said, would form "a full load for a good ship." In his treatise on relics (1543) he vehemently attacked the "anthill of bones" assembled by the faithful and the foolishness of a superstitious belief in the "magical" powers of relics.

THE MONSTER

Gilles de Laval de Retz (1404–1440) came from a distinguished Breton family; he was the grandson of De Guesclin (1320–1380), constable of France. He distinguished himself in the Hundred Years War, fighting beside Joan of Arc, and for his exploits he was made a marshal of France at the age of twenty-three. He was incredibly wealthy.

The Maid, his comrade-in-arms, went on to be burned as a witch and later canonized. Gilles too was executed for witchcraft, but he is recalled as a devil of depravity.

He lived sumptuously at Tiffauges and Machecoal, his castles on the border of Brittany, spending lavishly on books (then a big-ticket item), on gold and silver and velvet and jewels. Even his immense wealth could not survive such extravagance and he soon ran into debt. To recoup, he turned to alchemy, and when the philosopher's stone failed to materialize, he went on to magic. He brought the magician Francesco Prelati from Florence to teach him the black arts and sold his soul (they said) to the Devil.

Soon children began to disappear from peasant villages roundabout, young boys mostly. Stories began to circulate that they had been carried off by agents of Baron de Retz, but Gilles was too powerful for ordinary people to combat. Complaints went to ecclesiastical authorities, but still men hesitated. Then Gilles, for some reason, carried off a priest and held him prisoner, and this deed made him liable to action by the Church authorities. He was arrested and brought before an ecclesiastical court.

At first he was haughty and scornful, called his accusers simoniacs, and cursed them. But on the third day he broke down and confessed. He had indeed engaged in forbidden practices, he said, not only dealings with Satan but inspeakable cruelties to the children he had had kidnapped—sodomizing them, then cutting their throats and offering up their hearts and cut-off hands as part of the ritual he practiced. Sometimes he had them torn open so that he could predict the future by the condition of their entrails.

After this terrible confession, he burst into tears and prayed for mercy, but the court found him guilty and turned him over to the secular authorities for punishment. On October 26, 1440, he was hanged and his body partially burned. His servants were burned alive.

In her 1933 book, *The God of the Witches*, Dr. Margaret Murray suggested that all this was a trumped-up story, that Gilles was actually a ritual sacrifice along divine-victim lines and that he connived with certain church and secular authorities to make his execution seem plausible. Unfortunately for this theory, since then, Gilles's Breton castles have been excavated, and in the ruins nearly two hundred little skeletons have been found.

ALEISTER CROWLEY

Reputedly the most sinister of modern proponents of magic is the Englishman Aleister Crowley (1875–1947). As a child, he is supposed to have begun experimenting with animal sacrifice at the age of twelve, when he killed a kitten. He himself boasts, "Before I touched my teens, I was already aware that I was THE BEAST whose number is 666," a reference to Revelations 13:18. For the rest of his life, he liked to refer to himself as "the Great Beast" or its Greek equivalent, "Therion," and used the number 666 as a kind of signature.

A brilliant student at Cambridge, Crowley was first drawn to a serious study of magic by a clash with the master (dean) of St. John's College. The master had forbidden Crowley to put on a bawdy play, and in revenge Crowley and some friends made a wax image of the man and prepared to drive a needle through its heart; instead, Crowley's hand slipped, and the needle pierced the figure's leg. The following day, the master fell and broke his ankle.

In 1898, fresh out of Cambridge, Crowley joined the Order of the Golden Dawn and began to clash with that organization's other stormy petrel, S. L. MacGregor Mathers. Mathers managed to get Crowley expelled—or the rites were too tame for him, stories differ—and he withdrew to a lonely house in Scotland to continue magical experiments in private. When complaints were raised by neighbors about the strange goings on at Crowley's place, he retaliated by placing the complainers under a curse, causing two servants to commit suicide and a parish worker to turn alcoholic. (Or so it was claimed.) A butcher, who had received a check from Crowley covered with demonic signs, subsequently cut himself severely. (When Mathers died in 1918, it was claimed that Crowley had killed him by magic.)

In 1912, Crowley joined a German group called Ordo Templi Orientis ("Order of the Eastern Temple") and became head of its British section. When World War I broke out, he removed to the United States and spent the war years writing German propaganda. In 1920, having acquired some disciples and mistresses, he moved to Cefalu on the northern coast of Sicily.

There he set up what he called the Abbey of Thelema. (In Greek, *thelema* means "will, choice," so the place seems to have been named for Crowley's favorite motto: "Do what thou wilt shall be the whole of the law.") At the abbey he and his followers indulged in animal sacrifices, black masses, worship of Satan, and orgies and drug taking and sex. (Crowley was bisexual.) One follower is supposed to have died after drinking the blood of a sacrificed cat. Finally, in 1923, rumors began to circulate in the region that children had been sacrificed as well as animals. Crowley was expelled from Italy.

Dennis Wheatley in *The Devil and All His Works* (1971) relates a story of Crowley's attempt—successful, if Wheatley's information is not romancing—to raise the god Pan. The attempt is reported to have killed a follower and sent Crowley himself to a mental hospital for four months. If the tale is true, it presumably happened after the Sicily period and before the Great Beast returned to England to write *Magick in Theory and Practice*, an exposition of his ideas on the occult.

But from there on it was all downhill for Crowley. He tried but failed to break his addiction to heroin. His following fell away (the world had more important things to think about in the thirties and forties) and finally in 1947 he died. A black mass was performed at his funeral, concluding with a hymn to Pan.

Interest in Crowley revived somewhat during the 1960s, when anything that was unconventional won approval from some people and "wickedness" seemed glamorous and original. But this phase appears not to have lasted, and today—his "shocking" behavior dismissed as mere childish attention-getting—he is of interest chiefly to historians of magic.

8

A Few Frauds

IN the annals of fraud there may be few more egregious examples than can
be found among pretended magicians and purported witches, false
prophets and quack alchemists, humbug astrologers, flim-flam hocus-pocus.
It would be hard to beat the nerve of the Frenchman who forged and sold to
another Frenchman the supposed autographs of many characters in history,
including Julius Caesar and Adam and Eve—all in French. It would be hard
to beat the victim's credulity, too.

But deception has been a major element in magic for a long time, and
not only in stage magic, which is mere sleight of hand, admitted but
entertaining trickery. Men with pretensions to true sorcery have not
hesitated to claim fantastic results, in order to impress other men with their
esoteric knowledge and skill.

In this age of test-tube babies, can we believe that Paracelsus (1493–
1541) actually created a little man (*homunculus*) in an alchemist's alembic?
How about the eighteenth-century Abbé Geloni and Count Francis Joseph
Küffstein, who claimed that, after only five weeks' work in the laboratory,

they had produced ten *homunculi*: king, queen, architect, monk, miner, nun, knight, seraph, red spirit, blue spirit? Magic? Science? Ballyhoo?

Here are a few of the representative and interesting frauds in magic and witchcraft, some false ideas, and a zany or two.

THE GRAND FRAUD

Men didn't like him much; Giovanni Jacopo Casanova, who met him, said he was "short and badly hung." But women adored him. Baroness Oberkirch said he had "indescribable eyes" and then went on to describe them. Carlyle called him "Great Quack Face" and "King of Liars," and Dr. Howard W. Haggard said he was "one of the most successful charlatans of faith healing."

He may have been born Giuseppe Balsamo of Palermo, but the name he made famous was adopted from a Sicilian uncle: Cagliostro. He was "the last of the magicians" and perhaps the bravest fraud of them all.

A familiar figure at the glittering courts of Europe and in secret circles of Freemasonry, Cagliostro seems to have had some real psychic powers; when they failed, he faked. He invented the title "Count Alessandro di Cagliostro," and with his beautiful wife, Lorenza Feliciani, he traveled about to Egypt, Arabia, Persia, Rhodes, Malta, and many countries of Europe, dispensing love philters and elixirs of life, forging documents, healing, telling fortunes, treating rheumatism in a "magic" chair, changing coarse fabrics to "silk" and pebbles to "gold." In Paris, he got involved in the scandal of the queen's diamond necklace, though in this case he was only a pawn of the real defrauder, the countess of de la Motte.

Later he translated the names of Louis XVI and Marie Antoinette into "the language of the Magi," and by numerology predicted that they would both be beheaded. His friends urged him to warn the royal family, but he declined. First, he said, they would certainly not believe him. Second, if it were fated, how could warning them alter anything?

Through all the vicissitudes of his incredible life, Cagliostro maintained, in the spirit of Freemasonry, that the mystery was for the good of all. He wrote: "I am oppressed! I am accused! I am calumniated! Have I deserved this fate? . . . I probe my conscience; and there I find the peace which men deny me! I have traveled a great deal. . . . I have everywhere shown myself to be the friend of my fellow men. My knowledge, my time, my fortune have been employed in the relief of distress." He made a large fortune, let it be said, for all this "relief of distress" and spent it chiefly on show.

Despite the reason he gave for not warning the French monarchs, Cagliostro constantly tried to tamper with his own fate. But it caught up with him on April 7, 1791, when he was condemned by the Inquisition in Rome. Lorenza, whose cleverness and charm had more than once got him out of previous scrapes, could do nothing this time; she was compelled to "confess" her part in his swindles and sent off to a convent for life. Eventually Cagliostro's sentence was commuted to life—in a prison cell of the Castel Sant'Angelo. He tried to escape and was cast into a deep dungeon. There in 1795 his jailer strangled him.

Some said that was not the last of Cagliostro's influence. Gérard Encausse (1863–1916), known as Papus in magical circles, was born in Spain of a French father and a gypsy mother, who said she was descended from Cagliostro and had inherited his powers. Papus combined science (a medical degree and inventions) with the occult (he was clairvoyant to Czar Nicholas II for fifteen years) and excelled in magic. Cagliostro would have been proud of Papus. Others say Cagliostro was reincarnated as Aleister Crowley, and undoubtedly there were force and fakery in both.

TALL STORY

Nekhtnebf was one of the last native kings of Egypt (c. 358 B.C.). When a big navy was on the way to attack his kingdom, he put toy ships into a large bowl of Nile water and fought a battle in which the enemy toys were sunk. The real ships also were supposed to have perished.

The next time he tried it, his own ships' representations sank. Taking the hint, Nekhtnebf shaved his head and beard, put on rags, and with an immense fortune in gold and jewels ran off to Pella, Macedonia.

There he bought a nice house and set himself up as an Egyptian magician. One of his customers was the wife of Philip II of Macedon, Olympias. He convinced the queen that the god Ammon wished to visit her amorously by night.

Disguised as the god, Nekhtnebf then came at night and made love to the lady, who a reasonable time afterward gave birth to—Alexander the Great.

They do say that Alexander wasn't much like his father, King Philip.

MATHEMATICIAN AND ASTROLOGER

"James Hallett, Mathematician and Astrologer, New House, Chichester [England], Curer of All Diseases."

That's the inscription on a magical box of the eighteenth century that still exists. A sampler (dated June 20, 1791) testifies to one of Hallett's miraculous cures, but in the box when it was opened in modern times were found—two nutmeg halves.

Ladies and Gntleman waited on at their own Houfes, on the fhorteft notice.

₊ Nativities caſt for the Cure of Witcheraft and other Difeafes that are hard to be cured.

Advertisement of James Hallett, "Curer of Witchcraft" (1795).

PANACEAS

Magic and witchcraft or at least suggestions of the occult sciences were often used to give glamour (a word that means "magic") to all sorts of fraudulent cures and quack devices. Cagliostrio sold beds for painless childbirth. James Graham kept a Temple of Health in London (1779) that contained a sumptuous "celestial bed" guaranteed to produce conception. George O. Barnes of Kentucky preached that only the Devil caused disease, and this view is shared by many faith healers from the "bone setters" Valentine Greatrakes and "Crazy Sal" Mapp to Mary Baker Eddy.

In this country, where nostrums and tonics were hard-sell peddled with great success, there has been (and to a lesser extent still is) an especially promising market for every kind of cure from cancer to baldness and "loss of virility."

In his entertaining *Golden Age of Quackery* (1959), Stewart Holbrook describes the newspaper ads that touted some of them:

> There was no hedging about it, no qualification: Dr. King's New Discovery was the only Sure Cure for Consumption on earth; and for this reason "It Strikes Terror to the Doctors." There was Dr. Rupert Wells's Radiatized Fluid for Cancer. ("It will cure you at home without pain, plaster or operation.") Dr. Tucker had a specific for epilepsy. So did Dr. Kline and Dr. Grant. If the trouble had to do with kidney or liver, you need only to step into the nearest drugstore for a bottle of Dr. Kilmer's Swamp Root, which cured Bright's disease, Catarrh of the Bladder, Gravel, and trifles like Dropsy.

Consumer protection laws, beginning with the landmark Federal Pure Food and Drug Act of 1906, have put a halt to such advertising and driven many of these magical "cures" off the market. Nowadays, even people who frequent fortune-tellers and never miss the daily horoscope in the newspaper are likely to seek out a qualified physician when they are ill.

But there remain some, even today, who will pay large sums of money to con men for "magic earth" and "electrical belts," for treatment in machines that guarantee to drive out disease as the magician's wand was supposed to drive out demons, in short, who still believe in spells and incantations.

MARY TOFTS

At Godalming, Surrey, in 1726, Mary Tofts caused a sensation by announcing that she was giving birth to rabbits. King George I sent a royal physician, Sir Richard Manningham, to investigate, and her fraud was detected. William Hogarth depicted the lady in all the pangs of this incredible labor in his picture *Credulity, Superstition, and Fanaticism* (1762).

If you think we moderns are more sophisticated, examine the Amity-ville story of the seventies and its popular sequels. These impostures breed like rabbits.

"KATTERFELTO, WITH HIS HAIR ON END"

And here, for all of the miracle workers and spellbinders out there in Videoland, is an impressive example of fakery—an inspiration in Gustavus Katterfelto.

The self-proclaimed "Greatest Philosopher Since Isaac Newton" took London by storm. The eighteenth century was an age of patent nostrums, crank ideas, and pseudomedical nonsense. In 1755, when a disastrous earthquake shook Lisbon—and the complacency of Europeans—Katterfelto actually sold pills "for the earthquake." He cashed in on the plague (1782) and advertized a "solar microscope" to detect disease. To his "technological" approach he added the occult; his two "Morocco black cats" were known as the Doctor's Devils, and he did nothing to dispel the rumor that they were not pets but familiars. With them, and the patter, he peddled flu cures at five shillings a bottle in an age when the taverns literally guaranteed "drunk for a penny, dead drunk for tuppence."

His customers included George III and the largest royal family in British history. William Cowper mentioned him in his long poem *The Task* as one of the oddities of that flamboyant age:

> And Katterfelto, with his hair on end
> At his own wonders, wandering for his bread.

The vogue faded, and fashionable London was off on some other foolishness. Katterfelto wound up as a mountebank and cheap street conjuror, and died penniless in 1799.

LEVITATION

As we have seen elsewhere, many saints have been reported to float a foot or more off the ground—a phenomenon called levitation. People were also said to levitate when possessed of the Devil, and, of course, witches were supposed to fly off to sabbats on broomsticks.

Levitation was also attributed to various magicians and mediums, the most famous being the nineteenth-century notable medium D. D. Home. One English lord described in detail how he saw Home float out one window of a séance room and in at another.

On the stage the trick has been duplicated by a number of performers. Harry Kellar did it this way:

> A woman lay on a couch. She rose slowly in the air. Kellar was able to pass a hoop over the entire length of her body, "proving" that no wires were being used and that nothing was supporting her. Then in full sight of the audience she floated down until she rested once more on the couch.

The secret of the trick was that the top of the couch was detachable and connected to an iron bar worked by a pulley from backstage. Draperies concealed the rigid platform. The bar was painted so as to match the background perfectly and be undetectable from the audience. A U-bend in the bar enabled the solid hoop to be flipped backward and forward so that, from out front, the audience would "see" that it passed right over the reclining body. Then the hoop was drawn back again, and the platform was lowered.

Indian magicians perform the trick in much the same way, usually with a piece of drapery to cover the supporting rod.

A CONFESSED FRAUD

All too many innocent persons have been sent to the gallows for witchcraft or necromancy by means of lying testimony. All too seldom has the fraud been discovered in time. But in England in 1632, it did happen.

A man named Edmund Robinson—apparently out of no motive except malice toward his neighbors and perhaps a desire to have power over them—decided to lay charges of witchcraft. He taught his eleven-year-old son to tell a story: "In the fields he [the boy] had met with two dogs, which he urged to hunt a hare. They would not budge; and he in revenge tied them to a bush and whipped them; when suddenly one of them was transformed into an old woman and the other into a child, a witch and her imp."

The Robinson boy told this story, and it was so well received that the youngster became a local phenomenon. Robinson then began to tell people that his son could detect a witch at a glance, and he took the boy around to various local churches, where he was placed on a bench after the service and told to pick out the witches. He named seventeen persons, who were then arrested, tried at the local assizes, and found guilty of witchcraft.

The judge in the case, however, was skeptical. He postponed the sentence of hanging and sent four of the condemned "witches" to London, to be examined by the king's physicians (one of whom was William Harvey, who later discovered the circulation of the blood) and then by Charles I himself. These august personages could find no evidence that the accused had practiced black arts, so they summoned the Robinson boy and questioned him.

He broke down, confessed that it was all a fraud, and admitted his father's part in the affair. The seventeen were pardoned. It is not known what happened to Robinson.

LAMBE TO THE SLAUGHTER

In seventeenth century England, a certain Dr. John Lambe was convicted of practicing "execrable arts"—afflicting Thomas Lord Windsor with a terrible wasting disease by magic (or perhaps poison). Ordinarily that would have been enough to get him hanged, but he was "the duke's devil," which was to say that he had the protection of the first duke of Buckingham (1592–1628), boyfriend of the homosexual king, James I.

So John Lambe was not hanged, but he was sent to jail for fifteen years. In jail he continued to practice his astrology and other occult business and was allowed to have clients visit him and collect his fat fees. But eventually Buckingham began to lose confidence in Lambe.

Like all high rollers who depend on public credulity for their success, once his principal backer had defected, he went downhill fast. First he was deprived of the use of his jail cell as a consulting room, which lost him his clientele. Then, upon his release in 1640, he was set upon by the mob with cries of "Kill the wizard! . . . Kill the poisoner!" They caught him as he was on his way to the theater and beat him to death.

EGYPTIAN MAGIC TRICKS

The Egyptian priests understood the place of "magic" in overawing superstitious followers, and they often resorted to trickery to impose on the worshippers.

At the Temple of Luxor a fire lighted on the ancient altar, which was hollow, expanded the air within. This heated air forced water from a jar into a bucket. The bucket sank, which pulled a rope, and this caused a precisely hung door to swing open mysteriously. It may sound like Rube Goldberg, but its effect on superstitious worshippers must have been tremendous.

I. G. Edmonds in his book on stage magic, *The Magic Makers* (1976), tells of a trick performed by a famous Egyptian magician in the days of Cheops. Summoned to perform before the pharaoh, Teta offered to cut off the head of an animal and restore it again. When the king agreed, Teta brought forth a goose and beheaded it, laying the head on one end of the table and the body on the other.

> At his magical command, the two moved together. The severed head rejoined the body. The goose got up on its feet and cackled.
>
> Then, to prove his mastery of magic, Teta performed the trick on another bird. . . .
>
> The fact is that any magician can perform this simple trick—and through the centuries most magicians have. . . . All the trick requires is a trained bird and a carved wooden head and neck.

While the magician was pretending to cut off the head, the bird tucked its head under its wing. The magician palmed the realistically painted head and then laid it at the far end of the table. A few more passes, the "severed" head was again palmed, and the bird raised up its real head.

Egyptian priests were reported to have performed many feats of "magic" to impress the king and the common people—feats which modern stage magicians have no trouble duplicating. They caused ghostly images to appear on walls or in columns of smoke, which could be done by reflecting light off a mirrored surface through a hole in the ceiling of the temple. They hollowed out statues—at least one of these hollow images has been found—so that a priest could slip inside and cause the statue to "speak." Trumpets were made to play by remote control. Tubes, painted black so they could not be seen in the dark temple interior, led from an air bladder to the trumpet's mouthpiece; the priest stepped on the bladder, and air was forced through the instrument, blasting a long note.

They understood the function of air pressure in stopping the flow of liquids, and they used it in the bottle trick, in which three or four different liquids are made to flow from a single vessel. The bottle, specially made with several different (hidden) compartments each with a tiny air hole, is held so that the hand covers all the holes except one; the tilted bottle pours water, then the hand is clandestinely shifted to uncover a different hole, and wine emerges, and so on. Thus a priest could "change" water into wine and wine into milk and perhaps milk into beer.

Today most of these illusions are part of the repertoire of conjurors and stage magicians, used for pure entertainment. But how many other credulous people, aside from Egyptians, have they fooled, down through the ages, into thinking some charlatan was performing true magic?

9

Familiar Demons and Demon Familiars

MAGIC and witchcraft were worked, it was believed, not by the sorcerer or witch himself but by demons who did their masters' bidding. Magicians, who were powerful and learned men and knew the secret names of God and of the major Devils in Hell, forced these great spirits to submit to them. But witches were not thought to be so gifted. Poor, ignorant folk—and usually women at that—they could only make limited bargains with Satan. In return for their souls, he would give them a minor demon or imp, a "familiar," who would perform small magical chores like causing sickness or curing it.

Some demonologists argued that the Devil could not create something out of nothing, as God could, but he and his minions could change forms. An imp might appear as a dog or a black cat or a pet crow. However this changed form could never be perfect; some "imperfection" would eventually betray the evil spirit within. Interrogators, hoping to unmask witches, looked at the suspect's pet and asked about mysterious strangers who might have been seen in her company.

Tradition told of the Devil having appeared in tangible form to many people, even to Jesus Christ. The temptations of Saint Anthony in the desert involved evil spirits, which appeared to him in various forms, especially as a beautiful maiden. Hagiography was full of instances of the Devil appearing as a dwarf or a giant, as a beautiful and tempting person or a hideous monstrosity, of demons part human and part animal. Had not Martin Luther himself mentioned the Devil sixty-seven times in his *Greater Catechism* (and Christ only sixty-three times) and thrown his inkwell at the Devil when His Satanic Majesty dared to appear in Luther's study?

Our ancestors fully believed that evil spirits roamed the earth in dangerously deceptive human and animal forms.

HOW TO SELL YOUR SOUL

Here is how, according to seventeenth-century Germans, you sell your soul to the Devil.

On a piece of virgin parchment write in your own blood:

I promise GREAT DEMON to repay him in seven years for all he shall give me.
In witness whereof, I sign my name_____.

Then begin the invocation, holding the bit of parchment, within the magic circle:

LUCIFER, Emperor, Master of All Rebellious Spirits, I beseech thee be favorable to me in the calling upon thy GREAT MINISTER which I make, desiring to make a pact with him.

BEELZEBUB, Prince, I pray thee also, to protect me in my undertaking.

ASTAROTH, Count, be propitious to me and cause that this night the GREAT DEMON appear to me in human form and without any evil smell, and that he grant me, by means of the pact which I shall deliver to him, all the treasures of which I have need.

GREAT DEMON, I beseech thee, leave thy dwelling, in whatever part of the world you may be, to come to speak with me; if not, I shall thereto compel thee by the power of the mighty words of the Great Key of Solomon, whereof he made use to force the rebellious spirits to accept his pact.

Appear then instantly or I shall continually torment thee with the mighty words of the Key: *Aglon, Tetragrammaton, Vaycheon,*

Stimulamathon, Erohares, Retrasammathon, Clyoran, Icion, Esi-tion, Existien, Eryona, Onera, Erasyn, Moyn, Meffias, Soter, Em-manuel, Sabaoth, Adonai, I call you. Amen.

The Demon will then appear and demand the written promise of payment after seven years time, "that I may do with thee, body and soul, what shall please me."

The pact is then thrown to the Demon outside the circle, taken up and away, and commences in effect.

FAMILIARS

Pope Gregory IX (1147–1241) issued a bull to the German hierarchy explaining how the Devil took animal forms, and Reginald Scot in his *Discoverie of Witchcraft* recorded the English superstition that imps or little devils or demons could take animal form and that witches kept them as pets, feeding them human milk or blood, occasionally bits of chicken.

In the trials for witchcraft, familiars are often alleged to have accom-panied witches, and some witches confessed (or made up lies) about familiar spirits, even giving their names and descriptions.

Some poor old women who had nothing but a house cat or faithful dog as a companion were accused of being witches and had their pets used as "evidence" against them. Gray cats and black dogs were especially suspect, and people were frightened if a black cat even crossed their path. But two animal forms were said to be avoided by demons, the lamb and the dove, because of the Christian Agnus Dei (lamb of God) and Paraclete (Holy Ghost in the form of a dove).

Nonetheless, the Devil himself is supposed to have appeared to a witch named Agnes Webster (tried at Aberdeen in 1597) "in the liknes of a lamb, quhom thou callis thy god, and bletit on the, and thaireftir spak to the," though as a black and deformed lamb.

In fact, it was believed that the devils (superior evil spirits) and demons (under their jurisdiction) could take on any animal form whatsoever, even that of a human being living or dead. So when you saw a ghost, you could not always be sure that it was, indeed, the ghost of some soul departed or the Devil tempting you, and when you saw an animal, you could never be quite sure that it was not an evil force in disguise. Just as angels came to earth in human form, so could fallen angels.

INNOCENT AMUSEMENT

Giovanni Battista Cibo (1432–1492), who reigned as Pope Innocent VIII, believed that humans can mate with demons. He declared: "It has actually come to our knowledge and we are deeply grieved to hear that many persons of both sexes, completely forgetful of the salvation of their souls and straying far from the Catholic Faith, have [had intercourse] with evil spirits, both incubi and succubi." An incubus was a male demon who preyed on women, a succubus a female demon who preyed on men—thought nowadays to be the personifications of nightmares and sexual dreams.

CAVE CANEM!

The Devil has a black dog, and many demons and familiars are said to appear in canine form, an ironic comment on "man's best friend." In Goethe's *Faust* Mephistopheles first appears as a dog.

Dogs are common in Christian legends of saints too. Saint Roch, ill of the plague, was nursed by a dog. Saint John of the Cross was freed from prison by one. Saint Christopher was sometimes depicted with the head of a dog. Saint John Bosco (1815–1888) had a self-appointed guard dog named Grigio, which appeared one day when John was being set on by a robber, drove off the thief, and remained. But dogs are even commoner in pagan myth and demonology.

In ancient Britain a pack of hounds accompanied Gwynn ap Nudd (the god of the underworld) hunting souls. In Norse myth, Garm is the hound of Hell; in Greek myth, the many-headed Cerberus guards the shore of Styx. In Hindu myth, there are sun dogs and moon dogs (a twenty-four-hour patrol) of Yama, the god of death. In Persian myth, a dog guards the afterlife.

The Iroquois, Huron, Ojibway, Seminole, and other Native American groups all have a dog guarding their Hells; so do the Koryaks of Siberia.

The Chinese *p'eng hen* (black dogs without tails) are thought to be demons. The Muslims have a demonic black dog, and English tradition had the Black Dog of Newgate (the prison area), which consorted with "blacke conditioned people" and dwelt in the "bosom of traytors, murtherers, theives, cut-purses, cunny-catchers [coney-catchers, con men], and the like."

The Devil is said to have left Judas Iscariot in the form of a black dog, to have attacked Saint Stanislas Kostka in that form, and to have appeared in this form to many saints and anchorites. Some alchemists had big black dogs for pets that followed them everywhere and were popularly assumed to be familiars.

Dogs have been gods as well as devils. Set ruled Upper Egypt as a greyhound with a forked tail. Anubis, the Egyptian god of death, took a doglike jackal form. Hecate, queen of the witches, rejoiced in "the barking of dogs" and was accompanied by many a harpy or *empusa* or other vengeful night creature, some of whom took the form of bitches.

At the beginning of the eleventh century there was even a dog who reigned for three years in Norway. It was said he could speak several Norwegian words; in any case, all royal acts were signed with his paw. This King Sueining (or Saur) was thought by some Norwegians to be "the soul of a great lord of the past . . . reincarnated in the body of this dog" (as reported in Fernand Mery's *Life, History and Magic of the Dog*, 1970).

DEMON LETTER WRITER

If you want your love letters (or business letters, if you are more prosaic) to meet with wonderful success, you can enlist the aid of demons this way:

Take a sheet of virgin parchment (the real animal skin) and cover it on both sides with this invocation in black ink:

ADAMA, EVAH, EVEN AS THE ALL-POWERFUL CREATOR DID UNITE YOU IN THE EARTHLY PARADISE WITH A HOLY, MUTUAL AND INDISSOLUBLE LINK, SO MAY THE HEART OF THOSE TO WHOM I WRITE BE FAVOURABLE TO ME, AND BE ABLE TO REFUSE ME NOTHING:

✡ ELY   ✡ ELY   ✡ ELY.

Then you burn the parchment and add the ashes to the ink with which you write the letters you wish to make irresistible.

Paul Christian's *History and Practice of Magic* recommends you add to the ink ("which has never been used before") seven drops of milk from a mother suckling her firstborn and a pinch of powdered lodestone and suggests you write with a new quill pen sharpened with a never-used knife.

IN PERSON

At the beginning of Book V of his *Historia Sui Temporis* the medieval writer Raoul Glaber describes someone whose appearance you might want to be warned about: "At the foot of my bed I saw a little monster in human form. As far as I can remember, he had a thin neck and face, very black eyes, a narrow wrinkled forehead, a flat nose, a wide mouth with swollen lips, a short tapered chin, a goatee. . . . " And that's what a demon looks like.

MOURNFUL NUMBERS

According to James David Besser (in *The New Republic* of July 25, 1981), writing about the Moral Majority and the media evangelists on Station WABS ("We Always Broadcast Salvation") and so on, the Devil is still very active. "Satan," says the Rev. Jerry Falwell, "would love to silence the voice of the 'Old Time Gospel Hour,'" and the Devil has programs of his own. Besser reports: "David Weber warns that zip codes, Social Security numbers, and government computers are among the tools the Antichrist will soon use to identify his followers, who have been marked with the number 666. Already, he says, uniform product codes on food packages contain the dangerous digits." Hate campaigns count the letters in the name of Ronald Wilson Reagan.

GROTESQUE CREATURES

I remember my astonishment as a teenager when I found in my college library, at McGill University, a book with color plates purporting to portray the faces of various demons. Apparently people could not only call demons up; they could also get them down, drawing their likenesses.

The medieval imagination especially rejoiced in grotesques, and in the Middle Ages believed in the existence of extremely odd combinations of human and animal characteristics, in gargoyles and other monsters. In the Renaissance, Shakespeare had Othello charm Desdemona with his tales of

> . . . Cannibals that each other eat,
> The Anthropophagi, and men whose heads
> Do grow beneath their shoulders.

These latter were the Blemmyae that the historian Pliny placed in Libya and were (probably) men who hid behind shields so that their heads could not be seen in battle. How to explain the belief, though, in creatures such as the Astomi (whom Pliny said did not eat but subsisted entirely on smelling fruit and flowers, and could be killed by bad odors), the Sciopods (one-legged people who spent "their days lying on their backs protecting their heads from the sun with a single great foot"), and men with the heads of dogs, etc.? But none of the pygmies and giants and monsters are as grotesque and incredible as the demons.

Alphonse de Spina in *Fortalicium Fidei* ("Fortress of Faith," 1476) grouped demons in ten classes: Fates, Poltergeists, Incubi and Succubi, "Armies or Hordes," Familiars, Nightmares, Disguised Demons, Demons attacking saintly men, Demons who persuaded old women to go to the sabbat, and Demons created by "copulation" of human and inhuman creatures. The *Fortalicium*, however, denied the existence of this last class.

Satan ("Adversary") is the chief of the fallen angels in Hell, and demoted seraphim and cherubim there include various princes. Matthew gives Beelzebub ("Lord of the Flies") the title of Prince of Hell. Other princes are Mammon, Asmodeus, Belial, and Astaroth. De Spina says that 133,306,668 angels became devils. One of the discomforts of Hell: overcrowding.

TITLE OF RESPECT

Because God is called the Most High, the Devil is called the Most Low. Further information is presumably available from the public relations officer of Hell; his name is Nybras. It may be cold comfort to p.r. reps to learn that "he is treated as an inferior demon, prophet, and charlatan."

MOTHER REDCAP

The London *Sunday Chronicle* of September 9, 1928, published a startling story of a modern witch, Mother Redcap, who lived in a little village only fourteen miles from the University of Cambridge:

One day a black man called, produced a book and asked her to sign her name in it. The woman signed the book [not knowing what it was, which in true occult tradition, would invalidate the bargain], and the mysterious stranger then told her she would be the mistress of five imps who would carry out her orders. Shortly afterwards the woman was seen out accompanied by a rat, a cat, a toad, a ferret, and a mouse. Everybody believed she was a witch, and many people visited her to obtain cures.

The story, though only a typical piece of Sunday supplement sensationalism, does point up the dangers of a lonely old woman keeping pets. Mother Redcap, thanks to living in a relatively enlightened age, was left in peace, but how many similar old women, over the centuries, have found themselves paying dearly for the crime of giving house room to a cat?

FOREIGN DEVILS

The list of strange demons spoken of in other cultures is long, but just as a sample we may mention *Shui-mu Niang-niang* (the Chinese water demons who cause great rivers to flood), the Sumerian *Maskim* (the worst of all the seven classes of demons, "neither male nor female . . . they do not beget children . . . they are strangers to benevolence and heed neither prayers nor entreaties"), the *mutua* or *batwa* of Africa (pygmies about four feet tall, with one eye, webbed feet, and those on backward—if you see one, you die), and the *yara-ma* or *yara-ma-yha-who* of the Pacific Coast of Australia (also four feet tall, but with red and green scales—they can swallow a human being whole, dropping on him or her out of the trees).

DEMONIC ENERGY

Acts 19:11–16 tells the story of some vagabond exorcists who had seen Paul cast out demons of disease in Jesus' name and thought they would try their hand at it. Accordingly they went to work on some patients, ordering the possessing demons to leave and adding, "We adjure you by Jesus whom Paul preacheth."

One of the patients—or his demon—retorted, "Jesus I know, and Paul I know, but who are *ye*?" Then he leaped on them and knocked them about so severely that they "fled out of that house naked and wounded."

Exorcising is best left to professionals.

LUCIFER

Actually, there is no Lucifer.

The name "Lucifer" ("light bringer" in Latin) occurs once in the Bible (Isaiah 14:12), the King James Version calling him "Lucifer, son of the morning" and the Douai Version rendering it as "Lucifer, who didst rise in the morning." According to the Millers' *Harper's Bible Dictionary* (1961), this is a translation of the Hebrew "shining one," which refers not to fallen angels but to the king of Babylon, who boasted pridefully that he would ascend to Heaven and challenge God. But the Biblical attack might also refer to the Assyrian king Sargon II, father of Sennacherib. In any case, there is no devil named Lucifer, nor is this another term for Satan.

The Middle Ages were wrong. Lucifer is not Satan.

Tondriau and Villaneuve's *Dictionary of Devils and Demons* (1972) is also confused. They identify Lucifer (or Lucibel) as the most beautiful of the angels, "transformed for rebelliousness into a hairy monster and he became known as Satan" but then proceed to say that "Lucifer tempts men through vanity, while Satan tempts them through lust" and later that Lucifer is "King of Hell, superior even to Satan."

The authors are mistaken. It's true that the name "Lucifer" does turn up in medieval lists of demons or devils. But he never had any more reality than, say, Mammon ("riches"), another "person" created out of a misunderstanding of terminology. Sometimes men invented names for persons actually unnamed in the Bible: Dives and Lazarus, the Magi (Caspar, Melchior, Balthasar), the centurion whose spear pierced the side of Christ (Longinus), the "good thief" (Dismas). Lucifer is not even one of those—Lucifer is just a word mistaken for a name.

TAKING NO CHANCES

Readwald, king of the East Angles (died 627), was converted to the new religion (said Saint Bede in his ecclesiastical history) but was cautious not to abandon the Old Religion. He erected a church in which Mass was said at the high altar but on either side sacrifices were offered to the Devil. Early Christian churches often had Old Religion symbols decorating them as well as Christian symbols, especially at the north door. From the north, ancient Hebrews believed, came evil.

As Machiavelli (some swear) remarked on his deathbed when asked to abjure the Devil and all his works and pomps: "At a time like this I cannot afford to make enemies."

A DIFFERENT VISION

The Satan of Hieronymus Bosch is neither kingly (he has a kettle on his head) nor ordinary (he is shown as a creature with the head of a day-old chick impassively devouring people who emerge whole at the other end).

INFERNAL LEGIONS

Whereas de Spina, as we have seen, listed ten species of demons, Peter Binsfield (1540–1607) in his Latin treatise on "maleficers and sorcerers" connected seven demons with the Seven Deadly Sins. Lucifer was pride. Mammon (according to Biblical precedent) was avarice. Asmodeus, long associated with dissipation, was lust. Satan was anger. Beelzebub was confused with the watchman of Hell (Behemoth) and connected with his sin, gluttony. Leviathan, who as Lilith seduced Adam and as a serpent tempted Eve, was envy. Belphegor (the Moabite's Baal of Mount Phegor) was sloth.

Francisco Maria Guazzo and others arranged them a different way: demons of the upper atmosphere (not in touch with mankind), demons of our terrestrial plane (in the forests, the seas, the earth beneath our feet), demons of the day and demons of the night. Saint Athanasius averred that "the world is full of demons," but I suspect at least some were invented to fit those neat categories that medieval people liked to construct, paralleling with ranks of demons the Thrones, Dominions, Principalities, and so on, of the archangels and angels.

Creatures of disorder created by the desire for neatness!

THE DEVIL IN DISGUISE

When the Devil appeared to Saint Juliana of Izmir (303), he appeared in the shape of an angel. When he appeared to the old hag in the seventeenth-century play *The Witch of Edmonton,* he appeared as a dog and said his name was Tom.

SALT OF THE EARTH

In Derbyshire, England, people used to swear on salt, not the Bible. It is used at baptism and on the dead. It keeps away witches and (if you spill some and throw it over your left shoulder) the Devil. The Devil never serves salt at infernal banquets.

A MESSAGE FOR THE PREACHER

A Lutheran pastor named Carolstad preaching at Basel, Switzerland, on December 22, 1541, said the Devil appeared to him and told him he would not live through Christmas. He died by strangulation on December 25, 1541.

DOUBLE DEALING

The Bavarian painter Haizmann (died 1700) sold his soul to the Devil. In 1677 he went to Church authorities for help in breaking his bargain with the Devil and was exorcized. He drew portraits of the Devil who, he swore, appeared to him seven times as a dragon, a black dog, and in other shapes. Ecclesiastical authorities were convinced of the truth of his story and were delighted to have these Identikit likenesses of a Most Wanted personality, but Sigmund Freud long after used Haizmann's case as a *locus classicus* of paranoid schizophrenia.

MORE MALE CHAUVINIST PREJUDICE

The Kekchi Indians do a devil dance to banish the king of devils, who held court at Metnal (the Mayan Hell). Thomas Gann in the *London Illustrated News*, in 1926, reported this king "collected an army, consisting of his wife, his father and mother, four minor devils, a boar, five sows, a monkey, and Death." When Gann told his informant that this was impossible because he (as an anthropologist specializing in the Maya) knew there were no women in the Mayan Hell, the old informant replied *Ah Tat, Ma Xupal Ma Metnal.* I regret to tell the ladies that translates: "If there were no women, there would be no hell."

AMDUSCIAS

We've had Dr. John and the Night-Trippers and quite a few other pop groups more or less dabbling in the occult, right up to *nuevo wavo* punk. If any new group needs a moniker, I suggest that of Amduscias. He is grand duke of Hell, commands twenty-eight legions of demons, and is the patron of deafening noise.

LIVING ALONE IS PERILOUS

There has been a sharp upswing in America of people living alone. The Talmud advises: "It is indiscreet for one to sleep in a house as the sole occupant, for Lilith will seize him." Further, it warns: "Never go out alone on Wednesday or Saturday nights, for demons are abroad then, and eighteen legions of them, commanded by Agrath the daughter of Machlath, seek whom they may devour."

DEMONS IN THE DICE

In German tradition, the Devil is supposed to have invented dice, and in some old trials for witchcraft he was referred to as the Dicer, but the idea that dice are somehow diabolical and un-Christian goes back to Saint Cyprian (A.D. 200–258), who condemned them as inspired by the Devil.

In German folklore Jacob Grimm (1785–1863) found references to devils or demons living inside dice; that's why people bowed to dice on picking them up.

In India they say that Dvapara, an evil spirit, lies inside the dice and that you will always win with dice made from dead man's bones. In many other cultures dice are associated with magical things, often related to ancient forms of divination. They were part of the equipment (in the form of *urim* and *thurim*) provided in the magical breastplate of the High Priest of the Jews.

Dice may have been used first for magic and only later came to be playthings, used for gambling. It is, of course, magic to spit on the dice before throwing them.

THE IMP OF LINCOLN

High up in the choir of Lincoln Cathedral in England perches a half-human, half-animal creature that, legend says, was once not a carved statue but one of the little devils out of Hell.

The story is that in the thirteenth century the Devil sent two imps to bother the builders and clergy of Lincoln. One flew into the cathedral and pestered the bishop, knocked down the dean, and really raised Hell with the verger. The angels told him to cease and desist. "Stop me if you can!" he impishly replied.

So he was turned to stone, and to this day you can see him, about a foot high, way up in a cleft between two arches.

Gargoyles and similar creatures were a common decoration in medieval cathedrals; look for them even in modern imitations of such ancient buildings. You will see them perched, lurking, even "mooning" worshippers below in many otherwise sedate churches. But the Imp of Lincoln is the only one I know of that (at least legend claims) was once a real live devil.

THE DEVIL'S HELP

According to William Perkins, writing in 1608, all witches are in league with the Devil. "A witch is a magician who, either by open or secret league, wittingly and willingly consenteth to use the aid and assistance of the devil in the working of wonders." What, then, could be a so-called white witch? Without the Devil's help, there can be no witchcraft; what you have in "white magic" is nothing more than primitive pharmacy.

HOW A HELL FIRE CLUB WAS DISBANDED

The famous English Hell Fire Club had a counterpart in Ireland.

A story is told of a curate visiting Dublin who expressed a desire to attend a meeting of this notorious group and was invited to a lavish banquet. He expressed surprise that a black cat was given the place of honor and served first. The members assured him that was because the cat was "the oldest member."

"No," said the curate, "it is because the black cat is the Devil."

Their secret discovered, the members said they would kill the curate and gave him a few moments to say his prayers before being dispatched. As he did so, the cat turned into a demon and flew away, taking the roof of the building with him.

The prayers the curate had said were not for himself but an exorcism.

"FRIAR" RUSH

A German folktale, translated into English in 1568 as *Friar Rush*, told of the Devil sending a demon in human form up to earth, where he was admitted to a monastery to work as a scullion. He tempted the monks to gluttony, wantonness, and anger, but then was discovered and thrown out into the great world where he became a mischievous hobgoblin.

What he represented is clearer when you see his German name: *Bruder Rausch*. *Bruder* mistakenly suggested "Friar" (friars, who are ordained priests, are correctly addressed as "Father") but *Rausch* (drunkenness) is the clue; that's what drove the monks to sin.

HERE'S WHAT TO CALL YOUR CAT OR DOG

Oliver Cromwell is said to have had a familiar called Grimoald. Matthew Hopkins (*Discovery of Witches*, 1647) identified these familiars in the case of Elizabeth Clark: Holt ("a white kitling," or kitten), Jamara ("a fat spaniel without any legs at all" who "sucked blood from her body"), Vinegar Tom ("like a long-legged greyhound, with a head like an ox, with a long tail and broad [spaced] eyes" who could turn into a four-year-old child "without a head" and vanish), Sack and Sugar ("like a black rabbit"), and Newes ("like a polecat"). No Newes is good news.

WEREWOLF

Werewolves have been a standard bit of horror fare. Here's a story from 1590.

Peter Stubb (or Stump) of Bedburg, Germany, possessed a belt given him by the Devil, which enabled him to turn into a wolf at will. It was bad enough when the werewolf killed and ate cattle and sheep, murdered thirteen children and two pregnant women, and got his sister pregnant (though he had several "concubines" and a succubus the Devil sent him for his off hours), but when he killed and ate his own son, the populace had had enough.

Pursued across the countryside by irate citizens, lycanthropic Peter shed the wolfskin belt and turned back into an ordinary person. But they caught him, tortured him, and killed him, along with his daughter and mistress.

DRIVING OUT THE DEVIL

Recently a mother was arrested and jailed in New York City for having burned her infant child to death in an oven. She wanted, she said, to drive the devil out of him. Driving out demons has long been an excuse for abominable cruelties to the young.

From ancient times on, a child who cried too much—or too little—was considered a changeling or possessed of a demon; the least it could expect, even if it was still in its cradle, was a daily beating. Sometimes children were beaten regularly, whether they had misbehaved or not, just on general principles. Royalty was not excepted. The little dauphin who became Louis XIII when he was eight years old was beaten every morning from the age of two on. "I would rather do without so much obeisance and honor," he said once, "if they wouldn't have me whipped."

Infants were swaddled at birth—tightly wrapped from neck to feet so that they could not move—in order to prevent them from falling prey to evil tendencies. In this condition they were like little logs of wood, and servants sometimes played catch with them. When they reached the age of one or two, they were often strapped to chairs to prevent them from crawling on the floor "like an animal." And at night, they were told ghost stories and monster stories and bogeyman stories to terrify them into being good (and not bothering mother).

This was not enough for some, however. In 1771 a "holy man" appeared in Russia, claiming to be the brother of Jesus Christ and preaching a doctrine of avoiding sin (and especially sexual sin) by castrating young boys. He established a sect called the Skopsti, "the castraters."

In the 1920s in France, a woman calling herself the Holy Mother advocated severe beatings for children to make them good. She was tried at Bordeaux in 1926, but the outcome of her trial is not known to me.

In the United States a few years ago, a couple were jailed for having killed their two children by savage beatings to "discipline" them; interviewed in jail, they were outraged at the state for the treatment accorded them and had plans (on their release) only for moving to another state, having more children, and "disciplining" *them.*

When an adult mistreats a child to drive the demon out of it, you wonder in whom the demon really resides.

A REAL DEFINITION OF WITCH HUNTING

Jean Bodin (1529–1576), author of *République* and *Demonomanie des Sorciers* (ten editions up to 1604), argued that "not one sorcerer in a million would ever be accused or punished if one were to follow the regular legal practices" but thought also that anything was allowable in the face of the great threat that the populace felt, "and popular rumor is practically never wrong."

Bodin thought Satan had "a profound knowledge of all things" and could create beings. But is he not to be combated with justice and rationality and not ideas such as "suspicion is sufficient justification for torture"?

BAPHOMET

The church of St.-Merri in Paris has a representation of the demon Baphomet on its facade, and Aleister Crowley had his photo taken with this as a background, for Baphomet since the time of the Knights Templars has been regarded as useful in sex magic, one of Crowley's interests.

Some think Baphomet ought to be depicted as a herm (all head and phallus) and others suggest the Eternal Father, three-sided, three-genitaled, horned. Some wanted him to have the head of Mohammed or a hermaphroditic body because they thought the Knights Templars were getting heresies and homosexual practices from Islam. New York covens of gay witches worship him in the form that is a combination of kitsch and Ken Russell's *Lisztomania.*

NUMBERS GAME

The Talmud says there are 7,405,926 demons. Since the number of demons is fixed, every increase in the world's population improves our changes against the demonic enemy.

STAY TUCKED IN

Medieval Jews believed that a sick or dying man was especially vulnerable to demons if a hand, arm, foot, or leg stuck out from under the covers of the bed.

ARMENIAN GIANTS WERE ONCE DEMONS

The Armenians have such expressions as *devi ooj ounie* (he's as strong as a *dev*), *devi bes goudeh* (he eats like a *dev*), *devi hasag ounie* (he's as tall as a *dev*). A *dev* is a kind of giant, but formerly it was a demon who, in the form of a wild beast or snake or other horrible creature, terrified mankind. "There were giants in the earth in those days," says Genesis and it must have been to such demons the children of Adam and Eve were wed.

So we all must have some demonic relatives. Any genealogist will tell you there are strange creatures perched up in the family tree, and among ours are giants and demons.

A CALENDAR OF DEMONS

Watch out for the following in these months:

January: Belial, demon of pederasty, disorder, the Beast 666.
February: Leviathan, who in different sexes seduced both Adam and Eve.
March: Satan (the Adversary of God), not a demon but the Devil himself.
April: Astarte, not a demon but the Phoenician goddess of beauty.

May: Lucifer (the bringer of Light—the enemy's god of light became the Devil of the Jews), prince of Darkness, a fallen angel.

June: Baalberith, master of marriages, secretary and librarian of Hell.

July: Beelzebub (lord of the Flies), prince of Hell, master of the Living.

August: Astaroth, treasurer of Hell, grand duke of the Western Part of Hell.

September: Thamuz, the demon who is credited with inventing artillery and the Inquisition.

October: Baal, grand duke of Guile, a Phoenician god turned Christian demon.

November: Hecate, queen of the witches, a moon goddess gone wrong.

December: Moloch, Ammonite god turned Christian demon.

DEMON MATRIARCH

The Plantagenet kings of England were descended from William the Conqueror on the female side of the family and the counts of Anjou on the male, and their family name is taken from the plantagenista, or broom, which Geoffrey of Anjou wore in his helmet. The counts of Anjou, it was well known, were the offspring of a demon.

Their ancestor, Count Fulke, probably in the tenth century, went off on a journey and came home with a mysterious wife, Melusine. The couple seemed happy and produced four fine children, but the count was bothered by the fact that his wife would never remain in church through the Consecration of the mass, the solemn moment when bread and wine are changed to Christ's body and blood. One day, he gave orders for his knights to detain Melusine by force. She stood in the chapel, with two of her children on one side and two on the other. When it came time for the Consecration, she made as if to leave, but the knights stood on her dress and tried to hold her arms. But as the Host was elevated, she gave a terrible scream, wrenched herself free, and seizing the two children on her left, flew out of the chapel window.

This revealed the fact that Melusine was a demon. Her children inherited her demon blood, and thus England was ruled for 331 years by descendants of the Devil himself.

DEMON, STAY 'WAY FROM MY DOOR

Diners in Chinese restaurants are familiar with the traditional Chinese symbols of luck, longevity, prosperity. But you may not be aware that the character *shen*, hung over a doorway, prevents evil spirits from entering.

The Greeks use blue paint around doors and windows for the same purpose. So do some Frenchmen. In New Paltz, New York, there is a row of restored seventeenth-century French Huguenot houses, some of whose rooms are painted blue for good luck—despite the fact that blue is the most difficult color to obtain from vegetable dyes and in this case had to be wrung drop by drop from blueberries.

THE GEOGRAPHY OF DJINNS

The genies live in Ginnistan, banished there, legend says, by Taymour-al, a Persian prince. They are named for Gian ben Gian (Gian son of Gian), another Persian ruler; he was the first to discover there are two kinds. The good ones are *peris*, the bad ones are *dives*. The principal city of Ginnistan is Schadou Kiam. The country has two great deserts: Badiat-Goldare (Desert of Monsters) and Bidiat-Tealgim (Desert of Fairies); in the latter the *safar* (cold wind of the dead) never blows.

DEAD DOG

Here, you see, on Marston Moor outside York, a seventeenth-century soldier dispatch (with a magic silver bullet) a large poodle named Boy. But Boy was no ordinary pet. The gift of Lord Arundel to Prince Rupert, Boy was popularly believed to be a familiar, and it took "a valliant soldier, who had skill in Necromancy" to do him in. He is shown being mourned by a witch, not Prince Rupert, which is an error, but the Roundheads didn't worry about that and rejoiced that some magic helping the Cavalier cause in the English Civil War had been effectively countered.

ASMODEUS

Tales of the demon Asmodeus can be traced back at least as far as Aeshma Daeva, an ancient Persian deity who represented anger and devastation. Asmodeus appears in the apocryphal Book of Tobit (Chapters 3 and 7), written some time around 250 B.C. In the story, he falls in love with Sarah, daughter of Raguel, and is fiercely jealous of her seven husbands, whom he kills, one right after the other, on their wedding nights. When Sarah decides to marry her cousin Tobias, Tobias is afraid, but he follows the advice of the Archangel Raphael, who tells him to take the heart and gall of a fish and burn them in the bridal chamber. The odor drives the demon away.

Asmodeus flees to Egypt, where he is taken prisoner by Raphael. In time he escapes and now resides in Hell, from which he will come if called by certain rituals and sacrifices.

Asmodeus is depicted as having three heads (a bull, a man with fiery breath, a ram), and some Jewish writers say he is the chief demon of the *Shedim* (demons with vicious claws, haunting ruins and deserts). Traditional tales say that King Solomon forced him, by magic, to construct the First Temple. Later he is said to have dethroned Solomon and taken his place, committing the sins attributed to the king.

Demonologists of the Middle Ages tried hard to organize the denizens of the infernal world in the ranks of their own society, creating princes, dukes, and other officers of Hell. They made Asmodeus a sort of casino

manager, but sorcerers would say he is far more frightening—and useful—
than that. They call upon him to prosper adultery and wreck marriages, and
conversely, blame him for impotence and infidelity.

"CRAZY, AS NUTS AS THEY COME"

Stephen Cooper, defending Ronald K. Crumpley on a charge of
murdering two men and attempting to murder seven others on a November
19, 1980, rampage in Greenwich Village, New York City, said his client was
"crazy, as nuts as they come," and a defense psychiatrist testified that
Crumpley, an ex-transit policeman, was convinced that "demons in the guise
of homosexuals" were stalking him, and he was "merely protecting the
nation and himself" by destroying gay men.

Found not responsible by reason of mental illness, Crumpley, who
previously had done nothing much worse than stealing credit cards, was
turned over to the state for psychiatric treatment. The demons, if any, go
free.

THE CHURCH AND THE DEVIL

If God made everything, why did he make the Devil? If God is good,
why did he make evil?

Saint Thomas Aquinas, the Angelic Doctor, argues that evil is merely
"the absence of a due and necessary good"—so *God didn't make evil.* But we
still need someone to blame it on. If God is anthropomorphized as a
venerable old man with a long beard and a short temper, why not the Devil
as an anthropomorphized scapegoat? With a tail.

The Holy Office (this is the official name for what is better known as the
Inquisition), or Sacred Congregation for the Doctrine of the Faith (new
name), has announced: "The existence of the devil's world is revealed as a
fact of dogma in the Gospel" and is "a central tenet of the faith of the Church
and of its concept of redemption." To doubt the existence of the Devil and
his demons—to call the Devil just a convenient figment of our imaginations
or a useful poetic way of putting things—is "to trouble people's souls."

Rosette Dubal has psychoanalyzed him. Her *Psychoanalysis of the
Devil* (1953) puts the Devil on the Freudian couch and shows him up as a
wicked father figure, the embodiment of natural forces, the personification of

the libido. In Freudian analysis, he does not come through as the most interesting person around—as he unfortunately does in Milton's *Paradise Lost.*

Poor Old Nick! Now science wants to make him into a libido, and the Church won't let him retire, despite his advanced age!

A CHRISTIAN DEVIL DANCE

The *diabala* (devil dance) of Bolivian Indians presented at the Oduro Mission is not a remnant of pagan religion but is performed on the Feast of the Virgin of Sacavon for Christian purposes and is made up by the Indians out of bits of post-Conquest Hispanic culture. The dancers wear a headdress influenced by animal forms but also by the shape of Roman helmets in pictures of the Crucifixion that the padres showed them.

HARD TO HANDEL

Every time composer Domenico Scarlatti heard the music of Handel, he crossed himself. He believed (as some did of Paganini, the violin virtuoso) that such art was achieved with the help of the Devil.

"IN MY NAME SHALL THEY CAST OUT DEVILS"

This, from Mark 16:17, is only one of more than a hundred references to the Devil, devils, and demons in the Bible.

THE END OF THE DEVIL

In a parody of kissing the pope's shoe or the bishop's ring or the king's hands, it was rumored the sabbat witches performed the *osculum infame* on the Devil's posterior. The Knights Templars were accused of similar indecencies. One poor person on trial for witchcraft insisted she had "never seen the Devil from the rear." By the time this filtered through the confused mind of Caesarius of Heisterback, this appeared in his *Miraculorum* as the assertion that the Devil has no buttocks.

EVIL SPIRITS MUST BE FED

Mary Henrietta Kingsley (1862–1900) was a daring and indefatigable explorer of what used to be called the Dark Continent and at considerable personal risk went into the wilds to study the fetish of West Africa, starting in 1893. Among her interesting discoveries about "fourteen levels of the spirit world" is this about African familiars:

> It is held that a person who has the power of bewitching others has in his possession, under his control, a non-human spirit, and this non-human spirit is, in the case of witches, of a malevolent class. The spirit, among the true Negro Tschwi, is kept in a *suhman*. . . . I have reason to believe that among the true Negroes this malevolent spirit is kept in an external home as a general rule; still it has so close an inter-communion with the other souls of its owner, that if they get weakened it can injure them so as to cause his death. Among all the Bantu tribes I know, this spirit is kept in the witch's own inside; and it is held that it is liable to kill him, if he keeps it unemployed, *unfed*, too long. You will hear—when someone has been injured who does not seem to have merited injury in any particular way, someone who has not given any other person reason to hate him, or when a series of minor accidents and a run of ill-luck comes to a village— "Ah, someone is feeding his witchpower"; and means are, of course, taken to find out who that someone is, and put an end to him.

THE RITE OF EXORCISM

From the earliest times, people attempted exorcism, the driving out of devils and demons. It remains an integral part of baptism and certain other sacraments, but in recent times the Roman Catholic Church has much reduced the practice, and some Protestant sects have abandoned it entirely. The modern approach is to attribute cases of "possession" (with *glossolalia*, "speaking in tongues," violence, and so on) to psychopathology and to hand them over to psychiatrists, to treat them with drugs and doctors rather than bell, book, and candle.

Nowadays only certain priests of "piety and prudence" are empowered by their bishops to conduct the rites of exorcism, which used to be the province of men who had taken only three of the minor orders; exorcist was one rank below priest. The ordinary exorcisms involved in receiving a corpse into the church for a requiem, in consecrating a church, altar, church bells, and so on, are routinely done, but exorcism of persons—and priests will exorcise non-Catholics as well as coreligionists—is more strictly limited than previously.

When it becomes necessary to drive demons or devils out of certain possessed persons, an elaborate ceremony is available. This ritual was "set forth by order of the supreme pontiff, Paul V," who reigned as pope from 1605 to 1621. The text was printed in Latin by Maximilian van Eynatten (1619) and included in the collection of 1,200 pages called *Thesaurus Exorcismorum* and, with the imprimatur of Francis Cardinal Spellman of New York, in the *Rituale Romanum* edition of 1947.

The full exorcism ritual is too long and boring to present here, but anyone who is interested can find it in the above volume—if he can locate a copy.

10

The Good Neighbors

THE UNDERGROUND WORKERS

I N addition to believing in demons, people have believed that the Invisible World—and the rocks, streams, trees, caves, mines, mountains of the world we see—is inhabited by a host of other supernatural creatures: the jealous spirits of the dead (who we feared could return) or the helpful spirits abroad in the world (who we hoped would protect and assist us).

Animism and other ideas produced local sprites, who in time were promoted into the pantheon of organized religions. By the same token, as these religions faded, their gods and goddesses were demoted to elves, nymphs, pixies, hateful gnomes, mischievous leprechauns, helpful brownies, benevolent fairy godmothers. Some were conceived of as living much like human beings (mending pots, mining metals, weaving, cobbling, farming). Others led fantastic existences. They are our threatening hobgoblins and our "good neighbors" in the world.

THE REALM OF FAERIE

Fairies may have originated in spirits of nature or memories of earlier races that man drove away into hiding or unbaptized persons who belonged neither in Heaven nor in Hell. But whatever the source of the belief they have always been thought to live in an retreated underground realm—from which they ventured forth only warily among the sons of men.

Twelfth-century English chroniclers present as fact the story of the Green Children, a boy and a girl who somehow escaped the realm of Faerie and found themselves among the peasants at Wolfpitts in Suffolk. The children were lost, weeping in some foreign tongue, and oddly dressed— and green. They were taken to the home of Sir Richard de Calne and cared for but could eat nothing that was not green. In fact, the boy sickened on human food and died. The girl started with green beans and worked her way up to regular English cooking, learned the language, and gradually lost her green color, though she remained (as fairies are supposed to) "very wanton and lascivious." Eventually she was married to a human at King's Lynn in Norfolk.

Fairies, being half human to begin with (the other half being variously described as angelic or devilish), presumably can mate with earthlings. Perhaps those of us humans with "second sight," who can actually see the fairies with their bodies of "congealled Air" and perhaps even wings, have some strain of faerie in them and are distantly descended from marriages between our world and the realm of Faerie.

In 1556 a Dorset man, John Walsh, accused of witchcraft, swore that he could tell if a person was bewitched because "he knew it partly by the fairies, and saith that there be three kinds of fairies, white, green, and black, which, when he is disposed to use he speaketh to them upon hills whereas there is great heaps of earth, as namely in Dorsetshire." *The Examination of John Walsh* said one could consult fairies between twelve and one at noon or night but to be very careful of the black fairies, because "the black fairies be the worst."

Other old historians told of how the swineherd of William Peverell and others found entrances to the subterranean worlds of the fairies and elves and consorted with them in their kingdoms.

But these days, the folk wisdom or credulity that enabled sixteenth-century peasants to chat with the fairies of Dorset hills has gone forever. Our "little green people" now are expected in spaceships.

THE FAIRY BANNER

Dunvegan Castle on the Isle of Skye is the ancestral home of the McLeods, and it has been occupied by that family for more than eleven centuries. It is said to be protected by a fairy banner that, if waved in time of danger, will bring the hosts of fairies to the aid of the McLeods.

Other castles house many treasures, from the horn of Old King Cole to relics of the regal and damnable personages of Britain's past, but none but the castle of the McLeods' boasts such supernatural support, from a boggart, a special kind of supernatural creature we might now call a bogeyman.

FROM THE FAIRIES

Fairies work at night. Santa Claus comes during the night to pile presents under the Christmas tree. When baby teeth fall out, children put them under their pillows, to find money there in the morning, the gift of the Tooth Fairy.

The statue of Sir James M. Barrie's immortal Peter Pan was erected in the darkness of a single night in order to convince London children it had been put there by the fairies. When a duplicate was put up in Perth, Australia, it too was erected overnight and for the same reason.

FAIRY FASHIONS

Fairies always wear a long red mantle with a pointed hood; but witches do too. The Devil usually wears black, but in Scotland he has also been reported to wear green. Serious sorcerers need elaborate robes of different colors for different purposes and seasons, just as the chasubles worn by priests vary in color depending upon the occasion: red for the feasts of martyrs, purple or black for requiems, white or gold for solemn feasts, and so on. Leprechauns wear green. Most serious witchcraft is performed stark naked. Brownies wear brown, sometimes. Norwegian elves are blue but naked; maybe it's the cold. In the Faroes, elves wear a gray costume and black hats.

BRIDGET CLEARY

In March 1894, County Tipperary, one Bridget Cleary disappeared. When her burned and battered body was found, her husband Michael, her father, and seven other men—all but one of them relatives—were charged with her murder.

It seems that Michael Cleary and his relatives thought Bridget was a witch or a changeling—a fairy who had taken over the real Bridget Cleary's place. The mother of Michael Cleary "used to go to the fairies," and it was feared Bridget had too.

Yeats records this ancient belief in his *Irish Fairy and Folk Tales*: "Sometimes the fairies fancy mortals, and carry them away into their own country, leaving instead some sickly fairy child," or even marry mortals, keeping their supernatural nature a secret or revealing it only to a few— often under the threat of fire, of which they are afraid.

Trying to get Bridget to confess, Michael and his family forced her to take herbs and milk, tried countercharms, threw around a mixture of urine and chicken feces to get rid of the spells, and called in the parish priest to say mass in the house. (He later claimed he had no idea that witchcraft was suspected or he "would have given information to the police at once.") When those measures failed to force a confession from her, they threw oil from the lamp on her, burned her face, abdomen, and arm, and tortured her over the fire. But the woman died proclaiming that she was the real Bridget Cleary.

At the trial, the relatives told their strange story of superstition and murder. All were found guilty of manslaughter and sentenced to penal servitude. Michael Cleary got twenty years.

That was Ireland's last trial for witchcraft—or, rather, murder for witchcraft.

SYLPH CONSCIOUSNESS

Sylphs, salamanders, undines, and gnomes were elemental creatures, occupying (respectively) air, fire, water, and earth. They were believed to stand halfway between men and the immortals, being mortal in that they could eat and drink, become sick, beget children, and die, and being supernatural in that their bodies were transparent, they could move with great speed, and they could foretell the future.

Louis the Pious, son of the emperor Charlemagne, by royal edict banished from France all "sylphs." William Woods' *History of the Devil* (1975) comments:

> By forbidding them to appear, Louis was presumably forbidding people to see them—whereupon they were no longer seen. . . . [but] Charlemagne's world of faerie, almost contemporaneous with that of Arthur in Britain, has not died in France even today.

IGNIS FATUUS

The will-o'-the-wisp may lead you to destruction, like *ellylldan*, tiny little elves, only a foot high, that can appear and offer you a very unpleasant choice: either a flight through the air or a voyage upon the ground. If you choose the former, you are whisked up into the air and sped along only to be dropped from a great height; if you elect terra firma, you are dragged at great speed through briars and over jagged rocks, and dumped off one of the cliffs or precipices that the *ellylldan* call home. The twinkling lights of Will may be only the ghostly candles that are leading some soul to the grave—maybe yours.

In *Folklore in America* (1966) Coffin and Cohen write: "The Negroes are also very much afraid of the will-o'-the-wisp, or *ignis fatuus*. They believe that on a dark night it leads its victim, who is obliged to follow, either in the river, where he is drowned, or in bushes of thorns, which will tear him to pieces, the jack-o'-lantern exclaiming all the time, 'Aïe, aïe, mo gagnin toi'— 'Aïe, aïe, I have you.'"

They are not the only ones who are frightened. The *ignis fatuus* of marsh gas has led untold numbers of modern viewers to call the local sheriff to report invasions by flying saucers and little men.

WHERE FAIRIES CAME FROM

The *moira* (fate) of ancient Greece became the *Fata scribunda* (Fates who write down the destiny of each newborn child) of the Romans. The *Encyclopaedia Britannica* makes an striking point in a 1971 article on "fate":

This use of *fata* had an interesting development. When the neuter gender became extinct in spoken Latin, its plural came to be thought of as a feminine singular; hence Italian *fata*, French *fée*. The Fates had become a fairy.

HOW TO GET A FAIRY

The Ashmolean Museum in Oxford was founded by an antiquarian with a lifelong interest in the occult, so it may be no surprise that among its rare manuscripts is a fifteenth-century description of "An excellent way to get a Fayrie." Here it is:

> First get a broad square christall or Venus glasse, in length and breadth 3 inches; then lay that glasse or chrystall in the blood of a white Heene, 3 Wednesdays or 3 Fridays, then take it out and wash it with Holy Water and fumigate it [with incense]. Then take 3 hazel sticks or wands of a years growth, peel them fayre and white and make them so long as you write the spirits or fayries which you call 3 times on every sticke, being made flatt on one side. Then bury them under some hill, wheras you suppose fayries haunt, the Wednesday before you call her, and the Friday following, take them up and call her at 8, 3, and 10 of the clock which be good planets and hours, but when you call, be of cleane life and turn thy face towards the east, and when you have her, bind her to that stone or glasse.

This manuscript says you can summon up your own fairy at will, whether to give you secret information, endow a child with a good fate, protect an area, or even give you the precious diamond that some fairies are supposed to have in the middle of their forehead.

ANOTHER RECIPE

Raymond Lamont Brown's *Book of Witchcraft* (1971) does not say where he found this "Charm to See the Fairies":

> A pint of Sallet oyle and put it in a vial glasse; and first wash it with rose water; the flowers to be gathered towards the east.

Wash it till the oyle becomes white, and put it into the glasse, and then put thereto the budds of hollyhocke, the flowers of ma[r]ygolds the flowers or toppes of wild thyme, the budds of young hazle, and the thyme must be gathered near the side of a hill where fairies are used to be; and take the grasse of a fairy throne; then all these put into the glasse and set it to dissolve three days in the sunne and keep it for thy use.

Note that in the case of both recipes, you have first to know where the fairies are found.

WOMEN OF FAIRYLAND

Many noble houses were lucky enough to have an elf or fairy attached to each member of the family to help and guide them through life. Robert, count of Lusignan, even married a woman who was half human and half fairy: Her father was Elinas, king of Albanie (which could be Albania or Scotland), and her mother was Pressina *le Fay*.

In Ireland and the highlands of Scotland, the *bean sith* (women of fairyland) used to wail and lament under the windows of a house under their protection just before a member of the family was to die.

We call them banshees.

THE AIRMAN'S ELVES

Gremlins are clearly a twentieth-century creation, dating from the early days of flying, but exactly when they first appeared, or who coined the name, is not known and probably never will be.

The Dictionary of Phrase and Fable traces these "imaginary elves whom the R.A.F. in World War II blamed for all inexplicable failures in aeroplanes" back to the thirties, to "a Squadron of Bomber Command serving on the North West Frontier in India." Actually gremlins were known earlier than that.

Horror-story writer Roald Dahl claimed to have invented the term, but to refute him, B. J. Watson wrote to the *Radio Times* (December 1, 1979) to say that gremlins were mentioned a couple of times, by name, in a poem published in *The Aeroplane* (April 10, 1929), when Dahl was just entering his teens.

The late Eric Partridge, expert on all kinds of British slang and contributor of the RAF words to *Forces' Slang, 1939–1945* (1948), noted that "gremlins" had become Standard English. But when it was still slang, as Watson pointed out, it meant a creature that could bring good or evil; gremlins were "responsible for *all* unaccountable happenings—good or bad." Now gremlins—except in Australia, where the word describes a very young surfer, especially a showoff—bring pilots only bad news.

FAIRY NAMES AND NATURES

Novelist Gillian Edwards covers the incredible history of fairy lore in *Hobgoblin and Sweet Puck* (1974) and not only touches on fates and fays and fairies, elves and oafs and imps and urchins, but also dwarfs, gnomes, knockers, bugs, bogles, bogeys, boggarts, brownies, hobs, goblins, and hobgoblins, pookas, pucks, pixies, Queen Mab, Robin Goodfellow, Carabosse, the Elf-Queen, and other personages, from fetches to will-o'-the-wisps and gremlins. To this list Reginald Scot (of the famous *Discoverie of Witches*, 1584) would add "Bull-beggars, Spirits, Witches, . . . Hags, . . . Satyrs, Pans, . . . Sylens, Kit-wi-the-Can[dle]stick, Tritons, Centaurs, Gyants, . . . Calcars, Conjurors, Nymphs, Changelings, Incubus, . . . the Spoorn, the [Night]Mare, the Man-in-the-Oak, the Hell-wain, the Fired-rake [dragon], the Puckle, Tom-thombe, . . . Tom-tumbler, Boneless [and other bogeymen], and such other Bugs, that we are afraid of our shadow."

If your name is Alvin, it goes back to *aelf-wine* (friend of the fairies), and of course similarly derived names such as Oberon and Auberon and Aubrey were "fairy" names. There was a queen of England called Elfleda, and Alfred the Great had a daughter named Elfrida ("threatening elf"); were they fairy princesses?

PROTECTION

To avoid being *led willed* by will-o'-the-wisps, turn your left stocking inside out, or your cloak inside out, and put it on again. The old magical reverse! Usually a reverse (such as the Lord's Prayer or the Stations of the Cross backward) produces an evil result; this produces a good one.

SMALL TRUTHS

"How much is written of Pigme's, Fairies, Nymphs, Apparitions, which tho not the tenth Part true, yet could not spring of Nothing!"

That, in a nutshell, is the opinion of Robert Kirk, as found in his essay of 1691 entitled, in part, *Secret Commonwealth, an Essay of the Nature and Actions of the Subterranean (and, for the most Part) Invisible People, heretofioir going under the name of Elves, Faunes and Fairies, or the lyke, among the Low-Country Scots as they are described by those who have Second Sight . . .*

FAIRY POSSESSIONS

Everyone has heard of fairy gold (said to be found at the end of a rainbow), which vanishes when men try to take it home. But mankind has managed, it is said, to hold onto some fairy possessions. In the Victoria and Albert Museum in London you can see a glass vessel called the Luck of Eden Hall, reputed to have been stolen from the fairies by the Musgrave family in the old days. The intrepid Otto, count of Oldenburg, was said to have stolen the Oldenburg horn from the fairies; in Denmark, the church at Aagerup, Zealand, has a golden chalice stolen from the fairies.

But possession of anything belonging to them is uncertain; magical fairy things are likely to disappear as quickly as they appeared.

If you ever visit the fairies or elves, try to steal something (they are always stealing things from us) but be sure not to accept any refreshment. If you eat with them, you will not be able to return to our world.

FAIRY LORE

The legends about fairies and elves and such creatures may actually derive from exaggerated accounts by primitive peoples of strange nearby tribes with whom they had little communication. The fairies' hatred of iron, for example, may represent race memory of conquest of a Bronze Age people by invaders possessing iron weapons.

Early folklore got a big boost from the collections of the Brothers

Grimm (*Kinder- und Hausmärchen* in 1812–1814 and *Deutsche Mythologie* of 1835 started a whole school), and in England pioneers in folklore often wrote up and published old stories of the "little people": Peter Roberts' *Cambrian* [Welsh] *Popular Antiquities* in 1815, Thomas Keightley's *The Fairy Mythology* of 1828 (greatly expanded in 1850), and so on. Others found in the lore of fairies and elves and goblins some of our earliest memories and some of our most lasting and widespread oral literature.

By the way, it has been unlucky for you to be reading the word "fairy" here at all, which explains the section title, "The Good Neighbors." *They* like us to call them that, or "the little people," or some such name.

LITTLE RED MEN

The Europeans have their leprechauns and gnomes and fairies. In the New World we have our "little people" as well. A case in point is described in *Dictionary of Bahamian English* (1982):

> LITTLE RED MEN . . . *n.* mythical creatures said to inhabit the island of Andros: 1966. The little Red Men are about two feet high, have three fingers on each hand, and are "bright" or

Malicious little creatures crying "Hobyah! Hobyah! Hobyah!" are drawn by John D. Barton for More English Fairy Tales *(1894) collected by Joseph Jacobs. "Hob" means "devil."*

light-skinned. They wear long beards and black velvet waistcoats, but no trousers. They protect animals and try to keep humans out of the Andros interior and other isolated areas. They are said to come to the aid of birds or animals wounded by hunters. To show friendship and good will, Out Islanders hold up three fingers over their heads while walking through the high bush. . . .

SOCKS WITH WHITE TOES

Today there are some socks manufactured with white toes because of an ancient Irish belief that they will keep you from being tripped up by the "little people."

DON'T DAWDLE

In Britain the fairies come out to dance at night. If they do not find a well-swept hearth to dance on, they may dance in a ring outdoors. Where they dance, the grass withers and is called briza or dawdle. If you walk across it, you will get very drowsy and may fall into a sleep from which you will never wake, but if you leave a wad of cheese there (the favorite food of elves and fairies), you will gain their help. In Ireland it is considered mad to disturb the fairy rings marked on the grass.

Elsewhere, especially in Northern Europe, there are similar creatures called *duergar, nokke, droich, pixies, nixies,* and *kobbolds* (the latter related to the mineral cobalt).

THOMAS THE RHYMER

Fairies liked to carry off human beings to fairyland. Tales abound in Scotland and Ireland of young men or boys who, returning home late, happen to pass by a fairy mound when the door is open and see the revelries going on within; they are thereupon whisked away by the fairies and never heard from again.

Or fairies may steal away a human baby and leave a malevolent changeling in its place. Or they may simply invite some amenable human to visit them and later send him away, laden with extraordinary powers. The most famous real person to whom this is supposed to have happened was Thomas of Erceldoune (now Earlston) in Berwickshire, Scotland. Thomas was known as Thomas the Rhymer from the surviving fragments of rhymed prophecy attributed to his name.

His most famous prognostication concerned a great storm that was to sweep over Scotland March 20, 1286. But when the day came, it dawned clear and sunny, and people began to laugh at Thomas. But while they were still jeering, a messenger arrived with news: King Alexander III had died in an accident, leaving no heir.

"This is the storm of which I spoke," Thomas said, and indeed for the next century and longer Scotland was racked by dynastic wars and English invasion.

Thomas figures frequently in literature. Both Sir Walter Scott, in *The Bride of Lammermoor*, and Robert Louis Stevenson, in *The Master of Ballantrae*, have used prophecies of the Rhymer as plot devices. In 1921, the British government itself caused one of Thomas's prophecies to come true. He is supposed to have predicted this:

> . . . Whate'er betide
> Haig shall be Haig of Bemersyde.

The government purchased the estate of Bemersyde, which had been in the possession of the Haigs since the twelfth century but had recently passed into other hands, and donated it to the military leader of World War I, Field Marshal Sir Douglas Haig.

11

Magic and Witchcraft in the Modern World

THERE are very likely more active covens today then there have ever been before. Superstition is rife. Éliphas Lévi was the leading expert on ritual magic of the nineteenth century, yet in his whole life he attended only three such ceremonies. These days, in many cities in the world, you can do that well in a single weekend.

The present is marked by a great deal of the heritage of magic and witchcraft. We may think that we are less superstitious than our ancestors, but in many respects we are exactly the same. At the moment there is no witch hunt such as marred dark ages long past, but no one can deny that magic and witchcraft, though largely underground, are widespread in the modern world.

In fact, the modern world has produced newsletters for witches and mail-order magical daggers (though they come unconsecrated). There are far more covens in the United States today than in the seventeenth century, and more people (whether they will admit it publicly or not) are more guided by astrology than by conventional religion. Moreover, along with the cranks and crackpots, there is a highly educated and respectable segment of the population that increasingly believes that "there may be something in" occult happenings. The future, it is safe to say, holds surprises, and in the strange history of magic and witchcraft there may be hints.

HALLUCINATIONS

Many drugs used in witches' brew are reported to be able to cause visual or auditory hallucinations. You may start "seeing things" if you ingest any of these: amantadine, amphetamines, amyl nitrite, antihistamines, aspirin, atropinelike drugs (one of the witches' standbys), barbiturates, benzodiazepines, bromides, carbamazepine, cephalexin, cephaloglycin, chloroquine, cycloserine, digitalis (which witches brewed from foxglove), digoxin, disulfiram, ephedrine, furosemide, griseofulvin, haloperidol, hydroxychloroquine, indomethacin, isosorbide, levodopa, nialamide, oxphenbutazone, pargyline, pentazocine, phenothiazines, phenylbutazone, primidone, propranolol, quinine, various sedatives, sulfonamides, tetracyclines, tricyclic antidepressants (such as chlorpromazine), and tripelennamine. You may have auditory hallucinations as a result of amphetamines, aspirin, digitalis, diphenhydramine, indomethacin, morphine, and pentazocine.

Many of the "results" obtained in ritual magic may be attributed to the ingestion of such drugs, drunk or inhaled during the ceremonies. Or they may have been caused by the presence of nightshade and the burning of henbane and similar hallucinogens, or merely to the ill effects of burning charcoal in a closed room.

The "temple" that the Order of the Golden Dawn used had little room for the participants in the ceremonies, and some people were undoubtedly ill affected by the heat and the smoke. Also, some of the people used drugs. One cannot be too careful about the ingredients of magic oils applied to the body, either. Magic is supposed to deal in realities, not fantasies, objective results and not subjective hallucinations. An astral trip and a drug trip are not the same thing at all.

WITCH WEDDINGS

My researches show that ancient witch weddings were long on celebration but short on ceremony. One Spanish witch wedding ritual is simply (in translation): "This woman is good for you; take this woman."

Today, witch weddings are too much influenced, I think, by the do-it-yourself variation introduced by the hippies into their weddings in the sixties. I notice that the crowns of flowers are not even the correct combinations (to real witches flowers have individual powers and uses and are not to be thrown together haphazardly), and, of course, the inevitable circle is usually of the wrong size.

In today's Alexandrian circles of witches, the ceremony includes the old practice of the bride being spreadeagled naked in the circle and the groom mounting her naked. But spectators are required to look the other way while that goes on, and the actual consummation of the marriage is conducted later, in private. If the Alexandrians had known more of ancient witchcraft, they would have had the Horned God deflower the bride before the groom lay with her, a practice that long was honored and even came down to Christian times disguised as *le droit de seigneur* or *jus primae noctis*. I believe modern witches are too selfish or sophisticated for that.

WHITE WITCHES

One of the best writers on witchcraft, Christina Hole, has this to say in her brief but excellent *Witchcraft in England* (1947):

> The white witch, or wiseman, was the protector of the community, as his criminal opponent [the black witch] was its enemy. Like the black witch, he relied on magic, but he used it principally for benevolent purposes, to cure diseases, to defeat spells, detect thieves, or find stolen goods, and to protect his neighbours from every kind of ill. His influence at all times was very great, and is not yet entirely extinct. On the whole, perhaps, his activities did more good than harm. When doctors were few and not very highly skilled he was often able to cure simple ailments by the use of herbs and common sense, garnished with charms. He was the natural repository of the traditional lore of the countryside, which was not always so foolish as we tend to think today. . . .

One of the worst writers on the subject, the so-called Black Pope of San Francisco's Church of Satan (a materialist and hedonist organization), denounces white witches vehemently. In "Gay Witch" Leo Martello's *Weird Ways of Witchcraft* (1972) he is quoted thus:

They're tea shoppe witches, plump little women sitting around threatening to turn each other into toads. Most of them are neopagan Christians and they toy with the same notions other religions have, skulking around under a burden of guilt and afraid of being called evil.

The Satanist "religion of the flesh, the mundane, the carnal" seems to me to be a selfish and rather silly version of the Left-Hand Path, since the very essence of witchcraft involves a sense of community and unselfishness: "Do what thou wilt, so long as thou harm none other."

"MORMONS PULL PLUG ON MTV IN 1985"

Under the above headline, datelined Provo, Utah, comes this story about new restrictions on students at Brigham Young University:

Mormon bishops have pulled the plug on MTV [a TV channel showing rock music videos] for students living in church-approved housing, after condemning the popular cable music channel for containing "sex, drugs, witchcraft and the bizarre."

ARADIA

One of the most important books in the modern history of witchcraft is the *vangelo*, or gospel, of Italian witchcraft, written out by an Italian witch called Maddalena and published in 1899 as *Aradia: or the Gospel of the Witches*.

Charles G. Leland, the publisher, was aware of the survival into modern times of very ancient practices of an Old Religion, which he felt had long been a significant force in Western culture, whether on the surface of society or underground. Until the history and nature of that Old Religion are understood, he maintained, the history of the Establishment cannot be complete.

CONVICTED OF NOT PERFORMING WITCHCRAFT

Many gypsies in years gone by were executed for performing magic, but today we fine or jail them for pretending to do so. At the Portsmouth quarter sessions in 1939, Bessy Birch, a gypsy, was accused—under witchcraft laws that went all the way back to George II—of getting money and jewelry from a woman by falsely saying that as a gypsy she could take away the curse on the jewelry.

THE NECRONOMICON

The American fantasy writer H. P. Lovecraft and some of his followers used as the basis of some short stories an imaginary grimoire which Lovecraft called *Necronomicon*. Some people thought or hoped that such a book really did exist and, *presto!*, someone came up with one. Unfortunately, this *Necronomicon* was not only a forgery but a forgery based on a forgery, because its modern authors had "ripped off" the *Fourth Book* attributed to (by not authored by) Agrippa.

COURSES OF WITCHCRAFT

Many witches believe that they are not permitted to charge for teaching the craft, but teaching *about* witchcraft is something else again. Such courses have been offered, sometimes at fancy prices per credit, at the New School and New York University's School of Continuing Education in New York, at the University of Alabama and the University of South Carolina, and elsewhere.

THE PREVALENCE OF WITCHES

Louise Huebner in *Power Through Witchcraft* (1969): "Judging from the mail I receive, there is at least one person in every community who practices witchcraft. People in every walk of life are witches and wizards." Sybil Leek once claimed she heard from "a thousand people a week" who wanted to be witches.

"PEOPLE DON'T UNDERSTAND"

Christians used to believe that Jews kidnapped babies to be used in murderous blood rituals. Saint Hugh of Lincoln is supposed to have been such a victim. Black magicians have been accused of sacrificing babies, and one has at least to promise to do so to become a real Satanist.

Patty Dean Hawn, a witch, disturbed the mountain folk of Wartburg, Tennessee, by her adherence to *wicca*. But when rumors spread through the region that witch rites included the sacrificing of an eleven-year-old virgin, she denied it hotly:

> All the rumors are false. They say a devil worshipper sacrifices animals or people. We do not believe in any kind of sacrifice. Our lives are in danger because people don't understand.

Isaac Bashevis Singer recalls that as a boy he was very disturbed by the sacrifice of animals demanded in the ancient Jewish religion. Certainly Jews and Christians and "white witches" never sacrifice any living thing or person now.

POSSESSION AND EXORCISM

As the spirit of God can enter into people, making them holy, so too can the spirit of the Devil enter into them, making them evil. This is the basis of the belief in demonic possession. Diabolical possession was also thought to be the cause of madness and diseases like epilepsy, in which the victim suffers periodic seizures, or various hysterical afflictions.

Treatment of the possessed could be rough. He would surely be whipped, at least. He might be chained to a huge revolving wheel and whirled about at high speed until he lost consciousness. He might be burned or subjected to the same torture as witches were—all in the attempt to make the "demon" leave him.

If the possessed victim pointed the finger at some neighbor and accused him (or usually her) of being the person who had sent in the "demon," the accused was as good as dead. (This is exactly what happened at Salem in 1692.) In Burton-on-Trent, England, in 1596, the case of Thomas Darling occurred. Darling, a young boy, returned from a hunt one day and had a series of fits, during which he claimed to see green angels, a green cat, and a chamber pot from which flames were issuing. In his conscious moments, he produced a story of having had a run-in with an old woman with three warts on her face, and he blamed his troubles on her animosity. The neighbors thought the description sounded like one Alse Gooderidge, long suspected of witchcraft, and accordingly hauled the poor woman up before a judge.

Alse denied the charge, of course, but she was tried, convicted of witchcraft, and sent to prison, where she died before she could be hanged. Meanwhile, Thomas continued to have fits and visions, until one John Darrel, a self-appointed specialist in possession, appeared, prayed and fasted over the boy and (according to Peter Haining in *Witchcraft and Black Magic* [1972]) used ventriloquism to "converse" with the demon—and thus exorcised it.

Many churches still retain belief in the religious rite of exorcism and occasionally practice it. Recently in California, priests and doctors performed such a rite over the "possessed" boy John (the only name given) who was the original of the perturbed little girl in William Blatty's novel *The Exorcist*. John, fourteen, was exorcised more than twenty times over a two-month period.

In the eighteenth century exorcism was occasionally used by physicians in the treatment of the insane. Joseph Gassner in Germany reported remarkable results, probably with hysterics who are readily responsive to any kind of suggestion. In Germany as late as the 1830s, two leading physicians of Schwabia were treating cases of possession.

Today, vastly improved diagnosis and a broad armory of sophisticated drugs enable doctors to treat and cure many of the ailments that used to pass for possession. Medical hypnosis provides an efficient approach to cases of psychosomatic illness. But there remain a few odd cases, like John's, which—like the phenomenon of poltergeists, which they closely resemble in several particulars—remain a puzzle.

"SHALL WE JOIN THE LADIES?"

Hollywood bookshop owner Edward Gilbert recently reported that sales had tripled in the occult book market in the decade and said that "close to 90 percent of the books are bought by women."

POP GOES THE OCCULT

Coven, a pop music group out of Chicago, claim they invoke the Devil. Their lead singer is named Jinx, and they certainly raise the devil of a racket.

A MODERN CURSE

England, like America, has lost many elms lately to disease but someone stepped in to save an elm that was threatened by a planned housing development in Sussex. In March 1966 the *Evening Argus* of Brighton reported that affixed to the tree had been a public warning against cutting it down. Decorated with magical symbols, the notice read:

> Hear ye, hear ye, that any fool
> Who upon this tree shall lay a tool,
> Will have upon him a curse laid,
> Until for that sin he has paid.

Not much as poetry, but a nice idea.

JUST PLAIN FOLKS

According to Emile C. Schurmacher, author of *Witchcraft in America Today* (1970):

In present-day America witches are of all ages and of all shades from whitest white to blackest black. Few are weird or sinister in appearance or show any physical attributes which might lead one to suspect that they differ in any way from ordinary human beings.

BLACKSMITHS

Blacksmiths in olden days were often thought to have special magical powers, for, after all, they would force the hardest of known substances, iron, to take any shape they wished. To this day in Ethiopia, Morocco, and other parts of Africa, blacksmiths are believed able to change themselves into wild animals, especially hyenas. These *boudas*, as they are called, are something like our werewolves and are thought to rob graves.

Natives say that when changing themselves into wild animals, the blacksmiths sometimes fail to remove ornaments they are wearing, and so when the magic animals are killed, they are sometimes found to be wearing necklaces or other ornaments of men.

DEGREES

There are three degrees in witchcraft, Entered Apprentice being the first. (Once you join the cult, they'll tell you what the others are.) Philip Emmons Isaac Bonewits has a B.A. degree from the University of California at Berkeley, dated June 16, 1970—"with a Major in Magic." Some doctorates in history and other subjects touch more or less significantly on magic and witchcraft.

In a coven, all members are equal. At the witches' tables the salt dish is missing, not because the witches are frightened by that symbol of preservation and purity, but because in their company no one sits below the salt. They are brothers and sisters.

UNO WHO

Jehovah's Witnesses preach that "the Great Beast" of Revelations is the United Nations.

If you want to figure this out, remember that *U* and *N* correspond (in the Tarot) to the Pope and Death and to the numbers 6 and 50 (in gematria or numerology). Good luck!

BREATH OF LIFE

AMORC (Rosicrucian) advertisements used to feature Benjamin Franklin, supposedly a member. Now they depict Sir Francis Bacon. A more recent convert to the Rosy Cross was Sirhan Sirhan; he was expelled for not paying his dues but reapplied for membership after he had assassinated Robert Kennedy.

My favorite Rosicrucian, whom you will not see in the ads or the press, was a lawyer named Heydon (born in 1629), whose odd ideas included the conviction that man's Original Sin was—eating. He recommended that people give it up. There was, stated Heydon, plenty of nourishment in the air. For those who felt they needed more on their stomachs, Heydon had a compromise: Place a plate of cooked food on your stomach and inhale the aroma.

Some people would like to deny modern Rosicrucians the right to their name. They claim that, by definition, real Rosicrucians are members of a *secret* society. One eminent authority insists they have preserved their anonymity down the centuries because they all move every ten years, and, he says, they never advertise.

What is his evidence that this supersecret Rosicrucian Order has existed for centuries? Why, no trace of them has ever been found, that's how he knows.

MASQUERADE

Kit Williams's *Masquerade* was a best-selling fairy tale that involves a bejeweled golden pendant that a moon maiden sends to her love by a messenger named Jack Hare. The thirty-two-page illustrated book was a publishing phenomenon.

Williams in real life fashioned an amulet of seven ounces of gold and studded it with gems, enclosed it in a pottery rabbit, and buried it (1979) "Somewhere in the British Isles," on public property. It is supposed to be discovered (and kept) by whoever could figure out the clues in the book.

"'Masquerade' mavens," reported *Newsweek* (March 30, 1981), "use everything from astrology to trigonometry to fathom its mystical text and complex art" and are hot in pursuit of the bauble. It is worth between $20,000 and $36,000, depending on the price of gold, and the author's royalties have reached over $500,000.

Who would have thought that a modern international quest would involve thousands seeking an amulet described in a fairy tale?

HYPNO-TECHNICIANS

These are Los Angeles (and other) cops who, after a few days of training, can hypnotize witnesses in order to get information out of them that is not available to the witnesses' conscious minds: You *do* recall the license number after all; you *can* describe the man with the gun though you thought you were too scared to notice. Your subconscious holds hidden facts.

But, in truth, your unconscious mind can lie, and distort, too, and fall prey to suggestion by the inquisitor. The International Society of Hypnotism and the Society for Clinical and Experimental Hypnotism disapprove of information taken under hypnosis, and the courts may reject it as evidence. But the police find it useful as an aid to detection. Thus hypnosis, once thought occult, now may join fingerprinting among police procedures.

OM AND THE RANGE

TM (Transcendental Meditation) used to sell people a very personal mantra, a sound to chant for emptying the mind, facilitating concentration, and aiding meditation. Then someone revealed that the mantra you got just depended on your age; there was a list.

Actually, meditation is good for you, and mantras help. You can use any one you like, provided it is a monosyllable and you are not going to get bored repeating it. You can use *krim* or *hrim* or *shrim, vam* or *gam* or *ram,* whatever you like. A friend on Wall Street says he uses *cash,* and it has certainly worked for him.

SATAN'S POWER

In a *People* magazine article entitled "Five Things That Would Have Made George Orwell Happy in 1984," this is the first item:

Members of the congregation of the Cornerstone Assembly of God Church in Bowie, Md., destroyed a batch of phonograph records they said reflected "Satan's power." Among them were albums by Donny and Marie Osmond.

GREENING OF AMERICA

The old superstition that green is unlucky (because worn by fairies) has been translated into a folk belief that homosexuals wear green on Thursdays.

THE SECRET

The so-called Count of St.-Germain walks again!

In the eighteenth century he surrounded himself with a group of alchemical magicians who were supposed to have moved through various degrees (like Freemasons) until they became full-fledged adepts. At that point they were entitled to know the Secret. The count whispered to each that the secret was that there *was* no secret.

The Assassins, twelfth century followers of the murderous Hasan ibn al-Sabah, also learned at last that "nothing is true." The Tibetans are frequently told by their lamas, after a series of tests and mystical experiences, that it is all phony. But to many, as to the followers of the count, it comes as a stunning surprise.

Now, look at the group founded by Guy Warren Ballard called the Minute Men of St.-Germain. Ballard left Kansas a few years ago to start a new religion in California. It was called I AM, and the Minute Men was its paramilitary wing. The latter, claimed Ballard, was equipped with a death-dealing ray gun.

The secret is that, in Californian occult circles, anything goes.

OCCULT SUPERMARKET

The occult seems to be a thriving industry in America today. If you look in your local yellow pages, you may find magic and witchcraft suppliers, if not magicians and witches listed as such. "Magicians' Supplies" may simply mean equipment for sleight of hand, but there are warlock shops and many little sources of supply without a phone. Is there a real "magicians' supplies" store in your town, or are your local warlocks and witches creating their own equipment or making do with mail order?

A LITTLE STORY

In 1940, after Denmark had fallen to the Nazis, the great physicist Nils Bohr, still then working in his native Copenhagen on nuclear fission, telegraphed a message to British friends that concluded: "TELL COCKCROFT AND MAUD RAY KENT."

The British scientist Sir John Cockcroft was easily identified, but who or what was "Maud Ray Kent"? Some tried anagrams, and one scientist was sure it meant that U (uranium) and D (heavy water?) "may react." The British set up a MAUD Committee on the subject of atomic science and researches that might produce an atomic bomb.

Much later it was discovered there was a lady called Maud(e) Ray who lived in Kent. She had been governess to Bohr's children.

The point of this story is this: Ignorance can create mystery where there is actually none. Investigators of the paranormal and the supernatural ought to remember that, for the simplest explanation is most likely to be correct. And I feel that the simplest explanation for much magic and witchcraft is that the supernatural exists.

COMMUNIST CONSPIRACY

In 1960, a Senate Internal Security Subcommittee meeting, chaired by Sen. Thomas J. Dodd of Connecticut, heard Nigerian student Anthony G. Okotcha testify that he and twenty other African students were recruited elsewhere and trained in witchcraft at the University of Moscow. Their witchcraft professor, it was alleged, told them at the outset that the Soviet's purpose in this was "the eventual liquidation of American and British influence in Africa." Since that time it is not clear how well their lessons have been applied.

WORD WATCHING

The portable, often plastic, brightly colored cones placed in the road to divert traffic around road works are called witches' hats.

THE COVENANT OF THE GODDESS

A group of San Francisco women recently formed an organization they call the Covenant of the Goddess. It is dedicated to "Magic—the art of changing consciousness at will," which it celebrates in what it calls the Spiral Dance Ritual on "the witches' New Year," Halloween.

The Goddess, which the group describes as "the immanent life force," appears to be a kind of moon deity, worshipped in outdoor rituals. The main thrust of the the Covenant's teachings seem to be a combination of women's rights, artistic expression, and occultism.

HOLY TOLEDO!

Perhaps the city of the modern world most changed from its great days as a center for magic is Toledo in Spain, made immortal by El Greco's famous painting.

Today it still carries on some of its ancient Moorish craft of damascening metal, but it is no longer the university of sorcery that it was in the period when it brought together the magicians of North Africa, the cabalists of the Jews, and the Christian scholars who went there to absorb their knowledge of medicine, mathematics, and darker arts.

On the swords made in Toledo men used to swear the great oath, "the oath that kills." All we have left now is the slang expression "Holy Toledo!"

TRANSPORTATION

In 1969 in California, a U.S. Marine named Raphael Minichiello, en route to a court-martial for robbery, escaped from his guards, hijacked a TWA jet, and forced it to carry him 6,900 miles to Rome. He was seized by American authorities and returned to the States, but not before former friends in Melito Irpino, a village near Naples, had taken up a collection for him. They were going to pay a witch to whisk him out of the hands of the FBI and back to Italy.

The spell didn't work.

MAGIC IS BIG BUSINESS TODAY

Daniel Lawrence O'Keefe's magisterial book *Stolen Lightning: The Social History of Magic* (1982) makes a point often ignored in discussions of the subject:

Magic is big business; when practitioners succeed in avoiding taxes by having their ventures declared religions or charitable foundations they prosper. Magical products have cross-elasticities with all other goods and services in the economy; if other goods are taxed at up to 46 percent federally, and subjected also to regula-

242

tion of all kinds, then magical goods may partly drive non-magical goods out of circulation. If Transcendental Meditation is permitted to sell nonsense syllables for $150.00 a morpheme in every state in the union without a single regulatory agency lifting a finger, while a manufacturing company can be prosecuted for literally thousands of infringements of six centuries of business law, which product will prosper more? Magic also obtains large infusions of capital from crazy or reactionary sections of America's rich.

OLD IDEAS

"Little is known of the religion of the early Egyptians," wrote William MacQuitty in the first issue of *Museum Magazine* (1980), "but it is probable that they were fetishists, worshippers of objects considered to have special properties—the stone or stick with which a dangerous animal had been killed, a tree that had given shelter, and so on. Gradually, religion became more sophisticated, carvings and inscriptions reveal worship of the sun-god Atum."

Many people today are mere fetishists, ascribing power to a "lucky penny" or a pen with which they have signed successful contracts, or a "winning shirt." Certainly fetishists outnumber modern sun-god worshippers. Progress?

STILL THE MODERN VIEW

Probably the best statement of how most people today feel about magic is as old as Pliny the Elder (23–79) who, in his *Natural History*, said it was "frivolous and false" and yet "still contains some element of truth in it."

BEATING WITCHES

"In 1969," writes Richard Cavendish in *The Powers of Evil* (1975), "five men and a woman were tried in Zürich and found guilty of beating a girl of seventeen to death in an attempt to drive the Devil out of her."

The young girl, Bernadette Hasler, wrote an account of how she had had sexual relations with the Devil, "all black and furry." The six accused beat her for four hours on May 14, 1966, making her eat her own excrement and otherwise humiliating and injuring her.

In witchcraft circles, the apprentice to the coven has the Devil beaten *into* him or her. Scourging is part of the initiation rite, though gentle and more or less token in many modern covens. Some witches, however, report being very severely beaten before their induction into a coven.

The Hasler incident, which made *Time* of February 7, 1969, is only one of innumerable instances, most of which go unpublicized, in which religious persons literally try to beat the Hell out of people they believe to be possessed by Satan.

THE GOLDEN DAWN

Toward the end of the last century, a group of literary men in London formed an organization for the study of magic and the occult and called it the Hermetic Order of the Golden Dawn. The Golden Dawn liked to think of itself as having arcane and unique origins, but occult groups for literary types were not uncommon in the nineteenth century, and the Golden Dawn was probably not much different from that led by playwright and novelist Edward Bulwer-Lytton.

The Golden Dawn attracted a mixed bag of literary types, including A. E. Waite, William Butler Yeats, Arthur Machen, and Algernon Blackwood, some of whose interests in the occult inevitably appeared in their work and reached the general public. It also attracted the London coroner (a strange man who also headed the Rosicrucians), the rather loony Allan Bennett (who renounced Roman Catholicism at age sixteen when it was explained to him how God had arranged for children to be born), and the crazier Samuel MacGregor Mathers (who had translated various occult works) and Aleister Crowley. These latter two consummate egoists inevitably struggled for supremacy within the organization, constantly trying to discover or devise new ceremonies and to use them for personal power. In the battle over control of the Golden Dawn, Mathers sent a vampire (among other evils) to Crowley; Crowley replied with fifty demons (including Beelzebub). It was a deadly game—at least in their own estimations.

Mathers felt he owned the Golden Dawn. Had not the basic secrets of the organization come from a coded manuscript he, Mathers, had deciphered—with some help from his wife, a clairvoyant? Crowley also intended to run any group with which he was associated. Frustrated when Mathers created new levels of "secrets" and "degrees" which he would not share with Crowley, Crowley left the Golden Dawn, set up his own group called *Argentinum Astrum* ("Silver Constellation"), created some "secrets" of his own, and began to publish the "secrets" of the Golden Dawn in his magazine, *The Equinox*. Meanwhile there appeared on the Continent Crowley's four-volume work entitled (rather preciously) *Magick*. It was denounced as full of vile rituals, and copies were extremely hard to come by, but some eventually found their way to Britain, among other places.

Ultimately, The Golden Dawn collapsed, not so much because of the internecine struggles of ambitious members or the publication of its "secrets," but because of the good intentions of writer A. E. Waite, one of the least ambitious, and most serious, members. Waite strove to make the order more Christian, and when that happened, British membership melted away.

Eventually, even the closely guarded "secrets" of Aleister Crowley and the innermost "secrets" of the Golden Dawn were published in a revealing book, *The Golden Dawn*, by Francis Israel Regardie (born 1907), who once was Crowley's personal secretary. This infuriated other occultists (especially those in California, where Regardie went to live after leaving England), who wanted to keep Crowley's *Ordo Templi Orientis* ("Order of the Eastern Temple") their private mystery. But Regardie, who authored *The Tree of Life* and other useful books on magic and mind expansion (which went over big in California), knew the significance of what he was publishing. In *The Golden Dawn*, which went through several editions, one could "read all about it."

NEW YORK STORES

New York has always been rather tolerant of witches. Ralph and Mary Hall were tried for having cast spells in New Amsterdam (1665–1668) but were acquitted, and the accusations pooh-poohed. True, Edgar Cayce and Evangeline Adams were tried here for fortune-telling, but the objection seems to have been more to suspected fraud than to substantiated supernatural activities. (Today most "fortune-telling" consists of giving people numbers to play.)

New York has plenty of occult bookstores and some courses in witchcraft for students of various levels; it is also one of the best cities in the world to get the ingredients and paraphernalia for magic and sorcery.

MAGIC TRANSFORMATIONS

David Gerrard's documentary for the Year of the Child (1979) showed young Americans exercising and chanting:

Fee, fie, foh, fat;
This will make my tummy flat.

GOING THROUGH CHANGES

The *I Ching* ("Book of Mutations") is identified by Louis Pawels and Jacques Bergier in *The Morning of the Magician* (1968) as the "only oracular book the rules of which have come down to us from antiquity, and is composed of graphic figures: three continuous lines, and three discontinuous lines, in every possible order."

This ancient Chinese work needs little description here, for the *I Ching*, having been taken up in the psychedelic revolution of the sixties, is still a best-seller. Most of the people who swear by it hardly think of it as magic at all.

LOCAL DEVIL

This legend, concerning the Caquende Street fountain in Sabará, Brazil, is reported by contemporary Brazilian author Fernando Sabino:

At midnight on Fridays, a "colonial devil" is said to emerge from the fountain, cross the city toward the Velhas River, take a dip in the waters, and then disappear. That is, unless he encounters a woman on the road. Like all devils, he's crazy about women. He impregnates them, and the kids are born werewolves.

SHIVAREE

An old American custom is the shivaree, a noisy serenade to the bride and groom on their wedding night. The custom goes back to Europe, where it was called charivari and had as its original purpose not just teasing the newly married couple but actually frightening away demons who might prevent conception and the birth of a new soul.

A modern version of shivaree consists of a procession of cars following that of the bride and groom from the church to the place of the reception. The followers honk horns and create a loud and boisterous parade.

CALIFORNIA WITCHES

In 1965, during an entertainment in the Hollywood Bowl, Louise Huebner, who regards herself as a witch, offered an incantation "to increase the sexual vitality of Los Angeles," which one would hardly think was necessary.

However, Huebner's distribution of red candles, chalk, and garlic seems to indicate more familiarity with horror films than with ritual magic. Experts know that, to keep away vampires, you need garlic *flowers*; garlic only keeps away people. Nonetheless, the spell "Light the flame, bright the fire, red the color of desire," was happily chanted by the crowd, led by Huebner, dressed in a long silver robe.

Los Angeles County Supervisor Debs then jokingly gave the lady some recognition as "Official Witch of Los Angeles County." Later, when he saw the derisive press reception this was getting, he revoked her "appointment." She retaliated by revoking her spell.

Still, L.A. has many unofficial witches, so Huebner's dubious incantation can hardly be missed.

TOURIST GUIDE

In the 1970s Ernest Weatherall wrote from London for *Variety*, the show-biz bible: "For the visitor who has seen everything, the hotel concierge will probably know where you can attend the many witches' covens in town, where nude virgins will be 'sacrificed' to the spirits. The 'in-thing' in London today is to attend an exorcism ceremony, and watch one of the devil's disciples have the evil spirits knocked out of him."

But someone must have been pulling Mr. Weatherall's leg. "Nude virgins" are not all that common in London, and genuine witches' covens are Not Open to the General Public.

WITCHY BAHAMAS TODAY

In the Americas there are many places where European traditions of magic and witchcraft have been mingled with African Mumbo Jumbo (worship of an African deity) to create interesting customs, superstitions, and new religions. We may take the Bahamas as our example, for on both New Providence and the Out Islands, an active bush medicine is practiced by professors of plants (herbalists), witches involved in *fyak* (witchcraft), and medicine men with the charms and amulets of *mojo*, the fetishes and taboos of *juju* brought from West Africa. Also (though it is not a religion like the Voodoo of Haiti) there is the magic of Obeah.

A witch-man or old granny with Obeah can protect pregnant women from bad influences (with graveyard or crossroads dirt or foot-grass concoctions made from the grass growing around the house). He can fix a wayward husband or snare a lover (by putting menstrual blood in cuckoo soup and feeding it to the unwary). He can provide a guard (amulet) against other doctors' spells, or he can put a hant or ghost *on* someone or take one *off*.

You can have your house smoked to banish evil spirits or drive them away with *Petiveria alliacea* (a garlic-scented tropical American herb called Obeah bush, poor-man's strength, strong-man's weed, or guinea-hen weed). You can get an Obeah snake to protect your property from intruders or thieves, or set an Obeah trap for them, or hang a bottle or some other magic object in the trees to guard you. You can carry a good-luck bean or have someone with "the power" perform *macasee* (magic) for you, put the mouth on (curse) an enemy, drive off a plaguey spirit, or interpret your dreams for you with *King Tut* (a famous dream book that explains the significance of dreams).

Those who "live by olden days' time" keep the ancient ways inherited from British and other "massas" and likewise from slave ancestors brought to the islands from far-off Africa. Many of today's home remedies are tried-and-

248

true substitutes for the pharmacy's products, but in the use of some of them (as when one puts a leaf in one's shoe) magic enters in.

Jumbies—evil spirits whose name is derived from African roots and resembles the Haitian *zombie*—are thought to inhabit certain caves, trees, and so on, and even those who do not believe in such things are careful, nonetheless, not to disturb them. Jumby beans (seeds of the common lead tree, *Leucaena glauca*) can be placed at the wrists of children to protect them from these "ghosts." Children continue the traditions: Even when playing a favorite game of having one of their number lie down on the ground on a moonlight night to have his or her outline traced by the placement of shining pieces of shell or white stones, they always end with the very careful removal of every last piece of the outline, lest an evil spirit come and work against the moonlight child, whose outline somehow took on something of his identity.

AMERICAN ANTICHRIST

The *Ordo Templi Orientis* that Aleister Crowley established in Europe had certain appeals to Americans, especially those interested in sex magic. These disciples formed in California a group called Agape Lodge, but the Greek word *agape* (selfless and outgoing love) had little reference to their real activities, and especially those of Jack Parsons, a brilliant physical chemist. Parsons' sex life with real women had convinced him that he would be far better off with an "elemental" woman conjured up by sex magic. For a while Parsons had to be content with Crowleyan ceremonies that involved a lot of boring ritual magic and no sex but masturbation, but in the long run— lo and behold!—the "elemental" was produced. Some people said she was a would-be poetess from New York, but Parsons was ready to believe that she was his promised magical bride.

With this attractive woman, who was red-haired and green-eyed, Parsons undertook to produce in her womb Babalon, the Crowleyan "female principle" itself. Parsons and his girlfriend advanced the cause of heterosexual sex magic to the full extent of their energies, but no Babalon was conceived.

Ultimately (1952) Parsons blew himself up in an experiment with fulminate of mercury. He is remembered chiefly not for his sexual or magical prowess but for his legal name change—from "Jack Parsons" to "Balarion Armiluss al Daijal Antichrist."

DO YOU THINK THE AGE OF MAGIC IS DEAD?

"Many people delude themselves with the belief of living in a thoroughly rationalized era," wrote the author of the article "Magic" in *The New International Encyclopedia* (1930), "until some one in the room opens an umbrella."

The ancient beliefs in magic remain very much a part of modern lives. We knock on wood in hopes of averting bad luck, we refuse to light three cigarettes with one match, we avoid ladders and are careful with mirrors. Quite apart from such practices, we say things like "if something should happen to me" instead of "when I die." Thus we show our belief in the magical dictum which says that, by naming an event, one assists in making it happen.

BLASPHEMY

The *frisson* or thrill of doing something wicked and even dangerous is one of the attractions of witchcraft. Blasphemy and sacrilege can be said to introduce what some dabblers in the occult call "electricity" into magical ceremonies.

Blasphemy was part of the stock in trade of Aleister Crowley's magic. He spread the news that he had baptized a toad "Jesus Christ of Nazareth" and then crucified it. The Sixth Degree ritual of Crowley's *Ordo Templi Orientis* is a parody of Christ's Passion, involving scourging and the Crown of Thorns, the mocking and sponge of vinegar, even crucifixion. Crowleyan sects of one sort or another still exist, and some may still perform sex-magic-related crucifixions, although none involve death so far as I know. The terrible "Texas chainsaw murders" seem clearly attributable to dementia and not demonology, but they also involved some hideous practices—such as dressing up in the skins of flayed victims—that originated in ancient Teutonic magic.

Ritual magic appears to be growing somewhat more sedate, as we see in the increasing number of "robed covens" (witches traditionally celebrated stark naked). But on the fringes they may involve what we may describe as blasphemies against both humanity and the Godhead.

LOOKING FOR SYMBOLS OF WITCHCRAFT

For 103 years Proctor & Gamble used a trademark on its products of a crescent moon and thirteen stars. No longer. A rumor started about 1980 that the symbol was drawn from witchcraft. P & G fought the allegation of Satanism in the courts and won, set up a toll-free number the public could call for an explanation of the innocuous symbol, and finally decided, in 1985, that one cannot fight the public if they are willing to see 666 in the whiskers of the Man in the Moon or credit false reports that the company publicly admitted tithing to the Church of Satan.

Perhaps those same people would care to write to Washington. What do you know about that very curious mumbo jumbo of pyramid and eye and so on, on the back of the dollar bill? Perhaps they ought to look at every committee that boasts exactly thirteen members, from the College of Heralds in Britain to some small American town's Board of Selectmen. . . .

"DO DO THAT VOODOO THAT YOU DO SO WELL"

Frank Daminger of West Virginia sued seven neighbors for $50,000 for defaming him by saying that he attracted girls by witchcraft. The case was settled out of court.

THE END OF WITCHCRAFT?

Not long before his death, Gerald B. Gardner, whom one journalist unsympathetically called "the self-appointed Pope of British Witchcraft," wrote:

> I think we must say goodbye to the witch. The cult is doomed, I am afraid, partly because of modern conditions, housing shortage, the smallness of modern families, and chiefly by education. The modern child is not interested. He knows witches are all bunk.

As it turns out, Gardner was wrong: The interest in magic and witchcraft increases every year. The proliferation of occult shops and various courses in the black arts, available all over the globe, make it clear that witches are getting less bunkier all the time.

GERMAN CUSTOMS

When a German peasant woman thinks she has been zapped by the Evil Eye, she instantly reverts to ancient Teutonic religious practices. She removes her dress over her head. Then she turns it around three times. (This may be a later, Christian touch, though Christians are not the only ones to find power in the number 3.) Then, holding the dress open, she drops a burning coal through it three times before donning it again.

The burning coal is one with the torches, bonfires, shafts of light illuminating the altars in temples, and all the other remnants of the old religion of the Sun God.

The dress must be, like most things in magic, turned around *wiederschein* ("widdershins," we say in English, or counterclockwise, opposite the course of the sun through the heavens). The idea is that you are *unwinding* the spell cast on you.

TWO WORLDS

In the 1893 book, *Philosophical Studies*, one W. Wundt wrote an article entitled "Hypnotism and Suggestion." In it, he had this to say of magic and its adherents.

It is obvious that the world that surrounds us is composed of two quite different worlds. On the one hand there is the world of Copernicus, Newton, Leibniz and Kant; that is, the universe that is subject to immutable laws and where both big and small are unified in one harmonious whole. On the other hand, there exists, beside this grandiose and admirable universe, a small world of spirits, magicians and "mediums" which is the direct opposite of our great, sublime universe whose immutable laws are suspended for the profit of these most vulgar and frequently hysterical persons. So, we are led to believe that the laws of gravitation, the action of light and all the laws of our psychophysical organization must undergo a transformation as soon as they come before some "Madame Zara" [gypsy fortune-teller] . . . that they sleep a sort of magnetically-induced slumber, not so that she may predict some great universal catastrophe, but so that she may guess if some minor misfortune lies ahead of John Smith's small son. . . . Supposing all these absurdities were in fact true, can one imagine that a psychologist or a natural scientist, who is exempt from prejudice and who has free choice, would prefer the evidence of this small world of hysterical mediums to that of our great universe, whose order depends on immutable laws?

"HERE COMES THE ANTICHRIST"

To Jeffrey Burton Russell, whose books, *The Devil* (1977), *Satan*, (1981), and *Lucifer* (1985), explore the concept of God's Adversary, the modern world sounds much like that into which the Antichrist is prophesied as coming. He feels it is a world in which "a real force is actively present in the cosmos urging to evil." He concludes:

> This evil force has a purposive center that actively hates good, the cosmos, and every individual in the cosmos. . . . For Christians, then, the person of the Devil may be a metaphor for something that is real, that really brings horror to the world every day and threatens to lay the entire earth waste.

In our modern world, where the nuclear means of destruction of "the entire earth" are at our fingertips, the Devil is more to be feared than ever before. For we live in an age far more genuinely terrifying than any conceived by evil witches and sorcerers of the past.

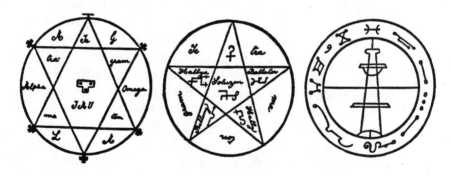

Afterword

ALL that is involved in or lies behind magical activities is too much for any single book. This one has attempted to touch authoritatively on some selected facts, chosen for their essential color and interest. To collect them, I have had to cast my net wide, and I am always ready to haul in new ones.

You may wish to write me your reactions to the book. I cannot promise to answer all your letters, but I assure you I shall read them with lively interest. I am signing below my real name and address.

Leonard is the name of the Inspector-General of Black Magic, the "great Black One" who presides at the sabbat as a giant goat with three horns and the ears of a fox and is worshipped by heirophants bearing green candles. My surname, *Ashley*, means a ring of ash trees in a field, the sacred grove where the Druids met, for the ash attracts spirits. Still, as an only child (therefore first-born), I should be immune to witchcraft, so I feel an affinity for both believers and unbelievers.

Now, hoping you have enjoyed the facts and fun of this truly marvelous subject, I conclude.

God bless you. Blessed be.

Brooklyn College of
The City University of New York

253

Index